The Cambridge Companion to International Criminal Law

This comprehensive introduction to international criminal law addresses the big issues in the subject from an interdisciplinary perspective. Expert contributors include international lawyers, judges, prosecutors, criminologists and historians, as well as the last surviving prosecutor of the Nuremberg Trials. Serving as a foundation for deeper study, each chapter explores key academic debates and provides guidelines for further reading. The book is organised around several themes, including institutions, crimes and trials. Purposes and principles place the discipline within a broader context, covering the relationship with human rights law, transitional justice, punishment and the imperatives of peace. Several tribunals are explored in depth, as are many emblematic trials. The book concludes with perspectives on the future.

William A. Schabas is Professor of International Law at Middlesex University, London. He also holds appointments at Leiden University and the National University of Ireland, Galway. He is the author of many books and articles on the abolition of capital punishment, genocide, human rights and the international criminal tribunals. Professor Schabas was a member of the Sierra Leone Truth and Reconciliation Commission and Chairman of the UN Commission of Inquiry on the 2014 Gaza Conflict.

The Cambridge Companion to International Criminal Law

Edited by
William A. Schabas

CAMBRIDGE
UNIVERSITY PRESS

CAMBRIDGE
UNIVERSITY PRESS

University Printing House, Cambridge CB2 8BS, United Kingdom

Cambridge University Press is part of the University of Cambridge.

It furthers the University's mission by disseminating knowledge in the pursuit of education, learning and research at the highest international levels of excellence.

www.cambridge.org
Information on this title: www.cambridge.org/9781107695689

© Cambridge University Press 2016

First published 2016

Printed in the United Kingdom by TJ International Ltd. Padstow Cornwall

A catalogue record for this publication is available from the British Library

Library of Congress Cataloguing in Publication Data
The Cambridge companion to international criminal law / edited by William A. Schabas.
    pages   cm. – (Cambridge companions to law)
Includes bibliographical references and index.
ISBN 978-1-107-05233-8 (hardback) – ISBN 978-1-107-69568-9 (pbk)
1. International criminal law.   I. Schabas, William A., 1950– editor.
KZ7000.C36   2015
345–dc23   2015027882

ISBN 978-1-107-05233-8 Hardback
ISBN 978-1-107-69568-9 Paperback

To Hans-Peter Kaul

Contents

Contributors

Diane Marie Amann is Associate Dean for International Programmes and Strategic Initiatives and Emily and Ernest Woodruff Chair in International Law, University of Georgia School of Law; Special Adviser to the International Criminal Court Prosecutor on Children in and affected by Armed Conflict.

Kai Ambos is Chair of Criminal Law, Criminal Procedure, Comparative Law and International Criminal Law, Georg August Universität Göttingen; Judge of the District Court Göttingen; Director, Centro de Estudios de Derecho Penal y Procesal Penal Latinoamericano (CEDPAL), Universität Göttingen; Editor in chief, Criminal Law Forum.

M. Cherif Bassiouni is Emeritus Professor, DePaul University College of Law; President, International Institute of Higher Studies in the Criminal Sciences; Honorary President, International Association of Penal Law.

Andrew Clapham is Professor of Public International Law at the Graduate Institute of International and Development Studies, Geneva.

Roger S. Clark is Board of Governors Professor at Rutgers Law.

Lawrence Douglas is James J. Grosfeld Professor of Law, Jurisprudence and Social Thought, Amherst College.

Mark Drumbl is Class of 1975 Alumni Professor of Law and Director, Transnational Law Institute, Washington and Lee University.

Benjamin B. Ferencz is a human rights advocate and was the Chief Prosecutor for the United States at Nuremberg in a case commonly referred to as the Einsatzgruppen Case (*United States* v. *Ohlendorf* et al.).

Donald M. Ferencz is the Convenor of the Global Institute for the Prevention of Aggression and a Visiting Professor at Middlesex University School of Law in London.

Charles Chernor Jalloh is Associate Professor, Florida International University College of Law, Miami.

Hans-Peter Kaul was a Judge at the International Criminal Court from 2003 until 2014. From 2009 to 2012, he served as its Second Vice-President.

Fannie Lafontaine is Associate Professor and holder of the Canada Research Chair on International Criminal Justice and Human Rights at Laval University.

Stephan Parmentier is Professor of Sociology of Crime, Law and Human Rights at the University of Leuven and Secretary-General of the International Society for Criminology.

Leila Sadat is Henry Oberschelp Professor of Law and Director, Whitney R. Harris World Law Institute, Washington University in St. Louis.

William A. Schabas is Professor of International Law, Middlesex University, London and Professor of International Criminal Law and Human Rights, Leiden University.

Michael Scharf is Dean and Joseph C. Hostetler-Baker Hostetler Professor of Law, Case Western Reserve University School of Law; from 1989 to 1993, Professor Scharf served as the United States Department of State lawyer responsible for issues relating to international war crimes' trials.

David Scheffer is Mayer Brown/Robert A. Helman Professor of Law and Director, Center for International Human Rights, Northwestern University School of Law; former United States Ambassador at Large for War Crimes Issues (1997–2001).

Göran Sluiter is Professor of International Criminal Law at the University of Amsterdam.

Alfred de Zayas is United Nations Independent Expert on the Promotion of a Democratic and Equitable International Order, retired senior lawyer with the Office of the United Nations High Commissioner for Human Rights and Secretary of the United Nations Human Rights Committee.

Abbreviations

AC	Appeal Cases
ILM	International Legal Materials
ILR	International Law Reports
IMT	Trial of the Major War Criminals before the International Military Tribunal
LNTS	League of Nations Treaty Series
TWC	Trials of the War Criminals before the Nuernberg Military Tribunals
UNTS	United Nations Treaty Series

William A. Schabas

Introduction

Three decades ago, international criminal law might charitably have been referred to as a niche interest area within the discipline of public international law. There were no academic journals dedicated to the subject. Only a handful of monographs and doctoral theses addressed issues of relevance. The subject matter did not normally figure on university curricula. If a course in the field were offered, it would have been viewed as the idiosyncrasy of a lecturer, an offering to satisfy some private obsession rather than a genuine demand from students. The situation has been completely transformed. Today, several academic journals focus almost exclusively on the subject, and books are released at a prodigious rate. Special post-graduate degrees are offered in the field and hundreds of doctoral students, in universities around the world, toil in research libraries and archives. Moreover, newspapers and television feature stories related to international criminal justice activities almost daily. Few areas in international law, or for that matter in law in general, have ever developed at such a pace.

The birthdate of this exciting project might be fixed in December 1981, when the United Nations General Assembly invited the International Law Commission to resume work on the Code of Crimes Against the Peace and Security of Mankind, a matter that had been virtually moribund since 1954. The Commission produced its initial report in 1983 and then subsequently delivered annual reports, politely appealing to the General Assembly to complete its vision by contemplating the establishment of an International Criminal Court. In the early 1980s, nobody could have imagined that within a decade there would be two *ad hoc* international criminal tribunals and that within two decades a permanent International Criminal Court would be fully operational.

Actually, the history really begins seventy years earlier with the declaration by the British, French and Russian governments of their intent to prosecute those responsible for 'these new crimes of Turkey against humanity and civilisation', the atrocities that today we call the genocide of the Armenians. The Treaty of Sèvres of July 1920 authorised prosecutions and reserved the right for these to take place before an international court '[i]n the event of the League of Nations having created in sufficient time a tribunal competent to deal with the said massacres'. Although the proposed trials did not take place, it was clear that important changes in international law were afoot. But this project was not yet ripe. The first effective efforts at international criminal justice had to wait for the Second World War.

Several of the chapters in this book consider the post–Second World War prosecutions. Despite their flaws, more a question of pangs of birth than genuine shortcomings, they not only delivered justice, they provoked a brief yet intense period of law-making. One of the participants in those activities, Benjamin Ferencz, who was prosecutor in the 1947 trial of SS officers at Nuremberg, is a contributor to this book. The crimes in the Rome Statute that comprise the subject matter jurisdiction of the International Criminal Court trace their ancestry to this time. In a more general sense, international law had begun a historic turn, leaving behind its traditional indifference to issues governing the treatment of the individual by his or her own State. The relationship between international human rights law and international criminal law can be traced to this point in time.

One of the classic criticisms of the post–Second World War prosecutions involves the retroactive application of criminal justice. Rather than rigid and mechanistic application of the maxim *nullum crimen sine lege*, judges at Nuremberg held that 'the accused knew or should have known that in matters of international concern he was guilty of participation in a nationally organised system of injustice and persecution shocking to the moral sense of mankind, and that he knew or should have known that he would be subject to punishment if caught'.[1] This issue arises less frequently in modern times, in large part because the International Criminal Court is unable to deal with acts that occurred before the entry into force of the Rome Statute in 2002. But the retroactivity argument is also less potent today because of the profound development of international human rights law.

---

1 *United States* v. *Alstötter* et al., 'The Justice Case', (1951) 3 TWC 954, at pp. 977–8.

The issue of retroactive criminality recurs throughout the chapters in this book. Although not directly connected, a second issue, that of 'victors' justice', features in most discussions of Nuremberg and the other early trials. There is no doubt that the efforts of the 1940s only addressed atrocities committed by one side in the conflict. Even today, it appears to be asking a lot of a State to undertake prosecution of its own leaders for international crimes committed in pursuit of governmental policy. One of the most steadfast advocates of international justice, the United States of America, has shown itself incapable of applying the provisions of the Convention for the Prevention of Torture and Other Cruel, Inhuman or Degrading Treatment or Punishment when its own leaders are concerned. It seems that it can acknowledge the commission of the crime to be an ugly, regrettable feature of its military adventures in the Middle East and Asia, yet sheepishly decline to prosecute those suspected of responsibility, adopting what amounts to a *de facto* amnesty.

Double standards

When the United States defies its obligations under the Torture Convention while continuing to hector other countries, in Africa, Asia and South America, about their obligations to bring perpetrators of international crimes to justice, this is not so much 'victors' justice' as a problem of double standards. It may be unfair to highlight this huge shortcoming of international justice given that double standards also afflict the enforcement of human rights principles and, more generally, international law as a whole. At the apex of the international law pyramid stands the International Court of Justice. Yet its jurisdiction is only mandatory for about one-third of the world's countries, those that have made declarations of acceptance. Some justice! It is probably better to see things as some unfinished jigsaw puzzle. It is no longer a jumble of single pieces, but only an incomplete picture has emerged. We know where the missing elements are to be found. Slowly, the gaps are being filled.

The first experiments with international justice manifested such double standards because they only really operated where a consensus of the most powerful could be found. The post–Second World War tribunals were established by mighty military powers whereas the more recent United Nations *ad hoc* institutions owe their creation to the Security Council. This is a distinction without necessarily much of a difference. Of course, there may be nothing necessarily perverse about addressing Nazi atrocities while giving a get out of jail free card to the victorious allies. The crimes of the former manifestly outweighed those of the latter, and by several orders of magnitude. Nor are we shocked by the initial choices of the United Nations Security Council in the early 1990s, given the horrors of the conflicts in the former Yugoslavia and, even more so, Rwanda. But why devote massive international efforts to the killings and other crimes attributed to the Khmer Rouge in Cambodia during the 1970s, with their bizarre attempt at social revolution, yet pass in silence on the extermination of hundreds of thousands of communist sympathisers in Indonesia only a few years earlier? Why establish a deluxe international court to deal with a single assassination in Lebanon in 2005 while studiously ignoring other atrocities in that country and neighbouring territories during the same period?

The International Criminal Court promises something better, a universal regime applicable to all. Yet its jurisdiction is mainly dependent upon acceptance by each individual State. The largest and most powerful, as well as some of the most brutal, have yet to join. Indeed, this jigsaw puzzle of jurisdiction looks woefully incomplete, especially in the face of appalling internal conflicts such as those in Sri Lanka and Syria. Nevertheless, the pieces are slowly finding their place. The coverage, though still very partial, is increasingly complete. In contrast with the International Court of Justice, which is a much older institution, the International Criminal Court seems already to be a phenomenal success. About twice as many States have recognised the jurisdiction of the International Criminal Court as have accepted the jurisdiction of the International Court of Justice.

This book appears at a time when international criminal law is passing through a phase of uncertainty about its future. The dynamic presence of temporary or *ad hoc* tribunals that has characterised the past two decades seems to be drawing to a conclusion. These institutions had always been viewed as a temporary substitute for the permanent institution, the International Criminal Court. However, the Court's first years of activity have been marred by frustrating delays, procedural missteps and an extraordinarily deceptive level of productivity. It might be simplistic to measure the health of international justice by the number of ongoing trials. But to the extent this gives even an imperfect insight into the vitality of the system, it is disappointing to observe that the level of activity in 2015 is significantly lower than it was in 2005. To some, this recalls a wave that is cresting or that has already crested.

In the early 1920s, no reasonable observer could have anticipated that the modest efforts at international justice associated with the First World War were actually the start of something great. The same is true for the post–Second World War years. After the International Law Commission halted its initial work on the creation of a permanent criminal court, in the early 1950s, there was nothing to suggest that the project was merely in hibernation and not frozen to death. The contrast with today is very stark. International criminal justice is firmly implanted within the international order. It is an expectation of the public conscience. It is considered one of the essential tools to deal with conflicts and transitions. Its implementation is demanded by international human rights institutions. Nothing resembling such consensus has ever existed in the past. Thus, although like everything else its growth may not be entirely linear, and it will encounter periods of difficulty as well as those of exceptional vitality, international criminal justice is here to stay.

International criminal justice is a matter not only for international criminal tribunals but also for the domestic system. The international courts have invariably been justified as a replacement for the failure of the relevant national mechanisms to do the job expected of them as institutions dedicated to the rule of law. Occasionally, domestic courts operate as surrogate international bodies when they act under the principle of universal jurisdiction, as in the legendary *Eichmann* trial. Even when national courts are willing and able to prosecute the most heinous crimes, they may be stymied because they require international co-operation in the form of extradition and evidence gathering. The first international criminal law treaty of general application, the 1948 Convention on the Prevention and Punishment of the Crime of Genocide, addressed such issues. Enlarging the regime of international co-operation has also proven to be a great challenge. Only now is the International Law Commission studying a proposed treaty aimed at extending the obligations of the Genocide Convention to the broader concept of crimes against humanity. This results from an initiative led by one of the contributors to this book, Professor Leila Sadat.

Peace, justice and the crime of aggression

Another persistent theme in this book is what might be called the 'peace v. justice' debate. International justice is often associated with transitional justice, a concept that underscores the utilitarian function. Accountability and prosecutions are said to make an important contribution when nasty regimes are replaced or when protracted conflict with an ethnic dimension is being calmed. There are even claims that without justice, peace cannot succeed in the long term, although this is a dubious assertion. In fact, some societies do manage a lasting peace in the absence of accountability; others return to conflict, but the reasons for this are usually more complex than a simplistic assertion that justice was not done. Regardless of whether justice actually assists in post-conflict reconciliation, there is also a strong case that it is an entitlement of victims. This proposition finds support in human rights law where a right to justice and to truth is deemed a corollary of the right to life and to protection against inhuman treatment.

The centrepiece of the Nuremberg prosecutions was the 'crime against peace'. Aggressive war was the evil lying at the core of the atrocities perpetrated by the Nazis and their allies, according to the International Military Tribunal. But when the immediate post-conflict period gave way to the early skirmishes in the Cold War, international law began to have more difficulty with the offence that was being rebranded as the 'crime of aggression'. Debate about its definition ultimately halted all further progress in international criminal law. Work did not resume until the early 1980s. By then, the waging of illegal war seemed to have migrated to the periphery of international criminal law. When the International Criminal Tribunal for the former Yugoslavia was established, in 1993, aggression was not even listed in the Statute.

There was no consensus at the Rome Conference on the importance of including the crime of aggression within the jurisdiction of the International Criminal Court. After protracted negotiations, a package was finally adopted in 2010 at the Kampala Review Conference. The amendments require a somewhat complicated process of ratification that should come to a successful conclusion in 2017. The United States arrived at Kampala after having boycotted the process of crafting the amendments for several years. It tried without real success to adjust a definition upon which consensus had already been reached. The intent was to carve out an exception so as to ensure that the use of force labelled as 'humanitarian intervention' would not fall within the ambit of the crime of aggression. Of course, this is entirely unnecessary as long as any use of force is authorised pursuant to the Charter of the United Nations.

At Rome, representatives of the permanent members of the United Nations Security Council argued that aggression could not be treated like the other crimes within the Court's jurisdiction. In particular, they contended that an independent prosecutor should not have the authority to initiate charges of aggression in the absence of a blessing from the Security Council. Their claims relied upon a particular interpretation of the Charter of the United Nations. Yet in Kampala, after again insisting that giving such power to the Prosecutor of the Court amounted to indirectly modifying the Charter, the United Kingdom and France sat on their hands and joined a consensus that allowed the unthinkable. Henceforth, unable to ensure impunity for themselves or their proxies by use of the veto, even they may find themselves called to account by the International Criminal Court for the unlawful use of force.

The amendments adopted at Kampala adjust the prerogatives of the permanent members of the Security Council. They continue a process that began in the 1990s as the Rome Statute was being drafted and that is reflected in some of its provisions. The Rome Statute, and the Kampala amendments, trim the authority of the Council, and thereby the extraordinary powers of its permanent members. This accomplishes indirectly what it seems it is impossible to do directly, namely, to amend the Charter. Small and middle powers have used the opportunities involved in the establishment of the International Criminal Court to reduce, ever so slightly, the powers of the five permanent members. These may only amount to small cracks in the system of the Charter. But they are signs of development, manifesting a tendency towards a more democratic and egalitarian world order, one in which double standards are reduced if not entirely eliminated. As Leonard Cohen wrote, '[t]here is a *crack*, a crack in everything. That's how *the light gets in*'.

Part I   Purposes and principles

Human rights and international criminal law 1

Andrew Clapham

One might expect the opening chapter of this *Cambridge Companion to International Criminal Law* to suggest that human rights came first and slowly developed a criminal law arm in order to prosecute the worst offenders. Indeed, a well-established account presents the process as passing from a preliminary enunciation of values stage through to declarations, prescription, enforcement, and finally criminalisation.[1] But the relationship between human rights and international criminal law is more complicated and, today, produces not only tension but also confrontation. This chapter will highlight tension over harmony, and suggest that the articulation of the relationship between these two branches of law remains very much 'work in progress'. Although many scholars and activists are involved in both branches, at certain points the dynamics diverge and the thirst for the prosecution of international crimes may not always take fully on board the human rights implications of such processes.

International criminal law can be seen as covering both crimes under treaties, which usually take effect through national legal orders, as well as what are increasingly called 'atrocity crimes' or 'core crimes', which may exist independently of national law and can be prosecuted in international courts. Such atrocity crimes can of course also be prosecuted at the national level, where the national courts enjoy such jurisdiction.

International criminal law, in the form of treaty crimes, has been traced back to classical times and to a treaty between the Kings of Cyprus, Alexandria, Egypt, Cyrene, and Syria aimed at preventing the harbouring of pirates.[2] The modern idea of international criminal law owes more,

---

1 M. Cherif Bassiouni, *Introduction to International Criminal Law*, 2nd rev. edn, Leiden: Nijhoff, 2013, pp. 217–8.

2 Neil Boister, 'Treaty-based Crimes', in Antonio Cassese, ed., *Oxford Companion to International Criminal Justice*, Oxford University Press, 2009, pp. 540–2, at pp. 540–1.

however, to the International Military Tribunals, established in Nuremberg and Tokyo after the Second World War. These courts, set up by the victorious Allies, focused on atrocity crimes (war crimes, crimes against humanity and genocide) as well as crimes against peace (aggression).

Strictly speaking, the Nuremberg International Military Tribunal had concluded its work before the drafting of the 1948 Universal Declaration of Human Rights had been completed. So it might seem that international criminal law came before international human rights law. But such a conclusion would ignore the key point that multiple commitments to fight for human rights were made by the Allies and popular movements throughout the Second World War.[3] The idea of human rights was already certainly in the air and politically significant, even if it took some time for human rights to be properly entrenched as legal rights in international law.

It is with the Nuremberg trials that we encounter a first tension between individual rights and the prosecution of international crimes. The UN Commission on Human Rights already requested in 1946 information concerning 'human rights arising from the trials of war criminals'. The eventual report produced by the UN War Crimes Commission explains the choice that faced the international community.

> One side, that of the Axis, asserted the absolute responsibility of the belligerents, who it was asserted were under no obligation to respect human rights, but were entitled to trample them underfoot wherever the military forces found them inconvenient for the waging of war. This is the totalitarian war as envisaged by the Axis powers. This doctrine was repudiated as contrary not only to morality but to recognised international law, which prescribed metes and bounds for the violation even in war of human rights. This latter doctrine involved also the further principle that there was individual responsibility for violations of human rights in wartime, beyond the limits permitted by the laws of war.[4]

So human rights violations were to be prosecuted as individual crimes at the end of the war. But the same report highlighted the human rights issues that arose for the defendants. A human rights principle, later entrenched in human rights treaties, protects the individual from being

---

3 Andrew Clapham, *Human Rights: A Very Short Introduction*, 2nd edn, Oxford University Press, 2015, at pp. 34–9.

4 Information Concerning Human Rights Arising from Trials of War Criminals, UN Doc. E/CN.4/W.19, p. ii. The report is very detailed and runs to 368 pages.

tried for an offence which was not a crime at the time it was committed (*nullum crimen sine lege*). The prosecution of crimes against peace in Nuremberg was novel and contested. Similarly, questions were raised about the rights of the accused who sought to rely on a defence of 'following orders'. Where disobedience could lead to punishment for the defendant and his family this was seen as pitting the rights of victims against the rights of defendants. The International Military Tribunal considered that those leaders in the dock must have known they were acting in defiance of international law. The claims by the defendants that the prosecution was in violation of their rights was not seen as precluding the criminal responsibility of these individuals; in some cases, these human rights concerns might be used to mitigate punishment. In the words of the UN War Crimes Commission, 'whenever a conflict may be said to have arisen between the rights of the victims and those of the accused at the time of the offence, the general rule appears to be that the conflict is solved in favour of the rights of the victims'.[5] At that time nearly every prosecution for an international crime was seen as the ultimate enforcement of the criminalisation of a human rights violation.

Today, almost every defendant facing charges of international crimes before an international court will at some point claim that the charges, the tribunal, the trial, or the punishment violates their human rights. Saddam Hussein and Slobodan Milošević both claimed that their trials violated their human rights, and brought cases before the European Court of Human Rights in Strasbourg.[6] In Saddam Hussein's case this included a claim that the punishment would violate his right to life. The international criminal tribunals for the former Yugoslavia, Rwanda, and Sierra Leone, for example, have all had to consider human rights law, not only to determine the scope of the crimes under consideration (especially in the context of torture, sexual violence, slavery, and recruitment of children), but also as part of the claims by the accused that their human rights were being violated by their conditions of detention, or by the long delays involved, or the defence rights according during the trial process itself.[7]

5 Ibid., p. 111.

6 *Saddam Hussein* v. *Albania* et al. (dec.), no. 23276/04, 14 March 2006; *Milošević* v. *the Netherlands* (dec.), no. 77631/01, 19 March 2002.

7 William A. Schabas, *The UN International Criminal Tribunals: The Former Yugoslavia, Rwanda and Sierra Leone*, Cambridge University Press, 2006, Ch. 13 ('Rights of the accused').

We might recall that Augusto Pinochet never faced the charges of torture on which he was being detained in the United Kingdom, because
the United Kingdom government ultimately determined that his apparent
poor mental health meant that he would not receive a fair trial in accordance with his human rights under the European Convention of Human
Rights.[8] This is a stark reminder that human rights is a double-edged
sword. Pinochet faced trial for human rights crimes and yet, remarkably
and perhaps exceptionally, his own human rights were said to be taken
into consideration in determining whether the trial could go ahead. Most
recently a detainee in Guantánamo, facing prosecution for international
crimes before the United States Military Commission, won his case in
Strasbourg against Poland for hosting him during his interrogation and
torture by the CIA.[9] The prosecution of international crimes can be seen
both as an effective way to punish human rights violations and, also, as
almost inevitably raising threats to well-established human rights protections. It rather depends on where you are standing.

This irony can pose severe dilemmas for human rights groups. The
prosecution of those who recruit children to fight in an armed conflict is
demanded by human rights law; but when exactly did recruiting those
under fifteen become an international crime?[10] On the one hand, one
wants justice for the victims of sexual violence, and the prosecution of
the perpetrators for such international crimes seems an essential step
towards this end. But what if this means introducing anonymous testimony, or other innovations to protect the victim? How does this fit for
organisations founded to defend the rights of the accused and ensure a
fair trial? Prosecuting the leaders for atrocities committed in a vicious
civil war seems the right thing to do to vindicate the rights of the victims;
but what if this means that those same leaders refuse to come to the table
to negotiate a peace? The slogan 'no peace without justice' rings hollow
when the people most affected simply yearn for peace and would rather
forgive and forget than live in terror waiting for a just solution. Again

---

8 'Pinochet Set Free', *BBC News*, 2 March 2000.
9 *Al Nashiri* v. *Poland*, no. 28761/11, 24 July 2014; see also *Husayn (Abu
   Zubaydah)* v. *Poland*, no. 7511/13, 24 July 2014.
10 This was the issue faced by the Special Court for Sierra Leone, see: *Prosecutor*
   v. *Norman* (SCSL-2004-14-AR72), Decision on Preliminary Motion Based on
   Lack of Jurisdiction (Child Recruitment), 31 May 2003.

an appeal to the combined framework for human rights and international criminal law may not provide the answers. We are faced with competing priorities rather than a neat global legal order.[11]

So, human rights principles can come into conflict with the dynamic of international criminal law from the stage of defining the offence, through the legality of the detention, the forms of interrogation, the rights of the defence at trial, the legality of the establishment of the tribunal, and of course the proportionality of the sentence at trial, including allegations of violations of the right to life. Moreover, statutes of limitations, amnesties and pardons will inevitably pit different interests, including the rights of the victims, against the rights of others. And yet, international criminal law is still to some extent an outgrowth of human rights law and celebrated as one of the most significant developments in the struggle to hold human rights violators accountable. Let us first look at how some human rights violations came to be criminalised and prosecuted as international crimes, and then in the second part return to see how various texts and courts have resolved the tension between the quest for prosecution and the need to protect the dignity and rights of the alleged perpetrators. In the third part, we consider the extent to which international human rights law is called on to oblige States to prosecute certain international crimes.

Human rights violations prosecuted under international criminal law

Crimes against humanity

At the end of the Second World War, international law recognised that foreigners had to be treated in accordance with minimum standards, otherwise their State of nationality could bring a complaint based on so-called 'diplomatic protection'. It also recognised that mistreating foreign prisoners of war or using civilians under enemy occupation for forced labour

---

11 For examples of how these competing priorities are being reconciled see: S. Vandeginste, 'Bypassing the Prohibition of Amnesty for Human Rights Crimes Under International Law: Lessons Learned from the Burundi Peace Process', (2011) 29 *Netherlands Quarterly of Human Rights* 189; R. C. Slye, 'The Legitimacy of Amnesties Under International Law and General Principles of Anglo-American Law: Is a Legitimate Amnesty Possible?', (2002) 43 *Virginia Journal of International Law* 173.

constituted violations of the laws of war. It had little to say about how a State treated its own population. These were matters for domestic law and national courts. The prosecution of German officials for crimes against humanity committed against Germans in Germany therefore represented something of a breakthrough. In fact this was considered so radical that the drafters of the Nuremberg Charter were careful to link the prosecution of these crimes to other crimes within the jurisdiction of the Tribunal (war crimes and crimes against peace). This was perhaps in part to avoid the allegation that the *nullum crimen sine lege* principle (no retroactive criminalisation of conduct) was being violated, and probably in part to ensure that they did not create a precedent that could be used against their own rulers for systematic human rights violations committed back home. The judgment of the International Military Tribunal fails to declare whether crimes committed by Germans against Germans in Germany before the war were crimes against humanity, and tends to exclude such acts from its reasoning, leading to a sense that such violations of human rights could not be prosecuted as crimes under international law at that time.[12] The Genocide Convention of 1948 (which demands no such link to war) is in part a response to the notion that at that time crimes against humanity as international crimes had to be linked to the Second World War and the other crimes in the jurisdiction of the Nuremberg and Tokyo Tribunals. Nevertheless the link with war was 'gradually dropped' as evidenced by national legislation and most recently in the Statutes of the International Criminal Tribunal for Rwanda and the International Criminal Court.[13]

The idea that these crimes were an individual criminalisation of gross and systematic violations of human rights is reflected in the International Law Commission's 1991 version of its Draft Code of Crimes Against the Peace and Security of Mankind which included these crimes under the heading 'systematic or mass violations of human rights'.[14] Although

12 Information Concerning Human Rights Arising from Trials of War Criminals, UN Doc. E/CN.4/W.19.

13 Antonio Cassese and Paola Gaeta, *Cassese's International Criminal Law*, 3rd edn, Oxford University Press, 2013, p. 90.

14 The evolution of the concept of crimes against humanity is very well described in Roger S. Clark, 'History of Efforts to Codify Crimes Against Humanity: From the Charter of Nuremberg to the Statute of Rome', in Leila Nadya Sadat, ed., *Forging a Convention for Crimes Against Humanity*, Cambridge University Press, 2011, pp. 8–27.

this heading was later lost and replaced with the phrase 'crimes against humanity', the link remains. Systematic violations of human rights are associated with the prospect of prosecuting the perpetrators for crimes against humanity. But if such acts are already violations of human rights law, what is the added value of criminalising them at the international level? Mass murder or torture could be prosecuted as simple crimes. One effect is certain: the international criminalisation allows for prosecution of the individual before an international tribunal. The other effects are less certain but are evolving: for example, there are rules which would forbid a statute of limitations being used to preclude a national prosecution for crimes against humanity, one could be denied refugee status if there were evidence of the commission of crimes against humanity, there could be a better case for arguing that universal jurisdiction allowed one to prosecute a crime committed by a non-national outside one's territory, the rules on State immunity may no longer protect a State official from another State's jurisdiction, one could be denied the defence of 'superior orders' in national law, and one could be prosecuted for command responsibility.[15] But perhaps the most practical day-to-day consequence, which deserves mentioning here, is that the expression 'crimes against humanity' concentrates the minds of policy makers and journalists. Human rights violations are around us all the time. Crimes against humanity deserve a meaningful response.

In this way, the threshold between human rights violations and crimes against humanity takes on a particular significance in the context of the recent doctrine of the 'Responsibility to Protect'.[16] This political commitment to act to save those in danger is triggered by crimes against humanity rather than human rights violations.[17] While no one has suggested

---

15 Paola Gaeta, 'International Criminalisation of Prohibited Conduct', in Antonio Cassese, ed., *Oxford Companion to International Criminal Justice*, Oxford University Press, 2009, pp. 63–74, at pp. 70–3.

16 G. Evans, *The Responsibility to Protect: Ending Mass Atrocity Crimes Once and for All*, Washington: Brookings Institution, 2008; Anne Orford, *International Authority and the Responsibility to Protect*, Cambridge University Press, 2011.

17 World Summit Outcome, UN Doc. A/RES/60/1: '139. The international community, through the United Nations, also has the responsibility to use appropriate diplomatic, humanitarian and other peaceful means, in accordance with Chapters IV and VIII of the Charter, to help protect populations from genocide, war crimes, ethnic cleansing and crimes against humanity'.

that crimes against humanity can legalise what would otherwise be an unlawful use of force in the form of a humanitarian intervention, the justification by the United Kingdom for a possible use of force against Syria in 2013 comes quite close, referring to the use of chemical weapons as a crime against humanity in its first substantive paragraph.[18] The recent Arms Trade Treaty draws a distinction between crimes against humanity and a serious violation of human rights. The treaty prohibits any arms transfer that would be used in the commission of crimes against humanity. On the other hand, an export that could be used to commit a serious violation of human rights is something to be assessed and mitigated against, and eventually prohibited, only if the risk is considered overriding.[19]

Crimes against humanity are discussed in more detail later in this book. For present purposes we need simply to caution at this point that by creating such international offences that criminalise a narrow category of human rights violators and violations there is an inevitable downgrading of other serious human rights violations.[20] Of course these acts remain violations of international and national law, but the emergence of crimes against humanity in contemporary discourse risks diluting our attention to human rights in general terms as well as distracting attention from the structural changes that need to be made to avoid all types of human rights violation. General questions of equality, the right to participate in decision-making, the rights of trade unions and political parties, freedom of expression, privacy, and rights to food, housing, and adequate health care all risk getting overlooked as the focus turns to the worst atrocities. But without a concentration on the structural changes that need to be taken to protect human rights in a sustainable way, there is not much chance of preventing the next round of atrocities.

18 Guidance, Chemical weapon use by Syrian regime: UK government legal position, 29 August 2013.
19 Arms Trade Treaty, UN Doc. A/CONF.217/2013/L.3, articles 6 and 7.
20 For a similar warning in the context of war crimes occluding other violations of international humanitarian law, see Paola Gaeta, 'The Interplay Between the Geneva Conventions and International Criminal Law', in Andrew Clapham, Paola Gaeta, and Marco Sassòli, eds., *The 1949 Geneva Conventions: A Commentary*, Oxford University Press, 2015, pp. 737–53.

Human rights and treaty crimes

Some human rights violations have been transformed by treaties into offences that States Parties to the treaties are under an obligation to incorporate into national law along with appropriate punishments. Furthermore, these treaties will usually give rise to an obligation to extradite or prosecute offenders within the jurisdiction. For example, the Convention against Torture generated the obligation on the United Kingdom to consider the prosecution of Augusto Pinochet (as may be now becoming obvious there are not in fact that many examples of these treaties actually directly leading to arrests!). The exact details vary from treaty to treaty. These issues are discussed in more detail elsewhere in this *Companion*. Interestingly, crimes against humanity have not yet been the subject of such a treaty.[21]

Scholars have sought to rationalise why some violations of international law have been criminalised in this way. They point to the transnational element, or the concern to the international community, or to the fundamental threat to the dignity of the victims concerned. I would suggest that the explanation is often rather more prosaic. Those who fought for the Conventions against Torture and Disappearances were continuing their human rights struggle by other means: the criminalisation of such violations with the incumbent obligations to extradite or consider prosecution. These were their concerns in the 1970s and 1980s. Had the movement been otherwise configured, or come into being only in the 1990s, the push might have been for the criminalisation of rape and sexual violence in internal armed conflict. The early human rights crimes were simply choices made by the human rights movement and a handful of non-governmental organisations in particular.[22]

---

21 In 2014, the International Law Commission decided to include the topic of crimes against humanity in its work programme and has appointed Sean D. Murphy as special rapporteur. For some of the issues that could be dealt with by a future treaty, see Leila Nadya Sadat, ed., *Forging a Convention for Crimes Against Humanity*, Cambridge University Press, 2011. Note that the Convention for the Suppression and Punishment of the Crime of *Apartheid* (1973) declared *apartheid* a crime against humanity. One could also consider the Genocide Convention under this rubric.

22 See, for details of the campaigns on torture and disappearances: A. M. Clark, *Diplomacy of Conscience: Amnesty International and Changing Human Rights Norms*, Princeton University Press, 2001, chapters 6 and 7. It has been argued

The list of treaties that define international offences is long and fuzzy around the edges. Is hostage-taking a human rights issue or something that belongs in the international terrorism box? It is worth recalling that the original charges against Pinochet when arrested in London included hostage-taking as defined by the relevant convention. Should we in fact see the suppression of *apartheid* and terrorism, as well as conventions on trafficking in persons and narcotics, as part of the struggle for human rights? Let us first mention the human rights treaties (as traditionally understood) that create offences and return to the 'suppression conventions' later: Convention against Torture and Other Cruel, Inhuman or Degrading Treatment or Punishment (1984); Inter-American Convention to Prevent and Punish Torture (1985); Inter-American Convention on the Forced Disappearance of Persons (1994); Optional Protocol to the Convention on the Rights of the Child on the Sale of Children, Child Prostitution and Child Pornography (2000); International Convention for the Protection of All Persons from Enforced Disappearance (2006).

These human rights treaties share several common features related to international criminal law: they oblige the States Parties to establish jurisdiction over the offences outlined in the treaties; they oblige the State to either extradite those accused of such offences or submit the case to its prosecutorial authorities; they can be used to ground individual complaints concerning violations; their compliance may be monitored by the relevant treaty monitoring body; and they operate as interstate treaties allowing even States that are not victims to demand compliance at the international level.[23] These treaties have generated the national law that allows for the prosecution of foreigners who have committed their crimes outside the jurisdiction. The challenge for those seeking to trigger such prosecutions is that national authorities may not want to disrupt their relations with the relevant foreign State. Moreover, any such prosecution is expensive and complicated, involving as it does witnesses and testimony from abroad. As the framework has become better understood

that one should really trace the criminalisation of human rights violations back to the slave trade: J. S. Martinez, *The Slave Trade and the Origins of International Human Rights Law*, New York: Oxford University Press, 2012; *contra* Philip Alston, 'Does the Past Matter? On the Origins of Human Rights', (2013) 126 *Harvard Law Review* 2043.

23 *Questions relating to the Obligation to Prosecute or Extradite (Belgium v. Senegal), Judgment, I.C.J. Reports 2012*, p. 422.

those who could eventually find themselves tangled up in this international web for prosecuting human rights crimes may seek to avoid the relevant jurisdictions or travel under the promise of State immunity. The result is that actual prosecutions are rather few and far between.[24]

As stated above, we can group another set of 'suppression conventions' which, while they are not written in a way that suggests that individuals hold rights that can be enforced against the State Party, nevertheless explicitly aim at protecting human rights and human dignity and have been incorporated into the armoury of texts deployed by human rights groups in their advocacy. These include: International Convention against the Taking of Hostages (1979); United Nations Convention against Transnational Organised Crime (2000); Protocol to Prevent, Suppress and Punish Trafficking in Persons, especially Women and Children, supplementing the United Nations Convention against Transnational Organised Crime (2000); Protocol against the Smuggling of Migrants by Land, Sea and Air, supplementing the United Nations Convention against Transnational Organised Crime (2000); Protocol against the Illicit Manufacturing and Trafficking in Firearms, their Parts and Components and Ammunition, supplementing the United Nations Convention against Transnational Organised Crime (2001); Council of Europe Convention on Cybercrime (2001); Council of Europe Convention on Action against Trafficking in Human Beings (2005); African Union Convention on Cyber-Security and Personal Data Protection (2014).

Lastly, when considering international criminal law treaties we can consider a slightly different type of suppression convention, where the stated aim may or may not be seen as enhancing human rights,[25] but where there is a recognition that the operation of the treaty could undermine existing human rights and the treaties therefore demand that measures taken under

24 Examples include the prosecution in England for torture and hostage-taking of the Afghan Warlord Zardad, and the prosecution in the United States of Chucky Taylor for torture in Liberia. See Rob Cryer, 'Zardad', in Antonio Cassese, ed., *Oxford Companion to International Criminal Justice*, Oxford University Press, 2009, pp. 979–80; J. Ku, 'U.S. Court Convicts "Chucky" Taylor of Torture', http://opiniojuris.org/2008/11/02/us-court-convicts-chucky-taylor-of-torture/. See also the prosecution *in absentia* in France of the Mauritanian Army Captain Ely Ould Dah for acts of torture between 1990 and 1991; the facts are explained in *Ould Dah* v. *France* (dec.), no. 13113/03, ECHR 2009.

25 One might also mention the United Nations Convention against Corruption (2003). The foreword to the United Nations publication containing the treaty is signed by Kofi Annan as UN Secretary-General and starts: 'Corruption is

the treaty are in conformity with human rights. See, for example, the United Nations Convention against Illicit Traffic in Narcotic Drugs and Psychotropic Substances (1988), article 14(2) of which demands that measures to eradicate plants containing narcotic or psychotropic substances shall respect fundamental human rights, and the International Convention for the Suppression of the Financing of Terrorism (1999), article 17 of which demands that individuals subjected to measures under the treaty are guaranteed fair treatment including applicable international human rights law.

But the threats to human rights from the suppression of drug trafficking or the financing of terrorism are of course much wider. As Boister explains, the application of the drug trafficking suppression conventions has enormous potential to involve human rights violations. While some of his points are particular to the drug trade, most will apply to other 'suppression conventions', and of course it is not hard to imagine the threats to human rights involved in the pursuit of terrorists through the opportunities presented by the wide-ranging offences and the facilitated inter-governmental co-operation.

> Cultivators of land may find their right to property threatened by eradication operations involving the use of herbicides. Innocent holders of property may find their property subject to forfeiture as the proceeds or instrumentalities of crime. The privacy rights of users may be threatened by the criminalisation of private behaviour. The rights of residents of urban areas may be threatened through police raids, curfews, and warrant-less searches. Suspected suppliers may be subject to detention without trial or the confiscation of property not proved to be linked to trafficking. Once arrested, alleged offenders may be denied fair pre-trial proceedings and a fair trial. Most of these processes will be entirely intra-State, away in many cases from international human rights exposure. When processes do become interstate, the extraterritorial nature of proceedings may serve as a veil for the denial of rights. Fugitive alleged offenders may be denied the right to be informed of an extradition request, the right to be heard, and

> an insidious plague that has a wide range of corrosive effects on societies. It undermines democracy and the rule of law, leads to violations of human rights, distorts markets, erodes the quality of life and allows organised crime, terrorism and other threats to human security to flourish'. The treaty demands *inter alia* respect for the 'rights of the defence', but the links to the world of human rights more generally are still rather underdeveloped. See further: *The Human Rights Case Against Corruption*, Geneva: Office of the High Commissioner for Human Rights, 2013.

the right to legal representation. International legal assistance in evidence gathering may only be used for inculpatory and not exculpatory purposes, violating the principle of equality of arms. Once in custody, alleged offenders may be subject to *ex post facto* laws. Once convicted, offenders may not receive fair conditions of detention and protection against cruel and unusual punishment. In particular, States that apply the death penalty for trafficking may threaten the right to life.[26]

This is not the place to enter into a discussion of all the possible threats to human rights that arise in the pursuit of those who are the target of the various 'suppression conventions', or indeed all the human rights complaints of those who are prosecuted in national and international tribunals for war crimes, genocide, and crimes against humanity.[27] There are, however, two areas where we should go a little deeper; they relate not only to the application of such conventions, but also to a more generalised tension between human rights and international criminal law. The first relates to the prosecution of international crimes that arguably did not already exist as offences under national or international law at the time of the offence. The second relates to the extent to which human rights law precludes the use of amnesties for international crimes.

Human rights in tension with the development of international crimes

The International Covenant on Civil and Political Rights contains a guarantee in article 15 that '[n]o one shall be held guilty of any criminal offence on account of any act or omission which did not constitute a criminal offence, under national or international law, at the time when it was committed'. And, for the avoidance of doubt, there follows a second clause stating: 'Nothing in this article shall prejudice the trial and

---

26 Neil Boister, 'Human Rights Protections in the Suppression Conventions', (2002) 2 *Human Rights Law Review* 199, at p. 201.

27 The Statute of the International Criminal Court explicitly references respect for human rights and non-discrimination in the context of the applicable law for the Court to apply; see article 21(3). For the way the *ad hoc* tribunals have developed the right to fair trial see Wolfgang Schomburg, 'The Role of International Criminal Tribunals in Promoting Respect for Human Rights', (2009) 8 *Northwestern Journal of International Human Rights* 1.

punishment of any person for any act or omission which, at the time when it was committed, was criminal according to the general principles of law recognised by the community of nations'. Other human rights treaties and declarations contain similar provisions.[28] Several defendants, both before national and international courts, have sought to show that the international crimes they are charged with did not exist at the time of the commission of the acts concerned. Where there is the possibility of appealing to an international human rights court this presents a real tension that has to be resolved one way or the other. While the reference to general principles quoted above will cover the principles of international law recognised by the Nuremberg Charter and the judgment of the International Military Tribunal,[29] what should be done about those accused of war crimes in an internal armed conflict, or crimes such as material support to terrorism,[30] or certain forms of conspiracy or joint criminal enterprise for war crimes or crimes against humanity? Of course where something is clearly criminal and heinous there might be little sympathy for a defendant seeking to get off on a 'human rights technicality', but human rights courts have to take a principled approach. The stakes are high because most of the future challenges in this area are more likely to be about widening the net to catch those accused of terrorism-related offences, and less about prosecuting crimes against humanity or genocide.

The cases before the European Court of Human Rights were brought by those who had been convicted of crimes against humanity, genocide, and war crimes. They are complicated and need not be summarised here.[31] The

28 Universal Declaration of Human Rights, article 11(2); European Convention on Human Rights, article 7; American Convention on Human Rights, article 9; African Convention on Human and Peoples' Rights, article 7(2); Arab Charter of Human Rights, article 15; Charter of Fundamental Rights of the European Union, article 49.

29 General Assembly Resolution 95(I) of 11 December 1946.

30 *Hamdan v. United States of America*, US Court of Appeals, DC Circuit, 12 October 2012, at p. 5: 'When Hamdan committed the conduct in question, the international law of war proscribed a variety of war crimes, including forms of terrorism. At that time, however, the international law of war did not proscribe material support for terrorism as a war crime.'

31 E.g., *Kolk and Kislyiy v. Estonia* (dec.), nos. 23052/04 and 24018/04, ECHR 2006-I; *Korbely v. Hungary* [GC], no. 9174/02, ECHR 2008; *Jorgić v. Germany*, no. 74613/01, ECHR 2007-III; *Kononov v. Latvia* [GC], no. 36376/04, ECHR 2010.

attitude of the Court has been to allow national courts a margin to interpret and apply the law, and to remind that all law involves judicial interpretation. In one case, the applicant (a Bosnian Serb) challenged the German courts' interpretation of the requisite intent to commit the crime of genocide, arguing that the crime did not extend to an intent to destroy Bosnian Muslims as a 'social unit' but rather should be confined to the physical destruction of living members of the group in question. The Court admitted that opinion on this question was divided, but concluded:

> while many authorities had favoured a narrow interpretation of the crime of genocide, there had already been several authorities at the material time which had construed the offence of genocide in the same wider way as the German courts. In these circumstances, the Court finds that the applicant, if need be with the assistance of a lawyer, could reasonably have foreseen that he risked being charged with and convicted of genocide for the acts he committed in 1992. In this context the Court also has regard to the fact that the applicant was found guilty of acts of a considerable severity and duration: the killing of several people and the detention and ill-treatment of a large number of people over a period of several months as the leader of a paramilitary group in pursuit of the policy of ethnic cleansing.[32]

We might expect, however, that where an applicant has been less involved in violence and is being tried for ancillary offences such as complicity, conspiracy, or joint criminal enterprise, the Court may take a stricter approach, recalling its principled position that this human right 'embodies, more generally, the principle that only the law can define a crime and prescribe a penalty (*nullum crimen, nulla poena sine lege*) and the principle that criminal law must not be extensively construed to the detriment of an accused, for instance by analogy'.[33]

International human rights supervision over a state's investigations, prosecution, and punishment of international crimes

In this last part, we consider a relatively new aspect of the relationship between human rights and international criminal law. International treaty bodies and courts, established to supervise the compliance by States with their treaty obligations, have started to become more and

32 *Jorgic* v. *Germany*, no. 74613/01, § 113, ECHR 2007-III.
33 Ibid., § 100.

more involved in determining what a State must do in the face of allegations that international crimes have been committed. This is particularly the case where these involve violence to the person as with the crimes of torture, enforced disappearances, or massacres that could amount to crimes against humanity. A recent in-depth study by Huneeus has highlighted that the Inter-American Court of Human Rights 'has decreed and is actively monitoring prosecutions of international crimes in roughly fifty-one cases across fifteen States'.[34] The study also found that '[p]ursuant to its orders in these cases, States have launched new criminal investigations, exhumed mass graves, moved cases from military to civil jurisdiction, overturned amnesties, bypassed statutes of limitations, and created new institutions and working methods to facilitate prosecution of such crimes. Indeed, at least thirty-nine prosecutions launched pursuant to the Court's orders have yielded convictions'.[35]

Similar, but less robust, supervision can be expected from other bodies such as the European and African Courts of Human Rights and the UN human rights treaty bodies. States may resist such supervision as an unwarranted interference in their prosecutorial discretion and national reconciliation processes, but they remain bound by their human rights treaty obligations. Two areas where human rights law has been deliberately excluded perhaps deserve special attention here. The first is where the laws of armed conflict are said to 'displace' the general human rights regime. The second is where the rights of victims of human rights violations are said to override any amnesty that might have been granted.

Overlap between human rights law and the law of armed conflict

The topic of the relationship between human rights law and the law of armed conflict has spawned multiple volumes and cannot be properly dealt with here.[36] For present purposes the point is that international

---

34 A. Huneeus, 'International Criminal Law by Other Means: The Quasi-Criminal Jurisdiction of the Human Rights Courts', (2013) 107 *American Journal of International Law* 1, at pp. 1–2.

35 Ibid., p. 2.

36 For a useful selection, see Robert Kolb and G. Gaggioli, eds., *Research Handbook on Human Rights and Humanitarian Law*, Cheltenham: Elgar, 2013; Orla Ben-Naftali, ed., *International Humanitarian Law and International Human*

criminal law is a part of both branches of law. An act of torture or killing can constitute both a violation of human rights law and the international humanitarian law of armed conflict. A prosecutor could choose to prosecute torture as a human rights violation or as a war crime. Some States have sought to argue that issues such as battlefield killing or detention of those captured in conflict should be exclusively dealt with under the law of armed conflict, and that therefore the human rights supervisory bodies should have no role. So far, the human rights bodies have ignored this approach and continued to apply human rights law pointing to the fact that States are free to derogate from certain obligations in times of armed conflict. The International Court of Justice has been faced with the issue and has upheld the continuing application of human rights treaties in times of armed conflict, simply stating that some human rights will have to be interpreted by reference to the applicable international humanitarian law.[37]

We should point out, however, that some of the treaties mentioned above do actually foresee that they would be inapplicable where the same issue is dealt with by the law of international armed conflict. These exceptions are worth mentioning as they reinforce the argument that, in the absence of an express exception, one should consider that human rights treaties continue to apply in times of armed conflict and that there may simply be overlap with the war crimes regime.

The Inter-American Convention on the Forced Disappearance of Persons is explicit that it does not apply in times of 'international armed conflict', and the Convention on Hostage Taking is inapplicable where the State Party is bound under the grave breaches regime of the Geneva Conventions to prosecute or hand over the alleged perpetrator. These

Rights Law, Oxford University Press, 2011; Christopher Greenwood, 'Human Rights and Humanitarian Law – Conflict of Convergence', (2010) 43 *Case Western Reserve Journal of International Law* 491; R. Cryer, 'The Interplay of Human Rights and Humanitarian Law: The Approach of the ICTY', (2010) 14 *Journal of Conflict and Security Law*, 511–27; Marco Sassòli and Laura Olson, 'The Relationship Between International Humanitarian Law and Human Rights Law Where it Matters: Admissible Killing and Internment of Fighters in Non-International Armed Conflicts', (2008) 871 *International Review of the Red Cross* 599.

37 *Legality of the Threat or Use of Nuclear Weapons, Advisory Opinion, I.C.J. Reports 1996*, p. 226, para. 25.

treaties are therefore not applicable in case of such an overlap, and the issues are therefore dealt with exclusively under the regime established by the 1949 Geneva Conventions and the first Additional Protocol thereto. More recent human rights treaties, however, such as the 2006 UN Convention on Enforced Disappearances, simply allow for the parallel application of the human rights treaty and the international humanitarian law treaties.[38]

Putting these technical issues aside, the debate continues and says a lot about the role of human rights in the international legal order. On the one side, we find remnants of the idea that war entitles you to do things that would be illegal at other times: killing, bombing, destruction, detention without charge, and the prosecution of war crimes under military commissions. On the other side, we find a network of human rights obligations which are said to apply at all times and in all places (unless a State chooses to derogate from some obligations). This leads to real differences. If a particular killing is not necessarily a war crime (perhaps because the victim was not a civilian, or because the death was proportionate to the anticipated military advantage) should this be a matter for those bodies that supervise respect for human rights? If the law on internal armed conflict is silent on the bases and review of detention of the opposing forces, should those detained in such a conflict enjoy the right to demand that their detention is in accordance with the law of human rights?

The law of war crimes is rather underdeveloped in the field of internal armed conflicts. It is argued here that just because something is not criminalised as a war crime in such conflicts should not necessarily mean that it is permitted under human rights law. The extent to which human rights bodies and courts are now holding States to account for their conduct and policies in the context of armed conflict is of course being resisted by the military and politicians who complain that this is reducing their capacity to fight effectively. Nevertheless, it has become quite clear that the human rights regime is not only more protective than the war crimes regime associated with the law of armed conflict, but it is also more effective as

---

38 These issues are explained in more detail in Andrew Clapham, 'The Complex Relationship between the 1949 Geneva Conventions and International Human Rights Law', in Andrew Clapham, Paola Gaeta, and Marco Sassòli, eds., *The 1949 Geneva Conventions: A Commentary*, Oxford University Press, 2015, pp. 701–35.

the rules are backed by multiple options for supervision at the national and international level.

Human rights and the issue of amnesties

Amnesties have been relied on to preclude the prosecution of international crimes. A typical amnesty would be adopted at the end of a civil war or as part of a transition away from dictatorship. It would prevent criminal courts from prosecuting a class of persons or certain types of acts committed over a certain period. International human rights bodies have had to deal with arguments demanding that such laws are incompatible with the human rights of the victims that have to be vindicated through prosecution. In turn, this asks us to consider whether such amnesties might serve a useful role in bringing peace and stability, or whether they are to be simply considered invalid. The answer of course lies somewhere in the middle as these questions are very context specific. A few things are nevertheless quite clear.

First, an amnesty proclaimed in one State will not be binding on the courts or the prosecutor of another State. Where a human rights violation is being prosecuted as an international crime in that second State, the amnesty will not present a bar to prosecution. The English courts did not consider that Pinochet's self-proclaimed amnesty precluded their jurisdiction. Secondly, an amnesty proclaimed at the national level will not preclude a prosecution in the International Criminal Court.[39] Thirdly, the UN Secretariat, including the Secretary-General, and the High Commissioner for Human Rights in particular, have discouraged amnesties in peace agreements and in national law.[40] Lastly, the international human rights

---

39 For thoughts on how the Prosecutor of the International Criminal Court might take an amnesty into account in deciding whether to prosecute see William A. Schabas, *Unimaginable Atrocities: Justice, Politics, and Rights and the War Crimes Tribunals*, Oxford University Press, 2012, pp. 188–98.

40 For a detailed examination see: *Rule of Law Tools for Post Conflict States: Amnesties*, Geneva: Office of the High Commissioner for Human Rights, 2009; M. Freeman, *Necessary Evils: Amnesties and the Search for Justice*, Cambridge University Press, 2010, ch. 6; N. Michel and K. Del Mar, 'Transitional Justice', in Andrew Clapham and Paola Gaeta, eds., *The Oxford Handbook of International Law in Armed Conflict*, Oxford University Press, 2014, pp. 840–83, especially pp. 865–71.

supervisory bodies have disapproved, invalidated, and ignored amnesties for human rights crimes.[41] In some cases the amnesty itself has been found to represent a violation of the victims' human right to a remedy.[42]

One of the most recent and reasoned judgments has come from the Grand Chamber of the European Court of Human Rights, building on the jurisprudence from the Inter-American Court and the UN Human Rights Committee. It reiterates its own case law that 'affirms that granting amnesty in respect of the killing and ill-treatment of civilians would run contrary to the State's obligations under articles 2 and 3 of the Convention, since it would hamper the investigation of such acts and necessarily lead to impunity for those responsible'.[43] The judgment then highlights the fact that some treaties including the Geneva Conventions and the Genocide Convention, as well as some of the human rights treaties we discussed above (such as the Convention against Torture), oblige States to prosecute certain offences, and considers that the possibility for a State to grant an amnesty 'may be circumscribed' by these treaty obligations under international criminal law.[44] But in its final conclusion it seems to leave the door ajar to allow some amnesties, where these are essential for reconciliation or accompanied by alternative procedures for ensuring compensation to victims.

> In the present case, the applicant was granted amnesty for acts which amounted to grave breaches of fundamental human rights such as the intentional killing of civilians and inflicting grave bodily injury on a child, and the County Court's reasoning referred to the applicant's merits as a military officer. A growing tendency in international law is to see such amnesties as unacceptable because they are incompatible with the unanimously recognised obligation of States to prosecute and punish grave breaches of fundamental human rights. Even if it were to be accepted that amnesties are possible where there are some particular circumstances, such as a reconciliation process and/or a form of compensation to the victims,

41 E.g., I/A Court H.R., Case of *Barrios Altos* v. *Peru*. Reparations and Costs. Judgment of November 30 2001. Series C No. 8; *Ould Dah* v. *France* (dec.), no. 13113/03, ECHR 2009.

42 African Commission of Human and Peoples' Rights, *Mouvement ivoirien des droits humains (MIDH)* v. *Côte d'Ivoire*, 246/02, para. 98: 'The granting of amnesty to absolve perpetrators of human rights violations from accountability violates the right of victims to an effective remedy.'

43 *Marguš* v. *Croatia* [GC], no. 4455/10, § 127, 27 May 2014.

44 Ibid., § 132.

the amnesty granted to the applicant in the instant case would still not be acceptable since there is nothing to indicate that there were any such circumstances.[45]

Concluding summary

We have seen that from the early days of international criminal law, as propounded by the Nuremberg Tribunal, there were inquiries as to how such prosecutions represented both an opportunity to address the massive violations committed during the war and, at the same time, a threat to the human rights of the defendants. We have also seen that international law has developed so that human rights violations that rise to the level of crimes against humanity can now be prosecuted as international crimes without any connection to an armed conflict. This criminalisation represents a huge opportunity to stigmatise as international criminals those who violate human rights in this way. We should be vigilant, however, that the chance to reformulate some human rights violations as crimes against humanity does not lead us to overlook those fundamental rights that are essential for building communities that guarantee social justice, the rule of law, and opportunities for all.

A parallel development has been the adoption of treaties that define certain human rights violations (for example torture and enforced disappearances) as offences and obligate States Parties not only to create jurisdiction over such crimes but also to prosecute or extradite anyone found within the jurisdiction who is alleged to have committed such human rights offences (even in times of armed conflict). But the same technique can actually threaten human rights; the applicability of treaties designed to suppress phenomena such as trafficking or terrorism may be part of the move to protect human rights, but actually be executed in ways that threaten a variety of human rights.

More generally the tension remains between the need to prosecute contemporary international crimes, and the right not to be tried for acts that could not be considered crimes at the time they were committed. On the one hand, where these crimes involve direct violence to the person, the principle of legality has been interpreted so as to allow international

---

45 Ibid., § 139.

criminal law to evolve in a way that encompasses such acts as crimes; courts have often considered it entirely foreseeable that such behaviour is criminal. On the other hand, this human rights principle, which protects the individual from retroactive application of the criminal law, remains essential for challenging the expanding reach of international criminal law, especially as new wide-ranging offences are imagined in the context of States' counter-terrorism measures.

While human rights law is now sometimes enforced through the prosecution of international crimes at either the national or international level, the same human rights law may constrain what investigators, prosecutors, and judges can do within the rule of law even in the quest to prosecute international crimes. In some cases both sides will be claiming that their arguments are based on human rights. Discovering new crimes may be in the interests of the rights of victims, while the accused will argue that this violates the right not to be tried for a crime that did not exist at the time the acts were committed. Although the criminal courts may be the focus for those thinking about international criminal law, human rights law provides the parameters within which these tribunals must work. And the human rights supervisory bodies now provide a measure of oversight, guiding not only the work of national and international prosecutions, but also obligating States to prosecute international crimes when it might be more convenient to forget all about them.

FURTHER READING

Tim Allen, *Trial Justice: The International Criminal Court and the Lord's Resistance Army*, London: Zed Books, 2006.

Neil Boister, 'Human Rights Protections in the Suppression Conventions', (2002) 2 *Human Rights Law Review* 199.

Alexandra Valeria Huneeus, 'International Criminal Law by Other Means: The Quasi-Criminal Jurisdiction of the Human Rights Courts', (2013) 107 *American Journal of International Law* 1.

Yasmin Q. Naqvi, *Impediments to Exercising Jurisdiction over International Crimes*, The Hague: T.M.C. Asser Press, 2010.

William A. Schabas, *Unimaginable Atrocities: Justice, Politics, and Rights and the War Crimes Tribunals*, Oxford University Press, 2012.

William A. Schabas, 'International Criminal Law and Tribunals and Human Rights', in Scott Sheeran and Nigel Rodley, eds., *Routledge Handbook of International Human Rights Law*, Abingdon: Routledge, 2013, pp. 215–29.

Evelyn Schmid, *Taking Economic, Social and Cultural Rights Seriously in International Criminal Law*, Cambridge University Press, 2015.

Wolfgang Schomburg, 'The Role of International Criminal Tribunals in Promoting Respect for Human Rights', (2009) 8 *Northwestern Journal of International Human Rights* 1.

Salvatore Zappalà, *Human Rights in International Criminal Proceedings*, Oxford University Press, 2003.

2 Truth and justice in atrocity trials

Lawrence Douglas

In 1997, the prominent French historian of Vichy, Henry Rousso, was asked to testify in the trial of Maurice Papon, the former French budget minister who stood accused of complicity in crimes against humanity for his actions as a police official during the Nazi occupation of France. Rousso declined the invitation. Worried that his testimony would contribute to what he called a 'judicialisation of the past', Rousso objected to trials in which 'beyond the judgment of particular individuals, the declared goal is to illuminate an entire era and its politics'.[1]

Rousso's concerns echoed those voiced thirty-five years earlier by Hannah Arendt in *Eichmann in Jerusalem*. In her famous 'report on the banality of evil', Arendt insisted, 'the purpose of a trial is to render justice and nothing else. Even the noblest of ulterior purposes – the making of a record of the Hitler regime which would withstand the test of history – can only detract from the law's main business'.[2] That is, rendering a just verdict.

Admittedly, the two positions are not identical. Rousso's concern seems to be what law does to history: when forced to speak in the law's Manichean idiom, the historian's voice loses nuance and subtlety, becomes somehow false. By contrast, Arendt's concern appears to be what history does to law: when burdened with the pressures of composing history, the trial wanders from the solemn dictates of justice. But taken together, the views of Rousso and Arendt can be seen as emblematic of a belief that has gained wide currency among scholars of law and history – that the interests of justice and truth are fundamentally incompatible.

---

1 Henry Rousso, *The Haunting Past: History, Memory and Justice in Contemporary France* (trans. Ralph Schoolcraft), Philadelphia: University of Pennsylvania Press, 2002, p. 50. See also Richard Evans, 'History, Memory and the Law: The Historian as Expert Witness', (2002) 41 *History and Theory* 326.
2 Hannah Arendt, *Eichmann in Jerusalem: A Report on the Banality of Evil*, New York: Viking, 1963, p. 254.

That such a belief should gain such wide acceptance seems, at first blush, deeply anomalous. Critics of the criminal justice system might bemoan how imperfectly truth is served, but to suggest that truth is irrelevant to the system is nothing short of extravagant. At the most basic, the criminal trial is an instrument for ascertaining truth: it is tasked with determining the truth of charges brought against the accused. Clearly, fixing the truth is not the sole goal of trial procedure. The system is prepared, for example, to bar highly probative evidence of factual guilt if such evidence was acquired in violation of the accused's constitutional or basic rights. Truth-seeking must, then, respect the dignity and autonomy of the accused. But if truth is not the exclusive goal of the criminal trial, it certainly cannot be said that the criminal trial is hostile to the truth. Indeed, the standard of proving the truth of the charges against the accused – beyond a reasonable doubt – is an exceptionally exacting one. Moreover, most would agree that a false conviction is an injustice *per se*, even in the absence of any visible procedural defect. Thus far from hostile to the truth, the criminal trial seems designed to serve it. But because the system is prepared to subordinate strict truth-seeking to the rights of the accused, we can say that truth is a necessary but not a sufficient condition to a finding of guilt.[3]

How then can we explain the perceived hostility of justice to truth? The arguments of Rousso and Arendt become more intelligible when we realise that the perceived antagonism does not infect all criminal trials equally, but rather appears to particularly vex a subset that I will call *atrocity trials*. Conventionally, law views criminal behaviour as a deviant act committed by an individual that harms community norms and interests. In this model, the most serious violation of community norms is murder, the planned, unjustified, unauthorised killing of one person by another. Here the criminal takes the familiar form of the deviant who clutters the evening news and police dramas – the creepy predator, the stalking sadist, the remorseless thug, the sociopathic freak.

In the classic model, the State serves as the defender and the locus of legality. It responds to acts of harmful deviance by deploying its coercive powers against the perpetrator, seeking to apprehend, prosecute and punish the perpetrator of crimes, and, in so doing, aims to defend and restore violated norms of community order. In such cases, the criminal

---

3 R. A. Duff, *Trials and Punishments*, Cambridge University Press, 1991.

trial plays the familiar role described above: it seeks to accurately identify persons deserving of the State's sanction. Here we detect no substantial gulf between justice and truth – except in cases in which, as noted, the system chooses to subordinate truth to superior values, or in cases in which it malfunctions, generating a false positive.

Crimes of atrocity turn this model on its head. In the wake of Germany's capitulation, the German philosopher Karl Jaspers described the Nazi regime as a *Verbrecherstaat,* a criminal State.[4] This idea – that the State *itself* was criminal – denoted a phenomenon that simply lay beyond the ken of the classic model of the criminal law. In the pages of Thomas Hobbes' *Leviathan*, arguably the greatest work of western political thought, the State is not simply the bulwark of all order; as the force that protects us from the violence committed in civil society, the State is the very source of Law itself.[5] Jaspers' formulation demanded that – *contra* Hobbes – the State be seen not as the defender of law and order but as the principal perpetrator of crimes, as the very agent of criminality.

What I am calling the *atrocity trial* can be understood as law's response to the advent of the *Verbrecherstaat.* The atrocity trial typically addresses the gravest violations of international law: war crimes, crimes against humanity, and genocide. The atrocity trial has given rise to a variety of specialised international courts, including the International Military Tribunal that tried the major Nazi war criminals in Nuremberg, the United Nations's *ad hoc* Yugoslavia and Rwanda tribunals, and the fledgling International Criminal Court housed in The Hague. But the atrocity trial need not have a strictly international character, and may assume a variety of forms. It may take on a hybrid cast, as in the case of the Extraordinary Chambers in the Courts of Cambodia tasked with trying former members of the Khmer Rouge for violations of both international and domestic Cambodian law. It can take the form of a special domestic national court, as was the case in the Israeli trial of Adolf Eichmann, who was tried, convicted, and executed under an Israeli law punishing crimes against humanity and crimes against the Jewish people, a sub-species of genocide. In France, the atrocity trials of Klaus Barbie and Maurice Papon took place before regular criminal courts that applied a domestic law

4 K. Jaspers, *Wohin Treibt die Bundesrepublik?* Munich: Reprint, 1988.
5 Thomas Hobbes, *Leviathan*, Richard Tuck, ed., Cambridge University Press, 1996, pp. 88–9.

incorporating crimes against humanity into the French legal code. And in Germany, John Demjanjuk, a death camp guard, was convicted by an ordinary German court applying Germany's ordinary law of murder.

Yet whatever its form, the atrocity trial invariably raises fraught questions of historical truth, as crimes of atrocity necessarily deal with large communities and actions perpetrated over broad swaths of space and time. In cases applying international incriminations such as crimes against humanity and genocide, this is true *by definition*: what constitutes a systematic attack on a civilian population or what constitutes an attempt to destroy members of a group *qua* group are legal questions that can only be answered by a thorough consideration of the historical record.

The strong connection between crimes of atrocity and patterns of history would seem to push against Rousso's and Arendt's positions. If anything, atrocity trials would appear to draw the interests of justice and truth all the more powerfully in concord. Certainly, the development of a jurisprudence of atrocity has revolutionised the use of historians in criminal trials. The very first witness to appear at the Jerusalem trial of Adolf Eichmann was Columbia historian Salo Baron, who essentially delivered a lengthy lecture connecting the Holocaust to the larger history of European anti-Semitism. When Israel tried John Demjanjuk as the notorious Treblinka guard known as Ivan the Terrible, the first witness called by the state was Yitzhak Arad, a prominent Israeli historian and at the time director of Yad Vashem, the Israeli Holocaust memorial and research centre. (Demjanjuk was convicted in one of the most notorious cases of mistaken identity in legal history, but later set free by the Israeli Supreme Court.) During the trial of Duško Tadić before the International Criminal Tribunal for the former Yugoslavia, Kings College historian James Gow was summoned to likewise anchor the case in the larger history of the war in the Balkans. In the United States, the Office of Special Investigations, the branch of the Justice Department responsible for preparing denaturalisation and deportation cases against Nazi collaborators in the United States, created its own staff of professional historians, something that marked a dramatic departure from Justice Department practice.

And yet it is precisely the intimacy of the relationship between jurists and historians in atrocity trials that has aroused the concern of scholars such as Rousso and Arendt. So let us look at their arguments in greater depth. At the outset, we should note that even the most critical scholars acknowledge history's indebtedness to law's power as a fact-finding tool.[6] It is widely accepted that many of the path-breaking early histories of the Holocaust, most notably Raul Hilberg's magisterial *The Destruction of the European Jews*, could not have been written without the astonishing documentary archive gathered at Nuremberg. More recent notable works, such as Daniel Goldhagen's *Hitler's Willing Executioners* and Christopher Browning's *Ordinary Men*, likewise drew largely on depositions and other documents assembled through the labour of German prosecutors. But this, we can agree, is a weak and grudging concession, one that sees the value of the atrocity trial simply in terms of the pile of archival material it makes available for future historians.

More to the point, it leaves intact the more basic insistence that the atrocity trial reveals a gulf between justice and historical truth.[7] So let us consider some of the structural constraints that are believed to contribute to this gulf. Firstly, it is noted that history and law are governed by differing epistemological and evidentiary conventions. Here it is argued that the formal procedures that constrain the production of knowledge in a criminal trial, at least in Anglo-American law, render this instrument a flawed tool for clarifying and comprehending complex historical truths. Geoffrey Nice, the British barrister who prosecuted Slobodan Milošević, once remarked: 'It is well nigh impossible to conduct complex war-crimes prosecutions, where evidence often comes from sensitive sources, using standard common-law rules of evidence'.[8] While these evidentiary and procedural norms might make sense and promote truth-seeking in the conventional model of criminal prosecution described earlier, they frustrate the interests of truth when applied to the atrocity paradigm.

A second and related argument insists that atrocity trials distort truth inasmuch as a complex historical record must be shoehorned to fit unsuitable legal categories. As one prominent historian has observed, 'the shape

---

6 See Carlo Ginzburg, *The Judge and the Historian: Marginal Notes on a Late-Twentieth-Century Miscarriage of Justice* (trans. Anthony Shugaar), London: Verso, 1999.

7 See Marti Koskenniemi, 'Between Impunity and Show Trials', (2002) 6 *Max Planck Yearbook of United Nations Law* 1; Mark Osiel, *Mass Atrocity, Collective Memory and the Law*, New Brunswick: Rutgers University Press, 1997; Donald Bloxham, *Genocide on Trial: War Crimes Trials and the Formation of Holocaust History and Memory*, Oxford University Press, 2001.

8 Conversation with the author.

of the stories told in trials ... follows the definition of the crimes with which the accused are charged, rather than an impartial assessment of the events themselves'.[9] Here the preoccupation is not with evidentiary norms but with the substantive incriminations through which history must be filtered. But the deeper concern is again specific to the atrocity paradigm. Incriminations designed to cope with conventional acts of criminality are stretched to their breaking point when applied to crimes of atrocity. The numerous Nazi atrocity trials conducted by the Federal Republic of Germany provide particularly dismaying examples of this phenomenon, as the entire exterminatory machinery of the Third Reich had to be juridi-cally digested through Germany's conventional murder statute, the most serious criminal offence that Nazi perpetrators could be charged with under the law of the Federal Republic – and, indeed, the *only* crime they could be charged with after the prescriptive period for other crimes, such as manslaughter, tolled in 1960.[10]

Under German law, murder was restricted to acts of killing commit-ted out of 'thirst of blood (*Mordlust*), satisfaction of ... sexual desires, avarice or other base motives (*niedrige Beweggründe*)' or perpetrated in a particularly 'malicious or brutal manner'. These requirements meant, for example, that in the famous Frankfurt-Auschwitz trial (1963–1965) the everyday horrors and killings of Auschwitz ended up serving as the baseline of normalcy against which the particularly base, malicious, or brutal conduct of certain guards or functionaries could be measured.[11] For the purposes of German law only those who had engaged in 'excessive acts' – had, for example, killed without authorisation to do so – could be considered murderers. In treating crimes of atrocity as conventional acts of murder, German trials grossly distorted the truth of State-sponsored extermination. As Arendt put it, these trials contributed to a 'pernicious

9 Michael Marrus, 'L'histoire et l'Holocauste dans le Prétoire', in F. Brayard, ed., *Le Génocide des Juifs Entre Procès et Histoire, 1943–2000*, Paris and Brussels: IHTP-CNRS/Complexe, 2000, pp. 25–50, at p. 48.

10 Adalbert Rückerl, *NS-Verbrechen vor Gericht: Versuch Einer*, Vergangenheitsbewältigung, Heidelberg: C.F. Müller, 1984.

11 Devin Pendas, *The Frankfurt Auschwitz Trial, 1963–1965: Genocide, History and the Limits of Law*, Cambridge University Press, 2005; Rebecca Wittmann, *Beyond Justice: The Auschwitz Trial*, Cambridge: Harvard University Press, 2005.

... understanding' – an 'illusion' that 'murder and extermination are essentially the same crime'.[12]

A third set of criticisms builds on this latter critique and focuses on what we may describe as the prosecutorial focus of atrocity trials. Here it is claimed that all criminal trials, by necessity, occupy themselves with the specific actions of an individual defendant or a group of defendants. As a result of this requirement, atrocity trials exaggerate the roles of individuals in events of greater historical sweep and compass. We find this argument in Arendt's insistence that the Eichmann proceedings revealed a disturbing disconnect between the vastness of the atrocities paraded before the court and the solitary drab individual in the dock – a disconnect that was overcome, Arendt claims, by transforming the defendant into an agent with demonic powers. Rousso makes much the same point when he raises his objection to trials in which 'beyond the judgment of particular individuals, the declared goal is to illuminate an entire era and its politics'. In his criticism of the Tadić trial by the International Criminal Tribunal for the former Yugoslavia, Geoffrey Robertson actually calls Tadić a 'scapegoat almost' whose punishment assumed a 'symbolic capacity' as 'less an example of individual responsibility than collective guilt'.[13] Taken to its logical conclusion, Robertson's criticism posits no antagonism between truth and justice in the atrocity trial. Rather, it insists that the trial threatens to fail in *both* regards.[14] By forcing individuals to answer for complex collective crimes, the atrocity trial risks distorting the historical record *and* treating the accused unjustly.

The claim that atrocity trials produce symbols and myths and not truth is related to a final criticism. Here the concern is that the atrocity trial can only produce Official History, a picture of the past that is rigid and refractory to the movement of historiography.[15] As Michael Marrus has put it,

---

12 Hannah Arendt, *Eichmann in Jerusalem: A Report on the Banality of Evil*, New York: Viking, 1963, p. 272.

13 Geoffrey Robertson, *Crimes Against Humanity: The Struggle for Global Justice*, London: Penguin Books, 2000, pp. 309–10.

14 Marti Koskenniemi, 'Between Impunity and Show Trials', (2002) 6 *Max Planck Yearbook of United Nations Law* 1.

15 In addition to the arguments of Michael Marrus, see also Martha Minow, *Between Vengeance and Forgiveness: Facing History after Genocide and Mass Violence*, Boston: Beacon, 1998; Tzvetan Todorov, 'Letter from Paris: The Papon Trial', in Richard Golsan, ed., *The Papon Affair: Memory and Justice on Trial*, New York: Routledge, 2000, pp. 217–222.

'while judgments of courts are fixed... historiography moves'.[16] The truths of history are tentative, available for complex amplification, retraction, and correction. The law, by contrast, frames its conclusions in the form of a verdict backed up by the coercive apparatus of the State. This finality and connection to State force turn the 'truths' framed in legal judgment into inflexible forms, tools of politics and power, not products of neutral inquiry.

Reconciling truth and justice

What are we to make of these arguments? Let us concede that the criminal trial is hardly the exclusive vehicle for coming to terms with the truth of atrocity. Episodes of mass atrocity may be just as satisfactorily – and perhaps even more satisfactorily – explored through the discourses of, say, history, philosophy, or literature – or through alternative forums, such as truth commissions.[17] We can grant all this and still reject the strong claim that would find the atrocity trial as the cause and occasion of an inseparable gulf between justice and truth.[18]

Let us begin with the matter of proof. History and law remain deeply committed to the notion of reliable proof, even if what counts as reliable proof differs across the disciplines. Admittedly, rules of evidence and procedure limit the utility of the criminal trial as a tool of seeking the truth of complex histories. But here we must bear in mind that the atrocity trial has imaginatively experimented with alternative evidentiary conventions in order to better equip it to make sense of complex history. For example, the Nuremberg trials – that is, both the trial of the major Nazi war criminals before the International Military Tribunal and the twelve 'successor' trials staged by the American military – were governed by relaxed rules of evidence that permitted the use of hearsay and

16 Michael Marrus, 'L'histoire et l'Holocauste dans le Prétoire', in F. Brayard, ed., *Le Génocide des Juifs Entre Procès et Histoire, 1943–2000*, Paris and Brussels: IHTP-CNRS/Complexe, 2000, pp. 25–50, at p. 45.

17 See generally Priscilla Hayner, *Unspeakable Truths: Confronting State Terror and Atrocity*, 2nd edn, New York: Routledge, 2011; Robert Rotberg and Dennis Thompson, eds., *Truth v. Justice: The Morality of Truth Commissions*, Princeton University Press, 2000.

18 Lawrence Douglas, *The Memory of Judgment: Making Law and History in the Trials of the Holocaust*, New Haven: Yale University Press, 2001.

embraced a more capacious notion of relevance. The Eichmann trial was likewise governed by more generous evidentiary rules, which, for example, permitted survivor testimonies to assume a more fluid narrative form, quite different from the tutored testimony produced at standard adversarial trials. The UN's *ad hoc* international criminal tribunals and the International Criminal Court are likewise controlled by evidentiary norms less formal than those tailored to the Anglo-American jury system. Do these norms compromise the fairness of these trials? In answering this, we must resist the parochial temptation to confuse Anglo-American norms of adversarial justice with justice writ large. Bars against hearsay may seem foundational to our system, but many continental legal systems, such as the German, allow hearsay and a less rigid approach to proof. Atrocity trials have tended, then, to follow the continental system, which, of course, protects rights of confrontation of witnesses and other core procedures foundational to a concept of trial fairness. By relaxing bars against hearsay and rules controlling relevance, the atrocity trial seeks to strengthen the law's truth-seeking powers without sacrificing principles of due process.

What of the problem of law's shoehorning history to fit restrictive legal categories? The concern is valid yet overlooks the law's bold attempts to shape incriminations adequate to the task of naming and condemning complex crimes of atrocity. Two critical legal innovations stand out, *crimes against humanity* and *genocide*. First recognised as an incrimination at Nuremberg, crimes against humanity provided the legal channel by which much of the evidence of the Holocaust entered the Nuremberg courtroom. Nuremberg, we need to recall, was not in the first instance a Holocaust trial. The twenty-two defendants were principally charged with 'crimes against peace', that is, with waging a war of aggression in violation of international law. At Nuremberg, 'crimes against humanity' described acts technically not considered war crimes, and prosecutors had to prove a nexus between these crimes and the Nazis' violations of the law of armed conflict.[19] Nonetheless, by elevating extermination and systematic attacks on a civilian population to the status of international crimes, 'crimes against humanity' marked a crucial conceptual innovation, and if Nuremberg failed to provide a perfectly adequate picture of Holocaust history, it nevertheless offered

19 Ibid., pp. 38–64.

to my mind a rather impressive first pass in the attempt to juridically digest unprecedented atrocities.

The second critical legal innovation was the articulation of the concept of 'genocide'.[20] In a book published in 1944, Raphael Lemkin, a Jewish refugee from Poland working as an advisor to the US War Department, proposed a new term to describe the Nazis' treatment of Jews in occupied countries. He called the new crime 'genocide' – wedding an ancient Greek word for group (γενος) to a Latin word for killing (*cide*). The resulting neologism meant to describe something distinct from mass murder. In Lemkin's words, it sought to 'signify a coordinated ... destruction of the essential foundations of the life of ... groups, with the aim of annihilating the groups themselves'.[21] The new term began to circulate widely – particularly in the twelve 'successor' trials staged by the American military at Nuremberg – and on 9 December 1948, the UN General Assembly voted to recognise genocide as denoting its own independent crime in international law.[22] Genocide now stands as the most extreme crime recognised by any legal code; it is, as William Schabas has put it, 'the crime of crimes'.[23]

These novel incriminations have made possible the prosecution of a large number of perpetrators of the most extreme international crimes, and so have served the interests of justice. But the point is deeper still. The creation of these new incriminations calls attention to a crucial point overlooked by the critics we have considered – namely, that the atrocity trial *has redefined the very meaning of justice itself.* In the conventional model which sees crime as deviance, justice is typically associated with the project of protecting the rights of the accused and safeguarding against false positives. In the atrocity model, by contrast, justice is served by *ending impunity.* This is not to suggest that the atrocity paradigm is not deeply concerned with conventional notions of procedural fairness;

---

20 See Samantha Power, *'A Problem from Hell': America and the Age of Genocide*, New York: Basic Books, 2002.

21 Raphael Lemkin, *Axis Rule in Occupied Europe: Laws of Occupation, Analysis of Government and Proposals for Redress*, Washington: Carnegie Endowment for International Peace, 1944, pp. 80–1.

22 The Convention on the Punishment and Prevention of the Crime of Genocide officially entered into force early in 1951.

23 William A. Schabas, *Genocide in International Law: The Crime of Crimes*, 2nd edn, Cambridge University Press, 2009.

clearly it is. But because the atrocity paradigm also understands justice as a battle against impunity, we are reminded that in weighing the fit between justice and history, we are also dealing with a different conception of justice itself, one that locates *injustice* in a failure to prosecute.

Thus, not only have these new incriminations served the interests of justice by expanding the reach of prosecutors, they have also liberated jurists from the strait-jacket of conventional categories of criminal wrongdoing, such as murder, unsuited to the historical and organisational complexities of crimes of atrocity. If German atrocity trials historically pigeonholed acts of State-sponsored extermination to fit the conventional statutory definition of murder, this was not because of the absence of alternative incriminations but because German jurists balked from applying them. Indeed, German courts, operating under the watchful eye of Allied occupiers, were familiar with the concept of crimes against humanity and regularly used the incrimination in trials of Nazi crimes. Unfortunately, the restoration of (West) German sovereignty was accompanied by a strong rejection of the Allied war crimes programme and the jurisprudence it had sponsored. German courts forthwith refused to charge former Nazis with crimes against humanity, arguing – wrongly to my mind – that the charge represented a violation of the Basic Law's bar against retroactivity (*Rückwirkungsverbot*).[24] In 1954, the crime of genocide was formally incorporated into the German criminal code, but here again jurists refused to apply the incrimination to former Nazis out of concerns about retroactivity. That the German law of murder proved itself ill-suited to deal with crimes of atrocity was hardly surprising. Thus, far from demonstrating the incompatibility of justice and truth in atrocity trials, the German case simply underscores the need to apply those incriminations specifically tailored to the historical and organisational complexities of State-sponsored extermination.

What of the distortions that arise from the trial's focus on the individual acts of discrete persons? First, it should be noted that this focus may serve the interests of both justice *and* truth by establishing a bulwark against collective punishment – a particularly strong temptation in the wake of

---

24 Lawrence Douglas, 'Was damals Recht war'...'*Nulla Poena*' and the Prosecution of Crimes Against Humanity in Occupied Germany', in Larry May and Elizabeth Edenberg, eds., *Jus Post Bellum and Transitional Justice*, Cambridge University Press, 2013, pp. 44–73.

mass atrocities. Still, the question remains whether the atrocity trial is capable of grasping the structural architecture of genocide – its corporate dimension, its dependence on an extensive apparatus of bureaucratic and logistical support. By way of response, we should note that the atrocity paradigm has experimented with novel theories of liability designed to better address the realities of mass crimes. Nuremberg, for example, was not simply a trial of leading Nazis; also on trial were a number of Nazi organisations, including the entire Gestapo. Robert Jackson, the lead American prosecutor, insisted that '[i]t would be a greater catastrophe to acquit these organisations than it would be to acquit the entire 22 individual defendants in the box'.[25] Nuremberg's controversial conspiracy count must also be seen as born of a prosecutorial effort to master the complexities of crimes of mass atrocity. More recently, the UN war crimes tribunals have developed a rich jurisprudence around the concept of the Joint Criminal Enterprise, a theory of liability designed to address the corporate nature of mass crimes. The doctrine of JCE seeks to serve the fight against impunity by expanding prosecutorial reach and addressing the complex reality of crimes of atrocity.

Second, inasmuch as an atrocity trial telescopes a broad history onto the actions of an Eichmann or even a lowly Tadić, this hardly turns the defendant into a scapegoat. A scapegoat is an innocent creature upon whom undeserved guilt has been *displaced*. In an atrocity trial, wrongdoing has not been displaced but *condensed* in the figure of the perpetrator or the accessory. Such a trial may indeed perform a 'symbolic function', but this is less a criticism than a statement of fact inasmuch as only a small percentage of those responsible for an episode of mass atrocity will ever be placed in the dock. Prosecutors will always aim to try principals, but an underling suffers no injustice when asked to answer for his or her role in crimes orchestrated by more prominent individuals or facilitated by groups or collectives. Indeed, the insistence that only architects of atrocity deserve to be prosecuted overlooks the multiple levels of complicity that make mass crimes possible.

Finally, there remains the concern that law's history threatens to become the Official History. While it is true that courts are not structured

25 Quoted in Lawrence Douglas, *The Memory of Judgment: Making Law and History in the Trials of the Holocaust*, New Haven: Yale University Press, 2001, p. 88.

in a manner that encourages acknowledging the limitations of their representations of the past, neither, I would argue, is the academy. The practice of history, even in the wake of the 'linguistic turn' and among those who recognise the constructed character of historical narrative, remains remarkably positivist in cast. This is not to deny the differences between the discourses of law and history, but only to caution that the differences may be overstated. Obviously a court's readings of the past may authorise the imposition of a punishment, but this fact arguably describes an advantage that atrocity trials hold over those quasi-legal forums typically considered more conducive to present history in its complexity, such as truth commissions. Because law's stories receive resolution in judgment and narratives find emphatic closure in juridically-sanctioned violence, atrocity trials have the power to galvanise public attention and so to serve as powerful tools of instruction.

And yet the fact that a trial court must render an unequivocal verdict does not mean that the historical truths presented in the courtroom or in the judgment become somehow fixed, inert, and unassailable. Any change to the trial court's judgment on appeal changes the understanding of the past framed at trial.[26] More to the point, because crimes of atrocity inevitably involve many participants, the legal response tends to take the form not of a one-off prosecution, but of a prosecutorial programme, involving multiple cases and defendants. As this prosecutorial programme unfolds – as prosecutors, judges, and other legal actors master the learning curve of complex crimes – atrocity trials typically come to frame a richer, more nuanced treatment of the larger historical complex.[27] By placing the destruction of European Jewry at the legal fore of the

26 Perhaps the best example of this in the context of atrocity trials remains the Israeli Supreme Court's vacating of Demjanjuk's 1987 conviction. Demjanjuk had been sentenced to death by a special Jerusalem court as Treblinka's Ivan the Terrible; the Supreme Court vacated the conviction once evidence emerged that Demjanjuk had served not at Treblinka, but at Sobibor, a less well known, though equally murderous, death camp. At the time, observers lamented the Supreme Court's decision as giving succour to Holocaust deniers. See Yoram Sheftel, *Show Trial: The Conspiracy to Convict John Demjanjuk as 'Ivan the Terrible'* (trans. Haim Watzman), London: Regnery, 1994, p. 342.

27 Shoshana Felman, 'Forms of Judicial Blindness: Traumatic Narratives and Legal Repetitions', in Austin Sarat and Thomas Kearns, eds., *History, Memory and the Law*, Ann Arbor: Michigan University Press, 1999, pp. 25–43.

proceedings, the Eichmann trial revised and refined the history of Nazi extermination presented in incomplete fashion at Nuremberg. In the case of French atrocity trials, the very definition of crimes against humanity – and the role that the Vichy state played in these crimes – became increasingly refined from the Barbie trial to the Touvier trial to the Papon trial.[28] Trials before the ICTY, such as the Foča case, have expanded the meaning of crimes against humanity to now include the crime of rape. And with the expansion of its legal meaning, the incrimination becomes a conduit for a broader range of historical material.

History and justice: a necessary collaboration

We must reject, then, the argument that atrocity trials invariably perform a disservice to the quest for historical truth. Indeed, the link between history and justice is so strong in atrocity trials that it is *impossible* to separate the two. If all historians were to follow Rousso's lead and were to refuse to lend their expertise to the court, far from preserving the purity of history and the sanctity of justice, the consequence would be the end of the atrocity trial altogether.

In the space that remains, I want to discuss an atrocity trial that underscores the inseparability of justice and historical truth – indeed, which provides a powerful example of the dependence of the former on the latter. In May 2011, a court in Munich convicted John Demjanjuk as an accessory to the murder of over 28,000 Jews. The Ukrainian-born Demjanjuk had emigrated to the United States after the Second World War; the exceptionally complicated and bizarre backstory of his case – which involved multiple denaturalisation and deportation proceedings in the States and the botched prosecution in Israel mentioned earlier – need not concern us here.[29] Suffice it to say that the Munich trial was based on Demjanjuk's service as a guard at the Sobibor death camp in

---

28 See Leila Nadya Sadat, 'The Legal Legacy of Maurice Papon', in Richard J. Golsan, ed., *The Papon Affair: Memory and Justice on Trial*, London: Routledge, 2000, pp. 131–60; Jean-Paul Jean and Denis Salas, *Barbie, Touvier, Papon ... Des Procès Pour la Mémoire*, Paris: Editions Autrement, 2002.

29 For the backstory and a description of the Munich trial, see Lawrence Douglas, 'Ivan the Recumbent, or Demjanjuk in Munich', *Harper's*, March 2012, pp. 45–52.

eastern Poland. Demjanjuk died in 2012 as his conviction was being appealed.

What was striking about Demjanjuk's Munich trial is not that it implicated important historical questions. Rather, at its core, it was a *trial by history*. Here basic legal questions were *unanswerable* without the insights of professional historians. Indeed, the Munich trial represented something altogether different from Rousso's observation that in atrocity trials, the individual defendant is used as a symbol to 'illuminate an entire era'. In Munich, detailed historical understanding of an elaborate exterminatory practice was deployed in order to illuminate the actions of a single individual. The juridical determination of individual guilt turned on basic answers to aggregate historical questions.

To appreciate this point, we need to bear three points in mind. First, as his case involved Nazi-era crimes, Demjanjuk could only, as I have noted, be charged under the German law of murder; no other incrimination was available to German prosecutors. Second, no witnesses could identify Demjanjuk; and third, there was no evidence concerning the accused's specific behaviour or personal actions while serving as a guard at Sobibor. The prosecution got around what might have been intractable obstacles to conviction with a theory as simple as it was irresistible. Tailored to the realities of Sobibor, one of the SS's three pure extermination facilities (along with Belzec and Treblinka), the prosecution's theory worked by simple syllogism:

> All Sobibor guards participated in the killing process.
> Demjanjuk was a Sobibor guard.
> *Therefore* Demjanjuk participated in the killing process.

The minor premise, that Demjanjuk was a Sobibor guard, was solidly established by documents. By contrast, the major premise – *All Sobibor guards participated in the killing process* – was an aggregate historical claim that could only be proved by a comprehensive historical study of Sobibor and its guard force. The historians consulted by the court established, first, that Sobibor was a death camp – hardly a novel insight, but nonetheless crucial to the theory of the case. If we compare Sobibor to Auschwitz, which was a hybrid facility – part death camp, part labour camp – the numbers are telling. Of the 1.2 million persons sent to Auschwitz, about 100,000 survived; of the approximately 1.5 million Jews sent to the pure extermination facilities of Treblinka, Belzec, and

Sobibor, no more than 125 lived. Sobibor had one purpose and one purpose only: to murder Jews.

As a second matter, historians demonstrated that *all* guards at Sobibor were generalists. Sobibor's entire guard force consisted of no more than twenty or so SS men and an additional 100–120 auxiliaries such as Demjanjuk. As a bare-bones operation, all the guards were mobilised when trainloads of Jews arrived; some served guard-tower duty to prevent escape while all others manned the train ramp and ran the well-rehearsed process of destruction. This historical evidence was essential, as any suggestion that some guards worked, say, exclusively as cooks, might have fatally weakened the prosecution's controlling premise.

Having established as a historical matter that Sobibor was a killing machine and that all guards participated in the process, the court was able to legally conclude that Demjanjuk *must have* participated in the killing process by virtue of his function. That, however, did not end the inquiry. One critical question remained: had the defendant participated voluntarily? This, of course, was a legal question that only the court could answer. A historian can no more tell a court that an action was voluntary than a ballistics expert can tell a court that a shooting was premeditated.

But here again the narrative fashioned by professional historians did not simply influence the court's response; it made it possible. Peter Black, a historian at the United States Holocaust Memorial Museum, exhaustively studied the 5,000 or so Eastern Europeans, mainly Ukrainians, trained by the SS to serve as death camp guards and auxiliaries to genocide. Of these 5,000 Black has estimated that one thousand men – one in five – deserted their posts.[30] The court concluded from this material that Demjanjuk had had a meaningful opportunity to desert and his failure to do so indicated the voluntariness of his service. Some have questioned this conclusion, though I take it to be correct. But that is not my main point. Rather, it is again to show the remarkable process by which a question of individual guilt was answered by recourse to larger patterns of historical action.

Some may find this trial by historical deduction disturbing. My own view is that in convicting Demjanjuk, the Munich court served the interests of both justice and truth. Indeed, the fact that the Munich court convicted in the *absence* of evidence of personal viciousness or excessive

---

30 Peter Black, 'Foot Soldiers of the Final Solution: The Trawniki Training Camp and Operation Reinhard', (2011) 25 *Holocaust and Genocide Studies* 1.

acts accounts for the ruling's importance. To convict only in the presence of proof of personal viciousness is to treat crimes of atrocity as ordinary criminal offences. Demjanjuk's Munich trial, by contrast, grasped an essential truth about mass killing: that it results not from individual acts of excess but from an exterminatory process. When it comes to State-sponsored atrocities, guilt is not to be measured by cruelty; guilt follows *function*.

Demjanjuk suffered, then, no injustice – and nor did the historical record. To the contrary, while compelled to rely upon an insufficient statutory tool – the conventional law of murder – the Munich court found a way to accommodate the logic of genocide, an achievement only made possible by the intimate collaboration between jurists and historians. The *trial by history* made possible a belated, yet crucial correction to German case law.[31] In so doing, it made clear how the accumulated knowledge of historians may serve jurists in shaping a verdict that comprehends the truth of State-sponsored atrocity.

FURTHER READING

Hannah Arendt, *Eichmann in Jerusalem: A Report on the Banality of Evil*, New York: Viking, 1963.

Donald Bloxham, *Genocide on Trial: War Crimes Trials and the Formation of Holocaust History and Memory*, Oxford University Press, 2001.

F. Brayard, ed., *Le Génocide des Juifs Entre Procès et Histoire, 1943–2000*, Paris/Brussels, IHTP-CNRS/Complexe, 2000.

Lawrence Douglas, *The Memory of Judgment: Making Law and History in the Trials of the Holocaust*, New Haven: Yale University Press, 2001.

Lawrence Douglas, *The Right Wrong Man: John Demjanjuk and the Last Great Nazi War Crimes Trial*, Princeton University Press, 2015.

Richard Evans, 'History, Memory and the Law: The Historian as Expert Witness', (2002) 41 *History and Theory* 326.

Priscilla Hayner, *Unspeakable Truths: Confronting State Terror and Atrocity*, 2nd edn, New York: Routledge, 2011.

Marti Koskenniemi, 'Between Impunity and Show Trials', (2002) 6 *Max Planck Yearbook of United Nations Law* 1.

---

31 For a contrasting view, see Thilo Kurz, 'Paradigmenwechsel bei der Strafverfolgung des Personals in den Deutschen Vernichtungslagern?', *Zeitschrift für International Strafrechtsdogmatik*, 3 (2013), 122–9.

Mark Osiel, *Mass Atrocity, Collective Memory and the Law*, New Brunswick: Rutgers University Press, 1997.

Henry Rousso, *The Haunting Past: History, Memory and Justice in Contemporary France* (trans. Ralph Schoolcraft), Philadelphia: University of Pennsylvania Press, 2002.

Richard Ashby Wilson, *Writing History in International Criminal Trials*, Cambridge University Press, 2011.

3 Transitional justice

Stephan Parmentier

Any volume on international criminal law would be incomplete without paying closer attention to the broader legal, political, and societal context within which this body of law is originating, as well as operating. Specifically, when countries are transitioning from violent conflict and war to the end of hostilities and peace, or when dictatorships are replaced by new forms of democracy, international criminal law becomes part of a larger agenda on how to address the crimes committed in the past or by a previous regime. More than ever before, the new power holders who may be democratically elected cannot avoid confronting the legacy of the country's past and the road towards the future. The latter half of the twentieth century and the first fifteen years of the new millennium are full of examples of such conflicts and the ensuing issues, including the Second World War, the restoration of democracy in Latin America, the period following the fall of the Berlin wall, post-*apartheid* South Africa, etc.[1] Frequently posed questions include: how to deal with the offenders of serious crimes in the past, whether it is better to remember or forget the horrors of the past, how to address the damage done to victims, and what is the room for independent decision-making by countries and regimes?

These issues, and the circumstances leading to them, are nowadays subsumed under the general concept of 'transitional justice', which has rapidly become entrenched in national and international research and policy-making. In this contribution, we first explain the origins and content of this notion, before going into the four main components considered to constitute transitional justice. We finish with some critiques and challenges for transitional justice.

---

1 Stephan Parmentier and Elmar Weitekamp, 'Political Crimes and Serious Violations of Human Rights: Towards a Criminology of International Crimes', in Stephan Parmentier and Elmar Weitekamp, eds., *Crime and Human Rights*, Amsterdam/Oxford: Elsevier/JAI Press, 2007, pp. 109–44.

Transitional justice: what's in a name?

The International Centre on Transitional Justice, one of the world's leading think tanks in this field, defines transitional justice as 'the set of judicial and non-judicial measures that have been implemented by different countries in order to redress the legacies of massive human rights abuses. These measures include criminal prosecutions, truth commissions, reparations programmes, and various kinds of institutional reforms.' While this definition refers to the current-day understanding of transitional justice, it should be noted that over the last quarter century considerable evolutions have taken place at the conceptual and also practical level. The specific term 'transitional justice' arose in the early 1990s, shortly after the unexpected and rapid implosion of the communist regimes in Central and Eastern Europe following the fall of the Berlin wall in November 1989. The genealogy of the term is quite interesting, if only to note that various authors claim its parenthood.[2] A couple of years later, it became the title of a three-volume book by Neil Kritz of the United States Institute of Peace, in which he collected a wide number of studies of countries that had passed to democracy and were facing the challenge of dealing with past crimes.[3] Also Richard Siegel, who wrote a review essay of the first decade of transitional justice research, clearly referred to political transitions in his working definition of transitional justice as 'the study of the choices made and the quality of justice rendered when states are replacing authoritarian regimes by democratic state institutions'.[4] This conception of transitional justice was situated against the background of the political science research by Schmitter, O'Donnell, and Whitehead who studied the worldwide trend away from authoritarianisms and towards democratisation.[5] It was echoed in the work of Samuel Huntington who

---

2 Paige Arthur, 'How "Transitions" Reshaped Human Rights: A Conceptual History of Transitional Justice', (2009) 31 *Human Rights Quarterly* 321; Ruti Teitel, *Transitional Justice*, New York: Oxford University Press, 2000.

3 Neil Kritz, ed., *Transitional Justice*, Washington: US Institute of Peace Press, 1995.

4 Richard L. Siegel, 'Transitional Justice: A Decade of Debate and Experience', (1998) 20 *Human Rights Quarterly* 431.

5 Philip Schmitter, Guillermo O'Donnell, and Laurence Whitehead, eds., *Transitions from Authoritarian Rule. Prospects for Democracy*, Baltimore: Johns Hopkins University Press, 1986.

talked about a 'third wave of democratization'.[6] This had started with the carnation revolution in Portugal and included the transitions in Latin America, Asia, and Central and Eastern Europe; and followed the first wave, from the early nineteenth century until the start of the Second World War, and the second one, between the end of the Second World War and the beginning of the decolonisation process in the early 1960s.

The conceptual framework of transitional justice was fundamentally altered in 2004, through a report on the rule of law and transitional justice by United Nations Secretary-General Kofi Annan to the UN Security Council. The report viewed transitional justice as 'the full range of processes and mechanisms associated with a society's attempts to come to terms with a legacy of large-scale past abuses, in order to ensure accountability, serve justice and achieve reconciliation'.[7] Firstly, this definition added a number of objectives for transitional justice actions and interventions, namely to ensure accountability, serve justice, and achieve reconciliation. And secondly, it substituted the idea of political transitions and regime changes with the notion of large-scale abuses in whatever context, also within democratic countries, thus bringing situations within the purview of transitional justice as diverse as the demobilisation during the ongoing violent conflict in Colombia and placement of indigenous children in residential schools in Canada and Australia where they suffered from sexual abuse. This definition was confirmed in the Secretary-General's 2011 report to the Security Council, and has thus obtained the status of 'acquis' in the field of international law and practice.[8]

In her work on the 'genealogy' of transitional justice, Ruti Teitel has specified that three broad categories of situations can be identified: Phase I, post–Second World War, starting in 1945 with the Nuremberg trials and ending just a couple of years later when the Cold War began; Phase II, post-Cold War, with the gradual disintegration and ultimate implosion of the Soviet Union and periods of 'accelerated democratisation' in Central and Eastern Europe, and around the world; and the steady-state phase III,

6 Samuel Huntington, *The Third Wave: Democratization in the Late Twentieth Century,* Oklahoma City: University of Oklahoma Press, 1991.

7 The Rule of Law and Transitional Justice in Conflict and Post-Conflict Societies, Report of the Secretary-General, UN Doc. S/2004/616, para. 8.

8 The Rule of Law and Transitional Justice in Conflict and Post-Conflict Societies, Report of the Secretary-General, UN Doc. S/2011/634.

with the acceleration of transitional justice phenomena associated with globalisation and characterised by political instability and violence.[9]

The scope of transitional justice continues to expand. Jon Elster, e.g., has traced transitional justice issues back to classical Greece, and to the English and French restorations, as well as to Latin America and South Africa in recent times.[10] And Jos Monballyu has studied the many changes in the Belgian criminal justice system in the post–First World War period (1918–1928) under the heading of transitional justice.[11]

Transitional justice has no monopoly in describing and analysing how regimes are facing the violations and crimes of the past. In some legal and social science literature, the same processes are coined as 'dealing with the past'.[12] Such a retrospective viewpoint, however, pays little attention to the reconstruction of societies. Another popular notion is 'post-conflict justice' which, in the words of Cherif Bassiouni – one of the godfathers of inter-national criminal justice – comprises two-related meanings, one referring to 'retributive and restorative justice with respect to human depredations that occur during violent conflicts' and the other relating to 'restoring and enhancing justice systems which have failed or become weakened as a result of internal conflicts'.[13] This notion is clearly more encompassing but also assumes a clear demarcation between a conflict and a post-conflict phase which, in the case of long-term authoritarianism (like communism), is anything but clear-cut. For these reasons, the broader notion of 'transi-tional justice' seems more useful, without being void of problems.[14]

9 Ruti Teitel, 'Transitional Justice Genealogy', (2003) 16 *Harvard Human Rights Journal* 69.

10 Jon Elster, *Closing the Books: Transitional Justice in Historical Perspective*. Cambridge University Press, 2004.

11 Jos Monballyu, 'La Justice Transitionnelle en Belgique dans les Affaires Pénales Après la Première Guerre Mondiale (1918–1928)', (2012) 80 *Tijdschrift voor Rechtsgeschiedenis / Revue d'Histoire du Droit / The Legal History Review* 443.

12 Luc Huyse, 'Justice after Transition: On the Choices Successor Elites, Make in Dealing with the Past', in A. Jongman, ed., *Contemporary Genocides*, Leiden: PIOOM, 1996, pp. 187–214.

13 M. Cherif Bassiouni, ed., *Post-Conflict Justice*, Ardsley: Transnational Publishers, 2003, p. xv.

14 Stephan Parmentier and Elmar Weitekamp, 'Political Crimes and Serious Violations of Human Rights: Towards a Criminology of International Crimes',

Finally, it should be highlighted that transitional justice is often associated with the fight against impunity. This connection was clearly established through the reports of the two special experts asked by the United Nations Commission on Human Rights to systematise and improve the principles against impunity. Both Louis Joinet and Diane Orentlicher refer to the three main pillars of the fight against impunity as being: (a) the right to know about the facts of the past, both for individuals and for society at large; (b) the right to justice, in the sense that perpetrators are prosecuted and tried before a court of law, and (c) the right to reparation for victims for the harm inflicted upon them.[15] These three pillars in the fight against impunity continue to constitute the hard core of transitional justice around the world and will also inform the analysis of the mechanisms below.

Criminal prosecutions

As analysed elsewhere, the classical way to deal with international crimes has for a long time been to try and punish them by means of the ordinary criminal justice system at the domestic level.[16] States are traditionally well-equipped to conduct criminal prosecutions against suspects of regular crimes through the various institutions of their criminal justice systems (notably the police, the Public Prosecutor's Service, the trial courts, and the prison system or other measures for the execution of criminal sanctions). However, crimes of mass violence bring with them new challenges. One of them concerns the political nature of the crimes in the sense that either the intent of the offenders or the object and context

in Stephan Parmentier and Elmar Weitekamp, eds., *Crime and Human Rights*, Amsterdam/Oxford: Elsevier/JAI Press, 2007, pp. 109–44.

15 Question of the Impunity of Perpetrators of Human Rights Violations (Civil and Political), Revised Final Report Prepared by Mr. Joinet Pursuant to Sub-Commission Decision 1996/119, UN Doc. E/CN.4/Sub.2/1997/20/Rev.1; Independent Study on Best Practices, Including Recommendations, to Assist States in Strengthening their Domestic Capacity to Combat All Aspects of Impunity, by Professor Diane Orentlicher, UN Doc. E/CN.4/2004/88.

16 Elmar Weitekamp and Stephan Parmentier, 'Restorative Justice and State Crime', in David Weisburd and Gerben Bruinsma, eds., *Encyclopedia of Criminology and Criminal Justice*, New York: Springer Verlag, 2014, pp. 4430–46.

of their crimes relate to politics and ideology. Another distinctive criterion between common crimes and international crimes lies in the massive numbers of victims of the latter and sometimes in the large numbers of perpetrators as well. Because of these difficulties, criminal justice systems in many countries, particularly if poorly equipped, tend to be reluctant to engage in widespread prosecutions.

The last three decades have witnessed two important shifts from domestic prosecutions to other levels.[17] The first shift relates to the development of so-called 'universal jurisdiction' legislation in a number of countries.[18] This allows third countries to prosecute and to try international crimes without the existence of a link between the third country and the place where the crimes have been committed, the nationality of the offender, or the nationality of the victim. The main rationale lies in the fact that international crimes are considered so heinous that they not only affect the victims and the criminal justice system of the country where they took place, but that they also affect humanity as such. For this reason also third countries put their criminal justice system at the disposal of the world community. Such cases of 'pure' universal jurisdiction are in fact rare in today's world, the former Belgian and Spanish legislations being among the exceptions. In fact, a number of countries – mostly European – have a limited form of universal jurisdiction and require at least one specific link with the crime in order to prosecute and try it. While welcomed by some as an ethical triumph for humanity, recent events in Western Europe suggest that the efforts to establish genuine systems of universal jurisdiction are often subject to the *Realpolitik* of international relations.

The second major shift to respond to mass atrocity lies in the establishment of criminal justice mechanisms at the international level. The forerunners of this tendency were the two *ad hoc* tribunals, for the former Yugoslavia and for Rwanda, set up by the Security Council of the United Nations in 1993 and 1994 respectively, for a limited period of time and with a limited territorial jurisdiction. They have been followed by the establishment of a permanent International Criminal Court, entering into

17 Ibid.
18 Anne-Marie Slaughter, 'Defining the Limits: Universal Jurisdiction and the National Courts', in S. Ratner, ed., *Universal Jurisdiction. National Courts and the Prosecution of Serious Crimes under International Law*, Philadelphia: University of Pennsylvania Press, 2006, pp. 168–92.

operation in 2002 and dealing with three main categories of international crimes, genocide, crimes against humanity and war crimes. While
the two *ad hoc* tribunals have a primary competence to deal with grave
breaches of humanitarian law and serious human rights violations, the
International Criminal Court has a complementary task to prosecute and
try international crimes when States Parties are 'unwilling or unable' to
do so, thus leaving the prime locus at the national level. It was followed
by a number of mixed international-national tribunals, for Sierra Leone,
East Timor, Kosovo, and Cambodia.

This short overview demonstrates that criminal prosecutions, as the
first pillar of transitional justice, rests on three main bodies of law, international humanitarian law, international human rights law, and international criminal law. Together, these constitute a 'justice cascade' that
has changed world politics over the last decades in the view of Kathryn
Sikkink.[19] The strong points of criminal prosecution for international
crimes have been well-documented.[20] The first is related to reconstructing
the moral order, i.e., the general idea that 'justice be done' to satisfy the
desire for justice of a society as a whole and of specific groups in particular. Another one is political in nature, in the sense that prosecution can
also strengthen the fragile democracy by confirming the principle of the
'rule of law', thus providing the firm foundation on which to construct
a human rights awareness and culture in the country. Moreover, there
are also aspects of legality involved. Orentlicher has argued in strong
terms that there exists 'a duty to prosecute in international human rights
law' for serious human rights violations, founding her arguments on the
various human rights treaties that contain passages to this effect and on
the ensuing case law. Nevertheless, she has also accepted the distinction
between the 'global norm' (criminal prosecution for the most responsible
perpetrators) and the 'local agency' of enforcing and interpreting this
norm (including non-prosecution for many low-level offenders).[21]

19 Kathryn Sikkink, *The Justice Cascade. How Human Rights Prosecutions are
    Changing World Politics*, New York: Norton Company, 2011.
20 Luc Huyse, 'Justice after Transition: On the Choices Successor Elites Make
    in Dealing with the Past', in A. Jongman, ed., *Contemporary Genocides*,
    Leiden: PIOOM, 1996, pp. 187–214.
21 Diane Orentlicher, '"Settling Accounts" Revisited: Reconciling Global Norms
    with Local Agency', (2007) 1 *International Journal of Transitional Justice* 10.

However, as much as they constitute a step forward against situations of amnesty provisions and thus large-scale impunity for crimes of the past, criminal prosecutions are not without problems or even risks.[22] While it may sound contradictory, criminal prosecutions of perpetrators can also undermine the 'rule of law' of the new State, as the principle of non-retroactivity of criminal law precludes new regimes from prosecuting crimes that were not prescribed or that were not punishable under the former regime. Another challenge for the new regime is to guarantee the independence and the impartiality of the criminal justice system. This is far from easy because the same police officers and judges appointed by the former regime may still be in their position and adhere to the values of the old system. Another category of risks is more of a political nature. Because the old political and military elites can be resisting and actively opposing the transitional government, many new democracies are truly fragile. Prosecuting well-known offenders, or even the threat thereof, can provoke the old elites and even seduce them to seizing power again, as the examples of Chile and Argentina clearly illustrate. Another problem relates to the capacity of the system. In long-term autocratic regimes, only a small minority tends to possess the knowledge and the skills required to govern a country in political and economic terms. To call to account, the members of this elite may lead to growing uncertainty about the future of the elites in general, and may even push them to emigrate from the country, a well-known scenario in Central Europe in the early 1990s and South Africa in the late 1990s. Thirdly, criminal justice systems that are confronted with the legacy of mass violence face some major logistical problems. In some cases, the sheer numbers of offenders and potential suspects is so large that the system would become completely clogged if too many prosecutions were to take place. Even in situations less extreme, it is unavoidable to be very selective and to only bring some perpetrators to the criminal court. A number of tough questions inevitably arise, namely, whether the prosecutorial agencies should aim at the heads and the planners of the crimes, who have ordered the crimes or were aware of them taking place, or whether they should target those who executed the orders and those who assisted them? And what about the so-called

---

22 Luc Huyse, 'Justice after Transition: On The Choices Successor Elites, Make in Dealing with the Past', in A. Jongman, ed., *Contemporary Genocides*, Leiden: PIOOM, 1996, pp. 187–214.

bystanders, who did not actively participate in committing the crimes, but nevertheless witnessed them and in some cases may have benefited from the consequences? Finally, criminal trials by their very nature are mostly focused on the offenders and on the rights of the accused, and pay far less attention to the victims and to the harm inflicted upon them. This is the case with ordinary criminal trials and it is by and large the same with international crimes and crimes of mass violence. The role of victims in the criminal process is often reduced to that of witnesses or in other ways.

Given the many difficulties associated with criminal prosecution, many choices have to be made. Therefore, it does not come as a surprise that in practice criminal prosecutions have often proved more the exception than the standard in the last quarter century. Some have even pleaded for a 'restorative justice approach' instead of a (criminal) retributive justice one.[23]

Truth commissions

Another innovative mechanism in the field of transitional justice are truth commissions. They stand for a completely different approach, since the basic idea is not to prosecute and try individuals according to strict legal procedures, but to unearth (sometimes literally) as many facts about the past as possible following non-judicial approaches. In this sense, they contribute primarily to 'the right to know' for victims and society at large,[24] as well as to 'historical justice'.[25]

Truth commissions constitute a relatively new phenomenon, and in the absence of a single definition various interpretations exist. Amongst the most widely accepted definitions is the one by Priscilla Hayner who proposes five major characteristics of a truth commission: (1) it is

---

23 Ivo Aertsen, Jana Arsovska, Holger-C. Rohne, Marta Valiñas, and Kris Vanspauwen, eds., *Restoring Justice after Large-Scale Violent Conflicts*, Cullompton: Willan Publishing, 2008.

24 Question of the Impunity of Perpetrators of Human Rights Violations (Civil and Political), Revised Final Report Prepared by Mr. Joinet Pursuant to Sub-Commission Decision 1996/119, UN Doc. E/CN.4/Sub.2/1997/20/Rev.1; Independent Study on Best Practices, Including Recommendations, to Assist States in Strengthening their Domestic Capacity to Combat All Aspects of Impunity, by Professor Diane Orentlicher, UN Doc. E/CN.4/2004/88.

25 Ruti Teitel, *Transitional Justice*, New York: Oxford University Press, 2000.

concerned with past events, not present ones; (2) it is investigating patterns of events, rather than individual events, over a certain period of
time; (3) it engages in a direct and broad manner with the people that are
affected, and collects information about their perceptions and needs; (4) it
is not a permanent but a temporary body that is supposed to produce a
final report; (5) and it enjoys the support and/or the powers provided by
the State being investigated.[26] This set of conditions very strongly echoes
the definition she gave back in 2001, with the exception of two points
(3 and 5) that were added after some criticism by Marc Freeman.[27] He had
argued that little attention was paid to the victim-centred nature of truth
commissions that provide an important forum for victims to tell their stories and voice their expectations; and that truth commissions direct their
attention to the crimes committed in the State that has provided them
with the support to investigate.

The State support is generally seen as particularly important because
while truth commissions are supposed to work in an independent manner,
they still need to operate within a State context: for their composition,
financial and logistical resources, and specific legal powers, they are heavily dependent upon the State apparatus, and even more so when it comes
to giving concrete effect to the recommendations that are finally issued.
This fifth feature also marks the difference between an official truth commission and a wide range of other, unofficial forms of truth-telling or
human rights investigations. In the latter category fall investigations and
reports from non-governmental organisations, trade unions, churches,
etc. Valuable as they may be to disclose facts about the past and pressur-
ise official bodies, these organisations and their reports generally cannot
rely on the State support and thus tend to face major problems in seeing
their recommendations implemented by State agencies.

In light of the above, it is clear that truth commissions adopt a strong
focus on victims and their families, as they are engaged in collecting individual stories about the horrors of the past, and thereby try to compose a
general picture of the underlying patterns and rationales of the violations
and crimes committed. To carry out this task, all truth commissions have

26 Priscilla Hayner, *Unspeakable Truths: Transitional Justice and the Challenge
    of Truth Commissions*, 2nd edn, New York: Routledge, 2011, pp. 11–2.
27 M. Mark Freeman, *Truth Commissions and Procedural Fairness*, Cambridge
    University Press, 2006, pp. 14–8.

adopted special procedures to take written statements from victims, and some have also organised public hearings with victims and the community that were often broadcast on radio and television. Some commissions have also tried to include direct perpetrators or representatives of the former powers, in the sense of persons willing to participate in the proceedings and disclose information about the command structure of the groups or regime that committed the violations and crimes or about specific events. Some commissions even have a mandate to force persons to participate or to seize documents.

It is interesting to note that, despite this general framework, truth commissions display different terminologies that reflect the specific objectives with which they are set up and the specific methods that guide their operation. Sometimes the scope is limited to a specific type of facts or group of persons, such as the National Commission on the Disappeared in Argentina. Other commissions highlight the specific objective of their work, for example, the Truth and Reconciliation Commission in South Africa, the Commission for Historical Clarification in Guatemala, the Commission for Reception, Truth and Reconciliation in Timor Leste, and the Equity and Reconciliation Commission in Morocco. These names not only reflect the specificities of the commission, they also make clear that truth and reconciliation may not always go hand in hand as many have started to believe after the strong publicity and impact of the South African Truth and Reconciliation Commission.[28] In Hayner's view, there have been five strong commissions thus far in terms of mandate, working procedures, and impact: South Africa, Guatemala, Peru, Timor Leste, and Morocco.[29]

Why then are truth commissions set up? Hayner elucidates the most important aims.[30] They 'discover, clarify and formally acknowledge past abuses' and thus generate more information about the facts, their origins and their qualifications; this fact-finding function is crucial to separate facts from rumours and reduces the space for denial about the past by

---

28 Charles Villa-Vicencio and Wilhelm Verwoerd, *Looking Back, Reaching Forward. Reflections on the Truth and Reconciliation Commission of South Africa*, Cape Town/London: UCT Press/Zed Books, 2000.

29 Priscilla Hayner, *Unspeakable Truths: Transitional Justice and the Challenge of Truth Commissions*, 2nd edn, New York: Routledge, 2011.

30 Ibid.

political opponents and certain sectors of society. Truth commissions also pay attention to the needs of victims who rarely receive the time and space to share their histories and interpretations of the past. Here lies one of their core functions, in contrast to the very limited space for victims during court proceedings. They 'counter impunity' and promote the accountability of individuals involved directly or indirectly in the commission of the violations and crimes. Although truth commissions are non-judicial bodies and cannot prosecute individuals, they sometimes can 'name names' of responsible persons and sometimes have the power to refer cases to a prosecutorial service. Furthermore, truth commissions highlight the responsibility of institutions and recommend reforms in order to avoid similar or new facts occurring again in the future. These recommendations often relate to a variety of legal, political, economic, social, cultural, and institutional matters and policies, which require follow up. Finally, they promote reconciliation between individuals and groups, and in society at large; this is probably the most difficult function, because reconciliation means different things to different people and is oscillating between process and result.[31]

A brief overview of the more than forty truth commissions established since the mid 1970s makes clear that the relationship between truth commissions and criminal justice organs can be diverse. Some truth commissions have been and are conceived of as an alternative to criminal prosecutions, in other words to satisfy the need to reveal facts about the past but also to avoid that offenders would be brought to criminal justice. Others are seen as complementary to and mutually reinforcing criminal justice, because they allow for a far broader investigation of patterns of violations and crime. In some exceptional cases, like Sierra Leone, a truth commission and a special criminal court have existed alongside one another.

Finally, it would be erroneous to assume that truth commissions have or are only operating in countries of the Global South. Some recent examples illustrate the usefulness of truth commissions for other contexts of large-scale abuses as well, e.g., the commissions in Canada (to investigate

---

31 David Bloomfield, Teresa Barnes, and Luc Huyse, eds., *Reconciliation after Violent Conflict. A Handbook*, Stockholm: International Idea, 2003; Erin Daly and Jeremy Sarkin, *Reconciliation in Divided Societies. Finding Common Ground*, Philadelphia: University of Pennsylvania Press, 2006.

the official policy of residential schools for First Nations children, and the ensuing sexual abuse taking place) and North Carolina (focusing on race-related violence in the late 1970s). This makes the model of a truth commission truly innovative and applicable to a variety of contexts, also western and northern, in which one or more of the above mentioned objectives are being pursued.

Reparation policies for victims

The third major mechanism of transitional justice is geared towards providing reparation to victims for the harm inflicted upon them. This is in line with 'the right to reparation' expressed in the Joinet and Orentlicher reports,[32] and fits the ideas of 'reparatory justice'[33] or 'reparative justice'.[34] It should be noted that the individual and subjective right to reparation is a relatively recent development in international law. For a long time, basically until the Second World War, the reparation of damage done to persons and goods was considered in legal terms as a 'duty of the State' to repair. This conception followed from the *Chorzów Factory* judgment of the Permanent Court of International Justice in public international law,[35] and the provisions of international humanitarian law. After the Second World War, the notion of a right to reparation began to emerge within international human rights law. Particularly, the Inter-American Court of Human Rights has developed an extensive case law on the content of victim reparations, e.g., by establishing the idea of a 'life project' (*proyecto de vida*) of individuals in order to determine the amount of monetary compensation, expanding the range of reparations – like conducting legal

---

32 Question of the Impunity of Perpetrators of Human Rights Violations (Civil and Political), Revised Final Report Prepared by Mr. Joinet Pursuant to Sub-Commission Decision 1996/119, UN Doc. E/CN.4/Sub.2/1997/20/Rev.1; Independent Study on Best Practices, Including Recommendations, to Assist States in Strengthening their Domestic Capacity to Combat All Aspects of Impunity, by Professor Diane Orentlicher, UN Doc. E/CN.4/2004/88.

33 Ruti Teitel, *Transitional Justice*, New York: Oxford University Press, 2000.

34 Rama Mani, *Beyond Retribution: Seeking Justice in the Shadows of War*, Cambridge: Polity Press, 2002.

35 *Case Concerning the Factory at Chorzów (Claim for Indemnity) (Merits)*, [1928] PCIJ Reports, Ser. A, No. 17.

investigations and establishing memorial sites[36] – and initiating forms of collective reparations.[37] Also the European Court of Human Rights, which for a long time adopted a very prudent position (a violation of the Convention counts as satisfaction), has gradually moved to a more expanding case law (e.g., ordering the release of a person in unlawful detention). Finally, the area of international criminal law is in full expansion in relation to victim reparations. Before 2002, none of the special tribunals (Nuremberg, the United Nations *ad hoc* tribunals) held any provisions on victim reparations. However, the Rome Statute establishing the International Criminal Court has incorporated the right to reparation in the case of individual criminal liability, while the Trust Fund for Victims is to provide services to victims of a situation before the Court.

The above makes clear that in the case of reparations to victims, important developments have taken place in at least four bodies of law: public international law, international humanitarian law, international human rights law, and international criminal law. While most of these sources can be considered 'hard law' at least one very important source of 'soft law' has emerged as squarely dealing with victim reparations, namely the United Nations Basic Principles and Guidelines on the Right to a Remedy and Reparation for Victims of Gross Violations of International Human Rights Law and Serious Violations of International Humanitarian Law. They were adopted by the United Nations General Assembly in December 2005, after a twenty-year period of negotiations and discussions at the highest level.[38]

The Basic Principles and Guidelines list five categories of victim reparations, thus expanding the scope enormously in comparison to other provisions. The first, restitution, is a very old concept dating back to Roman law based on the idea that victims are to be brought back into the position *ex ante*, that is, before their rights were violated. Examples of restitution are therefore not limited to giving back immovable or movable

---

36 I/A Court H.R., Case of *Myrna Mack Chang* v. *Guatemala*. Merits, Reparations and Costs. Judgment of November 25, 2003. Series C No. 101, paras. 246–286.

37 I/A Court H.R., Case of *Aloeboetoe et al.* v. *Suriname*. Reparations and Costs. Judgment of September 10, 1993. Series C No. 15.

38 United Nations Basic Principles and Guidelines on the Right to a Remedy and Reparation for Victims of Gross Violations of International Human Rights Law and Serious Violations of International Humanitarian Law, UN Doc. A/RES/60/147.

property (houses, furniture, land, cattle), but also include the restoration of citizenship, jobs, etc. The second is compensation, the second-best solution whenever restitution is not possible, and relates to financial reimbursement for all kinds of damage, including physical, material, and emotional damage. Various methods have been developed to 'calculate' the exact value of damage and the amount of financial compensation. The third, rehabilitation, is a form of reparation that encompasses medical and psychological assistance, as well as legal and other social services, that may be offered to victims of serious violations or crimes. The fourth, satisfaction, is definitely the broadest category of the Basic Principles and Guidelines and refers to many different activities.[39] These comprise: making the truth public, provided that such a disclosure will not cause any more harm to or jeopardise the safety of victims, surviving relatives, or others involved; looking for victims' remains and extending facilities for a dignified funeral or other ceremony in close consultation with the wishes of the surviving relatives; organising a memorial service or a tribute to the victims, or arranging a public apology, including an acknowledgement of the facts and an acceptance of responsibility; legal and administrative sanctions for those responsible for the violations. Guarantee of non-repetition constitutes the last category of reparations, the underlying idea being to avoid similar violent conflicts, violations and crimes in the future, or providing 'administrative justice' in the words of Teitel.[40] In essence, this category refers to a variety of fundamental reforms of specific institutions or the State as a whole; examples include both the hard core State institutions (towards democratic policing, judicial independence, functional detention systems, accountable intelligence services) and softer institutions (accessible education and health systems, democratic media, etc.); because this category forms part and parcel of the Basic Principles and Guidelines, it is discussed in this framework and not as a separate fourth mechanism of transitional justice following the definitions mentioned above.

39 Rianne Letschert and Stephan Parmentier, 'Repairing the Impossible: Victimological Approaches to International Crimes', in Inge Vanfraechem, Anthony Pemberton, and Felix Mukwiza Ndahinda, eds., *Justice for Victims. Perspectives on Rights, Transition and Reconciliation*, Abingdon: Routledge, 2014, pp. 226–43.
40 Ruti Teitel, *Transitional Justice*, New York: Oxford University Press, 2000.

As argued elsewhere,[41] the reparation measures of the Basic Principles and Guidelines can thus be ordered in three main categories: legal action, e.g., participation in trials that on the one hand bring a form of recognition and on the other hand can provide a means to receive financial compensation; symbolic measures that may lead to the recognition of victimhood, like public apologies or the establishment of memorial days; and financial measures that focus on monetary compensation of the damage suffered. Given this variety of measures, it is logical that distinct institutions are likely to play a role in giving effect to them. Regular or special courts and tribunals will primarily address legal actions and allow for financial reparation orders, but the latter can also take effect through administrative programmes, by means of individual payments (lump sums, pensions), compensation for school tuition, or collective investments in community projects. Symbolic actions, like apologies and memorials, are likely to come within the purview of administrative and political bodies, and sometimes also non-governmental associations (including victim groups) will play a prominent role in keeping memories of past atrocities alive. Because of the nature of the reparation measures, as well as the vast numbers of victims involved, it has sometimes been argued that it is impossible to repair the gigantic harm to victims and that reparation measures are for a large part symbolic.[42]

Challenges and future orientations

Transitional justice has become a very broad concept over the last two decades, encompassing both strategies to move away from conflict and authoritarianism through political transitions and strategies to deal with large-scale abuses outside of any political transition.[43] As such, it is now covering situations and cases in all parts of the world, not limited

41 Rianne Letschert and Stephan Parmentier, 'Repairing the Impossible: Victimological Approaches to International Crimes', in Inge Vanfraechem, Anthony Pemberton and Felix Mukwiza Ndahinda, eds., *Justice for Victims. Perspectives on Rights, Transition and Reconciliation*, Abingdon, UK: Routledge, 2014, pp. 226–243.

42 Brandon Hamber, *Transforming Societies after Political Violence: Truth, Reconciliation, and Mental Health*, Heidelberg: Springer, 2009.

43 *Contra*: Sandrine Lefranc, 'La justice transitionnelle n'est pas un concept', *Mouvements*, no. 53, March 2008, pp. 61–9.

to the Global South, but also including Europe, North America, and the Western world in general. Furthermore, transitional justice, once heavily dominated by law and political sciences, is gradually becoming an inter-disciplinary field of study with inputs from a variety of social science disciplines, like sociology, psychology, anthropology, history and, last but not least, criminology. It is fair to say that transitional justice has become one of the 'booming sectors' for research in the humanities, as well as for policy-making and practice.

The rapid development of transitional justice studies cannot obfuscate that some major critiques have been voiced and challenges identified. One set of such critiques and challenges is formulated by Phil Clark and Nicola Palmer.[44] In their view, transitional justice is an 'under-theorised field'. Some of the key concepts, like justice, peace, reconciliation, and the like, remain ill-defined and contested, and this has a bearing on complex debates cast in binary terms like peace versus justice, punishment versus reconciliation, local versus international, etc. They strongly plead for clarification of the key concepts, as well as more elaborate theoretical developments.[45]

Moreover, they point at a 'disciplinary disconnect' in transitional justice, which runs the real risk of reinventing the wheel in relation to understanding and dealing with the exceptional situations of massive human rights violations and international crimes. Yet, several disciplines have amply studied similar issues in past and present and can offer a lot of insight: on conceptions of justice in philosophy, on the impact of foreign interventions in international relations and anthropology, on punishment and deterrence in criminology, etc. In their view, transitional justice studies should look 'over their wall' and thus benefit from existing research findings in a variety of disciplines.

Furthermore, they call into question, the uneasy mixture between analysis and advocacy and plead for a stricter separation between a 'fact-based' and a 'faith-based' approach. While the prominent role of human rights organisations and individual activists has led to a strong

---

44 Phil Clark and Nicola Palmer, 'Challenging Transitional Justice', in Nicola Palmer, Phil Clark, and Danielle Granville, eds., *Critical Perspectives in Transitional Justice*, Cambridge/Antwerp/Portland: Intersentia Publishers, 2012, pp. 1–17.

45 Ibid.

emphasis on advocacy in the field of transitional justice, the authors warn of a lack of deep understanding of fundamental processes in the field of human rights and their short- and long-term effects. What is needed therefore is more scientific testing, theoretically and empirically, of many basic ideas, assumptions, and hypotheses in transitional justice.

Finally, Clark and Palmer highlight the importance of a context-specific approach. Despite the many similarities in conflict and post-conflict settings, no single situation is identical and therefore unique features must be taken into account. Specific needs and aims of victims, perpetrators, society, and all actors involved have to be mapped again and again, as solutions are tailored to these needs, in conjunction with the social, economic, and cultural infrastructure of any given society. The reality of transitional justice policies and practices is different, however, as ample recourse is made to a 'ready-made' model and a 'toolbox approach' that put institutions before objectives. The risk is the import of ideas and practices foreign and possibly hostile to the local environment.

While all of these critiques and challenges are very well-taken, they by no means constitute an exhaustive list. We therefore wish to add some other points. Firstly, the vast majority of transitional justice studies have focused on the violations of civil and political rights (e.g., right to life, freedom from torture, and enforced disappearances, etc.), or crimes against physical and moral integrity of the person (e.g., murder and attempted murder, rape, etc.). However, it is crystal clear that violent conflicts often find their root causes in social inequalities, inadequate distribution of resources, racism, and other forms of social and political exclusion. Although these underlying problems are often identified in truth commission reports and ensuing recommendations are formulated, it is striking that discussions about economic, social, and cultural rights and related crimes like corruption[46] have been virtually absent from transitional justice studies. This view, and the need to pay due attention to social and distributive justice, is echoed by Paul Gready and Simon Robins in their pleadings for 'transformative justice' aiming at treating causes of

---

46 Ruben Carranza, 'Plunder and Pain: Should Transitional Justice Engage with Corruption and Economic Crimes?', (2008) 2 *International Journal of Transitional Justice* 310.

conflicts rather than symptoms and emphasising the reformulation of power structures in conflict and post-conflict societies.[47]

Secondly, the dominant perspective on transitional justice remains a top-down one, paying ample attention to the viewpoints, proposals, initiatives, actions, and evaluations of elite actors. They encompass political and economic elites emerging from violent conflict and authoritarianism, but also intellectual and activist elites inside and outside the country concerned. What about the bottom-up perspective on transitional justice, the one represented by the affected populations at large, or by individual victims, perpetrators, bystanders, beneficiaries, etc.? In line with the strong arguments favouring a transitional justice approach 'from below',[48] we contend that much more attention needs to be paid to local and personal understandings of victimisation, attitudes on transitional justice, and actions towards societal reconstruction. The dozen or so population-based studies in post-conflict countries can generate very valuable insights into the facilitating and obstructing factors for justice, peace, and development.[49]

Finally, in line with the critique of conceptual lack of clarity raised by Clark and Palmer, we wish to emphasise the need to link the debates around justice with those around peace and around development.[50] In our view, the multiple connections between these three fields, including the factors facilitating and hampering them, need to be the object of in-depth research. This is crucial for countries and societies of the Global South, but equally for those from the North and the West. As a result, much more research is needed to study the theoretical frameworks that guide

47 Paul Gready and Simon Robins, 'From Transitional to Transformative Justice: A New Agenda for Practice', (2014) 8 *International Journal of Transitional Justice* 339.

48 Kieran McEvoy and Lorna McGregor, 'Transitional Justice from Below: An Agenda for Research, Policy and Praxis', in Kieran McEvoy and Lorna McGregor, eds., *Transitional Justice from Below: Grassroots Activism and the Struggle for Change*, London/Oxford: Hart, 2008, pp. 1–14.

49 Stephan Parmentier, Marta Valiñas, and Elmar Weitekamp, 'How to Repair the Harm After Violent Conflict in Bosnia? Results of a Population-Based Survey', (2009) 27 *Netherlands Quarterly of Human Rights* 27.

50 Pablo De Greiff and Roger Duthie, eds., *Transitional Justice and Development: Making Connections*, New York: Social Science Research Council, 2009.

transitional justice,[51] as well as the effects and impact of transitional justice processes.[52]

By way of conclusion

What happens in the present and future with large-scale abuses, serious human rights violations and international crimes committed in the past? This fundamental question lies at the heart of the emerging field of transitional justice research and policy-making, which focuses both on the ideals and the realities of justice as utopia as well as the institutions of justice. The question is both empirical ('what is actually happening if anything at all') and normative ('what should happen according to moral and legal standards'). And it can be addressed through the input of various scientific disciplines, criminal law just being one of them next to many other disciplines.

Over the past two-to-three decades multiple concepts have been developed, diverse policies formulated and many practices established to address these questions and issues. They have generated the 'transitional justice' industry, with its own raw materials and finished products, its intellectual and manual workers, and its systems of transportation and implementation.

Next to the many accomplishments, a number of important critiques and challenges are being formulated. To address these in an adequate manner is a major imperative for transitional justice studies, in order to move forward, thereby shedding old clothes and inhaling fresh air.

---

51 Susanne Buckley-Zistel, Teresa Koloma Beck, Christian Braun, and Friederike Mieth, *Transitional Justice Theories*, London/New York: Routledge, 2014; Naomi Roht-Arriaza and Javier Mariezcurrena, eds., *Transitional Justice in the Twenty-First Century. Beyond Truth versus Justice*, Cambridge University Press, 2006.
52 Tricia Olsen, Leigh Payne, and Andrew Reiter, *Transitional Justice in Balance. Comparing Processes, Weighing Efficacy*, Washington: United States Institute of Peace, 2010.

FURTHER READING

Koen De Feyter, Stephan Parmentier, Marc Bossuyt, and Paul Lemmens, eds., *Out of the Ashes. Reparation for Victims of Gross and Systematic Human Rights Violations*, Antwerp/Oxford: Intersentia Publishers, 2005.

Pablo De Greiff, ed., *The Handbook of Reparations*, Oxford University Press, 2006.

Priscilla Hayner, *Unspeakable Truths: Transitional Justice and the Challenge of Truth Commissions*, 2nd edn, New York: Routledge, 2011.

Rama Mani, 'Dilemmas of Expanding Transitional Justice, or Forging the Nexus between Transitional Justice and Development', (2008) 2 *International Journal of Transitional Justice* 253.

Kieran McEvoy and Lorna McGregor, eds., *Transitional Justice from Below: Grassroots Activism and the Struggle for Change*, London/Oxford: Hart, 2008.

Diane Orentlicher, ' "Settling Accounts" Revisited: Reconciling Global Norms with Local Agency', (2007) 1 *International Journal of Transitional Justice* 10.

Nicola Palmer, Phil Clark, and Danielle Granville, eds., *Critical Perspectives in Transitional Justice*, Cambridge/Antwerp/Portland: Intersentia Publishers, 2012.

Stephan Parmentier, 'Global Justice in the Aftermath of Mass Violence. The Role of the International Criminal Court in Dealing with Political Crimes', (2003) 41 *International Annals of Criminology* 203.

Naomi Roht-Arriaza and Xavier Mariezcurrena, eds., *Transitional Justice in the Twenty-First Century: Beyond Truth versus Justice*, Cambridge University Press, 2006.

Ruti Teitel, *Transitional Justice*, New York: Oxford University Press, 2000.

Independent Study on Best Practices, Including Recommendations, to Assist States in Strengthening their Domestic Capacity to Combat All Aspects of Impunity, by Professor Diane Orentlicher, UN Doc. E/CN.4/2004/88.

Question of the Impunity of Perpetrators of Human Rights Violations (Civil and Political), Revised Final Report Prepared by Mr. Joinet Pursuant to Sub-Commission Decision 1996/119, UN Doc. E/CN.4/Sub.2/1997/20/Rev.1.

The Rule of Law and Transitional Justice in Conflict and Post-Conflict Societies, Report of the Secretary-General, UN Doc. S/2004/616.

The Rule of Law and Transitional Justice in Conflict and Post-Conflict Societies, Report of the Secretary-General, UN Doc. S/2011/634.

United Nations Basic Principles and Guidelines on the Right to a Remedy and Reparation for Victims of Gross Violations of International Human Rights Law and Serious Violations of International Humanitarian Law, UN Doc. A/RES/60/147.

Punishment and sentencing 4

Mark Drumbl

How are individuals who are convicted of extraordinary international crimes punished? How ought they to be punished? Do current approaches to punishment attain their stated goals? Regrettably, these crucial questions are understudied. For the most part – as William Schabas has noted – punishment and sentencing linger as afterthoughts within the field of international criminal law.[1] This neglect is somewhat of a pity. After all, what ultimately happens to persons convicted of international crimes matters greatly to victims. Sentencing may also fulfil important narrative functions. Sentencing can serve as a venue to individuate differentiations among perpetrators, in particular within the context of group crimes, and thereby inject granularity into the attribution of responsibility.

Contemporary international criminal courts and tribunals predominantly punish through imprisonment. While restitutionary and reparative remedies can be awarded in some instances, these possibilities remain penumbral. The Trust Fund for Victims, established by the Rome Statute and funded by donor States, has nevertheless supported collective projects and, on this note, may come to more robustly instantiate reparative justice. The Trust Fund disclaims any punitive orientation and operates within a restorative paradigm.

A sentencing practice has emerged within international institutions. This practice can also be aggregated across institutions. The various international institutions are independent. When it comes to sentencing they nonetheless cite extensively to each other's jurisprudence. Such cross-references occur despite the formal absence of the doctrine of *stare decisis* and proof that the affirmed principle in fact constitutes a general principle of law. This cross-referencing also takes place notwithstanding

---

1 William A. Schabas, 'International Sentencing: From Leipzig (1923) to Arusha (1994)', in M. Cherif Bassiouni, ed., *International Criminal Law*, vol. 3 (Enforcement), Leiden: Martinus Nijhoff, 2008, pp. 613–34, at p. 613.

differences among the mandates and directives of these various institutions as enunciated by their enabling instruments. On the other hand, the need to individualise the penalty means that previous sentencing practices provide only limited assistance.

When national institutions are called upon to punish individuals convicted of genocide, crimes against humanity, and systematic war crimes, the national penological framework of the State in question governs the punishment that is meted out. Although greater diversity of sanction arises at national levels, incarceration once again emerges as the preferred modality of punishment.[2] Within the context of incarceration, considerable variation arises among national legal systems as to the norms of sentence severity (both in the case of international crimes and ordinary common crimes). Certain national mechanisms transcend courtrooms, for example truth commissions and customary ceremonies. These institutions deploy methods of sanction that diverge from the jailhouse and thereby push the conversation to the trickier question as to what, exactly, punishment means in the context of collective violence and communal repair.

Insofar as incarceration persists as the dominant modality of punishment, this chapter explores in detail the approaches of a variety of international courts and tribunals in this regard and concentrates on their sentencing practices. The ultimate point of this discussion, however, is to interrogate the ability of these institutions to engage in predictable and effective sentencing and also to prompt a conversation about alternate mechanisms.

Background: sentencing for Second World War atrocity perpetrators

Contemporary international or internationalised criminal tribunals – such as the International Criminal Tribunal for Rwanda, the International

---

2 National proceedings may jurisdictionally base themselves in territoriality, nationality, passive personality, universality, or some combination thereof. Prosecutions regarding atrocity in the former Yugoslavia and Rwanda have been brought in multiple national legal systems. By way of example, Désiré Munyaneza, who relocated to Canada following the Rwandan genocide, was found guilty in May 2009 on charges related to rape and civilian massacres. He was sentenced to life imprisonment. His conviction was upheld by the Québec Court of Appeal in May 2014. Munyaneza was the first person convicted pursuant to Canada's war crimes legislation.

Criminal Tribunal for the former Yugoslavia, East Timor Special Panels, the Mechanism for International Criminal Tribunals, the Special Court for Sierra Leone, and the International Criminal Court – inherit limited sentencing guidance from their predecessors, namely, the Nuremberg (International Military Tribunal) and Tokyo (International Military Tribunal for the Far East) Tribunals. Article 27 of the Nuremberg Charter gave judges 'the right to impose ... on conviction ... death or such other punishment as shall be determined ... to be just'. The sentencing provision of the Charter of the Tokyo Tribunal (article 16) read similarly. Accordingly, judges had nearly absolute discretion in the sentencing process.

Judges contoured the exercise of their discretion through inchoate development of aggravating and mitigating factors. Aggravating factors often were implied within the criminal conduct itself and received limited attention. Although (as was the case with Reichsmarschall Hermann Göring) judges often arrived rather quickly to the seemingly self-evident conclusion that there was 'nothing to be said in mitigation',[3] in other instances factors were accepted in mitigation, including not being a dominant organisational figure, evidence of abiding by the laws of war, following orders, and opposing certain official policies. Obedience to superior orders explicitly was recognised in article 8 of the Charter of the International Military Tribunal as a mitigating circumstance and not as a defence to the charges. Proof that 'British naval prisoners of war in camps under Doenitz's jurisdiction were treated strictly according to the [Geneva] Convention' was a 'fact' the International Military Tribunal took 'into consideration, regarding it as a mitigating circumstance' (Doenitz was sentenced to ten years' imprisonment). For Speer, it was recognised in mitigation that he opposed Hitler's scorched earth programme, 'deliberately sabotage[d] it at considerable personal risk', and that 'he was one of the few men who had the courage to tell Hitler that the war was lost and to take steps to prevent the senseless destruction of production facilities'. Speer received twenty years. With regard to von Neurath, it was emphasised in mitigation that he had intervened to release arrested Czechoslovaks, had resigned, and refused to act in certain capacities. He received a term sentence of fifteen years. Most defendants at the International Military Tribunal, however, were sentenced to death.

3 E.g., (1948) 22 IMT 411, at pp. 524 and 527.

Twelve further rounds also occurred at Nuremberg, albeit outside of the International Military Tribunal's jurisdiction. These rounds, which are colloquially referred to as the 'subsequent proceedings', involved members of criminal organisations (such as the SS and Gestapo), officials, notorious killers (e.g., *Einsatzgruppen*), industrialists, doctors, and jurists.[4] These proceedings, taken as a whole, implicated 177 individuals. In some cases, sentences were issued the same day the verdicts were read. Discussion of sentencing rationales was thin.

The *Einsatzgruppen* trial involved twenty-two leadership individuals. Among those sentenced, fourteen were sentenced to death, two to life, three to twenty years, one to fifteen years, and two to ten years.[5] Twelve of the death sentences later were commuted to a variety of lesser sentences ranging from life imprisonment to fixed terms of imprisonment. The social status and refined educations of the defendants – including that they were not 'untutored aborigines incapable of appreciation of the finer values of life and living' – were observed to their detriment. In the joint trials of industrialists, the sentences imposed ranged from one and a half to eight years (*I.G. Farben* trial) and from just under three to twelve years plus forfeiture of property (*Krupp* trial). In the *Justice* trial, fifteen former jurists were prosecuted. Six were acquitted and released. Nine were convicted and sentenced: three to ten years, one to five years, one to seven years, and four to life imprisonment. In one case, Lautz (Chief Public Prosecutor at the People's Court in Berlin), the report reveals a reference to mitigation, citing non-activity in Nazi Party matters and his resistance to efforts by Party officials to influence his conduct (although he was found to have yielded to Hitler's influence and guidance). Lautz received ten years' imprisonment.[6] In the *Hostages* trial, the tribunal opined generally that the degree of mitigation depends on many factors, including the nature of the crime, the age and experience of the person, the motives for the criminal act, the circumstances under which the crime

---

4 Article II(3) of Control Council Law No. 10 referenced the following sanctions: death, imprisonment for life or for a term of years (with or without hard labour), fines, forfeiture of property, restitution, and deprivation of some or all civil rights.

5 James Waller, *Becoming Evil: How Ordinary People Commit Genocide and Mass Killing*, New York: Oxford University Press, 2002, p. 92.

6 *United States* v. *Alstötter* et al., 'The Justice Case', (1951) 3 TWC 954, at p. 1128.

was committed, and provocation.[7] In the *Flick* trial, the Tribunal delved into 'incidents' in the lives of two of the convicted defendants, 'some of which involved strange contradictions', including interceding to protect certain Jewish friends and saving survivors of a sunken ship, to mitigate sentences to seven and five years.[8]

The International Military Tribunal for the Far East indicted twenty-eight individuals in proceedings that began in 1946 and ended in 1948. These individuals ('Class A' criminals) mostly were military and political leaders. Seven were sentenced to death, including General Tojo, Japan's Prime Minister during much of the Second World War, who was executed in 1948. Sixteen others were sentenced to life in prison and two to fixed terms of confinement. Two of the accused died of natural causes before trial; another had a nervous breakdown and was removed. No acquittals were rendered. Over time, though, many of the convicts were pardoned. For example, of the sixteen individuals given life sentences, three died in prison while the remaining thirteen were paroled in the 1950s. Three convicts assumed senior government posts after their release. One defendant whose sentence was mitigated was Mamoru Shigemitsu, the former Japanese Foreign Minister, who was found not to be involved in the formulation of the war conspiracy. By the time, he acceded to his ministerial post, the Tribunal noted that the machinery of war crimes and war of aggression had already been established. Shigemitsu received a seven-year sentence; he was paroled in 1950 and subsequently served in the Japanese cabinet.

Many proceedings involving Axis crimes were held at the national level in a large number of jurisdictions. In some instances, the death penalty was issued. Such was the case with the Supreme National Tribunal of Poland in the cases of Rudolph Höss (Auschwitz *Kommandant*), Amon Göth (commander of the Kraków-Płaszów labour camp), and Arthur Greiser (Governor of the Warthegau). Such also was the case with the Chinese Military Tribunal at Nanking in the case of Takashi Sakai, briefly Japanese Governor of Hong Kong in 1942, who was executed by firing squad in 1946; and the Israeli Supreme Court in the case of Adolf Eichmann. In other cases, for example proceedings against Auschwitz personnel held in the 1960s in Frankfurt, comparatively light sentences were issued.

---

7 *United States* v. *List* et al., 'The Hostage Case', (1950) 11 TWC 1230, at p. 1377.
8 *United States* v. *Flick* et al., (1952) 6 TWC 1187, at p. 1222.

To be clear, judges tasked with punishing Second World War–era criminals exercised their discretion to vary punishment according to the individual defendant. These judges did so, however, without providing a rigorous heuristic to account for the exercise of this discretion, although they did develop a rudimentary typology of facts in mitigation that continues to inform international criminal law to this date. In the ensuing decades, the death penalty has disappeared as a sanction in international institutions. The death penalty, however, has not disappeared from all national legal frameworks. The Bangladesh International Crimes Tribunal, for example, in November 2013 sentenced two individuals *in absentia* to death by hanging for their involvement in the murder of pro-independence activists during Bangladesh's 1971 war of independence from Pakistan. Twenty-two defendants sentenced to death by Rwandan national courts for their role in the genocide were publicly executed in 1998. Rwanda, however, abjured the death penalty in 2007.

Enabling instruments of contemporary international institutions

Article 24(1) of the Statute of the International Criminal Tribunal for the former Yugoslavia limits penalty to imprisonment and stipulates that, in the determination of the terms of imprisonment, the Tribunal shall have recourse to the general practice regarding prison sentences in the courts of the former Yugoslavia. Article 23(1) of the Statute of the International Criminal Tribunal for Rwanda reads identically, except that it refers to the courts of Rwanda instead of the courts of the former Yugoslavia. The Rwanda Tribunal has concluded that this provision does not imply an obligation to conform to the relevant national practice, though there is an obligation to consider this practice.[9] The Yugoslavia Tribunal's approach is basically identical. Although similar cases (that is, prior sentences awarded by the *ad hoc* tribunals) are instructive, the International Criminal Tribunal for Rwanda ruled that these are not binding as benchmarks.[10] In addition to imprisonment, the statutes of the *ad hoc* tribunals permit the return of property and proceeds.

---

9 *Prosecutor* v. *Semanza* (ICTR-97-20-A), Judgment, 20 May 2005, para. 345.
10 *Prosecutor* v. *Nyiramasuhuko* et al. (ICTR-98-42-T), Judgment and Sentence, 24 June 2011, para. 6190.

When it comes to determining sentence, the International Criminal Tribunals for the former Yugoslavia and Rwanda are to take into account 'the gravity of the offence and the individual circumstances of the convicted person'.[11] A convict may be incarcerated for a term up to life. Therefore, since there is no mandatory minimum sentence, judges of the Tribunals have the power to impose any sentence ranging from one-day imprisonment to life imprisonment for any crime over which the tribunal has jurisdiction.

Both tribunals have emphasised their discretion to determine sentence.[12] For example, in the *Butare Six* case, rendered in 2011 and subject to appeal, the Trial Chamber of the Rwanda Tribunal ruled that it 'has considerable, though not unlimited, discretion on account of its obligation to individualise penalties to fit the individual circumstances of an accused and to reflect the gravity of the crimes for which the accused has been convicted'.[13] The Mechanism adheres to a similar methodological approach. Determination of sentence, then, proceeds through two steps: first, assessment of the gravity of the offence and, second, determination of the individual circumstances. It is in this second step that aggravating and mitigating factors are to be considered. Rule 101 of the Rules of Procedure and Evidence (common to both Tribunals) in fact requires Trial Chambers to take into account mitigating and/or aggravating circumstances in determining sentences. With one exception (substantial co-operation by the offender), Rule 101 does not enumerate mitigating or aggravating circumstances. Both Statutes provide that following superior orders may be considered a mitigating circumstance. In practice, however, it is difficult to disentangle criteria that touch upon the gravity of the offence from criteria that may constitute aggravating factors, thereby invoking the risk of unfairness to the convict.[14]

11 Statute of the International Criminal Tribunal for the former Yugoslavia, article 24(2); Statute of the International Criminal Tribunal for Rwanda, article 23(2).

12 *Prosecutor* v. *Kambanda* (ICTR-97-23-S), Judgment, 4 September 1998, para. 30; *Prosecutor* v. *Kvočka* et al. (IT-98-30/1-A), 28 February 2005, 668–669, 715.

13 *Prosecutor* v. *Nyiramasuhuko* et al. (ICTR-98-42-T), Judgment and Sentence, 24 June 2011, para. 6188.

14 Barbora Holá, 'Sentencing of International Crimes at the ICTY and ICTR', (2012) 4 *Amsterdam Law Forum* 3.

In cases where an accused is convicted of multiple charges, the Rules of Procedure and Evidence enable the Trial Chambers the option to impose either a single sentence reflecting the totality of the criminal conduct or a sentence in respect of each conviction with a declaration regarding whether these sentences are to be served consecutively or concurrently.[15] Holá notes that, in the case of the *ad hoc* tribunals, defendants are mostly convicted on multiple counts but only one global sentence is issued.[16] While this approach of totality/globality is economical, it also shrouds many of the factors that influence the determination of sentence and complicates matters when the Appeals Chamber revisits sentence in light of the quashing or the addition of convictions. Procedurally, in the early years of the *ad hoc* tribunals separate sentencing hearings were held, but the Rules were soon amended to unify the trial and sentencing hearing process.[17] Parties are entitled to present evidence related to sentencing in the course of the trial but, as per Rule 86(C), submissions regarding sentencing should be rendered during closing arguments.

The International Criminal Court can sentence an offender to up to thirty years' imprisonment, with a possibility of 'life imprisonment when justified by the extreme gravity of the crime and the individual circumstances of the convicted person'.[18] Sentence is to be joint, that is, cumulative of all the convictions.[19] Thus far at the International Criminal Court (two convictions at the time of writing), a specific sentence was given as to each charge for which a conviction was entered and then a global sentence was issued which corresponded to the most severe among these concurrent sentences. The International Criminal Court Rules of Procedure and Evidence indicatively list some aggravating and mitigating factors.[20] These replicate many of the factors jurisprudentially developed

---

15 Rule 87(C). See also *Prosecutor* v. *Delalić* (IT-96-21), Judgment, 20 February 2011, para. 771.

16 Barbora Holá, 'Sentencing of International Crimes at the ICTY and ICTR', (2012) 4 *Amsterdam Law Forum* 3, at p. 9.

17 Kai Ambos, *Treatise on International Criminal Law, Vol. II: The Crimes and Sentencing*, Oxford University Press, 2014, p. 278. At the International Criminal Court, pursuant to article 76(2) of the Rome Statute, a separate sentencing hearing may occur upon the discretion of the Trial Chamber or upon the request of either the prosecutor or the accused.

18 Rome Statute of the International Criminal Court, article 77(1).

19 Ibid., article 78(3).

20 Rules of Procedure and Evidence, Rule 145.

by the judges of the *ad hoc* tribunals, however, including the nature of the harm caused, degree of intent, personal characteristics and prior criminal record of the convicted person, abuse of power, any demonstrated co-operation and compensation to victims, vulnerability of victims, particular cruelty, and the mental capacity of the convict. No ordering principle is provided as to the relative weight to attribute to any of these factors; 'one or more aggravating circumstances' may justify the imposition of life imprisonment.[21]

The Statute of the Special Court for Sierra Leone precludes life sentences so convicts are to be imprisoned for a specified number of years. Juvenile offenders (persons between fifteen and eighteen years of age), moreover, are to be treated with clemency so as to encourage their rehabilitation.[22] The Court has sentenced its nine convicts with comparative severity: an average term of nearly thirty-nine years and a maximum term of fifty-two years.[23]

The agreements between the United Nations and Cambodia regarding the Extraordinary Chambers in the Courts of Cambodia are virtually silent on penalty and the determination of sentence although, taken together, they provide a minimum sentence of five years' imprisonment and a maximum sentence of life imprisonment (with the possibility of combining this with seizure of personal and real property acquired by criminal conduct, which is to be returned to the State). Kaing Guek Eav (*aka* Duch, the Commander of the Tuol Sleng prison) was ultimately sentenced by the Extraordinary Chambers to life in prison despite his guilty plea and stated remorse. The East Timor Special Panels could punish through a fixed term of imprisonment, capped at twenty-five years for a single crime. Special Panel judges received a mandate very similar to those of the *ad hoc* Tribunals and the International Criminal Court, that is, to take into account the gravity of the offence and the

---

21 Ibid, Rule 145(3).

22 Statute of the Special Court for Sierra Leone, articles 7 and 19; Rules of Procedure and Evidence, Rule 101. No indictment was ever brought against a juvenile. The Special Court was required to consult ICTR sentencing practices and Sierra Leonean national practices.

23 Alette Smeulers, Barbora Holá, and Tom van den Berg, 'Sixty-Five Years of International Criminal Justice: The Facts and Figures', (2013) 13 *International Criminal Law Review* 7, at p. 22.

individual circumstances of the convicted person in fashioning a sentence.[24]

In addition to imprisonment, as mentioned previously, the positive law of international criminal justice institutions permits restitution (the return of illegally obtained property), forfeiture, or fines. Restitution has not been awarded in the sentences of the *ad hoc* international criminal tribunals, however. The International Criminal Court can impose fines and order forfeiture, but these remedies shall be imposed only if imprisonment is insufficient and with regard to the convict's financial capacity and motivation. These remedies were declined in the *Lubanga* and *Katanga* cases owing *inter alia* to the convict's indigence. The International Criminal Court can also make reparative orders through the Trust Fund for Victims, for which regulations have been developed.[25] The Fund is to be capitalised by compensation orders entered against convicts (in theory) and also by voluntary grants from organisations and governments (in actuality). The total Trust Fund for Victims income by April 2013 was €12.8 million.[26] Leading donors include Germany, the United Kingdom, Sweden, and Finland. The Fund has supported projects in Northern Uganda and the Democratic Republic of the Congo. Projects include vocational training, counselling, reconciliation workshops, and reconstructive surgery. The Fund's programming involves individual assistance (to victims of crimes) and also collective projects to help communities rebound. Planned programmes in the Central African Republic have been suspended owing to security concerns.

Contemporary international criminal tribunals permit sentences to be pardoned or commuted and early release to be granted.[27] Persons convicted by the Special Panels, for example, had the right to be released from prison after two-thirds of their sentence was served as long as they

---

24 On the Establishment of Panels with Exclusive Jurisdiction over Serious Criminal Offences, UN Doc. UNTAET/REG/2000/15.

25 Rome Statute, article 79; Rules of Procedure and Evidence, Rule 98. The *Lubanga* proceedings also saw (in August 2012) the issuance of a decision establishing the principles and procedures to be applied to reparations.

26 Trust Fund for Victims Financial Statements for the Period 1 January to 31 December 2013, ICC-ASP/13/13.

27 Statute of the International Criminal Tribunal for Rwanda, article 27; Statute of the International Criminal Tribunal for the former Yugoslavia, article 28; Statute of the Special Court for Sierra Leone, article 23.

behaved well while in custody and the release would not threaten public safety and security.[28] At the *ad hoc* tribunals, the timing of early release textually is determined by the national laws of the State in which the convict serves sentence. That said, the International Criminal Tribunal for the former Yugoslavia adopted a 'rule of thumb' to permit eligibility for early release upon completion of at least two-thirds of the sentence, despite the fact that this benchmark did not reflect the municipal law of all enforcing states.[29] The Mechanism, which now oversees the enforcement of sentences of both the Yugoslav and Rwanda tribunals, replicates this benchmark. Rule 151 of the Mechanism Rules of Procedure and Evidence identifies a number of illustrative factors that the Mechanism President shall take into account in such determinations. These are: the gravity of the crime or crimes for which the prisoner was convicted; the treatment of similarly situated prisoners; the prisoner's demonstration of rehabilitation; and any substantial co-operation on the part of the prisoner with the Prosecutor. In addition, the President may consider the interests of justice and the general principles of law (Mechanism Statute, article 26); any other information that he or she considers relevant; along with the views of any judges of the sentencing chamber who are MICT judges.

Article 110 of the Rome Statute states that when the convict has served two-thirds of the sentence, or twenty-five years in the case of life imprisonment, the Court shall review the sentence to determine whether it should be reduced. A sentence reduction may be issued if the Court determines the existence of one or more of the following factors: (1) 'early and continuing willingness' of co-operation by the convict; (2) the convict's 'voluntary assistance ... in particular providing assistance in locating assets subject to orders of fine, forfeiture or reparation which may be used for the benefit of victims'; or (3) other factors 'establishing a clear and significant change of circumstances sufficient to justify the reduction of sentence, as provided in the Rules'. Although the prospect of early release may be anticipated at the time the sentence initially is fixed, judges of the International Criminal Tribunal for the former Yugoslavia have held

---

28 *Prosecutor* v. *Mau*, 08/C.G/2003/TD.DIL (Dili District Court Serious Crimes Special Panel, 23 February 2004); *Prosecutor* v. *Gusmão*, 07/C.G/2003 (Dili District Court Serious Crimes Special Panel, 28 February 2003).

29 Roísín Mulgrew, *Towards the Development of the International Penal System*, Cambridge University Press, 2013, pp. 57–8.

that this prospect should not factor into the determination of the length of the sentence.[30] In other words, it is improper to gross up the length of sentence to absorb the possibility of early release.

One under-discussed yet disturbing phenomenon at the International Criminal Tribunal for Rwanda is that seven acquitted individuals and three released convicts are currently residing in a safe house in Arusha, Tanzania.[31] They do not yet have anywhere else to go. These individuals (some of them were acquitted over a decade ago) need to be relocated – a point repeatedly raised by the Tribunal's President. The fact that they remain stuck, so to speak, presents serious due process challenges for the international criminal tribunals. At the International Criminal Court, what to do with witnesses and acquitted persons who might fear persecution were they to return home? In such instances, should The Netherlands as host state grant refugee or resident status?

Sentencing practice and determining factors

The two *ad hoc* tribunals – the International Criminal Tribunal for Rwanda and the International Criminal Tribunal for the former Yugoslavia – are winding down; these institutions are transitioning to the Mechanism, with branches in Arusha and The Hague, which continues some of their activities in a phase-out period.[32] The relationship between the *ad hoc* tribunals and the Mechanism is complex and is discussed elsewhere in this *Companion*. In any event, the Mechanism has assumed responsibility for the supervision of all sentences pronounced by the *ad hoc* tribunals as of 1 July 2012, and 1 July 2013, respectively, including the process of early release. As of July 2013, nearly half of all international convicts had been released, the vast majority of this group having been granted early release.

---

30 *Prosecutor* v. *Dragan Nikolić* (IT-94-2-A), Judgment on Sentencing Appeal, 4 February 2005, para. 97.

31 Patrick W. Hayden and Katerina I. Kappos, 'Current Developments at the *Ad Hoc* International Criminal Tribunals', (2014) 12 *Journal of International Criminal Justice* 367, at p. 390.

32 Upon closure of the Special Court for Sierra Leone, a residual mechanism also was established to supervise the institution's on-going legal obligations which include administrative and archival management, witness protection, and fulfilment of prison sentences.

Sentencing practice

Individuals convicted of crimes by the *ad hoc* tribunals serve their sentences in States that have concluded enforcement agreements with these tribunals or with the Mechanism. Those sentenced by the International Criminal Tribunal for the former Yugoslavia have been incarcerated in Germany, Austria, Spain, Italy, Denmark, Finland, Norway, the United Kingdom, Sweden, Portugal, Estonia, and France. Rwandan convicts have been incarcerated in Mali, Bénin, Italy, and Sweden (nearly all in Mali and Bénin, however). Some individuals are detained at the United Nations Detention Facility, but these are largely convicted persons awaiting judgments on appeal by the *ad hoc* tribunals or the Mechanism.

As of the time of writing, the two *ad hoc* tribunals, when taken together, have issued approximately 120 finalised sentences (i.e., no longer subject to appeal). The differentiation of finalised sentences and sentences subject to appeal is relevant. The Appeals Chamber, after all, can revisit the sentence by reviewing the determined aggravating or mitigating factors: this sort of appellate intervention is not particularly common, however, in light of the broadly understood sentencing discretion of the trial judges who are owed considerable deference.[33] That said, the Appeals Chamber also can revisit the quantum of sentence by altering the actual convictions (or acquittals) entered by the Trial Chamber. For example, on 11 February 2014, in the *Military II* case, the Appeals Chamber of the International Criminal Tribunal for Rwanda entirely reversed the convictions of two of the defendants and, in the case of a third (Sagahutu), reversed certain convictions and reduced the sentence from twenty to fifteen years. While Sagahutu had been convicted at trial *inter alia* for the murder of Rwandese Prime Minister Agathe Uwilingiyimana on 7 April 1994, the Appeals Chamber found that he could not be held criminally responsible for this crime.

The International Criminal Tribunal for the former Yugoslavia has issued final sentences in seventy-two cases, including two life sentences and fixed-term sentences ranging from two to forty years (among term sentences, the median sentence is fifteen years and the mean sentence

---

33 Barbora Holá, 'Sentencing of International Crimes at the ICTY and ICTR', (2012) 4 *Amsterdam Law Forum* 3, at p. 15. Sentences can be revised (or reversed) only in cases where discernible error is found in the exercise of discretion by the Trial Chambers.

is a touch over fifteen years). At the Rwanda Tribunal, the number of finalised convictions stands at forty-seven; there have been fourteen life sentences (constituting slightly under 30 per cent of the total number) and the average term sentence is 22⅓ years.[34] An evident disparity can be noted between sentencing practices at the two tribunals. While instinctively it may seem that the greater focus on genocide at the International Criminal Tribunal for Rwanda might explain this differential, the sentencing jurisprudence of the *ad hoc* tribunals has not consistently stated that certain crimes *per se* are more serious than others in an ordinal hierarchy of gravity.[35]

The East Timor Special Panels had convicted eighty-four individuals (arising out of fifty-five trials) before ceasing operations (after funding ran out) on 20 May 2005. The Special Panels issued a broad range of terms of imprisonment: from eleven months to fifteen years for ordinary crimes and from two to 33⅓ years for extraordinary international crimes. The Special Panels' enabling instruments precluded them from awarding a life sentence. Mean and median sentences issued by the Special Panels were 9.9 and eight years, respectively, in cases of international crimes. The length of Special Panel sentences shrinks, however, when the effects of conditional release and Presidential Decrees (pardons) are considered.

Two separate Trial Chambers have issued the International Criminal Court's first two sentences in the cases of Thomas Lubanga and Germain Katanga, two rebel leaders in the Democratic Republic of the Congo, who were prosecuted separately. Lubanga was convicted, as a co-perpetrator, of the war crime of conscripting and enlisting children under the age of fifteen years and using them to participate actively in hostilities in a non-international conflict in the DRC's Ituri region. He was sentenced on 10 July 2012, to a term of fourteen years.[36] Katanga was convicted as an accessory to murder as a crime against humanity and to four counts

---

34 ICTR research conducted by Barbora Holá for the NWO funded project Vertical (In)consistency of International Sentencing, shared by email, 29 May 2014.

35 *Prosecutor* v. *Mrksic and Sljivancanin* (IT-95-13/1-A), Judgment, 5 May 2009, para. 375.

36 *Prosecutor* v. *Lubanga* (ICC-01/04-01/06), Decision on Sentence Pursuant to Article 76 of the Statute, 10 July 2012, para. 106. Specifically, the majority concurrently sentenced Lubanga to thirteen years' imprisonment for the crime of conscription, twelve years for the crime of enlistment, and fourteen years for the crime of using children to participate actively in hostilities. In dissent,

of war crimes (murder, attacking a civilian population, destruction of property, and pillaging) for a 2003 attack also in Ituri. On 23 May 2014, Katanga was sentenced to a term of twelve years' imprisonment.[37] The Office of the Prosecutor had requested a thirty-year sentence in Lubanga's case and a twenty-two to twenty-five year sentence in Katanga's case. In neither case was a fine imposed in addition to the prison term in light of the financial situation of the convict. International Criminal Court Trial Chamber I deducted the six years that Lubanga had already spent in detention (his surrender to the International Criminal Court occurred on 16 March 2006) from the sentence; Trial Chamber II deducted the time Katanga spent in detention – between 18 September 2007 and 23 May 2014 – from his sentence. Both of these convicts would be eligible to apply for early release in accordance with the Rome Statute. In the *Lubanga* proceedings, the Prosecutor proposed a minimum sentence of 80 per cent of the maximum term sentence (twenty-four years) in all cases; the Trial Chamber rejected this proposal, suggesting that it flouted principles of proportionality and was nowhere mentioned in the International Criminal Court's enabling instruments.

Insofar as the International Criminal Court is a permanent institution operative at the time of writing in eight situations (with other preliminary investigations ongoing), it is worthwhile to consider these sentencing judgments in greater detail. In *Lubanga*, Trial Chamber I held that evidence admitted for sentencing 'can exceed the facts and circumstances set out in the Confirmation Decision, provided the defence has had a reasonable opportunity to address them'.[38] Also as a preliminary matter, and in line with settled jurisprudence from the *ad hoc* tribunals, the trial

Judge Odio Benito would have increased the sentence by one year, to fifteen years. The Appeals Chamber, on 1 December 2014, affirmed the sentence.

37 *Prosecutor* v. *Katanga* (ICC-01/04-01/07), Décision Relative à la Peine (article 76 du Statut), 23 May 2014. Specifically, Katanga was sentenced to twelve years for the convictions for his accessorial role in murder as a crime against humanity, murder as a war crime, and attacks on a civilian population as a war crime; and ten years each for the convictions for pillage and destruction of property as war crimes. Ibid., para. 146. The Trial Chamber in *Katanga* distinguished the gravity of crimes that targeted individuals from crimes that targeted goods. Ibid., para. 145. In dissent, Judge Van den Wyngaert would have acquitted the accused on all counts.

38 *Prosecutor* v. *Lubanga* (ICC-01/04-01/06), Decision on Sentence Pursuant to Article 76 of the Statute, 10 July 2012, para. 29.

chambers in both *Lubanga* and *Katanga* concluded that aggravating factors need to be established beyond a reasonable doubt, while mitigating
circumstances need to be established on a balance of probabilities.[39] Any
factors to be taken into account in ascertaining the gravity of the crime
are not to be considered as aggravating circumstances.

These sentencing judgments begin with a discussion of gravity followed
by a discussion of aggravating and mitigating circumstances within the
context of individualisation. The *Katanga* and *Lubanga* judgments delineate and compartmentalise these steps so as to guard against the possibility of double-counting. The gravity of the crime is a principal factor in
determining sentence. On this note, Trial Chamber I determined Lubanga's
crimes to be 'undoubtedly very serious'.[40] Trial Chamber I referenced the
vulnerability of the affected children, how they were compelled, and how
their use in hostilities rendered them potential targets. Trial Chamber I also
underscored the large-scale, significant, and widespread nature of child
soldier recruitment in the armed group; it also linked Lubanga's degree
of participation and intent, his position of authority, and his individual
circumstances (namely, that he 'is clearly an intelligent and well-educated
individual') to the gravity of the crimes.[41] In *Katanga*, the cruelty of the
crimes, including the suffering of the victims prior to their murder, figured
prominently in Trial Chamber II's assessments of gravity.

In neither case were any aggravating circumstances established. In
Katanga, in fact, Trial Chamber II found no abuse of Katanga's leadership position.[42] Turning to mitigating factors, Trial Chamber I found that
Lubanga's hope that peace would return to Ituri once he had secured
his military objectives was 'only of limited relevance' since, regardless
of any such intention, 'in order to achieve his goals, he used children
as part of the armed forces over which he had control'.[43] Trial Chamber
I also highlighted Lubanga's notable and consistent co-operation with

---

39 Ibid., paras. 33–4; *Prosecutor* v. *Katanga* (ICC-01/04-01/07), Décision Relative
    à la Peine (article 76 du Statut), 23 May 2014, para. 34. See also *Prosecutor*
    v. *Simić* (IT-95-9), Judgment, 17 October 2003, para. 1064.
40 *Prosecutor* v. *Lubanga* (ICC-01/04-01/06), Decision on Sentence Pursuant to
    Article 76 of the Statute, 10 July 2012, para. 37.   41 Ibid., para. 56.
42 *Prosecutor* v. *Katanga* (ICC-01/04-01/07), Décision Relative à la Peine (article
    76 du Statut), 23 May 2014, para. 75.
43 *Prosecutor* v. *Lubanga* (ICC-01/04-01/06), Decision on Sentence Pursuant to
    Article 76 of the Statute, 10 July 2012, para. 87.

the International Criminal Court and determined that he 'was respectful and cooperative throughout the proceedings, notwithstanding some particularly onerous circumstances'.[44] In *Katanga*, Trial Chamber II accorded some weight to the convict's young age at the time of the offences (twenty-four years) and his family situation (including his six children).[45] Trial Chamber II found that Katanga did not fully recognise the crimes he had committed and, hence, rejected remorse as a mitigating factor.[46] Much more germane, however, were Katanga's *post hoc* efforts to help demobilise and disarm child soldiers – which Trial Chamber II lauded.[47] In this regard, Katanga could be characterised as having contributed to reintegration and reconciliation. The credit that Katanga received for this conduct contrasts with the prosecutor's inability to actually convict him on child-soldiering charges – he was in fact acquitted on these allegations at trial. While noting the endemic nature of child soldiering in Ituri, Trial Chamber II did not find a sufficient nexus between Katanga and the recruitment of these child soldiers.

Whereas Lubanga was convicted solely for the enlistment, conscription, and active use in hostilities of children under the age of fifteen, Katanga was convicted as an accessory to murder and war crimes involving attacks on both people and property. Yet Lubanga received the more severe sentence. Even disregarding the potential for early release, Lubanga's fourteen-year sentence is lower than that of other defendants ultimately convicted internationally on child-soldier-related charges. Trial Chamber I noted that, at the time, the Special Court of Sierra Leone had entered seven convictions in four cases for the crime of using child soldiers under the age of fifteen.[48] In the best known of these cases (the RUF case), separate sentences were issued on the child-soldier-related convictions: Issa Sesay was awarded a fifty-year sentence and Morris Kallon a thirty-five-year sentence.[49] When it came to determining the 'exceptionally high' gravity of

---

44 Ibid., paras. 91 and 97.
45 *Prosecutor* v. *Katanga* (ICC-01/04-01/07), Décision Relative à la Peine (article 76 du Statut), 23 May 2014, para. 144.
46 Ibid., paras. 119 and 121.
47 Ibid., paras. 88, 115, and 144.
48 *Prosecutor* v. *Lubanga* (ICC-01/04-01/06), Decision on Sentence Pursuant to Article 76 of the Statute, 10 July 2012, para. 12.
49 Ibid., para 13. Sesay and Kallon received fifty-two years and forty years in total, respectively, on all convictions.

the criminal acts, the Special Court emphasised the large-scale nature of the use of child soldiers (including in the commission of gruesome atrocities), the prevalence of abduction, the cruel training, the very young age of some of the recruits, and the forced ingestion of narcotics.[50]

Individualisation: factors to consider in aggravation and mitigation

The *ad hoc* tribunals developed an array of factors to consider in aggravation and mitigation, which other sentencing institutions have referenced. These factors help operationalise principles of individualisation and gradation. Whereas factors in mitigation need to be established only on the balance of probabilities, aggravating factors need to be proven beyond a reasonable doubt.[51]

The following aggravating circumstances have arisen in the jurisprudence of the *ad hoc* tribunals: the breadth of the crimes (e.g., numbers of victims) and the suffering inflicted; the youth of the victims or their general vulnerability; the nature, degree, and form of the perpetrator's involvement (active role, principal perpetrator, or secondary/indirect involvement – this factor, however, remains rather controversial);[52] premeditation and discriminatory intent; abuse of a leadership position; depraved motivations, zeal, and enthusiasm in committing the crimes;

---

50 Ibid., para 13.
51 *Prosecutor* v. *Siméon Nchamihigo* (ICTR-01-63-T), Judgment, 12 November 2008, para. 389.
52 In the *Taylor* Appeals Chamber judgment, the Appeals Chamber of the Special Court for Sierra Leone resisted the submission that aiding and abetting generally triggers a lower sentence. The Appeals Chamber found no textual support for this proposition in the SCSL Statute. It noted that presuming a lower sentence in such instances would depart from the obligations to individualise punishment, to consider the convict's actual conduct, and to respect due process rights. *Prosecutor* v. *Taylor* (SCSL-03-01-A), Judgment, 26 September 2013, paras. 663–70. But see *contra* on nature of involvement: *Prosecutor* v. *Ntagerura* (ICTR-99-46-T), Judgment and Sentence, 25 February 2004, para. 813 (systematising sentencing patterns of fifteen years to life for principal perpetrators, and lower sentences for secondary or indirect forms of participation); *Prosecutor* v. *Ndahimana* (ICTR-01-68-A), Judgment, 16 December 2013, para. 252 (noting that a conviction for participating in a Joint Criminal Enterprise, as opposed to aiding and abetting (which has generally warranted

and deportment of the accused during trial.[53] At the Special Court for Sierra Leone, Charles Taylor – sixty-four years old – was sentenced to fifty years (this sentence was affirmed by the Appeals Chamber in 2013). In sentencing, the Trial Chamber emphasised as aggravating factors the extraterritoriality of Taylor's acts (that is, he meddled in Sierra Leone from his perch in Liberia) and also, in particular, his status as Head of State.

Preserving these differentiations between elements of the crime, factors that pertain to gravity, and factors to consider in individualising (aggravation and/or mitigation) can be tricky. The due process rights of the defendant and the principle of legality, however, require vigilance in this regard so as to avoid double-counting. When slippage happens across cases (namely, conduct is viewed as pertinent to gravity in one case, while analogous conduct taken as pertinent to aggravation in another, and to both aggravation and gravity in a third case), the outcome is inconsistency and a lack of predictability.

Commonly referenced mitigating factors include: whether and when the accused pled guilty and/or admitted guilt; substantial co-operation by the offender with the prosecution; the remote or tangential nature of the convict's involvement in the crime; voluntary surrender; the youth, advanced age, health, and other personal circumstances of the offender (including whether married and with children); the extent to which the offender was subject to duress, orders, or coercion; the good character of the offender; the chaos of constant armed conflict; that the offender did not have a previous criminal record for ordinary common crimes; assistance to victims; and human rights violations suffered by the offender during pre-trial or trial proceedings. At times, a factor may be referenced in mitigation, and established on the facts, but then not be assigned any weight. Mitigating factors, to be clear, attenuate the punishment and do not diminish the gravity of the crime. They do not need to be linked

a lesser sentence), suggests an increase in overall culpability in cases where the underlying crime is the same); *Prosecutor* v. *Krstić* (IT-98-33-A), Judgment, 19 April 2004, paras. 266–8; *Prosecutor* v. *Vasiljević* (IT-98-32-A), Judgment, 25 February 2004, para. 182 ('[A]iding and abetting is a form of responsibility which generally warrants a lower sentence than is appropriate to responsibility as a co-perpetrator').

53 *Prosecutor* v. *Kayishema* et al. (ICTR-95-1-T), Sentence, 21 May 1999, para. 17 (sentence influenced by the fact one of the defendants repeatedly smiled and laughed while genocide survivors testified).

specifically to the impugned conduct. The Special Court for Sierra Leone also has insisted that mitigation should not be granted based on the perceived 'just cause' for which a convict may have fought.

In addition to pleading guilty, the East Timor Special Panels claimed similar aggravating and mitigating factors as those at the *ad hoc* tribunals. A review of the Special Panels' jurisprudence reveals considerable attention paid to gravity, vulnerability of victims, superior responsibility, and political context as aggravating factors; and, as mitigating factors, remorse, personal/family circumstance, and position as a subordinate/coercive environment.[54] The Special Panels had occasionally referred to traditional indigenous principles in sentencing, such as *adat* (taking responsibility/paying respect to authority).[55]

Conclusion

International judges retain considerable discretion in sentencing. Formalised guidelines are lacking, although this discretion is tempered with the development – both jurisprudentially and in enabling instruments – of criteria to consider in gravity and individualised factors to weigh in aggravation and mitigation. In the case of Rwanda, a contrast arises between the Rwanda Tribunal's discretion and the domestic *gacaca* legislation which deployed comprehensive sentencing guidelines keyed to the categorisation of the offence and whether or not (and when) the accused tendered a guilty plea. The domestic *gacaca* legislation also contemplates community service as a remedy, unlike international sentencing practice.

In the initial years of their work, the *ad hoc* tribunals sentenced somewhat erratically. Nevertheless, and on a positive note, some consistency has emerged over time,[56] at least in the case of the identification of

54 *Prosecutor* v. *Sufa* (4a/2003, Dili District Court Serious Crimes Special Panel, 25 November 2004), para. 34.
55 *Prosecutor* v. *Beno* (4b/2003, Dili District Court Serious Crimes Special Panel, 16 November 2004), para. 20 (deferring the start of a five-year sentence by four weeks from the time sentence was issued so that the defendant may prepare his farm and noting that the risk of flight was 'comparatively small due to the strong Timorese tradition, rooted in 'Adat', of taking responsibility and paying respect to authority').
56 Silvia D'Ascoli, *Sentencing in International Criminal Law, The UN Ad Hoc Tribunals and Future Perspectives for the ICC*, Oxford: Hart, 2011; Barbora

principles to guide gravity and individualisation of sentence. Importantly, however, Holá identifies lingering concerns as to transparency and clarity.[57] This opacity may be exacerbated by certain institutional practices, for example, the imposition of a global sentence. Even more problematic, however, is the question whether the international sentences are actually attaining – or can ever attain – their avowed penological objectives.

Penological objectives

International criminal judges gesture towards important rationales when they impose sentences. Retribution and general deterrence are the two most prominently cited punishment goals.[58]

Although there are many divergent schools of retributivism, what retributivists generally share is an understanding that the infliction of punishment rectifies the moral balance, in particular, through condemnation of the criminal conduct.[59] Simply put, punishment is what the perpetrator deserves. Punishment, therefore, is to be proportionate to the extent of the harm caused by the crime and also to the perpetrator's degree of responsibility. The ICTY Appeals Chamber has nevertheless emphasised that 'retribution should not be misunderstood as a way of expressing

Holá, Catrien Bijleveld, and Alette Smeulers, 'Consistency of International Sentencing – ICTY and ICTR Case Study', (2012) 9 *European Journal of Criminology* 539; Kai Ambos, *Treatise on International Criminal Law, Vol. II: The Crimes and Sentencing*, Oxford University Press, 2014, p. 268; Barbora Holá, Alette Smeulers, and Catrien Bijleveld, 'International Sentencing Facts and Figures: Sentencing Practice at the ICTY and ICTR', (2011) 9 *Journal of International Criminal Justice* 411.

57 Barbora Holá, 'Sentencing of International Crimes at the ICTY and ICTR', (2012) 4 *Amsterdam Law Forum* 3.

58 *Prosecutor* v. *Stakić* (IT-97-24-A), Judgment, 22 March 2006, para. 402 (stating that 'the Appeals Chamber notes that the jurisprudence of the Tribunal and the ICTR consistently points out that the two main purposes of sentencing are deterrence and retribution'); *Prosecutor* v. *Marqués* et al. (09/2000, Dili District Court Serious Crimes Special Panel, 11 December 2001), para. 979; *Prosecutor* v. *Katanga* (ICC-01/04-01/07), Décision Relative à la Peine (article 76 du Statut), 23 May 2014, para. 38.

59 See generally H. L. A. Hart, *Punishment and Responsibility*, Oxford: Clarendon Press, 1968, pp. 234–5.

revenge or vengeance'.[60] Rather, it has conceived of the retribution as the 'expression of condemnation and outrage of the international community'.[61] In this regard, retributive motivations may move in the direction of expressivism. The expressivist punishes to strengthen faith in rule of law among the general public, as opposed to punishing simply because the perpetrator deserves it or will be deterred by it. From an expressivist perspective, punishment proactively embeds the normative value of law within the community.[62] This leads to positive general prevention. Expressivism also transcends retribution and deterrence in claiming as a central goal the edification of historical narratives and the public dissemination thereof.

General deterrence considers that the purpose of prosecuting and punishing individuals who commit mass atrocity is utilitarian in nature, that is, to dissuade others from offending in the future. Specific deterrence implies that punishing the offender will deter that one offender from reoffending. When the activity of international criminal justice institutions is taken as a whole, the focus of deterrence remains oriented towards general deterrence. From a deterrence perspective, punishment is inflicted because of the consequentialist effect of reducing the incidence of crime.

On occasion, international judges also refer to other penological rationales including rehabilitation,[63] incapacitation, and reconciliation. These rationales, however, are not particularly salient. Reconciliation overall

60 *Prosecutor* v. *Kordić and Čerkez* (IT-95-14/2-A), Appeals Judgment, 17 December 2004, para. 1075; *Prosecutor* v. *Katanga* (ICC-01/04-01/07), Décision Relative à la Peine (article 76 du Statut), 23 May 2014, para. 38.

61 *Prosecutor* v. *Momir Nikolić* (IT-02-60/1-S), Judgment, 2 December 2003, para. 86.

62 On expressivism generally, see Mark A. Drumbl, 'Collective Violence and Individual Punishment: The Criminality of Mass Atrocity', (2005) 99 *Northwestern University Law Review* 539; Robert Sloane, 'The Expressive Capacity of International Punishment: The Limits of the National Law Analogy and the Potential of International Criminal Law', (2007) 43 *Stanford Journal of International Law* 39.

63 Rehabilitation is among the more frequently referenced among this group of subjacent objectives, but is often described as not deserving of undue weight (*Prosecutor* v. *Milutinović* et al. (IT-05-87-T), Judgment, 26 February 2009, para. 1146) or as something to be de-emphasised because of the international nature of the sentencing institution (*Prosecutor* v. *Fofana and Kondewa* (SCSL-04-14-T), Sentencing Judgment, 9 August 2007, para. 28).

has not received much more than lip service, although it arose in the *Katanga* judgment where an International Criminal Court Trial Chamber affirmatively recognised the convict's *post hoc* efforts to demobilise and disarm child soldiers as a mitigating factor.[64] Certain transitional justice modalities operative at the national level (such as truth commissions, customary cleansing ceremonies, or tort-based claims) invoke sanctions such as apologies, community service, sharing the truth, lustration, and reparations – each of which may better serve reintegrative, rehabilitative, and reconciliatory goals. In the case of lower-level offenders, such modalities may involve principles of reciprocity and obligation that could help build a robust sense of citizenship.

Whether the sentencing practice of international institutions attains their avowed penological goals remains an unsettled question. The evidence is mixed regarding whether and to what extent punishing a perpetrator dissuades other perpetrators, either in the same region or elsewhere, from offending, in particular in the case of ecological discrimination-oriented crimes such as genocide and persecution. The likelihood of getting caught is more influential than any other factor in discouraging criminal conduct. Yet the likelihood of getting caught and prosecuted by an international institution in cases of atrocity crimes sadly remains low. In terms of retribution, the severity of a prison sentence may never be able to reciprocate the gravity of egregious international crimes (if determined by the harms caused). Meting out just deserts in such cases ominously suggests the abandonment of core principles of international human rights law (whether in terms of the length of sentence or conditions of confinement). Many convicts at the International Criminal Tribunal for the former Yugoslavia, and both Katanga and Lubanga at the International Criminal Court, received sentences that were not any longer than what ordinary common criminals receive in many national justice systems.

Conclusion

International criminal law's turn to the courtroom and jailhouse instantiates what Frédéric Mégret describes as the discipline's 'radical transformation of the legal function away from the traditional mediation role

---

64 *Prosecutor* v. *Katanga* (ICC-01/04-01/07), Décision Relative à la Peine (article 76 du Statut), 23 May 2014, paras. 88, 115, and 144.

of classical international justice and towards a much thicker ability to condemn'.[65] Sentencing is the lens through which this condemnation is refracted. Ultimately, however, as the field matures diversifying the lenses and welcoming other goals, in particular restoration and reintegration, may prove salutary. A cognate challenge for international lawyers is to develop a vocabulary to address persons other than the most notorious offenders, for example bystanders and lower-level participants, whose conduct is not readily intelligible in the language of punitive criminal law but remains essential for violence to become normalised and explode into mass atrocity.

FURTHER READING

Kai Ambos, *Treatise on International Criminal Law, Vol. II: The Crimes and Sentencing*, Oxford University Press, 2014.

Christine Bishai, 'Superior Responsibility, Inferior Sentencing: Sentencing Practice at the International Criminal Tribunals', (2013) 11 *Northwestern Journal of International Human Rights* 86.

Silvia D'Ascoli, *Sentencing in International Criminal Law, The UN Ad Hoc Tribunals and Future Perspectives for the ICC*, Oxford: Hart, 2011.

Mark B. Harmon and Fergal Gaynor, 'The Sentencing Practice of International Criminal Tribunals: Ordinary Sentences for Extraordinary Crimes', (2007) 5 *Journal of International Criminal Justice* 683.

Ralph Henham, 'Developing Contextualised Rationales for Sentencing in International Criminal Trials', (2007) 5 *Journal of International Criminal Justice* 757.

Barbora Holá, Alette Smeulers, and Catrien Bijleveld, 'International Sentencing Facts and Figures: Sentencing Practice at the ICTY and ICTR', (2011) 9 *Journal of International Criminal Justice*, 411.

Barbora Holá, Catrien Bijleveld, and Alette Smeulers, 'Consistency of International Sentencing – ICTY and ICTR Case Study', (2012) 9 *European Journal of Criminology* 539.

Jakob von Holderstein Holtermann, 'A "Slice of Cheese" – A Deterrence-Based Argument for the International Criminal Court', (2010) 11 *Human Rights Review* 289.

65 Frédéric Mégret, *Anxiety, Practices, and the Construction of the Field of International Criminal Justice*, Paper presented at the International Studies Association Annual Meeting (Toronto), March 2014 at p. 13.

Peace 5

Alfred de Zayas

Peace is not an eschatological phenomenon, but a continuous work-in-progress. It encompasses multiple legal commitments undertaken by all member States of the United Nations pursuant to the UN Charter and numerous regional and universal treaties on issues such as collective security, disarmament, and international criminal law. Moreover, it is *de lege ferenda* a soon to be codified human right with both individual and collective dimensions. In 2012, the Advisory Committee of the Human Rights Council elaborated a Draft Declaration on the Right to Peace, with a view to reaching a consensus text for adoption and referral to the General Assembly for proclamation. However, it has proven difficult to bring some of the major powers on board. They remain reluctant to accept the limitations of article 2 paragraphs 3 and 4 of the Charter of the United Nations, which, however, constitute a *jus cogens* obligation of all States members of the United Nations, a veritable *jus contra bellum*. It is sad to observe how States persist in claiming that there is no legal basis for a human right to peace, and that the Human Rights Council is not the proper venue to discuss this fundamental right.

There is no generally accepted legal definition of peace. Obviously the concept is incompatible with historical precedents of the destruction of the enemy, as Rome perpetrated on the Carthaginians 146 BCE at the end of the third Punic War (*Carthago delenda est,* Cato the elder). Nor is peace the silence of cemeteries described by Tacitus in *Agricola,* that prerogative of the stronger to devastate the weaker and then to make a desert of its homeland (*ubi solitudinem faciunt, pacem appellant*). Peace is a state of harmonious national and international relations based on the rule of law, justice, and solidarity, consistent with the motto of the International Labour Office: 'if we want peace, we must cultivate social justice' (*si vis pacem, cole justitiam*).

Besides its philosophical, sociological, and religious components, peace encompasses important legal commitments. As emphasised by the United Nations Security Council, the rule of law is a vital element of conflict prevention and peacekeeping.[1] The breach of the peace by aggression constitutes an internationally wrongful act giving rise to State responsibility, the obligation to make reparation, and personal criminal liability.

Over the centuries, peace has gradually emerged as a principle of international relations whose breach constitutes a new category in international criminal law and which awaits further elaboration and application in the form of international case law. For the purposes of this chapter, the author endeavours to give a holistic view of peace and refers the reader to the more specific chapters on aggression by Benjamin and Donald Ferencz, on the future of international criminal justice by M. Cherif Bassiouni, and to the human rights introduction by Andrew Clapham.

As many observers have noted, peace is not merely the absence of war (negative peace), it is a comprehensive concept that implies the absence of structural violence, of economic pressures, unilateral coercive measures and political blackmail, and the proactive promotion of an equitable international order based on fair trade, international co-operation, and solidarity (positive peace). It goes beyond mere positivism, beyond the *jus cogens* prohibition of the threat and the use of force stipulated in article 2, paragraph 4, of the Charter of the United Nations. It has a natural law component and should be understood as a general principle of law in the sense of article 38 of the Statute of the International Court of Justice. As a general principle, it predates the codification of international criminal law, the Kellogg-Briand Pact of 1928 and article 6(a) of the Statute of the International Military Tribunal at Nuremberg, which defines the 'crime against peace'.

Undoubtedly, international criminal law experienced a significant impulse at the Nuremberg trials, which produced legal precedents, subsequently proclaimed by the United Nations General Assembly as the *Nuremberg Principles*. Alas, there have been countless wars and aggressions since the Nuremberg and Tokyo trials, and whereas tribunals have produced significant case law on war crimes and crimes against humanity, there has been no progress with regard to the prosecution of the crime against peace.

1 UN Doc. S/PV.7113, pp. 3–4.

The Purposes and Principles of the United Nations Charter lay out a *mode d'emploi* to spare future generations from the scourge of war. Admittedly, no world war has been fought since 1945, but there have been continuous wars and foreign interventions in all regions of the world, causing many millions of victims, primarily among civilians. The United Nations General Assembly has adopted numerous resolutions condemning the breach of the peace and the ensuing war crimes. It has repeatedly emphasised the need to promote friendly relations among nations (Resolution 2625) and to prevent aggression (see definition contained in Resolution 3314).

The punishment of the crime of aggression

In the seven decades since the end of the Second World War, the crime of aggression has enjoyed general impunity, notwithstanding the Nuremberg Judgment: 23 out of the 24 Nazi accused were indicted for the crime against peace and eight were convicted pursuant to article 6(a) of the Statute which defines the crime as: 'planning, preparation, initiation or waging of a war of aggression, or a war in violation of international treaties, agreements or assurances, or participation in a common plan or conspiracy for the accomplishment of any of the foregoing'. In this context, it is worth recalling that, at the opening of the Nuremberg trials, United States Chief Prosecutor Robert Jackson stated: 'We must never forget that the record on which we judge these defendants today is the record on which history will judge us tomorrow ... While this law is first applied against German aggressors, the law includes, and if it is to serve a useful purpose it must condemn, aggression by any other nations, including those which sit here now in judgment'.[2] In this sense, the judgment of the tribunal stated that '[t]o initiate a war of aggression ... is ... the supreme international crime differing only from other war crimes in that it contains within itself the accumulated evil of the whole'.[3]

Alas, these noble words were not followed by international action, and no subsequent trial of other aggressors has taken place. The application of the Nuremberg precedent on the crime of aggression could have been tested in hundreds of cases, e.g., the Warsaw Pact's invasion of Hungary in 1956, the Warsaw Pact's invasion of Czechoslovakia in

2 (1947) 2 IMT 101.   3 (1948) 22 IMT 411, at p. 427.

1968, the bombing of Vietnam, Laos, and Cambodia by the United States 1964–1973, the United States military interventions in Grenada in 1983, Nicaragua 1982–1986, Panama 1989, the NATO bombardment of Serbia in 1999, the ongoing blockade of Gaza, the assault on a humanitarian flotilla in the high seas in 2010 and, of course, the assault on Iraq by the 'coalition of the willing' in March 2003, which remains one of the most flagrant violations of the Charter of the United Nations and of the international rule of law. Even Secretary-General Kofi Annan called this geopolitically motivated war an 'illegal war'.[4] In 2003, no international tribunal existed with jurisdiction over the culprits. The only possibility of prosecution would have been through the exercise of universal jurisdiction by a State with appropriate universal jurisdiction legislation and not overly vulnerable to economic and political intimidation or to the imposition of sanctions by the powerful.

International people's tribunals have, however, taken up the matter, but these tribunals are only moral instances devoid of legal powers of execution, and continue being largely ignored by the mainstream media. On 16 July 2005, Professor Richard Falk reported in an article in *The Nation*:

> The World Tribunal on Iraq (WTI) held its culminating session in Istanbul June 24–27, the last and most elaborate of 16 condemnations of the Iraq War held worldwide in the past two years, in Barcelona, Tokyo, Brussels, Seoul, New York, London, Mumbai and other cities. The Istanbul session used the verdicts and some of the testimony from the earlier sessions; the cumulative nature of the sessions built interest among peace activists, resulting in this final session having by far the strongest international flavour. The cumulative process, described by organisers as 'the tribunal movement', is unique in history: Never before has a war aroused this level of protest on a global scale – first to prevent it (the huge February 15, 2003, demonstrations in eighty countries) and then to condemn its inception and conduct. The WTI expresses the opposition of global civil society to the Iraq War, a project perhaps best described as a form of 'moral globalisation'.

More recently, the Kuala Lumpur War Crimes Tribunal found both George W. Bush and Tony Blair guilty of waging aggressive war. In its judgment of 22 November 2011, the Tribunal concluded:

> The essence of legality is the principled, predictable, and consistent application of a single standard for the strong and the weak alike. Selective

---

4 'Iraq War Illegal, says Annan', *BBC News*, 16 September 2004.

manipulation of international law by powerful states undermines its legitimacy. The 2003 invasion of Iraq was an unlawful act of aggression and an international crime. It cannot be justified under any reasonable interpretation of international law. It violates the outer limits of laws regulating the use of force. It amounts to mass murder. Unlawful use of force in Iraq threatens to return us to a world in which the law of the jungle prevails over the rule of law, with potentially disastrous consequences for the human rights not only of the Iraqis but of people throughout the region and the world.

Although the UN General Assembly, the old Commission on Human Rights, the new Human Rights Council and the UN Human Rights Committee, among others, have repeatedly condemned impunity, until recently there has been no mechanism with recognised competence to try and sentence aggressors. The most significant step toward the punishment of the 'crime against peace', now known as the crime of aggression, was achieved at the Diplomatic Conference in Rome in 1998, which adopted the Statute of the International Criminal Court, article 5 of which gives jurisdiction to the Court over the crime of aggression. At the July 2010 Review Conference of the Rome Statute held in Kampala, Uganda, a consensus definition of aggression was finally adopted. Admittedly, the new amendment has no retroactive application and will not allow the prosecution of aggressors in previous wars, e.g., the war against Iraq of March 2003. But the perpetrators of the crime of aggression in that war could be indicted for their responsibility for the ensuing war crimes and crimes against humanity committed during that war.

Justifications for the use of force

At present there are only two legitimate justifications for the use of force (*jus ad bellum*). The exercise of self-defence is customary international law, but since the entry into force of the UN Charter and its article 51, self-defence can only be exercised 'until the Security Council has taken measures necessary to maintain international peace and security'. Thus it is a temporary right of self-help, which necessarily ceases when the Security Council becomes seised of the matter. Following an 'armed attack', any self-defence measure must be notified to the Security Council so that the United Nations can exercise its peace restoring function. Moreover, a mere border skirmish does not justify all-out war under the pretext of self-defence, since there must be a 'threshold of gravity', as the International Court of Justice determined in the *Nicaragua Judgment* of 27 June 1986. In this context, it is also important to recall that the right to self-defence does not allow the preventive or so-called pre-emptive use of force. A previous armed attack is a necessary precondition for invoking article 51 of the Charter.

Another legitimate use of force exists when the Security Council, acting under Chapter VII of the Charter, authorises it. The Security Council, how-ever, is not above the Charter and can only authorise the use of force in a manner consistent with the Purposes and Principles of the Organisation, particularly the maintenance of peace, as stipulated in Article 24 of the Charter: 'the Security Council shall act in accordance with the Purposes and Principles of the United Nations'. In this context, the relatively new doctrines of 'humanitarian intervention' and 'responsibility to protect' cannot be understood as a *lex specialis* that can derogate from Charter obligations to resolve all disputes through peaceful means (article 2(3)), to refrain from the threat and the use of force (article 2(4)), and to refrain from intervening in the domestic affairs of other States (article 2(7)). 'Responsibility to protect' cannot be used as a pretext to facilitate military intervention, but must be read in conjunction with the overall obligation to protect succeeding generations from the scourge of war, and therefore to prevent armed conflict. Thus, contrary to some journalistic trends and misconceptions, which would like to see the United Nations transformed from a peacekeeping to a war-making organisation, the 'responsibility to protect' idea contained in General Assembly resolution 60/1, the World Summit Outcome, does not and cannot replace the Charter-mandated rule of non-interference in the internal affairs of sovereign States. This is all the more true as in 2005 world leaders declared that '[e]ach individual State has the responsibility to protect its populations from genocide, war crimes, ethnic cleansing and crimes against humanity'. The principle of non-intervention remains very much valid and is confirmed in count-less resolutions of the General Assembly and the Human Rights Council. Therefore, responsibility to protect must not be abused to circumvent the Charter or engage in sabre-rattling or propaganda for war, which is spe-cifically prohibited by article 20(1) of the International Covenant on Civil and Political Rights.

Any intervention in other States must satisfy strictly defined bench-marks and take place only as *ultima ratio*. In July 2009, the General

Assembly revisited the responsibility to protect doctrine, holding a plenary debate on the question. The President of the Assembly identified four benchmark questions that should determine whether and when the system of collective security could implement the responsibility to protect: (a) Do the rules apply in principle, and is it likely that they will be applied in practice equally to all States, or, in the nature of things, is it more likely that the principle would be applied only by the strong against the weak?; (b) Will the adoption of the responsibility to protect principle in the practice of collective security be more likely to enhance or undermine respect for international law?; (c) Is the doctrine of responsibility to protect necessary and, conversely, does it guarantee that States will intervene to prevent another situation like the one that occurred in Rwanda?; (d) Does the international community have the capacity to enforce accountability upon those who might abuse the right that the responsibility to protect principle would give States to resort to the use of force against other States?[5] Moreover, it should be recalled that the Charter of the United Nations imposes certain *erga omnes* obligations on States, including the obligation to condemn the illegal use of force and to deny recognition of territorial changes arising from the illegal use of force. While there is an international responsibility to protect, there is, first and foremost, an international responsibility to protect humanity from the scourge of war and, most importantly, to protect humanity from weapons of mass destruction, including biological, chemical, and nuclear weapons.

Obstacles to maintaining peace

A significant obstacle to maintaining the peace in the world is the prevalence of belligerent rhetoric, sabre-rattling, and war-mongering, including irresponsible media-hype and blatant propaganda for war in contravention of article 20 of the International Covenant on Civil and Political Rights. Indeed, many armed conflicts have begun because of incitement by politicians and the media, pursuing a logic of war and rejecting other options for the solution of international disputes by negotiation and diplomacy.

5 Interim Report of the Independent Expert on the Promotion of a Democratic and Equitable International Order, Alfred-Maurice de Zayas, UN Doc. A/67/277, paras. 14 and 15.

Humanity's best hope thus rests on a revitalised United Nations and a proactive General Assembly capable to deploy preventive strategies. As the most representative world body, the General Assembly should not only voice the international community's rejection of war and war-mongering, but also develop early warning mechanisms to detect and neutralise disinformation, insidious propaganda for war, and the panoply of pretexts used by some States to justify the use of force. Similarly, the UN Secretary-General could use his good offices and deploy preventive strategies against the uncontrolled dynamics of war propaganda. He can exercise a more proactive role in referring belligerent tensions not only to the Security Council but also to the General Assembly and to the Human Rights Council, bearing in mind that armed conflicts always impact negatively on the most fundamental human rights. In this context, the creation of the function of a Special Advisor to the Secretary-General on the prevention of war and the suppression of war-mongering could be considered. The United Nations should provide a friendly forum where politicians who have galloped away in their belligerent rhetoric can lower their tone, defuse the tension, and discretely withdraw without losing too much face.[6]

Another important obstacle to the maintenance of world peace is the continued arms race and the enormous commerce in arms. Both effectively fuel wars worldwide. Many observers have long concluded that as long as there are big profits to be made, there will be wars. The undemocratic impact of the military-industrial complex on governments and the general lack of budget and fiscal transparency in most countries constitute a major problem. Effective measures must be adopted to reduce the undemocratic influence of the arms industry on government officials, also concerning decisions on the use of force, the privatisation of war, the globalisation of militarism, and the expansion of military bases at home and abroad.

Disarmament

In the light of the above, the international community has adopted a number of important legal commitments concerning the necessity of global disarmament. Already in 1960, the United Nations Office in Geneva

6 Statement by Alfred-Maurice de Zayas, Independent Expert on the promotion of a democratic and equitable international order at the 68th session of the General Assembly, 28 November 2013.

hosted the Ten Nation Committee on Disarmament, which was followed by the Eighteen-Nation Committee (1962–1968) and the Conference of the Committee on Disarmament (1969–1978). Since 1979, the United Nations Conference on Disarmament, a multilateral negotiating forum composed of sixty-five countries, meets three times a year in Geneva. Currently the Conference on Disarmament focuses on the cessation of the nuclear arms race and the promotion of nuclear disarmament; prevention of nuclear war, including all related matters; prevention of an arms race in outer space; effective international arrangements to assure non-nuclear-weapon States against the use or threat of use of nuclear weapons; new types of weapons of mass destruction and new systems of such weapons including radiological weapons; comprehensive programme of disarmament and transparency in armaments.

Among the many treaties the observance of which contribute to peace, the Nuclear Non-Proliferation Treaty of 1968 (190 States Parties) stipulates in article 6: 'Each of the Parties to the Treaty undertakes to pursue negotiations in good faith on effective measures relating to cessation of the nuclear arms race at an early date and to nuclear disarmament, and on a treaty on general and complete disarmament under strict and effective international control'. Notwithstanding the above commitment, the Nuclear States have continued producing, modernising, and stockpiling nuclear weapons. Some commentators point out that this entails not only a failure to abide by the NPT commitment to negotiate in good faith, but also amounts to a contravention of article 6 of the International Covenant on Civil and Political Rights, which protects the right to life. The first General Comment of the Human Rights Committee on article 6 stipulates: 'Every effort they make to avert the danger of war, especially thermonuclear war, and to strengthen international peace and security would constitute the most important condition and guarantee for the safeguarding of the right to life'.[7] Similarly, in the second General Comment on article 6 the Committee stated:

> 3. While remaining deeply concerned by the toll of human life taken by conventional weapons in armed conflicts, the Committee has noted that, during successive sessions of the General Assembly, representatives from all geographical regions have expressed their growing concern at the

7 General Comment No. 6: Article 6 (Right to life), UN Doc. HRI/GEN/1/Rev.1, p. 4, para. 2.

development and proliferation of increasingly awesome weapons of mass destruction, which not only threaten human life but also absorb resources that could otherwise be used for vital economic and social purposes, particularly for the benefit of developing countries, and thereby for promoting and securing the enjoyment of human rights for all...

4. The Committee associates itself with this concern. It is evident that the designing, testing, manufacture, possession and deployment of nuclear weapons are among the greatest threats to the right to life which confront mankind today. This threat is compounded by the danger that the actual use of such weapons may be brought about, not only in the event of war, but even through human or mechanical error or failure.

5. Furthermore, the very existence and gravity of this threat generates a climate of suspicion and fear between States, which is in itself antagonistic to the promotion of universal respect for and observance of human rights and fundamental freedoms in accordance with the Charter of the United Nations and the International Covenants on Human Rights.

6. The production, testing, possession, deployment and use of nuclear weapons should be prohibited and recognised as crimes against humanity.

7. The Committee accordingly, in the interest of mankind, calls upon all States, whether Parties to the Covenant or not, to take urgent steps, unilaterally and by agreement, to rid the world of this menace.[8]

These were courageous words from the most respected universal human rights treaty body, the Human Rights Committee. Unfortunately, its pronouncements are only 'soft law' and not legally binding.

In this context, it is important to welcome the emergence of several demilitarised zones in the world, the first being Antarctica, pursuant to the Antarctic Treaty of 1959. There are also important Nuclear-Weapon Free zones and nuclear-free countries, including countries like Austria, Finland, Norway, Sweden, and many cities in individual countries including the United Kingdom and the United States. Of regional significance is the Tlatelolco Treaty of 1967, also known as the Treaty for the Prohibition of Nuclear Weapons in Latin America and the Caribbean, which committed thirty-three States to a regional nuclear weapon-free zone. Pursuant to the South Pacific Nuclear-Free Zone Treaty (Rarotonga Treaty) of 1985, fourteen States, including Australia and New Zealand, declared a large area of the Pacific, a nuclear weapon-free area. Similarly, pursuant to the African Nuclear-Weapon Free Zone Treaty (Pelindaba Treaty) of 1996,

8 General Comment No. 14: Article 6 (Right to life), UN Doc. HRI/GEN/1/Rev.1, p. 18.

the entire African continent and many islands in the Atlantic Ocean such as the Canary Islands and Cape Verde, and islands in the Indian Ocean including Comoros, Madagascar, Mauritius, and Seychelles, constitute a nuclear weapon-free zone. Proposals for other nuclear weapon-free zones are on the table. So, for instance, in 2010 the General Assembly proposed a nuclear weapon-free zone in the Middle East.[9] This follows-up on Security Council Resolution 687 (1991), which specifically recalled 'the objective of the establishment of a nuclear weapon-free zone in the region of the Middle East'.

Other legal commitments concerning disarmament include the Biological Weapons Convention (1972), the Chemical Weapons Convention (1993), the Anti-Personnel Landmines Convention (1997), the Convention on Certain Conventional Weapons (2001), and the Convention on Cluster Munitions (2008). Besides treaties, some regions have issued Declarations proclaiming themselves 'zones of peace'. On 29 January 2014 at the conclusion of the second CELAC Summit (Community of Latin America and Caribbean States), held in Havana, Cuba, the thirty-three member States adopted by consensus a Declaration proclaiming:

> Latin America and the Caribbean as a Zone of Peace based on respect for the principles and rules of International Law, including the international instruments to which Member States are a party to, the Principles and Purposes of the United Nations Charter;
> Our permanent commitment to solve disputes through peaceful means with the aim of uprooting forever threat or use of force in our region;
> The commitment of the States of the region with their strict obligation not to intervene, directly or indirectly, in the internal affairs of any other State and observe the principles of national sovereignty, equal rights and self-determination of peoples...

On 2 February 2014, the Independent Expert issued a press release welcoming this Declaration.

Peace as a human right

The General Assembly has been at the vanguard in the efforts to recognise peace not only as a general principle, but also as a human right. Already

---

9 Establishment of a nuclear-weapon-free zone in the region of the Middle East, UN Doc. A/67/RES/64/26.

General Assembly Resolution 33/73, Declaration on the Preparation of Societies for Life in Peace, adopted on 15 December 1978 without opposition, stipulated that 'every nation and every human being, regardless of race, conscience, language or sex, has the inherent right to life in peace'. On 12 November 1984, the Assembly adopted Resolution 39/11, Declaration of the Right of Peoples to Peace, which 'solemnly proclaims that the peoples of our planet have a sacred right to peace'. Ninety-two States voted in favour, no State voted against. Moreover, it should be noted that 105 States have incorporated the universal value of peace in their national constitutions as a governing principle of their domestic legal systems. Some constitutions explicitly recognise peace as a fundamental right of peoples and individuals, in particular article 10.1 of the Constitution of Bolivia ('Bolivia is a pacifist State, which promotes the culture of peace and the right to peace ...), article 22 of the Constitution of Colombia ('Peace is a right and a duty whose compliance is mandatory') and the Preamble of the Constitution of Japan ('we recognise that all peoples of the world have the right to live in peace, free from fear and from want'). Other States have chosen to abolish their armies. Thus, article 12 of the Costa Rican Constitution stipulates: 'The Army as a permanent institution is abolished.' And in the context of regional co-operation, the African Charter of Human and Peoples' Rights stipulates in article 23(1): 'All peoples shall have the right to national and international peace and security'. Notwithstanding these legal commitments, the world is still very far away from developing a culture of peace.

Pursuant to Human Rights Council Resolution A/HRC/11/4 entitled 'Promotion of the rights of peoples to peace', the Office of the UN High Commissioner for Human Rights convened in December 2009 an expert workshop on the Human Right to Peace, among whose expert panellists were Professor William Schabas, Judge Antonio Cançado Trindade of the International Court of Justice, Fatimata-Binta Dah, who is President of the Committee for the Elimination of Racial Discrimination, and the author of this chapter. The workshop concluded that there was a human right to peace with individual and collective dimensions and that the Human Rights Council should establish a working group to elaborate all aspects of this right.[10]

---

10 Report of the Office of the High Commissioner on the outcome of the expert workshop on the right of peoples to peace, UN Doc. A/HRC/14/38.

On 10 December 2010, the Spanish Society for International Human Rights Law, an association of professors of international law in Spain and elsewhere, adopted the *Declaración de Santiago de Compostela*, which was subsequently transmitted to the United Nations Human Rights Council and referred to its Advisory Committee for further elaboration. On 18–21 February 2013, the first open-ended inter-governmental working group on the right to peace met in Geneva. Among the issues discussed was the *legal basis* for the contention that peace is a human right. The Independent Expert was invited to contribute to the proceedings, agreeing with some of the speakers that the Working Group's mandate necessarily encompassed the progressive development of international law and mechanisms of implementation, for law is a living instrument. Here lies the added value of the draft Declaration as dynamic development – not mere reaffirmation of norms.

It is indicative of the enhanced role played by civil society that this standard-setting exercise was spearheaded not by governments but by scholars, in response to the worldwide aspiration of individuals and peoples to live in peace. This confirms the spirit of the Charter of the United Nations, which begins with the words 'We the Peoples'. At the session, some delegates expressed scepticism about the legal basis of the right to peace. Some participants, however, pointed out that the legal basis rests solidly on the Charter's preamble and articles 1 and 2. Legal basis is also provided by article 28 of the Universal Declaration of Human Rights, which stipulates that everyone is entitled to a social and international order in which the rights and freedoms set forth in the Declaration can be fully realised, and by the United Nations human rights treaties.

Many of the elements of the right to peace have been codified as articles of the International Covenant on Civil and Political Rights, the International Covenant on Economic, Social and Cultural Rights, and other United Nations treaties. While some States still harbour doubts about the justiciability of the right to peace as a norm of international law, participants indicated that constitutive elements of the right to peace already exist and that a significant body of regional and international jurisprudence has emerged. Just to name an example, Costa Rican lawyer Luis Roberto Zamora filed a suit against the participation of Costa Rica in the 'Coalition of the Willing', which resulted in the 2004 Judgment of the Supreme Court of Costa Rica holding Costa Rican association contrary to the Costa Rican Constitution, its neutrality declaration, international law and the United Nations system.

Seen from the perspective of individual rights, the Human Rights Committee is competent to examine individual complaints concerning violations of the International Covenant on Civil and Political Rights. Thus, a breach of the right to life such as extrajudicial executions and potentially also illegal wars can be considered as a breach of article 6. Bearing in mind that two general comments on article 6 and General Comment No. 29 on states of emergency postulate the State obligation to disarmament, a test case in this context may be justiciable. Threats to the right to peace may potentially be examined under article 9, which imposes on the State an obligation to ensure security of the person. Freedom to engage in anti-war activities, to demonstrate for peace and to create pacifist organisations is protected under articles 19, 21, and 22. The prohibition of the recruitment of children as soldiers in armed conflicts breaches article 24 and the Optional Protocol to the Convention on the Rights of the Child on the involvement of children in armed conflict, and will be justiciable under the third protocol to the Convention which entered into force on 14 April 2014. The right of conscientious objection to military service has been repeatedly affirmed in the general comments of the Human Rights Committee and case law as inherent to article 18, which stipulates the right to freedom of conviction and belief. Conscientious objectors and other persons have the right to leave any country, including their own, pursuant to article 12. Persons who have fled armed conflict and persecution or who have left their countries of origin because of conscientious objection have a right to seek asylum; as refugees, they have a right not to be subjected to *refoulement*, a right protected under article 7 of the International Covenant on Civil and Political Rights, article 3 of the Convention against Torture, and the 1951 Convention relating to the Status of Refugees. They also have the right to return in safety and dignity to their countries of origin pursuant to article 12 of the International Covenant on Civil and Political Rights. Propaganda for war is specifically prohibited under article 20 of the Covenant. The liability of State officials for war-mongering and State responsibility for incitement by non-State actors may be considered by the Human Rights Committee under the State reporting and the Optional Protocol procedures. In case of violation of these constitutive elements of the right to peace, victims have a right to a remedy under article 2 of the Covenant.

The human right to peace also has important economic, social, and cultural components. Following the entry into force of the Optional Protocol to the International Covenant on Economic, Social and Cultural Rights on 5 May 2013, individuals can invoke violations before the Committee on Economic, Social and Cultural Rights. Thus, the right to, *inter alia*, health, a safe environment, food, water, and education has acquired even more resonance in the life of each individual.

Following the successful February 2013 session of the open-ended Working Group,[11] 1,792 non-governmental organisations and cities worldwide submitted to the Human Rights Council a joint written statement endorsing the Working Group and supporting its continuous efforts to achieve consensus among States.[12] The second session of the Working Group made some modest progress in July 2014.[13] A third session, held in April 2015,[14], failed to reach consensus. It is likely that the new chairman-rapporteur of the Working Group will abandon the vain hope of obtaining consensus and move forward with a robust text to be adopted by majority vote. Unfortunately, some States seem to equate 'consensus' with the right to impose *a veto* on the progressive development of international law. Recognition of peace as a human right will promote a democratic and equitable international order and that national and international democratisation will reduce conflict, since peoples want peace. It is governments that stumble into war.

Other civil society initiatives include the work of the Writers for Peace Committee of PEN International. In 2013 at its Bled session, the Committee adopted the Bled Manifesto on Peace. It was endorsed by the Assembly of Delegates at the seventy-ninth PEN International Congress in Reykjavik. Article 1 of the Manifesto stipulates: 'All individuals and peoples have a right to peace and this right should be recognised by the United Nations as a universal human right'.

Attention must be given to the penal consequences of violations of the right to peace, including the punishment by domestic courts or in due time by the International Criminal Court of those who have engaged in aggression, propaganda for war, and incitement to violence. Among the

---

11 UN Doc. A/HRC/WG.13/1/2.

12 UN Doc. A/HRC/23/NGO/96.

13 www.ohchr.org/EN/HRBodies/HRC/RightPeace/Pages/SecondSession.aspx

14 www.ohchr.org/EN/Issues/IntOrder/Pages/HRCPeace.aspx

elements of the crime against peace that could be subject to prosecution are blockades, targeted assassination, the use of indiscriminate weapons including drones, demolition of homes, forced population transfers, and other forms of State terrorism. The International Criminal Tribunal for Rwanda has established an important precedent condemning incitement to genocide and crimes against humanity[15] that *mutatis mutandis* can be used to prosecute those who incite war, in particular those politicians and senior military who deliberately disseminate wrong information to induce a form of fear psychosis and make the necessity of the use of force appear plausible. The international criminal aspects of war propaganda are being addressed by several think tanks and foundations, including the Kuala Lumpur Foundation to criminalise war, which has set up the Kuala Lumpur War Crimes Tribunal (reminiscent of the Russell Tribunal on Vietnam), and conducted several quasi-judicial proceedings, largely ignored, however, by the mainstream press.

Advancing toward world peace?

It has been said that the arms trade fuels wars, since weapons are built so as to be used and destroyed, so that ever more weapons can be produced and sold. Only in this manner can the arms industry make a profit. Therefore, it is imperative to develop an effective strategy for disarmament – not only nuclear disarmament, but also disarmament of conventional weapons. The adoption by the General Assembly of the Arms Trade Treaty on 2 April 2013[16] is a small step in the right direction, but it is imperative not merely to regulate the trade but to significantly reduce it and the corruption and commission-taking that accompany it, which must be subject to national and international penal sanctions.[17]

It is in the hands of international civil society to demand budget and fiscal transparency, a significant reduction in military spending and a reorienting of the work force away from war industries toward peace activities. The Geneva-based Conference on Disarmament has a major

---

15 *Prosecutor* v. *Nahimana* (ICTR-99-52-A), Judgment, 28 November 2007.
16 The Arms Trade Treaty, UN Doc. A/RES/67/234 B. The Treaty itself is an annex to UN Doc. A/CONF.217/2013/L.3.
17 Jonathan Turley, 'Perpetual War And America's Military-Industrial Complex 50 Years After Eisenhower's Farewell Address', *Al Jazeera*, 12 January 2014.

task in achieving effective and verifiable disarmament both with respect of weapons of mass destruction and conventional weapons. Peace is not only threatened by megalomaniacs, but also by business-oriented profit seekers.

Perhaps there is some truth to the observation by Oscar Wilde: 'As long as war is regarded as wicked, it will always have its fascination. When it is looked upon as vulgar, it will cease to be popular'. Hence, public and general education for peace and a responsible media have a role to play in creating a culture of peace and its corollary: a culture of no impunity to aggressors, no matter from which country they come. Civil society should demonstrate resolve in telling democratically elected leaders 'not in our name', when it comes to military threats against other countries or an intransigent refusal to negotiate and settle disputes through peaceful means in conformity with the Charter of the United Nations.

FURTHER READING

Michael Kearney, *The Prohibition of Propaganda for War in International Law*, Oxford University Press, 2007.

Jakob Th. Möller and Alfred de Zayas, *United Nations Human Rights Committee Case Law*, Kehl: N.P. Engel, 2009.

William A. Schabas, 'The Human Right to Peace', in Asbjørn Eide, Jakob Th. Möller, and Ineta Ziemele, eds., *Making Peoples Heard*, Leiden: Martinus Nijhoff, 2011, pp. 43–58.

Carlos Villán and Carmelo Faleh, eds., *Paz, Migraciones y Libre Determinación de Los Pueblos*, Luarca: AEDIDH, 2012.

Carlos Villán and Carmelo Faleh, eds., *The International Observatory of the Human Right to Peace*, Luarca: AEDIDH, 2013.

Carlos Villán and Carmelo Faleh, eds., *Contribuciones Regionales Para una Declaración Universal del Derecho Humano a la paz*, Luarca: AEDIDH, 2010.

Alfred de Zayas, 'Peace as a Human Right: The *Jus Cogens* Prohibition of Aggression', in Asbjørn Eide, Jakob Th. Möller, and Ineta Ziemele, eds., *Making Peoples Heard*, Leiden: Martinus Nijhoff, 2011, pp. 27–42.

Part II   Institutions

Ad hoc international criminal tribunals (Yugoslavia, Rwanda, Sierra Leone) 6

Göran Sluiter

After the end of the Cold War, the time was ripe for further and spectacular developments in international criminal law. For a long time after the creation of the post–Second World War tribunals of Nuremberg and Tokyo the efforts to establish successors were fruitless. Progress was made in the field of standard-setting, as is demonstrated by the adoption of the Genocide Convention, the Geneva Conventions and Additional Protocols, and the Convention against Torture. This progress was not matched by the creation of international judicial mechanisms aimed at ending – or at least reducing – impunity for the commission of international crimes.

This changed in the 1990s, when *ad hoc* international criminal tribunals were created by the United Nations directly (the International Criminal Tribunal for the former Yugoslavia and the International Criminal Tribunal for Rwanda) or by means of a treaty between the United Nations and a State (Special Court for Sierra Leone). The creation of the International Criminal Tribunal for the former Yugoslavia in 1993 and the International Criminal Tribunal for Rwanda in 1994, in particular, set in motion an almost unsaturated development of international criminal law. It was the upbeat to the later creation of the International Criminal Court, other international criminal justice mechanisms and renewed attention to prosecution of international crimes domestically. It made the relatively dormant field of international criminal law fully come to life. If the United Nations *ad hoc* tribunals made one thing clear it must have been that international criminal law can be a very powerful tool and that impunity for the most serious crimes is not self-evident.

One can hardly overestimate the importance of the United Nations *ad hoc* tribunals for the development and operationalisation of international criminal law. This chapter cannot do justice to their impressive achievements and contributions to the field. It is confined to a sketch and outline of what I perceive to be essential information on the *ad hoc* tribunals and also what I perceive to be their most significant contributions to the field of international criminal law. This analysis and the underlying choices are by definition selective. One is thus encouraged to engage in further reading within the rich variety of available literature on the topic.

The present chapter deals with the International Criminal Tribunal for the former Yugoslavia, the International Criminal Tribunal for Rwanda, and the Special Court for Sierra Leone. I am aware that the Special Court is of quite a different nature than the two Tribunals, because it has not been established directly by the United Nations. Nevertheless, because of the important role of the United Nations in the establishment of the Special Court and its similarities in its law and practice to the *ad hoc* tribunals, it is included in the present chapter.

Establishment

Unfortunately, international criminal tribunals of an *ad hoc* nature are a response to the occurrence of large-scale atrocities that have been committed and shock the international community. This was the case of the post–Second World War tribunals and this is no different for the *ad hoc* tribunals. The International Criminal Tribunal for the former Yugoslavia was established in 1993 in response to serious violations of humanitarian law that occurred in the Balkan war in the former Yugoslavia since 1991.[1] The International Criminal Tribunal for Rwanda was created in response to the genocide committed in Rwanda in 1994.[2] The Special Court for Sierra Leone was set up because of the serious crimes that were committed in the context of the civil war in Sierra Leone since 30 November 1996.[3]

All three institutions have in common that their creation is due to the initiatives taken by the United Nations Security Council, acting under Chapter VII of the Charter. The Yugoslavia and Rwanda Tribunals were established directly pursuant to a United Nations Security Council resolution, whereas the Special Court for Sierra Leone's legal birth is a treaty

---

1 The International Criminal Tribunal for the former Yugoslavia was established by Security Council Resolution 827 (1993) after the Council had decided in its Resolution 808 (1993) that the Tribunal 'shall be established'.

2 The International Criminal Tribunal for Rwanda was created – and its Statute adopted – by Security Council Resolution 955 (1994).

3 The Agreement between the United Nations and Sierra Leone creating the Special Court was concluded on 16 January 2002.

between the United Nations and Sierra Leone, although it would not have been concluded without an important encouraging role of the Council.[4]

Whether the Security Council is legally empowered under the Charter of the United Nations to set up judicial institutions of a penal nature was litigated in the first cases at the Rwanda Tribunal, and especially the Yugoslavia Tribunal. In the first case, *Tadić*, the defence argued that the Tribunal should review the decision from the Security Council that led to its creation and determine that this decision was in violation of the Charter of the United Nations. The issue was decided by the seminal Appeals Chamber decision of 2 October 1995.[5] The majority of the judges, interestingly, did not shy away from claiming and exercising the competence on the part of the Tribunal to review the legality of the decisions taken by its parent body, the Security Council. This was indeed a wise course of action, as one would not like to see such a new institution being burdened with continuing question marks as to whether it was in fact lawfully established. The Appeals Chamber also ruled that the Security Council has a wide margin of discretion in taking the measures necessary to maintain and restore international peace and security. The legality of establishment of the Rwanda Tribunal was confirmed on identical grounds.[6]

Outside the realm of litigation at these tribunals, it has been a matter of debate for some time – maybe even it still is – whether the creation of international criminal tribunals is an appropriate and positive measure for maintaining international peace and security. The maxim 'no peace without justice' is highly sympathetic but empirically largely unproven. On the other hand, the sceptics who feared that the creation of the International Criminal Tribunal for the former Yugoslavia would be an obstacle to peace agreements between the warring factions in the former Yugoslavia have equally no proof for these assertions.

---

4 In Resolution 1315 (2000), the United Nations Security Council requested the Secretary-General to negotiate an agreement with the Government of Sierra Leone to create an independent special court to prosecute persons who bear the greatest responsibility for the commission of serious violations of international humanitarian law and crimes committed under Sierra Leonean law.

5 *Prosecutor* v. *Tadić* (IT-94-1-AR72), Decision on the Defence Motion for Interlocutory Appeal on Jurisdiction, 2 October 1995.

6 *Prosecutor* v. *Kanyabashi* (ICTR-96-15-T), Decision on the Defence Motion on Jurisdiction, 18 June 1997.

The creation of the Special Court for Sierra Leone also spurred litiga-tion about its legality. This litigation focused in part on some issues of powers incumbent upon United Nations organs and on issues of Sierra Leonean constitutional law.[7] It also dealt with whether an international criminal tribunal can lawfully be created in derogation of a treaty in which amnesty had been granted to members of the warring factions. This matter was resolved in favour of the generally accepted rule that amnes-ties in respect of international crimes have no value.[8]

The first case law of the *ad hoc* tribunals has confirmed that the United Nations, especially the Security Council, can lawfully play a vital role in holding individuals criminally accountable for international crimes.

Jurisdiction

The matter of jurisdiction is key in the establishment of all of the *ad hoc* tribunals. What powers can be exercised in terms of crimes, persons, time, and space (or, in Latin: jurisdiction *ratione materiae, ratione perso-nae, ratione temporis, ratione loci*)? This was by far the most important question to be decided in the course of drafting the statutes of the *ad hoc* tribunals. Since the tribunals were meant to be of a temporary nature only, confined to a few specific (small) States, and had to be operational and effective on relatively short notice, the statutes that were created were short and simple. Details of the procedure and functioning of the

7 *Prosecutor v. Kallon, Norman and Kamara* (SCSL-2004-15-AR72(E), SCSL-2004-14-AR72(E) and SCSL-2004-16-AR72), Decision on Constitutionality and Lack of Jurisdiction, 13 March 2004; *Prosecutor v. Gbao* (SCSL-2004-15-AR72), Decision on Preliminary Motion on the Invalidity of the Agreement between the United Nations and the Government of Sierra Leone on the Establishment of the Special Court, 25 May 2004; *Prosecutor v. Fofana* (SCSL-2004-14-AR72), Decision on Preliminary Motion on Lack of Jurisdiction: Illegal Delegation of Jurisdiction by Sierra Leone, 25 May 2004; *Prosecutor v. Fofana* (SCSL-2004-14-AR72), Decision on Preliminary Motion on Lack of Jurisdiction Materiae: Illegal Delegation of Powers by the United Nations, 25 May 2004.

8 *Prosecutor v. Kallon and Kamara* (SCSL-2004-15-AR72 and SCSL-2004-16-AR72), Decision on Challenge to Jurisdiction: Lomé Accord Amnesty, 13 March 2004; *Prosecutor v. Kondewa* (SCSL-2004-14-AR72), Decision on Lack of Jurisdiction / Abuse of Process: Amnesty provided by the Lomé Accord, 25 May 2004.

tribunals had to be worked out in so-called rules of procedure and evidence, to be adopted by the judges. However, the statutes of the *ad hoc* tribunals set out their jurisdictional limitations.

The jurisdiction was limited to the territories of the States where the crimes were committed (states of the former Yugoslavia, Rwanda (and states neighbouring Rwanda) and Sierra Leone). As a starting date, the year was chosen in which the conflict started (Yugoslavia Tribunal), or the period in the conflict from which moment on the most serious crimes were considered to have been committed (Special Court), or the year in which the genocide took place (Rwanda Tribunal). The Statute of the International Criminal Tribunal for the former Yugoslavia does not set an end date to its jurisdiction, as the Tribunal was created when the armed conflict in the former Yugoslavia was still ongoing. The open-ended temporal jurisdiction permitted the Yugoslavia Tribunal to also deal with the crimes committed in the context of the later Kosovo and Macedonia independence wars. Also the temporal jurisdiction of the Special Court for Sierra Leone, starting on 30 November 1996, is open-ended, but there was no renewed escalation of violence that triggered new investigations.

The personal jurisdiction of all *ad hoc* tribunals appears restricted to natural persons (all Statutes refer to 'persons'). A vital aspect of all *ad hoc* tribunals' personal jurisdiction is that there are no exceptions on account of immunities under international law, such as State or diplomatic immunities. This is codified in the Statutes by the provision that the official position of an accused person, such as Head of State, shall not relieve that person from criminal responsibility.[9] A unique feature of the personal jurisdiction of the Special Court for Sierra Leone is that it specifically allows in its Statute for jurisdiction over minors, starting age fifteen.[10] This jurisdictional expansion has been criticised a lot; the Special Court for Sierra Leone has never indicted any minor.

For the development of international criminal law the scope and content of the *ad hoc* tribunals' subject matter jurisdiction has been of most significance. Two basic starting points underlie the subject matter jurisdiction in the statutes of the *ad hoc* tribunals. First, the choice of crimes

---

9 Statute of the International Criminal Tribunal for the former Yugoslavia, article 7(2); Statute of the International Criminal Tribunal for Rwanda, article 6(2); Statute of the Special Court for Sierra Leone, article 6(2).

10 Statute of the Special Court for Sierra Leone, article 7.

should as much as possible reflect the conflicts and the severity of atrocities committed in that context. Second, the definition of the selected crimes should correspond to international law, in order to ensure respect for the principle *nullum crimen sine lege.*[11]

The first contemporary *ad hoc* tribunal, the International Criminal Tribunal for the former Yugoslavia, includes war crimes – in the form of grave breaches and the violations of the laws or customs of war, genocide, and crimes against humanity. These three categories are generally referred to as 'core crimes'. Especially because the conflict was still ongoing at the time of creation of the Tribunal, it was difficult to envisage the crimes that would be most the focus of its prosecution. However, in its report accompanying the Statute of the International Criminal Tribunal for the former Yugoslavia, the United Nations Secretary-General did refer to a particular crime against humanity that already at the time of creation symbolised the atrocities committed in the Balkan wars: ethnic cleansing.[12]

As far as the International Criminal Tribunal for Rwanda is concerned, being established after the 1994 genocide and with jurisdiction confined to the year 1994, the drafters had a better idea as to the nature and scope of crimes that had to be in the Statute. Genocide was included, of course, just like crimes against humanity. The interesting deviation from the Yugoslavia Statute concerned war crimes. For the Rwanda Tribunal, jurisdiction over war crimes was restricted to violations of common article 3 of the Geneva Conventions and Additional Protocol II to these Conventions. The reason for this jurisdictional limitation is that the conflict in Rwanda in 1994 was regarded beforehand as being exclusively of an internal character, whereas this matter was left open for judges of the International Criminal Tribunal for the former Yugoslavia to decide.

Finally, the subject matter jurisdiction of the Special Court for Sierra Leone has taken shape on account of it being a hybrid, or mixed, tribunal, in which there is also a place for the application of national law. Thus, the Special Court for Sierra Leone also has jurisdiction over two categories of crimes under Sierra Leonean law: abuse of young girls and wanton destruction of property.[13] Although insertion of these crimes might have

---

11 See Report of the Secretary-General Pursuant to Paragraph 2 of Security Council Resolution 808 (1993), UN Doc. S/25704 (1993), para. 34.

12 Ibid., para. 6.

13 Statute of the Special Court for Sierra Leone, article 5.

served the function to fill certain gaps and to deal with serious ordinary crimes that frequently occurred during the conflict, there was no need for it in practice. There has never been an indictment issued by the Special Court Prosecutor for crimes under Sierra Leonean law.

It should furthermore be noted that genocide is not included in the jurisdiction of the Special Court for Sierra Leone, as there was no evidence of commission of this crime in the Sierra Leonean context. War crimes are essentially confined to the situation of an internal armed conflict. The Statute of the Special Court copies the provision in the Statute of the International Criminal Tribunal for Rwanda penalising violations of common article 3 of the Geneva Conventions and Additional Protocol II. However, contrary to the Rwanda Statute, the Special Court Statute contains a residual war crimes provision penalising other serious violations of international humanitarian law. This clause also penalises the use of child soldiers. Of course, crimes against humanity are also penalised; they were the focus of the Special Court indictments.

Substantive criminal law

In their practice, the *ad hoc* tribunals have strongly contributed to the field of substantive international criminal law. What follows is just a very small selection of their contributions and points of criticism.

General principles: *nullum crimen* and legal certainty

It is a recurring debate in the field of international criminal law how one should strike a balance between progressive development of the law and the demands of legal certainty and prohibition on retroactive application of substantive criminal law. It is clear from the report of the United Nations Secretary-General accompanying the Statute of the International Criminal Tribunal for the former Yugoslavia that he wished to avoid the criticism generally voiced in relation to the retroactive application of the law by the Nuremberg and Tokyo Tribunals.[14] Yet, it is also clear that in the set-up of the *ad hoc* tribunals, the judges were given a vital role in the development of the law. This was inevitable, because the judges were

---

14 Report of the Secretary-General Pursuant to Paragraph 2 of Security Council Resolution 808 (1993), UN Doc. S/25704 (1993).

called to apply the law not on the basis of clearly articulated written rules but by resorting to the elusive sources of customary international law. The methods the judges applied in interpreting the substantive criminal law were not always clear and convincing. Considering especially the earlier jurisprudence of the Yugoslavia and Rwanda Tribunals – which share their Appeals Chamber – it would be safe to conclude that the desire to maximise protection of victims and to end impunity outweighed the adherence to fundamental notions of substantive criminal law such as the *nullum crimen* rule, legal certainty, and *in dubio pro reo*. Sometimes this is even explicitly acknowledged. The following was said by the Trial Chamber of the International Criminal Tribunal for the former Yugoslavia in *Milutinović* et al.: 'In order to give full effect to the object and purpose of customary international law prohibiting crimes against humanity, it is necessary to adopt a broad definition of the key terms that extends as much protection as possible'.[15]

In its candour, this Trial Chamber confirmed the reduced role for substantive criminal law principles of legal certainty and strict interpretation. It is therefore important to bear in mind that while the *ad hoc* tribunals have greatly contributed to the development of substantive international criminal law, such judicial development has met with criticism, especially from criminal lawyers.[16]

Definition of crimes

The *ad hoc* tribunals have produced a rich body of jurisprudence, in which they have contributed to the clarification and elucidation of virtually every element of the crimes in their subject matter jurisdiction. As follows from the previous section, often the issues of interpretation and scope of application of the crimes were entrenched in favour of maximum protection and ending impunity. This can be exemplified by the famous Appeals Chamber decision of 2 October 1995 in the *Tadić* case, dealing with a range of challenges to the jurisdiction of the International Criminal Tribunal for the former Yugoslavia. Among other things, the defence in

15 *Prosecutor* v. *Milutinović* et al. (IT-05-87-T), Judgment, 26 February 2009, para. 147.
16 Just one example: George P. Fletcher and Jens D. Ohlin, 'Reclaiming Fundamental Principles of Criminal Law in the Darfur Case', (2005) 3 *Journal of International Criminal Justice* 539.

the *Tadić* case claimed lack of subject matter jurisdiction, because the crimes set out in article 3 – violations of the laws or customs of war – were allegedly confined to an internal armed conflict. The Appeals Chamber paved the way for synchronisation between war crimes in international and internal armed conflict. Not only did the Appeals Chamber rule that customary rules have developed to govern internal strife,[17] it also ruled that serious violations of humanitarian law applicable to internal armed conflict triggered individual criminal responsibility under international law. Although this finding was in part based on customary international law, the Chamber also said that criminalising violations of humanitarian law in internal armed conflict is 'fully warranted from the point of view of substantive justice and equity'.[18]

Another example of expansive interpretation of crimes, in favour of protection of victims and ending impunity, can be found in Special Court for Sierra Leone case law confirming the use of child soldiers as a war crime. At the time the Rome Statute was negotiated, in 1998, it was unclear whether the recruitment of children and their use in hostilities had already crystallised into a crime under customary international law, and if so, to what extent. The Appeals Chamber of the Special Court for Sierra Leone held that recruiting children has been a crime under customary international law since at least November 1996. In its reasoning the Appeals Chamber relied heavily on the Appeals Chamber in *Tadić*, which ruled largely in favour of criminalisation of all serious violations of international humanitarian law.[19] However, dissenting judge Geoffrey Robertson was convinced that the crime of non-forcible child enlistment did not enter international criminal law until the Rome Treaty in July 1998.[20]

Modes of liability

With respect to the modes of liability, one can discern a similar approach to enlarging individual criminal liability in the case law of the *ad hoc*

---

17 *Prosecutor* v. *Tadić* (IT-94-1-AR72), Decision on the Defence Motion for Interlocutory Appeal on Jurisdiction, 2 October 1995, para. 127.

18 Ibid., para. 135.

19 *Prosecutor* v. *Norman* (SCSL-2004-14-AR72), Decision on Preliminary Motion based on Lack of Jurisdiction (Child Recruitment), 31 May 2004, especially paras. 30–51.

20 Ibid., Dissenting Opinion of Justice Robertson.

tribunals. It must be acknowledged that the statutes of the tribunals lack elaboration on the modes of liability. The articles on individual criminal responsibility are as good as identical in all three statutes. They contain as modes of liability: planning, instigating, ordering, committing, aiding and abetting, and command responsibility. The provisions do not mention forms of liability such as co-perpetration, incitement, attempt, or conspiracy.[21]

In its case law, the International Criminal Tribunal for the former Yugoslavia has spectacularly developed the modes of liability. The other two tribunals have followed suit. In the *Tadić* appeals judgment of 15 July 1999, the Chamber addressed the question whether criminal responsibility for participating in a common criminal purpose falls within the ambit of the modes of liability explicitly set out in the Statute. The Appeals Chamber answered the question in the affirmative: commission of one of the crimes in the Tribunal's jurisdiction might also occur through participation in the realisation of a common design or purpose.[22] The Chamber justified this holding by saying that the notion of common design as a form of accomplice liability is firmly established in customary international law and in addition is upheld, albeit implicitly, in the Statute.[23] The 'common purpose' liability was later referred to as joint criminal enterprise, a form of co-perpetration designed to hold especially the 'masterminds' behind the commission of international crimes criminally accountable.

The notion of joint criminal enterprise has since its inception in 1999 played a vital role in the case law of all of the *ad hoc* tribunals. It has greatly facilitated the prosecution of suspects in leadership positions, who have not physically killed or tortured victims, but who have designed or otherwise contributed to a broader criminal plan, such as the creation of greater Serbia. When suspects are considered to be part of a joint criminal enterprise, the presentation of evidence in subsequent trials by the prosecutor is much easier. Judicial notice can be taken of facts established in previous trials dealing with the same joint criminal enterprise. However, the inception and further use of joint criminal enterprise in the practice of the *ad hoc* tribunals has also triggered a good deal of criticism, especially

---

21 It must be noted that, following the language of the Genocide Convention, attempt, conspiracy, incitement and complicity are punishable modes of liability in relation to the crime of genocide.

22 *Prosecutor* v. *Tadić* (IT-94-1-A), Judgment, 15 July 1999, para. 188.

23 Ibid., para. 220.

from criminal law scholars. They pointed out the risk of collectivisation of guilt, or of guilt by association.

In addition to the development of joint criminal enterprise, the practice of the *ad hoc* tribunals has been vital to the interpretation and application of criminal liability under the notion of command responsibility. Command responsibility has been available under humanitarian law and makes the superior criminally responsible for international crimes committed by his/her subordinates, when the superior fails to prevent or punish commission. The case law of the *ad hoc* tribunals has developed parameters for each of the three elements of command responsibility: effective control, knowledge, and duty to prevent/punish. The case law has applied command responsibility – in principle a notion confined to the military – also to civilian commanders.[24]

Defences – grounds excluding criminal responsibility

The statutes of the *ad hoc* tribunals do not contain any defence that may be invoked to exclude criminal responsibility. The statutes do, however, explicitly exclude the applicability of certain, anticipated, defences, namely: irrelevance of official capacity and non-applicability of a defence of superior orders. This exclusion is, understandably, based on the extremely serious nature of the crimes and can be traced back to the post–Second World War tribunals.

The exclusion of the aforementioned two specific defences leaves unanswered the question if other defences – although not mentioned in the statutes – might nevertheless be applicable. The matter became directly relevant in one of the first cases at the International Criminal Tribunal for the former Yugoslavia. The suspect, Dražen Erdemović, invoked the defence of duress, because if he would not comply with the order to kill civilians in Srebrenica, he would be killed himself. The Appeals Chamber, dealing with the issue in the context of the validity of a plea of guilt, ruled – by majority – that duress does not afford a complete defence to a person charged with a crime against humanity and/or war crime.[25] However, the Appeals Chamber was split over the issue. Two judges, in a joint separate opinion found that duress cannot afford a complete defence

---

24 *Prosecutor* v. *Delalić* et al. (IT-96-21-T), Judgment, 16 November 1998, para. 377.

25 *Prosecutor* v. *Erdemović* (IT-96-22-A), Judgment, 7 October 1997, para. 19.

to a soldier charged with crimes against humanity or war crimes involving the taking of innocent lives.[26] Judge Cassese, in a dissenting opinion, argued, however, that the customary rule of international law on duress does not exclude the applicability of duress to war crimes and crimes against humanity whose underlying offence is murder or unlawful killing.[27]

This diametrically opposed outcome goes to show two things. First, judges appear inclined to exclude generally accepted notions, rules and principles of substantive criminal law – or to reduce their applicability – because of the extremely serious nature of the indicted crimes at international criminal tribunals. Second, for the applicability of generally accepted notions, rules, and principles of substantive criminal law, it seems decisive whether one seeks rules of (customary) international law to confirm the applicability or to confirm the exclusion of applicability.

After the *Erdemović* case, the *ad hoc* tribunals were from time to time called upon to rule on defences not specifically available in their applicable law. However, at no time was the difficulty in finding and applying substantive defences in the context of the newly established *ad hoc* tribunals better exemplified than in the *Erdemović* case.

Procedure and co-operation

In the early years of the *ad hoc* tribunals, there was not yet much attention to procedural issues. However, problems in procedure and co-operation with States soon became essential matters in ensuring the effective functioning of the *ad hoc* tribunals. The law of international criminal procedure also developed as a new and relatively independent field of law.[28] As in previous sections, only a very small selection of topics can be discussed.

An adversarial model of procedure

When setting up a procedural system governing the functioning of the *ad hoc* tribunals, there was a choice between the two major procedural models of criminal justice. One is used in the Anglo-Saxon justice

26 Ibid., Joint Separate Opinion of Judges McDonald and Vohrah, para. 88.
27 Ibid., Dissenting Opinion of Judge Cassese, para. 44.
28 For an attempt to codify the rules and principles of international criminal procedure, see Göran Sluiter, Håkan Friman, Suzannah Linton, Sergey Vasiliev, and Salvatore Zappala, eds., *International Criminal Procedure – Principles and Rules*, Oxford University Press, 2013.

systems and is generally referred to as the adversarial model. The other belongs to continental European countries and is known as the inquisitorial model. It exceeds the scope of this chapter to explain in detail the difference between the two models. The most essential difference is that in the adversarial system criminal proceedings are regarded as a contest between two equal parties, whereas in the inquisitorial system proceedings, including fact-finding, are dominated and controlled by the judge.

The procedural design of the *ad hoc* tribunals can only to a very limited degree be found in their statutes. The task of developing the Rules of Procedure and Evidence was assigned to the judges. The Rules of Procedure and Evidence of the Yugoslavia Tribunal were also used at the tribunals for Rwanda and Sierra Leone. The Rules of Procedure and Evidence – and thus the judges – hold the key in choosing the appropriate model and corresponding rules for the procedures of the *ad hoc* tribunals.

It follows from the content of the Rules of Procedure and Evidence that the choice was made in favour of a predominantly adversarial procedure. This choice can be explained by three factors. First, the post–Second World War precedents also applied by and large an adversarial procedural model. Second, the judges of the International Criminal Tribunal for the former Yugoslavia made use of various draft Rules of Procedure and Evidence, of which the Americans' draft proposal proved to be most detailed, reasoned, and therefore influential. Third, it has been submitted that the adversarial model would correspond better to the requirements of a fair trial.

This is not to say that the judges opted for a purely adversarial system. In its first annual report, the International Criminal Tribunal for the former Yugoslavia pointed out three so-called elements of the inquisitorial system which found a place in its procedural edifice. First, it was said that the Tribunal does not allow for plea bargaining; second, the law of evidence of the Tribunal was supposed to be flexible, without strict exclusionary rules and allowing, for example, for hearsay evidence; third and finally, contrary to the adversarial judge, the Tribunal judge was allowed to put questions to witnesses and to engage in additional fact-finding, by calling additional witnesses *proprio motu*.[29]

---

29 Annual Report of the International Tribunal for the Prosecution of Persons Responsible for Serious Violations of International Humanitarian Law Committed in the Territory of the Former Yugoslavia since 1991, 29 August 1994, UN Doc. A/49/342-S/1994/1007, para. 71.

One can but conclude that the perceived vital differences from common law systems have withered over time and are in practice not as important as presented in the first annual report. Plea bargaining, for one, became since the *Erdemović* case an important mechanism for the Tribunal to cope with its many indictments. Of the 161 indictments at the International Criminal Tribunal for the former Yugoslavia, ninety-two were (or are ongoing) contested trials, twenty resulted in a short trial following a plea of guilt, and thirteen indictments were referred to the Bosnian War Crimes Chamber; twenty indictments were withdrawn, ten persons died before transfer to the Tribunal, and six died after transfer. Plea bargaining was for a long time less popular at the Rwanda Tribunal, because the first person pleading guilty, former prime minister Kambanda, nevertheless received the maximum sentence: life imprisonment. Later on in the life-span of the Rwanda Tribunal plea bargaining returned to the surface, and was used in nine cases, on a total of seventy-five cases (completed and ongoing). At the Special Court for Sierra Leone, plea bargaining has not taken place at all, but this can be explained by the very limited number of indictments at that Court.

As far as the perceived flexibility of the law of evidence is concerned, it needs to be mentioned that in one of its very first decisions, the Yugoslavia Tribunal admitted hearsay evidence without cross-examination.[30] However, in subsequent practice this decision was not followed to its logical conclusion; rather, especially compared to inquisitorial justice systems, the *ad hoc* tribunals have continually attached great value to live testimony and securing the right to cross-examination. The law of evidence is thus not as flexible as indicated in the Yugoslavia Tribunal's very early years.

It also needs to be mentioned that the judges' powers in respect of fact-finding, calling witnesses, and asking questions to witnesses have never been very strong in practice. In any event, it is far away from a judge-led investigation, such as the *juge d'instruction* in certain inquisitorial systems or at the Extraordinary Chambers in the Courts of Cambodia.

The jury is still out on the question whether in international criminal proceedings one should prefer the adversarial model – party driven – over the inquisitorial model – judicial control. The problem is that both models

---

30 *Prosecutor* v. *Tadić* (IT-94-1-T), Decision on the Defence Motion on Hearsay, 5 August 1996.

do not function in a vacuum, but are connected to a justice system's roots and development over decades, even centuries.[31] In spite of perceived shortcomings of the adversarial model, such as the fact that it does not really cater for victim participation, it must also be acknowledged that the adversarial model has served the *ad hoc* tribunals well. In particular, the emphasis on presentation of evidence – witnesses – at trial has enhanced the public and transparent nature of these trials, a matter of fundamental importance for international criminal tribunals.

Efficiency and fairness

The quality of criminal proceedings will eventually be based on the parameters of efficiency and fairness. This is not different for the *ad hoc* tribunals. Statistics show that the *ad hoc* tribunals have been very efficient in the overall processing of cases, when compared to other contemporary international criminal tribunals, such as the International Criminal Court or the Extraordinary Chambers in the Courts of Cambodia. In twenty years of existence, the International Criminal Tribunal for the former Yugoslavia has – almost – disposed of 125 cases, of which twenty were dealt with after a plea of guilt, and thirteen referred to national courts. The figures for the International Criminal Tribunal for Rwanda are more modest, but still impressive: seventy-five (almost) completed cases. The Special Court for Sierra Leone is certainly far less productive, with less than ten completed cases, but it needs emphasising that it was meant to prosecute only a handful of suspects. If there was budget for a longer lifespan, it could have capitalised on its first cases and been more efficient on possible follow up cases.

The efficient functioning of the Yugoslavia and Rwanda Tribunals can be explained by a number of reasons. First, both institutions were provided with sufficient time and resources to process a relatively high number of cases. This allowed the tribunals, especially the Prosecutor, to build up an institutional memory and to learn from past mistakes. Second, the availability of plea bargaining and referral of less important indictments to national courts counterbalanced a number of very lengthy and complex trials, such as the one of Vojislav Šešelj – still ongoing – and of

---

31 M. R. Damaska, *The Faces of Justice and State Authority – A Comparative Approach to the Legal Process*, New Haven: Yale University Press, 1986.

Slobodan Milošević – who died before the end of his trial was reached. Third, the procedural system was flexible enough to allow for changes in the law adopted by the judges, in cases required by demands of efficiency and fairness.

Of course, gains in efficiency should not compromise the fairness of the proceedings. It is clear from the report of the Secretary-General accompanying the Statute of the International Criminal Tribunal for the former Yugoslavia that the proceedings had to meet the highest standards of fairness. This even went as far as ruling out proceedings in the absence of the accused, although this is not as such prohibited by international human rights law.[32] All in all, fair trial rights have received adequate protection at the *ad hoc* tribunals. There is sufficient funding for defence teams, allowing for investigations and effective preparation of a defence. The taking of testimony at trial generally ensures adequate protection of the right to challenge witnesses.

There is more criticism in respect of lengthy periods of detention. Especially at the International Criminal Tribunal for Rwanda, accused persons had to wait many years before the start of their trials and then again many years in detention before the completion of their trials; during this period all accused remained in custody. This appears inconsistent with the right to liberty. The approach of the *ad hoc* tribunals to the right to liberty started on the wrong foot, because detention of the suspect was for some years regarded as the rule and not the exception, as provided for in Rule 65 of the Rules of Procedure and Evidence. At the International Criminal Tribunal for the former Yugoslavia, in its later years and following an amendment to Rule 65, a practice developed in which provisional release was granted in case of delays in the proceedings. This functioned, with the assistance of the States in the former Yugoslavia, relatively well. However, at the International Criminal Tribunal for Rwanda and the Special Court for Sierra Leone no person was ever provisionally released awaiting and during trial.

Regarding the lengthy periods of pre-trial detention, one can also wonder whether the individual's right to a speedy trial has been adequately respected at the *ad hoc* tribunals. This is more difficult to determine, as there is no generally accepted standard of 'speedy trial' that applies to

---

32 Report of the Secretary-General Pursuant to Paragraph 2 of Security Council Resolution 808 (1993), UN Doc. S/25704 (1993), paras. 101 and 106.

cases of such magnitude and complexity. Moreover, it seems that delays in proceedings are regularly also requested or occasioned by the defendant.

Building the vertical co-operation model

No international criminal tribunal can function effectively without assistance from States and also non-State entities. This assistance is especially required in securing the arrest of indicted persons and the collection of evidence. Although the International Criminal Tribunal for the former Yugoslavia has especially faced difficulties in securing co-operation from certain States in the former Yugoslavia, both the Yugoslavia and Rwanda Tribunals have eventually managed in securing the required co-operation.[33] The Special Court for Sierra Leone, being an internationalised court seated in Sierra Leone, never suffered significant co-operation problems in practice.

Although I will offer some observations on the legal dimension of co-operation, it is self-evident that the political side to it is just as important – perhaps even more important. Nearing the end of the lifespan of all the *ad hoc* tribunals, one can safely conclude that at critical moments in their existence, especially with regard to the International Criminal Tribunal for the former Yugoslavia, the political context and developments were in its favour, as evidenced by the arrest and surrender of fugitives Milošević, Karadžić, and Mladić.

The legal assistance relationship between States and international criminal tribunals has been characterised as 'vertical'. The concept of a vertical legal assistance relationship was introduced by the Appeals Chamber of the Yugoslavia Tribunal in the *Blaškić* case, with a view to indicating the hierarchy between the jurisdiction of the *ad hoc* tribunals and national criminal jurisdictions, and in order to indicate the consequences for the provision of legal assistance by States.[34] From the perspective of the trial forum, it has become synonymous with highly effective legal assistance regimes. Its distinctive features are the existence of far-reaching duties

33 Although it must be mentioned that at the time of writing nine persons accused by the International Criminal Tribunal for Rwanda are reported to be still at large.

34 *Prosecutor* v. *Blaškić* (IT-95-14-AR108bis), Judgment on the Request of the Republic of Croatia for Review of the Decision of Trial Chamber II of 18 July 1997, 29 October 1997.

to co-operate, the absence of a reciprocal co-operation relationship (the *ad hoc* tribunals have no duty to provide assistance to States), and – most importantly – the unilateral settlement of disputes by the tribunal requesting the co-operation.

This newly coined 'vertical' legal assistance regime differs considerably from the traditional horizontal model of co-operation in criminal matters between sovereign States, in which the obligation to co-operate does not exist at all or tends to be subject to grounds justifying refusal, such as the requirement of double criminality or the political offence exception. The vertical model of legal assistance, as developed in the *Blaškić* case, undoubtedly best enables the fair and effective prosecution of crimes. In combination with the fact that all United Nations members are bound by this vertical co-operation law, the Yugoslavia and Rwanda Tribunals have attained the most effective co-operation model, from a legal perspective. In addition, the International Criminal Tribunal for the former Yugoslavia has especially benefited from effective enforcement support, such as that coming from the European Union, aimed at securing the arrests of fugitives like Karadžić and Mladić.

Efforts to transpose to the International Criminal Court the vertical co-operation model of the *ad hoc* tribunals have been in part unsuccessful. The co-operation law of the International Criminal Court is far less vertical, which is – among other things – demonstrated by the inclusion in the Rome Statute of grounds justifying refusal of co-operation. However, even more harmful for the effective functioning of the International Criminal Court is that – contrary to the Yugoslavia and Rwanda Tribunals – it does not enjoy the benefit of co-operation obligations for almost every State in the world. States that have not ratified the Rome Statute have no co-operation obligations towards the ICC.[35] In the area of co-operation, the *ad hoc* tribunals represent an almost perfect situation for contemporary international criminal justice.

Conclusion

The Rome Statute of the International Criminal Court and the Court's Rules of Procedure and Evidence were drafted while the Yugoslavia and

---

35 The exception here is the imposition of co-operation obligations on Sudan and Libya by virtue of Security Council resolutions.

Rwanda Tribunals were operating. There were attempts to improve on certain perceived shortcomings of the *ad hoc* tribunals. For example, victim participations is provided for in the Rome Statute, and a procedure for confirmation of the charges was put in place. With a considerable number of years of practice at the International Criminal Court behind us, it does not go too far to say that the prestige and impressive legacy of the *ad hoc* tribunals increases with each day. With the problems facing the International Criminal Court at present, especially in terms of procedure, one can indeed raise the question whether it will and can get ever any better than the International Criminal Tribunal for the former Yugoslavia and the International Criminal Tribunal for Rwanda.

It follows from the above analysis that I evaluate the legacy of the *ad hoc* tribunals relatively critically in respect of their contributions to substantive criminal law. It is my view that the fundamental criminal law notions of legal certainty and *in dubio pro reo* should have been better protected. Especially in the early years of the tribunals, the drive among prosecutors, judges, and staff to contribute to the laudable goal of ending impunity should have been moderated at times. It would have undeniably led to a more modest development of substantive international criminal law, but at the same time would have further enhanced the quality, credibility, and authority of the judgments of the *ad hoc* tribunals.

I am more positive about the legacy of the *ad hoc* tribunals in terms of procedure and co-operation. This positive evaluation is growing with the benefit of hindsight and in observing the procedural and co-operation problems troubling the International Criminal Court. The adversarial model has served the *ad hoc* tribunals well, as is evidenced by the impressive number of completed cases. The adversarial model embodies fairness and ensures the transparency of trials, while it also allows for quick disposal of certain cases via plea bargaining. The criticism of the adversarial model that seems to be fashionable these days in international criminal justice is in my view already simply contradicted by the impressive performances of the *ad hoc* tribunals. The *ad hoc* tribunals, notably the International Criminal Tribunal for the former Yugoslavia and International Criminal Tribunal for Rwanda, have also greatly contributed to the development of a co-operation regime that is exclusively geared towards the effective functioning of international criminal tribunals.

The lessons learned in terms of procedure and co-operation seem to be that longer preparation and drafting of the law, such as occurred for the International Criminal Court, does not necessarily result in well-functioning international criminal tribunals. When setting up a new international criminal justice mechanism, without a solid and supportive societal context, a minimalist approach to procedure may be preferable, in the sense that it should be kept as simple as possible. While the major features of the proceedings should be clearly laid down in the Statute, there should also be built-in a certain degree of flexibility. In particular, the judges should be allowed to adjust the procedure – via amendments to the Rules of Procedure and Evidence – if this is required for the effective functioning of the international criminal tribunal.

FURTHER READING

M. Cherif Bassiouni and Peter Manikas, *The Law of the International Criminal Tribunal for the Former Yugoslavia*, Irvington-on-Hudson, NY: Transnational Publishers, 1996.

Virginia Morris and Michael P. Scharf, *An Insider's Guide to the International Criminal Tribunal for the Former Yugoslavia*, Irvington-on-Hudson, NY: Transnational Publishers, 1995.

Virginia Morris and Michael P. Scharf, *The International Criminal Tribunal for Rwanda*, Irvington-on-Hudson, NY: Transnational Publishers, 1998.

William A. Schabas, *The UN International Criminal Tribunals – The Former Yugoslavia, Rwanda and Sierra Leone*, Cambridge University Press, 2006.

Bert Swart, Alexander Zahar, and Göran Sluiter, eds., *The Legacy of the International Criminal Tribunal for the Former Yugoslavia*, Oxford University Press, 2011.

The International Criminal Court 7

Leila Sadat

On 17 July 1998, a Statute for a new, permanent International Criminal Court was adopted at a Diplomatic Conference held in the city of Rome, in an emotional vote of 120 to seven, with twenty-one States abstaining.[1] The vote was, for many, unexpected, for the road to the establishment of the Court had been long with many twists and turns along the way. Indeed, when the Diplomatic Conference opened on 15 June, it was unclear whether it would lead to a concrete outcome. Some seventeen years later, the Court now has 123 State Parties and has been in existence since July 2002. Permanent premises are nearing delivery, and several trials have been completed or are close to completion. This chapter will briefly explore the efforts that led to the establishment of the Court in 1998, outline the basic structure and operations of the Court as well as its current proceedings, and, finally, elaborate upon some of the challenges it faces as it proceeds through its second decade.

The road to Rome

The notion that a criminal court established by States could try individuals accused of committing crimes under international law was too radical for most statesmen – and even most scholars – in the early twentieth century. Although the Treaty of Versailles that followed the First World War provided that a 'special tribunal' would try William II of Hohenzollern for the 'supreme offence against international morality and the sanctity of treaties', the American members of the Commission on the Responsibility

---

1 L. N. Sadat and S. R. Carden, 'The New International Criminal Court: An Uneasy Revolution', (2000) 88 *Georgetown Law Journal* 381. For a fuller treatment of the issues raised in this chapter, see William A. Schabas, *The International Criminal Court: A Commentary on the Rome Statute*, Oxford University Press, 2010.

of the Authors of the War expressed reservations about the legality and the appropriateness of such an exercise, and the Netherlands refused to extradite Kaiser Wilhelm for trial. Following this disappointing precedent, in the 1920s, expert bodies, including the Committee of Jurists of the League of Nations, the International Association of Penal Law, and the International Law Association proposed the creation of a permanent international criminal court, but these proposals did not immediately bear fruit. Many experts concluded that the creation of a court to try individuals was an affront to State sovereignty, and to the 'right' to be judged under domestic law and by one's countrymen. They also argued that heads of State could not be liable to the international community but were accountable only to their own citizens, and noted that there was no international criminal code with which potential defendants could be charged. Finally, arguments were raised suggesting that such a court might not only fail to prevent war, but make matters worse, as the lawyers would 'begin a war of accusation and counter accusation and recrimination', preventing soldiers and sailors of opposite sides from shaking hands and settling matters peaceably.[2]

It was only with the decision of the Allies to conduct trials after the Second World War that the concept of an international criminal court achieved a certain momentum. The Allies announced their intentions to hold trials in declarations issued at St. James in 1942 and in Moscow in 1943, but holding a trial rather than simply executing Axis prisoners was not a foregone conclusion. Winston Churchill wanted the Nazi leaders executed, and President Roosevelt's cabinet was divided. Morgenthau, Secretary of the Treasury, called for the execution of 'German arch-criminals'; Stimson, Secretary of War, advocated for trials. Ultimately, Stimson's view prevailed, and the four Allied Powers negotiated and adopted, on 8 August 1945, the Charter of the International Military Tribunal.[3] The Charter provided for the trial of the 'major war criminals of the Axis powers', and included three crimes in article 6 setting forth its jurisdiction: crimes against peace, war crimes, and crimes

---

2 Leila Nadya Sadat, 'The Proposed Permanent International Criminal Court: An Appraisal', (1996) 29 *Cornell International Law Journal* 665, at p. 672 (formerly Wexler) (discussing the International Law Association draft of 1926).

3 Whitney Harris, *Tyranny on Trial*, 2nd edn, New York: Barnes and Noble, 1999, pp. 9–24.

against humanity. Twenty-four accused were indicted, twenty-two were tried, nineteen were convicted, and three were acquitted. Twelve were sentenced to be executed by hanging. The remainder received prison sentences ranging from ten years to life.[4] Although the proceedings were undoubtedly a form of 'victor's justice', their procedural fairness and the fact that twenty-three nations ultimately ratified the Nuremberg Charter helped to ensure their continued importance and legacy. Moreover, the principles established by the Charter and the International Military Tribunal itself were endorsed by the General Assembly of the newly created United Nations in 1946.[5]

In contrast with the vociferous Allied response to war criminality in Europe was their comparative silence regarding issues of alleged Japanese war criminality.[6] Following Japan's unconditional surrender, a tribunal similar to the International Military Tribunal was established by proclamation of the Supreme Commander of the Allied Powers, General Douglas MacArthur, as modified by the Far Eastern Council (on which the four Allied Powers as well as China, Australia, Canada, the Netherlands, the Philippines, and New Zealand sat). The Charter of the Tokyo Tribunal (also known as the International Military Tribunal for the Far East) largely tracked the Nuremberg Tribunal; however the bench was expanded to encompass eleven members (the Far Eastern Council members as well as India). The Tribunal tried twenty-eight Japanese military and political leaders. Seven were sentenced to death, three died of natural causes or were found mentally unfit and eighteen received prison sentences. The proceedings resulted in a lengthy judgment and a stinging dissent rendered by the Indian judge who objected to the exclusion of Allied crimes and the lack of judges from the vanquished nations on the bench, allegations that were compounded by the doubtful procedural fairness of the trial itself. Thus, unlike the Nuremberg tribunal, although the International Military Tribunal for the Far East undoubtedly left a legacy in Japan itself, until very recently, it has had little or no legacy effect in the West.[7]

---

4 (1948) 22 IMT 411.
5 GA Res. 95(I). See also Principles of International Law Recognised in the Charter of Nuremberg and in the Judgment of the Tribunal, UN Doc. A/1316.
6 Neil Boister and Rob Cryer, *The Tokyo International Military Tribunal: A Reappraisal*, Oxford University Press, 2008, p. 17.
7 Ibid., pp. 323–7.

Following the war, the United Nations embarked upon a codification and institution building effort using the Nuremberg Charter as a guide. The Convention on the Prevention and Punishment of Genocide was adopted by the General Assembly in 1948, and the four Geneva Conventions relating to the conduct of war followed one year later. In a resolution accompanying its adoption of the Genocide Convention, the General Assembly invited the International Law Commission to 'study the desirability and possibility of establishing an international judicial organ for the trial of persons charged with genocide or other crimes'.[8] Thus instructed, the International Law Commission embarked upon a fifty-year long odyssey, voting initially in 1950 to support the desirability and feasibility of creating an international criminal court, only to have the question of the court's establishment taken away from it by the General Assembly, which handed it over to a Committee on International Criminal Jurisdiction composed of the representatives of Member States. Although the Committee and a successor Committee did produce drafts of a statute for a new international criminal court, their work was shelved as the Cold War made it impossible to achieve consensus.

In 1989, the question of an international criminal jurisdiction found its way back onto the agenda of the General Assembly. The International Law Commission was again instructed to proceed. It adopted a new version of a Draft Code of Crimes in 1991 and in 1992 established a Working Group that produced a report laying out the basis for the adoption of an international criminal court. The General Assembly responded positively, and the International Law Commission adopted a final draft statute in 1994 that served as the basic text upon which the provisions of the International Criminal Court were established.[9]

The International Law Commission's 1994 draft included five categories (but not definitions) of crimes: genocide, crimes against humanity, war crimes, aggression, and 'treaty crimes' that would be set forth in an annex. It was premised on a new principle, the notion of 'complementarity' which meant that the proposed court would complement national criminal justice systems which would have priority over cases that might

---

8 Study by the International Law Commission of the Question of an International Criminal Jurisdiction, GA Res. 260B(III).

9 Leila Nadya Sadat, 'The Proposed Permanent International Criminal Court: An Appraisal', (1996) 29 *Cornell International Law Journal* 665, at pp. 676–86.

otherwise come to it. The 1994 draft conditioned all cases upon either the consent of the implicated State or the Security Council, except in cases in genocide over which the jurisdiction of the proposed court was automatic. Finally, the 1994 draft suggested that the prosecutor and deputy prosecutor could be elected on a 'stand-by' basis and that the judges – except for the President – would only be paid when actually sitting.

The General Assembly convened an *ad hoc* committee to discuss the International Law Commission 1994 draft, and subsequently established a Preparatory Committee to begin the extraordinarily difficult process – both technical and political – of developing a statute that could be acceptable to States as well as civil society. The Preparatory Committee, composed of representatives of UN Member States, held fifteen weeks of meetings beginning in March 1996 and ending in April 1998,[10] and between the six official meetings of the Preparatory Committee, several inter-sessional meetings were held.[11] The text that emerged from these protracted and intense negotiations, which were closely followed by a global coalition of non-governmental organisations, was a complex document containing more than 1,300 'bracketed' provisions, representing divergences of views between governments. When the Diplomatic Conference convened on 15 June 1998, it faced a herculean task: to bring the 160 States attending the conference to a consensus not only on the Court's ultimate establishment, the desirability of which was far from unanimously agreed, but the principles under which it would operate, the crimes it would punish, and the jurisdictional reach and strength of the Court's statute and its enforcement capabilities.

The Rome diplomatic conference of plenipotentiaries

In the summer of 1998, the text of what we now know as the Rome Statute for the International Criminal Court was negotiated and ultimately adopted. The conference was held in the United Nations Food and Agricultural Organisation building in Rome, and was well-attended, both by States and non-governmental organisations. The mood of the

---

10 F. Benedetti, K. Bonneau, and J. L. Washburn, *Negotiating the International Criminal Court*, The Hague: Martinus Nijhof, 2014, p. 39.

11 L. N. Sadat and S. R. Carden, 'The New International Criminal Court: An Uneasy Revolution', (2000) 88 *Georgetown Law Journal* 381, at p. 383.

conference alternated between anxiety and exhilaration as delegates took up the extraordinarily complex draft text that had been submitted to the Diplomatic Conference by the Preparatory Committee, and attempted to achieve consensus on the difficult issues the conference needed to address. The negotiations would undoubtedly have failed but for several propitious factors: first, the emergence of a group of approximately sixty 'like-minded' States, that had started as a caucus in 1994 and evolved into a formal and powerful group of countries committed to the Court's ultimate establishment based upon certain core principles;[12] second, the emergence of a powerful NGO coalition – the Coalition for the International Criminal Court – that engaged in a tireless campaign in support of the Court and served as a crucial information dissemination function during the conference by providing information to small delegations that could not possibly cover the entire conference in its various working groups, and by recounting on a daily basis in email, a newsletter and on the radio the status of the negotiations; third, a strong commitment to the successful outcome of the conference by key UN leaders, including former Secretary-General Kofi Annan and Under-Secretary-General for Legal Affairs Hans Corell; fourth, the successful establishment of the *ad hoc* international criminal tribunals for the former Yugoslavia and Rwanda, which demonstrated the feasibility of conducting modern international criminal proceedings; and finally, the serendipitous good fortune of having able and experienced diplomats undertake the negotiations, most of whom had also participated in the Preparatory Committee meetings and understood each other and the issues well.

During the negotiations, the 'complementarity principle' underlying the structure of the proposed new institution was quickly agreed upon; but less clear was whether its jurisdiction would be 'inherent' meaning that States joining the treaty would automatically be subject to the proposed Court's jurisdiction, or whether they would have to opt-in to a particular case before jurisdiction could attach. Many other issues faced the drafters as well, including whether or not the Security Council would act as a filter for cases coming to the Court (essentially giving the Permanent Members of that body a veto over all future cases, which was a non-starter for most other UN Member States); whether war crimes in non-international armed

---

12 F. Benedetti, K. Bonneau and J. L. Washburn, *Negotiating the International Criminal Court*, The Hague: Martinus Nijhof, 2014, p. 65.

conflicts and the crime of aggression would be included in the statute; whether the prosecutor would have independent powers of investigation or would require a referral from States or the Security Council prior to engaging the Court's investigative powers; what the organisational structure and trial procedures of the Court would be; how to accommodate the interests of victims and witnesses as well as defendants and the prosecution; and what the Court's relationship would be with the United Nations, given that it was to be created as a free-standing institution rather than as a UN organ created via an amendment to the UN Charter. Indeed, some of the debates became so fractious that NGO representatives, who were generally allowed access to meetings, were asked to leave as the Conference's leaders endeavoured to achieve consensus.

On 17 July 1998, after five weeks of difficult negotiations, the Conference leaders (the 'Bureau') proposed a compromise text they hoped would accommodate the various positions represented at the Conference. There was much agreement amongst delegates on the proposed Court's major features, but a few sticking points remained. On the final day of the Conference, both India and the United States attempted to undo the Bureau's 'package' proposal by offering amendments; these were met with 'no-action' motions proposed by Norway, which carried overwhelmingly. The United States delegation had argued throughout the negotiations that the Statute should not permit any trials of individuals without the consent of their state of nationality unless the Security Council referred the case (thereby insulating nationals of the United States from prosecution before the Court). Not willing to accept the defeat of its amendments, the United States then called for a vote on the Statute as a whole – which it lost, 120 in favour, seven opposed and twenty-one States abstaining. China, Iraq, Israel, Libya, Qatar, and Yemen joined the United States in opposing the Rome Statute. Delegates supporting the Statute – and NGO representatives – erupted in cheering and crying as the tensions of the past five weeks gave way to the realisation that more than seventy-five years of hard work and false starts had just born fruit.

The organisational structure and operational features of the Court

The negotiators of the Rome Statute created an institution almost breathtaking in its complexity and organisational structure. The 128-article

Statute is divided into thirteen Parts, each addressing some feature of the Court's establishment, jurisdiction, or operation. The Statute is supplemented by important ancillary documents negotiated following the Rome Conference (but prior to the Statute's entry into force), including, importantly, the Elements of Crimes, the Court's Rules of Procedure and Evidence, a relationship agreement between the Court and the United Nations, an agreement on the privileges and immunities of the Court and the rules of procedure for the Court's Assembly of States Parties that would ultimately provide the Court's management and oversight. The drafting of these ancillary documents was taken up by a Preparatory Commission composed of representatives of States that had signed the Final Act of the Rome Diplomatic Conference and other States invited to participate in the Rome Conference.[13] Like the Preparatory Committee that had prepared the draft Statute taken up in Rome, the Preparatory Commission was composed of State delegates, many of whom had represented their governments during the Preparatory Committee meetings and the Diplomatic Conference. This facilitated the work of preparing the Statute's entry into force. The Statute attained the requisite ratifications needed for entry into force with the deposit of eleven ratifications in April 2002, bringing the total number of States Parties to sixty-six.[14] On 1 July 2002, the Rome Statute entered into force.

Jurisdiction and admissibility

Pursuant to article 11(1), the Court only has jurisdiction with respect to crimes committed after the entry into force of the Rome Statute, on 1 July 2002. Additionally, with respect to States ratifying the Statute after 1 July 2002, the Court only has jurisdiction with respect to crimes committed

---

13 Final Act of the United Nations Diplomatic Conference of Plenipotentiaries on the Establishment of the International Criminal Court on 17 July 1998, Annex I, Resolution F, UN Doc. A/CONF.183/10. See also Philippe Kirsch, 'The Work of the Preparatory Commission', in Roy S. Lee, ed., *The International Criminal Court, Elements of Crimes and Rules of Procedure and Evidence*, Ardsley: Transnational Publishers, 2001, pp. xlv–lii.

14 Leila Nadya Sadat, 'Summer in Rome, Spring in the Hague, Winter in Washington?: U.S. Policy Towards the International Criminal Court', (2003) 21 *Wisconsin International Law Journal* 557, at p. 575.

after the entry into force of the Statute for that State, unless that State decides otherwise.

In terms of jurisdiction *ratione materiae,* although the negotiators of the Rome Statute contemplated adding many crimes to the Court's jurisdiction including terrorism, drug trafficking, hostage-taking, and aggression, it was ultimately decided that it would be preferable to begin with universal 'core crimes' defined in treaties or found in customary international law rather than add treaty crimes, the universality of which could be questioned. Moreover, although there was little doubt that the crime of aggression was a 'core crime', and the Nuremberg judgment declared aggression to be 'the supreme international crime differing only from other war crimes in that it contains within itself the accumulated evil of the whole',[15] many States were opposed to its inclusion in the Rome Statute. Thus, the Rome Statute initially defined only three crimes: genocide (article 6), crimes against humanity (article 7), and war crimes (article 8), which were the only offences immediately chargeable.

As a compromise between those desiring the inclusion of the crime of aggression and those opposing it, article 5 listed aggression as one of the crimes within the Court's jurisdiction, but specified that the Court could not exercise jurisdiction over aggression until it was defined by the Assembly of States Parties at a future time. In June 2010, the Assembly of States Parties held a Review Conference in Kampala, Uganda, during which a definition of aggression was agreed upon, and a new article 8 *bis* was added to the Rome Statute. However, pursuant to the text adopted, which includes two separate articles on the exercise of jurisdiction over the crime of aggression, articles 15 *bis* and 15 *ter,* the Court cannot exercise jurisdiction over the crime until the Kampala amendments have entered into force for at least thirty States (i.e., those States have ratified the amendments) *and* the States Parties to the Rome Statute so agree under the provisions of the Statute governing amendments thereto which require either a consensus vote or an absolute two-thirds majority *and* in any event not before, at the earliest, 2 January 2017.

Finally, Resolution E of the Rome Conference's Final Act provided that terrorism and drug crimes should be taken up at a future Review Conference, and proposals for their inclusion in the Statute have been

---

15 (1948) 22 IMT 411, at p. 427.

taken up by Working Groups of the Assembly of States Parties. However, they have never been included in the Court's jurisdiction and progress on this issue has been very slow to date.[16]

Preconditions on the exercise of the Court's jurisdiction

Some of the most difficult features to negotiate were the provisions on how the Court's jurisdiction could be activated in particular cases, and when a case would be admissible before the Court. As noted earlier, some States wished to be able to opt out of the Court's jurisdiction in cases involving their nationals, or to require all cases to be filtered through the Security Council. Conversely, civil society and eventually the members of the Like Minded Group of States wanted a Court with a simple and automatic jurisdictional regime rather than a 'Court á la carte'. The compromise is found in articles 12–15 which set forth the 'Preconditions' and conditions for the Court's exercise of its jurisdiction. These provisions allow referrals to be made by a State Party, by the Security Council and by the Prosecutor on his or her own initiative, using *proprio motu* powers. If the aggression amendments enter into force, the uniform jurisdictional regime of the Statute will be impaired as States are not bound by those amendments unless they choose to be, and in cases brought to the Court by a State Party or the Prosecutor, the Court has no jurisdiction over the nationals or territory of non-party States (which was the outcome desired by the United States at Rome with respect to all crimes within the Court's jurisdiction).

While there has been a great deal of discussion as to whether jurisdiction in the Statute is 'universal' or consent-based, it is undoubtedly the case that the prescriptive jurisdiction of the Statute is premised on the universality principle, which is why the Statute provides that the Security Council may refer a situation to the Court whether or not it involves crimes committed on the territory of a State Party or by a national of a State Party.[17] However, the adjudicative jurisdiction of the Court is more limited. In cases involving a referral by either a State Party or the

---

16 E.g., Report on the Working Group on Amendments, ICC-ASP/10/32, pp. 2–4 (consideration of proposals on terrorism from the Netherlands and drug trafficking from Trinidad and Tobago and Belize).

17 Rome Statute, article 13(b).

Prosecutor on his or her own initiative, although the universality principle does not disappear, layered upon it is a State consent regime based upon two additional principles, which are disjunctive: either the territorial State or the State of the accused's nationality must be a party to the Statute or have accepted the jurisdiction of the Court. Finally, in case of a referral by the Prosecutor using his or her *proprio motu* powers, an additional precondition is found in article 15 which requires the Prosecutor to apply to a Pre-Trial Chamber for authorisation to open an investigation before proceedings as such.

Admissibility

In addition to jurisdiction, the Rome Statute requires that a case be admissible before the Court to proceed. Admissibility is linked to the principle of complementarity found in the Preamble and articles 1 and 17 of the Statute. The International Criminal Court is envisioned as a Court of last, not first, resort, and may exercise jurisdiction only if: (1) national jurisdictions are 'unwilling or unable' to; (2) the crime is of sufficient gravity; and (3) the person has not already been tried for the conduct on which the complaint is based. Although the inclusion of the complementarity principle undoubtedly increased State support for the Court, it makes the Court's operation more difficult and litigation regarding admissibility has complicated several of the Court's early cases. For example, in the Kenyan situation, the Prosecutor initiated the case under article 15 of the Statute, claiming that Kenya was 'unwilling' (and presumably unable) to prosecute individuals who had perpetrated crimes during the post-election violence that wracked Kenya in the wake of the 2007 elections there. An investigation was authorised by Pre-Trial Chamber II in March 2010. However, nearly one year later, Kenya then challenged the admissibility of the case. Litigation ensued for several additional months and ultimately both the Pre-Trial Chamber and the Appeals Chamber concluded that the cases were admissible because the Kenyan government had failed to provide sufficient evidence to substantiate that it was investigating the six suspects charged before the Court for the crimes alleged against them. The Appeals Chamber clarified the meaning of 'inadmissibility' by holding that for a case to be inadmissible under article 17(1)(a) of the Rome Statute, the national investigation must cover the same individual and substantially the same conduct as alleged in the proceedings before the Court.[18] Conversely, in the *Al-Senussi* case, involving the situation in Libya, the Pre-Trial Chamber concluded that Libya was investigating Al-Senussi for the conduct with which he was charged at the International Criminal Court, and that Libya was neither unwilling nor unable to carry out the investigation. Thus, it concluded that the case was inadmissible although it recognised that the absence of defence counsel and the security concerns in Libya were serious issues.[19] Indeed, Al-Senussi expressed a clear preference to have his case heard before the International Criminal Court, undoubtedly believing the trial would be fairer before an international court. Thus, even with respect to a particular situation, some accused will be tried before the International Criminal Court, whereas others will be tried in national courts.[20]

Organisational structure

The Court's organisational structure is much more complex than predecessor international tribunals. The four organs of the Court are the Presidency, the Judiciary (composed of three divisions: Appeals, Trial, and Pre-Trial Divisions), the Office of the Prosecutor, and the Registry. In addition, the Assembly of States Parties established by Part 11 of the Statute oversees the operations of the Court (including its budget) and the Trust Fund for Victims, established by a decision of the Assembly of States Parties under article 79. The Trust Fund administers funds and other forms of assistance for the benefit of victims of crimes within the jurisdiction of the Court. It advocates for victims and mobilises individuals, institutions with resources and the goodwill of those in power for the benefit of victims and their communities. As of this writing, the Court's annual budget is just short of €122 million, €10 million of which are allocated to the Judiciary, €33 million to the Office of the Prosecutor, and €66 million to the Registry, and the staff number in the several hundred.

---

18 *Prosecutor* v. *Muthaura* et al. (ICC-01/09-02/11 OA), Judgment on the Appeal of the Republic of Kenya against the decision of Pre-Trial Chamber II of 31 May 2011 entitled 'Decision on the Application by the Government of Kenya Challenging the Admissibility of the Case Pursuant to Article 19(2)(b) of the Statute', 30 August 2011, para. 39.

19 *Prosecutor* v. *Gaddafi* et al. (ICC-01/11-01/11), Decision on the admissibility of the case against Abdullah Al-Senussi, 11 October 2013.

20 Ibid.

The Court has eighteen judges, nominated and elected by secret ballot by the Assembly of States Parties. Each judge must be a national of a State Party and be a person of 'high moral character, impartiality and integrity' who possesses the qualifications required in his or her States for appointment to the highest judicial office. In choosing, article 36 of the Statute requires the Assembly to 'take into account' the need for gender balance, equitable geographical representation, and the representation of the principal legal systems of the world. Each judge serves one non-renewable nine-year term, and at least nine of the judges must have established competence and experience in criminal law and procedure; five must have competence and experience in relevant areas of international law. The judges organise themselves into Divisions upon their election, and elect the members of the Presidency, who serve for a term of three years. Five judges sit as members of the Appeals Chamber, which decides upon a Presiding Judge for each appeal. Three judges sit in each Trial Chamber and Pre-Trial Chamber, although the functions of the Pre-Trial Chamber may be carried out by a single judge if the Statute so provides. The Pre-Trial Chamber oversees the initiation of a case until confirmation of the charges against the accused, after which time the accused is committed to a Trial Chamber for trial.

It was initially thought that the addition of the Pre-Trial Chamber would assist with the streamlining of cases by preparing them for trial and avoiding some of the procedural delays experienced at the *ad hoc* international criminal tribunals, which averaged three years between arrest and judgment.[21] Thus far, however, the addition of the Pre-Trial Chamber seems not to have had this effect: in the *Lubanga* case, for example, the accused was transferred to The Hague on 16 March 2006, the decision confirming the charges was issued in January 2007, but trial did not begin until two years later, and the judgment was not issued until 14 March 2012, six years after arrest. Likewise, the *Katanga* case took nearly seven years between arrest and judgment. Moreover, there has been some confusion about the respective roles of the Pre-Trial and Trial Chambers,

---

21 International Criminal Tribunal for the former Yugoslavia, Weekly Press Briefing, 15 January 2003, (noting that a typical trial at the Tribunal is sixteen months); see also Report on the Completion Strategy of the International Criminal Tribunal for Rwanda, UN Doc. S/2009/247 (stating that the average length for a trial is from two to four years).

perhaps due to the fact that the functions and operation of the divisions are spread throughout the Statute and difficult to discern, and because the addition of this preliminary phase of the proceedings is new to international criminal justice. In contrast, the first case before the International Criminal Tribunal for the former Yugoslavia took less than a year to try, and the trial judgment was rendered two years following the accused's transfer to the Tribunal.

Like the judges of the Court, the Prosecutor and Deputy Prosecutors are elected by the Assembly of States Parties, and serve one non-renewable, nine-year term. Although the Prosecutor and Deputy Prosecutor(s) must be of different nationalities, unlike the judges they need not be nationals of a State Party to the Rome Statute. It is the Prosecutor who drives the caseload of the Court, and it is thus not surprising that during the Statute's negotiation, both during and prior to Rome, defining the powers of the Prosecutor was highly contentious. In particular, one innovation of the Rome Statute is that the Prosecutor can initiate cases on his or her own initiative, using the '*proprio motu*' powers set forth in the Statute, and subject to the jurisdiction and admissibility requirements of the Statute. As a response to concerns about the potential overreaching, the Statute contains extensive checks on the Prosecutor's power including a requirement that the Pre-Trial Chamber must authorise any investigation brought on the Prosecutor's own initiative only if it independently determines that a 'reasonable basis' exists that crimes within the jurisdiction of the Court have been committed.

Finally, the Registry is the administrative organ of the Court for non-judicial matters. A full-time member of the Court, the Registrar is elected by the judges for a five-year term and exercises his or her functions under the authority of the President of the Court. Although the Statute has very little to say about either the Registrar or the Registry, this organ is by far the largest at the Court with a great deal of control over the Court's operations. The Registry is responsible for initiating staff regulations governing the court's personnel, and for the establishment and operation of the Victims and Witnesses Unit. It also performs outreach activities, and is responsible for information technology. Perhaps most importantly, it creates and maintains the list of defence counsel from whom the accused may choose if counsel is to be provided and otherwise supports the defence in its work.

The Court's current caseload

The Court has eight situations on its docket, involving twenty-one cases brought against thirty individuals. All eight situations involve African nations, five of which referred their own situations to the Court including the Central African Republic, Côte d'Ivoire, the Democratic Republic of the Congo, Mali, and Uganda. Two situations, Darfur, Sudan, and Libya, were referred to the Court by the Security Council in 2005 and 2011, respectively.[22] One situation, Kenya, was brought by the Prosecutor on his own initiative, pursuant to article 15 of the Statute.[23] Of those accused in these situations, one has been acquitted, two have died, and charges have not been confirmed against four persons. Three trials have been completed and two are ongoing; three more will commence shortly. The three completed trials have resulted in two convictions and an acquittal, and each involved accused from the Democratic Republic of the Congo. Several appeals – by both the Prosecution and the defence – are pending. More than a third of the accused remain at large. In addition to the eight situations currently on its docket, the Office of the Prosecutor is currently conducting preliminary examinations in a number of situations, including Afghanistan, Colombia, Georgia, Nigeria, Guinea, Honduras, Iraq, Palestine, and Ukraine.

Challenges and future prospects

The International Criminal Court has faced significant challenges during its first twelve years. Many have been political. It weathered a brutal campaign waged by the United States during the first term of President George W. Bush that explicitly advocated for its 'wither and collapse'[24] and involved the adoption of anti-International Criminal Court legislation

---

22 UN Doc. S/RES/1593 (2005); UN Doc. S/RES/1970 (2011).
23 Côte d'Ivoire was technically a *proprio motu* case and authorisation to the Prosecutor to proceed was given by the Pre-Trial Chamber. It was not a party to the Rome Statute at the time the investigation began, but had accepted the jurisdiction of the Court and requested the Prosecutor to proceed. It has now ratified the Rome Statute.
24 Paula R. Kaufman, 'Bolton is on Duty as America's Sentry', *Insight on the News*, 22 July 2002 (quoting Bush administration official John Bolton).

by Congress, the negotiation of bilateral immunity agreements with more than 100 countries, the extraction of concessions in Security Council resolutions on peacekeeping exempting non-party State nationals from the Court's jurisdiction and perhaps, most famously, the sending of a letter attempting to 'un-sign' or nullify the signature by the United States of the Statute. The punishing treatment from Washington notwithstanding, membership in the Court grew due to the unceasing work of civil society, particularly the NGO Coalition for the International Criminal Court, the successful work of the *ad hoc* international criminal tribunals for Rwanda, the former Yugoslavia and Sierra Leone, and increasing support from regional organisations. The Obama administration has taken a much more positive view of the International Criminal Court, sending a high-level delegation to Assembly of States Parties meetings, co-operating to the extent possible given the anti-Court legislation adopted by Congress, assisting with arrests and more generally adopting a positive and productive tone towards the Court and its activities. Although it is unlikely to submit the treaty for ratification in the Senate, current policy is to 'engage' with States Parties to the Rome Statute on issues of concern and support the prosecution of cases that advance United States interests and values.[25]

At the same time, as United States opposition has diminished, other political opposition has surfaced. The leaders of many African Union member states have challenged the Court on the basis that it has 'targeted' Africa. These objections have increased over the years, centred first upon the Prosecutor's decision to issue an arrest warrant directed to Sudanese President Omar al-Bashir, which resulted in efforts to get the Security Council to use article 16 to defer the proceedings against him as well as a proposal to extend the possibility of deferral (for ongoing cases) to the General Assembly.[26] Subsequently, with the election of indictees Uhuru Kenyatta and William Ruto as President and Deputy President of Kenya, respectively, the Assembly of States Parties yielded to political pressure and amended the Rules of Procedure and Evidence to permit them to be

---

25 The White House, National Security Strategy 48 (May 2010).

26 Assembly of States Parties to the Rome Statute of the International Criminal Court, ICC-ASP/8/20 (vol. I), Annex II, pp. 59–62. See also: 'Braced for the Aftershock', *The Economist*, 7 March 2009, p. 67 (citing efforts pushing for the deferral from African-Arab groups at the United Nations); Franklin Graham, 'Put Peace before Justice', *New York Times*, 3 March 2009, p. A27.

absent from their trials (subject to judicial approval) to perform 'extra-ordinary public duties'.[27] Although most of the African situations cur-rently before the Court were referred by African states themselves, the African Union's anger at the International Criminal Court and threats of a mass withdrawal of African states parties pose a significant threat to the Court's real and perceived legitimacy and public support. It also highlights another challenge – which is the need for universal ratification and support from the seventy states which are currently outside the Rome Statute system and which represent approximately three-fifths of the world's population. This includes China, India, Russia and, as aforemen-tioned, the United States. The absence of three permanent members of the Security Council is particularly damaging to the Court's effectiveness and credibility as those states have the power to block or refer situations that might be heard by the Court.

Finally, the Court has challenges of a more mundane nature – financ-ing, public outreach, streamlining trial procedures, arresting the accused. Amongst these challenges, both mundane and extraordinary, it is easy to lose sight of the Court's successes and the achievement of the Rome Conference. The International Criminal Court was the last international institution established in the twentieth century, a tribute to the judgment of reason over power, to paraphrase Justice Jackson's famous opening address at Nuremberg. It is an institution dedicated to the prevention and punishment of serious crimes that threaten the security of humankind, a living tribute to the idealism of Nuremberg. Given the values its establish-ment represents, one can only hope it prospers and that the States that created it provide it with the political and financial support it needs to thrive.

FURTHER READING

M. Cherif Bassiouni, *Introduction to International Criminal Law*, 2nd rev. edn, Leiden: Nijhoff, 2013.

---

27 M. Plachta, 'African Union Requests Deferral of Trial by the International Criminal Court', (2014) 30 *International Enforcement Law Reporter*, 29–32; see also: 'Kenya's "Victory" At Assembly of States Parties Meeting', AllAfrica, 28 November 2013.

F. Benedetti, K. Bonneau, and J. L. Washburn, *Negotiating the International Criminal Court*, The Hague: Martinus Nijhoff, 2014.

Leila Nadya Sadat and S. R. Carden, 'The New International Criminal Court: An Uneasy Revolution', (2000) 88 *Georgetown Law Journal* 381.

Leila Nadya Sadat, *The International Criminal Court and the Transformation of International Law*, Ardsley: Transnational, 2002.

William A. Schabas, *The International Criminal Court: A Commentary on the Rome Statute*, Oxford University Press, 2010.

Otto Triffterer, ed., *Commentary on the Rome Statute of the International Criminal Court, Observers' Notes, Article by Article*, 2nd edn, Munich: C.H. Beck; Baden-Baden: Nomos; Oxford: Hart, 2008.

National jurisdictions 8

Fannie Lafontaine

Eichmann, Pinochet, Barbie, Touvier, Rios Montt, Fujimori, Scilingo, Munyaneza, and Simbikangwa: a few among the thousands that have been processed, in the spotlight or below the radar, through national courts for the commission of atrocity crimes. The role of national jurisdictions in the fight against impunity for international crimes is the object of this chapter.

One of the justifications for the creation of international criminal institutions is the traditional failure of States where the crimes occurred, or of which the perpetrator is a national, to undertake investigations and prosecutions in respect of such crimes. The same rationale explains the development of the principle of universal jurisdiction. Universal jurisdiction is indeed based on the notion that some crimes – including genocide, crimes against humanity, war crimes, enforced disappearances, and torture – are of such exceptional gravity that they affect the fundamental interests of the international community as a whole. Every member of the international community therefore has a right – or an obligation, as we shall see – to ensure that these crimes do not go unpunished.

Interestingly, despite this fundamental rationale for the existence of international courts, the International Criminal Court has not followed the model of the *ad hoc* tribunals for the former Yugoslavia and Rwanda, based on the primacy of the international jurisdictions over national jurisdictions. The Court is 'complementary to national jurisdictions' and its Statute further affirms in the Preamble that it is 'the duty of every State to exercise its criminal jurisdiction over those responsible for international crimes' and that 'the most serious crimes of concern to the international community as a whole must not go unpunished and that their effective prosecution must be ensured by taking measures at the national level and by enhancing international cooperation'. The Assembly of States Parties reaffirms this commitment at every meeting.

The International Criminal Court is thus based on the hope that classical assumptions to the effect that the post-conflict domestic dynamic prevents war crimes trials can be reversed. It is also based arguably on the idea that it forms part of a system of accountability for core international crimes, composed of a web of national jurisdictions able and willing to investigate and prosecute such crimes wherever they were committed, with the international institution ready to act to close the impunity gap where no State can or does so genuinely.

The attention given to the duties of national jurisdictions to prosecute core crimes has followed more or less the same curve as that dedicated to international tribunals. Although the idea of national trials for war crimes has a long history in international humanitarian law,[1] the best-known exercises of national jurisdiction relate to crimes committed during the Second World War, with the various military trials held by the victorious powers pursuant to Control Council No. 10 and other legislative basis, and by Germany itself.[2] The international treaties adopted in the aftermath of the Second World War – in particular the Genocide Convention and the Geneva Conventions – logically provide, at different degrees, for States' duties to investigate and prosecute, or extradite, *génocidaires* and war criminals, and the 1951 Refugee Convention declares that those suspected of involvement in the commission of international crimes are undeserving of refugee protection. 'Never again' was going to be translated among other things by a strong resolve to fight against impunity – if it did happen again – and to commit national courts to this global endeavour.

But the 'dark ages' of the idea of individual criminal responsibility for violations of international law that followed Nuremberg and Tokyo, caused by the Cold War, also affected the development of the idea of justice at the national level. After the thousands of convictions post–Second World War, there was a considerable loss of appetite for justice for war

---

1 E.g. Institute of International Law, *Manual of the Laws of War on Land* (adopted 9 September 1880), Part III (Chapeau and Article 84); James W. Garner, 'Punishment of Offenders Against the Laws and Customs of War', (1920) 14 *American Journal of International Law* 76.

2 Michael Wahid Hanna, 'An Historical Overview of National Prosecutions for International Crimes', in M. Cherif Bassiouni, ed., *International Criminal Law*, vol. 3 (Enforcement), Leiden: Martinus Nijhoff, 2008, pp. 297–328, at pp. 304–9.

crimes. The new East-West tensions had accelerated the need to secure the co-operation of former members of the secret services of Axis countries. Also, the arrest of Nazi war criminals and their collaborators was seen as a less crucial issue than the economical reconstruction of the victorious nations, and the anti-communist perspective of these possible new immigrants fitted quite well the dominant ideology of the fifties.[3] There certainly were national efforts here and there, with uneven success, such as the trials held in Hungary to address crimes committed during the 1956 revolution; in the Baltic States – Estonia, Latvia, and Lithuania – to prosecute offences against international law committed in their territories by the Soviet authorities during and after the Second World War; and the later and under-reported Ethiopian massive efforts in the 1990s to investigate and prosecute the 'Red Terror' massive human rights violations of the Derg era.[4] The best-known trials that occurred during this later period for Nazi war crimes are surely those of Adolf Eichmann in Israel and of Paul Touvier and Klaus Barbie in France, who were initially convicted *in absentia* and retried in 1994 and 1987, respectively, for crimes against humanity.

However, similarly to the enforcement of international criminal law through international tribunals, it is principally with the conflicts in the former Yugoslavia and Rwanda that enforcement through national courts regained some speed. With suspects of crimes committed during these conflicts roaming around the world among refugee populations and the reviving of the legal principles of Nuremberg through the statutes of the *ad hoc* tribunals, States began to adopt laws or enforce existing ones (for instance the implementing legislations of the Geneva Conventions), giving life to the principle of universal jurisdiction. Belgium and Spain famously adopted an expansive version of the concept, Pinochet was arrested in London in 1998 on an extradition request from Spain who wished to exercise jurisdiction for the crimes committed in Chile, the Statute of the International Criminal Court was adopted in Rome, inciting States into action at the domestic level: it seemed that States would concretise Beccaria's belief, stated as long ago as 1764, that 'the conviction of

---

3 Ibid., p. 308; Fannie Lafontaine, *Prosecuting Genocide, Crimes against Humanity and War Crimes in Canadian Courts*, Toronto: Carswell, 2012, p. 48.

4 Kevin Jon Heller and Gerry Simpson, eds., *The Hidden Histories of War Crimes Trials*, Oxford University Press, 2013, ch. 11, 12, 14, and 15.

finding nowhere a span of earth where real crimes were pardoned might be the most efficacious way of preventing their occurrence'.[5] This renewed enthusiasm was followed by inevitable setbacks – Belgium and Spain amended their laws, the African Union has decried an 'abusive' recourse to universal jurisdiction – and innumerable writings announced the fall of universal jurisdiction.

Yet, despite obstacles facing national prosecutions for international crimes, States do prosecute. Numbers will always be difficult to ascertain, but scholars and organisations count that over thirty-five countries have been involved in the prosecution of international crimes over the last fifteen years, including some twenty where the crimes had taken place. Many thousands of perpetrators would have been brought to justice in these States, and a few dozens in almost fifteen States on the basis of universal jurisdiction.[6] Courts of States where crimes occurred are indeed very busy: the closing *ad hoc* international tribunals are transferring cases to Serbia, Bosnia, and Rwanda, for instance, where national courts have already tried thousands of perpetrators.[7] Latin American countries have now prosecuted hundreds of suspects of international crimes associated with the brutal dictatorships of the 1970s.[8] Universal jurisdiction is not on the wane, law enforcement officials in States such as Argentina, Canada, Denmark, Finland, France, Germany, the Netherlands, Norway, Senegal, South Africa, Spain, Sweden, Switzerland, and the United Kingdom, have been involved in universal jurisdiction cases

---

5 Cesare Beccaria, *Del delitti e delle pene*, translated in J. Farrar, Crimes and Punishment, 1880, at pp. 193–4.

6 Robert J. Currie and Joseph Rikhof, *International and Transnational Criminal Law*, 2nd edn, Toronto: Irwin Law, 2013, pp. 233, 284–8; Maximo Langer, 'The Diplomacy of Universal Jurisdiction: The Political Branches and the Transnational Prosecution of International Crimes', (2011) 105 *American Journal of International Law* 1.

7 Rwanda has prosecuted over 10,000 perpetrators in its criminal courts, and more than 1 million others have been processed through the *gacaca*: see e.g., William A. Schabas, 'Genocide Trials and *Gacaca* Courts', (2005) 3 *Journal of International Criminal Justice* 879.

8 A March 2015 report of the special section of the Attorney General's office in Argentina highlights that 456 cases are active, with over 500 previous convictions: Procuraduría de Crímenes contra la Humanidad, *Actualización de datos sobre el proceso de justicia por crímenes de lesa humanidad. Datos al 18 de marzo de 2015.*

in recent years,[9] and the topic features quite highly on international and regional political and judicial agendas.[10]

In this context, where States bear the primary responsibility to prosecute those responsible for genocide, crimes against humanity and war crimes, and because international tribunals cannot meet the full demands of justice due to restrictions on their jurisdiction and limited resources, it has become commonplace to affirm that the future of the international criminal justice system lies with States. National prosecutions are indeed called to play an increasingly important role in the global system put in place to fight against the impunity of those responsible for these crimes. On that front, however, as we shall see, there is a gap between the promise of the new international criminal justice system, which places States as the primary duty-bearers for ensuring accountability for international crimes, and the actual obligations flowing from international law in that regard.

This chapter will first offer an overview of the definitions and relevant principles regarding States' jurisdiction in international law. It will then discuss conventional and customary international law rules concerning States' obligations over atrocity crimes and the gaps in the existing regime, before turning to some crucial conditions for the 'reasonable' exercise of universal jurisdiction.

---

9   E.g., Amnesty International, *Universal Jurisdiction: Strengthening this Essential Tool of International Justice*, October 2012, Index: IOR 53/020/2012, at p. 25.

10 As examples, the topic of universal jurisdiction is discussed at the Sixth Committee of the United Nations General Assembly; the closely related concept of the obligation *aut dedere aut judicare* was on the agenda of the International Law Commission; the International Court of Justice in 2012 delivered a judgment on the issue of *aut dedere aut judicare* and universal jurisdiction pursuant to the Convention against Torture; the Council of the European Union established a 'European Network of contact points in respect of persons responsible for genocide, crimes against humanity and war crimes' to strengthen Member States' capacities in the investigation and prosecution of the core crimes, including on the basis of universal jurisdiction (*Strategy of the EU Genocide Network to combat impunity for the crime of genocide, crimes against humanity and war crimes within the European Union and its Member States*, The Hague, November 2014); Interpol launched projects to help international courts, but also States, in locating fugitives suspected of atrocity crimes.

Jurisdiction: basic principles

Any study of the role of national jurisdictions in the pursuit of justice for violations of international criminal law must begin by an understanding of the rules governing when and how States can exercise criminal jurisdiction over such crimes. This question bears particular importance in the context of international criminality for at least two reasons. First, the exercise of jurisdiction is an important function of State sovereignty. Considering that at international law, all States are sovereign equals, States have a duty not to interfere in each other's internal affairs. The exercise of extraterritorial jurisdiction is susceptible of causing infringements on State sovereignty and jurisdictional principles of international law aim at avoiding this. Second, if the Westphalian system and very much still the United Nations model of international affairs are based on borders as the outer limits of State sovereignty, crimes and criminals have never respected borders, and international crimes and criminals even less so. Not only do international crimes often implicate perpetrators and victims from various States, as well as transnational theatres of operations, but also victims and perpetrators often migrate during and after the conflict, incidentally involving third States and a distinct set of applicable international rules.

A State's 'jurisdiction' in this context refers to its authority under international law to apply and enforce rules of conduct upon persons. A distinction must be made between jurisdiction to prescribe and jurisdiction to enforce:

> Jurisdiction is not a unitary concept. ...[it] must be understood in its two distinct aspects, viz. jurisdiction to prescribe and jurisdiction to enforce. Jurisdiction to prescribe or prescriptive jurisdiction...refers, in the criminal context, to a State's authority under international law to assert the applicability of its criminal law to a given conduct.... Jurisdiction to enforce or enforcement jurisdiction...refers to a State's authority under international law actually to apply its criminal law, through police and other executive action, and through the courts. More simply, jurisdiction to prescribe refers to a State's authority to criminalise given conduct, jurisdiction to enforce the authority, inter alia, to arrest and detain, to prosecute, try and sentence, and to punish persons for the commission of acts so criminalised.[11]

11 Roger O'Keefe, 'Universal Jurisdiction: Clarifying the Basic Concept', (2004) 2 *Journal of International Criminal Justice* 735, at pp. 736–7 (footnotes omitted).

Jurisdiction to enforce is, save a few exceptions (on the high seas or during occupation, for instance), strictly territorial: a State cannot enforce its laws in another State without such State's consent; this would clearly violate State sovereignty. In order to secure the presence of a suspect on their territory to enforce their criminal laws, States have recourse to extradition, a consensual transfer of custody usually based on a treaty, which will be discussed below. It is useful to note that States also use extra-legal means of securing the presence of a suspect in their territory, for instance by abducting the suspect from the foreign State. Such conduct clearly violates State sovereignty, but it might not affect the legality of the subsequent prosecution, according to the *mala captus bene detentus* principle. Pursuant to a rigid application of this principle, the illegality of an arrest does not affect a court's jurisdiction over the accused. A famous application of this principle occurred in the trial of Adolf Eichmann. The Israeli courts upheld their jurisdiction, and tried and convicted the accused despite the fact that he had been illegally kidnapped from Argentina. The principle is applied unequally throughout the world and has gradually been eroded, particularly where the abduction is accompanied by torture or other grave human rights violations. In such cases, courts might conclude there had been an abuse of process and refuse to exercise jurisdiction. However, in the case of a trial for genocide, crimes against humanity, war crimes, or other serious international crimes, the violations of State sovereignty or human rights of the suspect in the course of his abduction would likely be balanced with the imperative of ensuring justice for international crimes and the rights of victims, with an outcome that could very well resemble the *Eichmann* version of the traditional *mala captus bene detentus* principle.[12]

If jurisdiction to enforce is strictly territorial, jurisdiction to prescribe can be territorial or extraterritorial. International law recognises various bases or 'heads' of jurisdiction.[13] These include, first and foremost,

12 See discussion in William A. Schabas, 'The Contribution of the Eichmann Trial to International Law', (2013) 26 *Leiden Journal of International Law* 667, at pp. 683–7; Louise Arbour, 'In Our Name and on Our Behalf', Speech at Chatham House and the British Institute of International and Comparative Law, 15 February 2006.

13 It is not the place to discuss the dictum in *The S. S. Lotus (France* v. *Turkey)*, 1928 PCIJ Series A, No. 10, which put forward the idea that States could assert extraterritorial jurisdiction to the extent that it is not limited by prohibitive rules of international law. It is generally accepted that the main 'prohibitive

the territorial principle, according to which a State has jurisdiction over persons of any nationality who commit crimes within its territory. The territoriality principle is often defined as including subjective and object-ive territoriality: the former referring to the assertion of jurisdiction by a State over 'an offence that begins on its territory but is completed outside the territory' and the latter referring to a State's jurisdiction 'over a crime that is completed within its territory'.[14] The other principles provide for extraterritorial jurisdiction. They include the active nationality principle, or active personality principle, giving jurisdiction to a State where the perpetrator of the crime is a national of that State; the passive personality (or nationality) principle, according to which a State may exercise crim-inal jurisdiction over extraterritorial acts by non-nationals when the vic-tim of the crime is a national of that State; the protective principle, which essentially entitles States to assert jurisdiction over extraterritorial activ-ities that threaten State security or some vital interest of that State; and the universal principle, which 'amounts to the assertion of jurisdiction to prescribe in the absence of any other accepted jurisdictional nexus at the time of the relevant conduct'.[15] In other words, universal jurisdiction is

> [t]he assertion by one State of its jurisdiction over crimes allegedly commit-ted in the territory of another State by nationals of another State against nationals of another State where the crime alleged poses no direct threat to the vital interests of the State asserting jurisdiction. In other words, uni-versal jurisdiction amounts to the claim by a State to prosecute crimes in circumstances where none of the traditional links of territoriality, national-ity, passive personality or the protective principle exists at the time of the commission of the alleged offence.[16]

rule' is respect for the sovereignty of other States and that international law rather provides for jurisdictional principles that allow States to assert extra-territorial jurisdiction while respecting State sovereignty.

14 Robert J. Currie and Joseph Rikhof, *International and Transnational Criminal Law*, 2nd edn, Toronto: Irwin Law, 2013, pp. 64–5.

15 Roger O'Keefe, 'Universal Jurisdiction: Clarifying the Basic Concept', (2004) 2 *Journal of International Criminal Justice* 735, at p. 737.

16 AU-EU Technical *Ad hoc* Expert Group on the Principle of Universal Jurisdiction: EC, Council, *The AU-EU Expert Report on the Principle of Universal Jurisdiction*, Brussels: European Commission, 2009, para. 8. See also the various versions of the definition provided by States to the Secretary-General of the United Nations in the course of the study by the Sixth (Legal) Committee of the UN General Assembly of the scope and application

Importantly, the proper base upon which a State bases its jurisdiction in a given case must be assessed with respect to the link that existed *at the time of the commission of the offence*. Therefore, the presence of the accused on a State's territory after the commission of the crime, his or her subsequent residence, or any other link to the State after the crime is committed that is imposed by domestic legislation as a condition for investigations or prosecutions, have no impact on the characterisation of the head of jurisdiction as one of universality, where at the time of commission of the crimes there was no territorial or national link with the State in question. Whether the presence of the accused should be a precondition to the exercise or enforcement of universal jurisdiction is a distinct issue and will be touched upon below.

Finally, it should be noted that a State's jurisdiction over a certain criminal conduct is not necessarily exclusive. Two or more States can have concurrent jurisdiction over the same event. For instance, State A can have jurisdiction over the accused because the war crime was committed on its territory (territorial jurisdiction), while State B can also have jurisdiction because the accused is a national (active personality jurisdiction) and State C, where the accused sought refuge, has universal jurisdiction. The prevailing view is that '[p]ositive international law recognises no hierarchy among the various bases of jurisdiction that it permits'[17] although, as we shall see below, there is a growing tendency to consider, at least as a matter of good policy, that the territorial State should be given priority in the prosecution of atrocity crimes. Conflicts arising from competing claims of jurisdiction are usually resolved through extradition law or by extra-legal approaches such as 'practicality (the State with custody prosecutes), *Realpolitik* (powerful State threatens/induces weaker States into yielding jurisdiction), or outright illegality'[18] (abduction, referred to above).

of universal jurisdiction; the first report being, The Scope and Application of the Principle of Universal Jurisdiction – Report of the Secretary-General prepared on the basis of comments and observations of Governments, UN Doc. A/65/181 (2010).

17 Ibid., para. 14.
18 Robert J. Currie and Joseph Rikhof, *International and Transnational Criminal Law*, 2nd edn, Toronto: Irwin Law, 2013, p. 81.

Obligations and gaps at international law regarding international crimes

Applicable rules and principles

Obligations at international law relate to three distinct but related concepts, namely the obligation to criminalise the offence in domestic law; the obligation to give national courts jurisdiction over the core crimes (prescriptive jurisdiction, which can be territorial or extraterritorial, including on the basis of universality); and the obligation to exercise jurisdiction, most often where a suspect is found on a State's territory, and that is embodied in the obligation *aut dedere aut judicare*, or the obligation to prosecute or extradite.

As noted above, the Rome Statute, in its preamble and by implication of the complementarity principle, provides for States Parties' duty to prosecute the international crimes contemplated therein. The Appeals Chamber has recognised that States 'have a duty to exercise their criminal jurisdiction over international crimes'.[19] However, there is no explicit obligation in the Rome Statute on the part of States Parties to criminalise the crimes *qua* genocide, crimes against humanity, and war crimes, to establish jurisdiction over the crimes and certainly no obligation to assert jurisdiction on the basis of universality. The Rome Statute does not either provide for an *aut dedere aut judicare* obligation for States Parties, although it provides for obligations to arrest and surrender a person if so requested by the Court (article 89) and provides for certain rules regarding competing requests, i.e., where a State receives a request from the Court for the surrender of a person and also receives a request from any other State for the extradition of the same person for the same conduct (article 90).

Regardless of the absence of a clear obligation in this regard in the Statute, many States have taken the opportunity presented by the need to modify their domestic law to implement their (co-operation) obligations to criminalise the 'ICC crimes' in domestic law and to give their domestic courts jurisdiction to try these crimes, including on the basis

19 *Prosecutor* v. *Katanga* et al. (ICC-01/04-01/07), Judgment on the Appeal of Mr. Germain Katanga against the Oral Decision of Trial Chamber II of 12 June 2009 on the Admissibility of the Case, 25 September 2009, para. 85.

of universality. It may be, as discussed elsewhere in this book, that the mere existence of the principle of complementarity acts as an incentive to States to adapt their legislation, investigate and prosecute, an idea that is reinforced by the positive view of complementarity espoused by the Office of the Prosecutor and its view of the impact of preliminary investigations on national proceedings, for instance.[20] Still, the only legal consequence that might flow from the absence of genuine proceedings – including objections based on a lack of criminal basis or of jurisdiction to investigate or prosecute in domestic law – is that a case may be declared admissible before the Court,[21] an encroachment on State sovereignty that is, however, a far cry from a finding that a State violated international law for failing to prosecute, which an obligation to do so would entail.

Other widely ratified treaties do provide for obligations to enact domestic legislation making the international offence a crime under domestic law, to assert specific bases of prescriptive jurisdiction, including universal jurisdiction, and to prosecute or extradite suspects found on a State Party's territory. It may be apposite to clarify that the obligation *aut dedere aut judicare* is distinct from universal jurisdiction, but it overlaps with it to some extent. As a practical matter, 'when the *aut dedere aut judicare* rule applies, the State where the suspect is found must ensure that its courts can exercise all possible forms of geographic jurisdiction, including universal jurisdiction'.[22] In fact, an *aut dedere aut judicare* obligation is a direction as to how to 'enforce' jurisdiction, which may or

---

20 Office of the Prosecutor, Prosecutorial Strategy 2009–2012, 1 February 2010; OTP Strategic Plan June 2012–2015, 11 October 2013; Policy Paper on Preliminary Examinations, November 2013, para. 100.

21 Note that the lack of criminalisation of genocide, crimes against humanity or war crimes *qua* international crimes in domestic law might not necessarily lead to a finding of admissibility. The standard is rather whether the national proceedings concern the 'same person/same conduct', possibly regardless of the legal characterisation of the conduct as a domestic or international crime: see discussion in Sarah M. H. Nouwen, *Complementarity in the Line of Fire: The Catalysing Effect of the International Criminal Court in Uganda and Sudan,* Cambridge University Press, 2013, p. 45.

22 Amnesty International, *Universal Jurisdiction: The Duty of States to Enact and Implement Legislation,* London: Amnesty International, 2001, ch. 1, p. 11; Preliminary report on the obligation to extradite or prosecute ('aut dedere aut judicare') by Mr. Zdzislaw Galicki, Special Rapporteur, UN Doc. A/CN.4/571, ch. II.

may not have been 'prescribed' on the basis of universality. International law may allow or mandate the assertion by States of prescriptive universal jurisdiction and may also oblige them to act in a certain way when an alleged offender is found on their territory. The obligation to extradite or prosecute imposed on custodial States is an obligation to exercise jurisdiction they were either obliged or allowed to prescribe. As per the International Law Commission, 'when the crime was allegedly committed abroad with no nexus to the forum State, the obligation to extradite or prosecute would necessarily reflect an exercise of universal jurisdiction'.[23]

The obligation to extradite or prosecute is mandated for grave breaches of the Geneva Conventions and the first Additional Protocol, and for some crimes against humanity that are the subject of a specific convention, notably *apartheid*, enforced disappearances, and torture. These treaties also mandate States to establish prescriptive jurisdiction on the basis of territoriality, active nationality, passive nationality, and universality and to criminalise the offences in their domestic law. The Genocide Convention is more limited: it imposes prosecution obligations upon territorial States and provides for a general duty with respect to extradition. As noted by Andrew Clapham in this *Companion*, various regional and international human rights treaties also provide for a general duty to repress serious violations of human rights that can be qualified as crimes against humanity. Importantly, however, such human rights treaties provide very limited extraterritorial obligations and certainly do not oblige States to repress violations that have occurred on other States' territories.

The *aut dedere aut judicare* obligations in the treaties create a powerful tool to achieve justice. Interpreting the regime of the Convention against Torture, the International Court of Justice has confirmed that '[e]xtradition is an option offered to the State by the Convention, whereas prosecution is an international obligation under the Convention, the violation of which is a wrongful act engaging the responsibility of the State'.[24] However, numerous atrocity crimes are not covered by such a treaty obligation to extradite or prosecute:

23 Report of the Working Group on the Obligation to Extradite or Prosecute (*aut dedere aut judicare*), UN Doc. A/CN.4/L.829, para. 24.
24 *Questions relating to the Obligation to Prosecute or Extradite (Belgium v. Senegal), Judgment, I.C.J. Reports 2012*, p. 422, para. 95.

there are important gaps in the present conventional regime governing the obligation to extradite or prosecute which may need to be closed. Notably, *there is a lack of international conventions with this obligation in relation to most crimes against humanity, war crimes other than grave breaches, and war crimes in non-international armed conflict.* In relation to genocide, the international cooperation regime could be strengthened beyond the rudimentary regime under the Convention for the Prevention and Punishment of the Crime of Genocide of 1948.[25]

It may be that customary international law imposes an obligation to extradite or prosecute all core crimes. It is outside the scope of this chapter to fully address the complex and controversial issue. Suffice it to say that such a rule may be emerging, but a safer view at the moment is that the existing rule is permissive rather than mandatory.[26]

Consequences of the gaps in international law

The gaps in the international law regime concerning the obligations imposed on States in the fight against impunity are at odds with the increasing reliance on national jurisdictions to close the impunity gap. The lack of international obligations over many of the most serious international crimes has as a main consequence that States criminalise and assert jurisdiction in an incoherent and unequal fashion as regards all core crimes and that the web meant to close the impunity gap is filled with holes. Any attempt to document how States criminalise and assert jurisdiction over the core crimes meets confusion and chaos. The crucial and Herculean efforts of organisations such as Amnesty International, the International Committee of the Red Cross, Parliamentarians for Global Action, the Coalition for the International Criminal Court, and the International Criminal Court Legal Tools, to systematise and render accessible such information, must be commended and encouraged. Amnesty International, in its 2012 survey of legislation around the world, to assist the Sixth (Legal) Committee of the United Nations General Assembly in its annual discussions of universal jurisdiction, found that definitions of crimes worldwide were 'seriously flawed' and that the

---

25 Report of the Working Group on the Obligation to Extradite or Prosecute (*aut dedere aut judicare*), UN Doc. A/CN.4/L.829, para. 20 (my emphasis).

26 Final Report of the Working Group on the Obligation to Extradite or Prosecute (*aut dedere aut judicare*), UN Doc. A/CN.4/L.844, paras. 8–14.

assertion of universal jurisdiction over international crimes was widespread but incoherent.[27]

Now, various States have made no distinction in their laws for the core crimes, and have criminalised and provided for universal jurisdiction for all of them. A natural reaction would be to think that the existence of a formal obligation would be unnecessary or even redundant. Indeed, why differentiate, at the execution stage, between crimes of similar gravity? In Canada, for instance, the two prosecutions thus far, of Désiré Munyaneza and Jacques Mungwarere for the Rwandan genocide, concerned genocide and crimes against humanity as well as, in the case of Munyaneza, war crimes committed in a non-international armed conflict, making no distinction based on existing international obligations. These prosecutions as well as numerous others worldwide, would seem to signal such a non-discriminatory vision. But, in fact, the existence of formal obligations at international law can potentially have three major impacts.

First, the existence of obligations can influence in a significant manner the exercise of prosecutorial discretion, by will or (judicial) force, actually leading to effective results. To begin with, one would think that an obligation at international law to investigate (and to submit the case to its competent authorities for the purpose of prosecution) would be taken into account by a State's prosecution authorities in the exercise of their discretion to launch a criminal prosecution. Faced with a treaty obligation, it is presumed that authorities will act with a view of not breaching the international obligation.

Interestingly, on whether to prosecute, treaties with an obligation *aut dedere aut judicare* provide that upon examination of the information available, 'authorities shall take their decision in the same manner as in the case of any ordinary offence of a serious nature under the law of that State' (Convention against Torture, article 7(1)(2)). This apparently innocuous prescription can actually carry great weight. In Canada, for instance, the decision to prosecute in general cases takes into account two criteria: the existence of a reasonable prospect of conviction and public interest. Generally, the graver the offence, the more likely it is that a prosecution will take place. Provided there is sufficient evidence, it is certain,

---

27 Amnesty International, *Universal Jurisdiction: A Preliminary Survey of Legislation Around the World – 2012 Update*, London: Amnesty International Publications, 2012.

for instance, that a prosecutor will launch a prosecution for the crime of murder. Where international crimes are concerned, however, these criteria become almost irrelevant and the main guiding principle is very different than for ordinary crimes, and not glamorous: it is, essentially, money. Financial considerations greatly restrict the capacity to investigate and prosecute. The absence of clear obligations at international law allows States to exercise prosecutorial discretion in a manner that is quite different than that applicable to ordinary serious crimes and that is not justifiable – as would be the lack of evidence, lack of co-operation from third State, risk to security and, arguably, serious diplomatic countermeasures.

Furthermore, more than an incentive to exercise prosecutorial discretion with a favourable view toward prosecution, the existence of clear international obligations can have legal implications 'forcing' authorities to implement them. Internally, the international obligation to investigate and prosecute can be mentioned in domestic law, in the preamble of a statute implementing the crime, for instance, or in guidelines for the exercise of prosecution, which can have the effect of incorporating the international norm into domestic law, possibly giving a basis to review in domestic courts the decision (not to) prosecute. Prosecutorial discretion may be reviewable in courts depending upon the legal system at play. But the mention in domestic law that a State has an obligation to investigate and prosecute gives a legal basis (and more weight to victims and groups pressing for prosecution in a given case) to formally or informally dispute the decision of the authorities. The recent example of South Africa is telling in this regard. The Constitutional Court recognised an obligation to investigate international crimes; a powerful judicial confirmation of the impact that genuine consideration of the State's responsibilities in the international fight against impunity can have in practice.[28] In addition to enforceable criteria at the domestic level, a State could also be held liable for an internationally wrongful act if it failed to respect its obligation to prosecute or extradite. The International Court of Justice case concerning Senegal and Belgium shows the power of such an international obligation at international law. Senegal had the obligation to prosecute (if it chose not to extradite), based on the Convention against Torture, and the international proceedings led to the historic trial of Hissène Habré on the

---

28 *National Commissioner of the South African Police Service* v. *Southern African Human Rights Litigation Centre and Another* [2014] ZACC 30, paras. 55–60.

basis of universal jurisdiction. Imagine, even without romanticising the power of international law, the potential for enforcement if there was a clear obligation to prosecute all core crimes.

A second tangible impact that explicit obligations at international law to exercise jurisdiction (*aut dedere aut judicare*) could have is that, *a contrario*, the absence of clear obligations could then not be invoked as a justification to *not* use existing legislation to investigate or prosecute, where other motives may wrongly justify the refusal to do so. If the cases of *Munyaneza* and *Mungwarere* in Canada and dozens of cases elsewhere were positive indications of the non-selective approach of the legal authorities to prosecute international crimes on the basis of universal jurisdiction, the political authorities, however, have not hesitated to exploit the gap, justifying the expulsions (not extraditions) of dozens of alleged war criminals from the country on the basis that 'Canada is not the UN. It's not our responsibility to make sure each one of these [alleged war criminals present in Canada] faces justice'.[29] The absence of certain obligations at international law can also serve, as in Spain in 2014, as a justification to cut back on existing universal jurisdiction legislation, where in reality, political, diplomatic, or ideological reasons are at play.[30]

Clearly, the lightness of international obligations can provide a powerful justification for the lack of political will. The gaps in the existing system favour arbitrary distinctions not based on traditional factors as to whether to initiate criminal proceedings. This creates an environment that is not conducive to a sense of ownership and responsibility by States in the fight against impunity.

Third, the lack of obligations to extradite or prosecute at international law regarding many atrocity crimes has an under-reported consequence: it does not favour interstate co-operation in the context of the fight against impunity for international crimes, affecting mutual legal assistance and extradition. Extraterritorial prosecutions rely extensively on co-operation by the territorial State and effective mutual legal assistance may often

29 Laura Payton, 'War Crimes Prosecution not up to Canada, Toews Says: 6th War Crimes Suspect in Canadian Custody', *CBC News*, 3 August 2011, citing the then Public Safety Minister.

30 *Ley Orgánica 1/2014, de 13 de Marzo, de Modificación de la Ley Orgánica 6/1985, de 1 de Julio, del Poder Judicial, Relativa a la Justicia Universal.* Exposición de motivos.

be the deciding factor in a State's capacity to conduct trials (fair and impartial trials that also allow co-operation with the accused). Extradition is obviously a central element in the 'obligation to prosecute or extradite' and despite such central role, it is in fact rarely used, constituting, in my view, the missing limb of the international enforcement system. Apart from a recent surge of extraditions to Rwanda, after numerous years of refusals to do so, there are, basically, very few extraditions for international crimes worldwide. This is partly due to the fact that the horizontal, or indirect, enforcement of international criminal law through State co-operation is weakly provided for in international multinational treaties. Recent human rights treaties such as the Conventions against Torture and Enforced Disappearances provide for sophisticated regimes of mutual legal assistance and extradition, facilitating the implementation of the alternative obligation to 'extradite' or 'prosecute', but they are of limited application. The Rome Statute contemplates an extensive vertical co-operation regime that has its own challenges, but it does not provide anything as regards horizontal co-operation to implement effectively the complementarity principle (except for a mention about competing requests, as noted above). Interstate co-operation for the core crimes thus relies almost exclusively on bilateral and regional treaties as well as domestic law. Despite the high number of such treaties, States where suspects are found often lack agreements with the State where the crimes were committed.[31] While the absence of a treaty is not necessary fatal (sometimes States can enter into *ad hoc* arrangements), it remains an extra hurdle and a justification to use other means less respectful of the spirit and letter of the *aut dedere aut judicare* idea, such as immigration measures. As an example, the lack of an extradition treaty with Rwanda for many years provided Canada with a justification for ignoring Rwanda's extradition request in the case of Léon Mugesera. Mugesera was eventually deported to Rwanda and was welcomed by the police who arrested him upon arrival. The removal constituted a disguised extradition, without the safeguards and mutual trust it entails.[32]

31 E.g., Maarten P. Bolhuis, Louis P. Middelkoop, and Joris van Wijk, 'Refugee Exclusion and Extradition in the Netherlands: Rwanda as Precedent?', (2014) 12 *Journal of International Criminal Justice* 1115.

32 See other examples in Ward Ferdinandusse, 'Improving Interstate Cooperation for the National Prosecution of International Crimes: Towards a New Treaty?', *ASIL Insight*, 18, 15.

In order to alleviate some limitations of the current system, at least two initiatives are worth mentioning.[33] First, the International Law Commission at its sixty-fifth session, in 2013, decided to include the topic 'crimes against humanity' in its programme of work.[34] The draft Convention on crimes against humanity prepared by the Crimes Against Humanity Initiative[35] alleviates many of the concerns identified here as regards these crimes, issues that the International Law Commission agrees need to be discussed: it would oblige States to criminalise these crimes in their domestic law and establish jurisdiction, it provides for an obligation *aut dedere aut judicare* and establishes a sophisticated regime of State co-operation on mutual legal assistance and extradition. This eventual convention would fill some of the gaps as regards the core crimes. Obviously, it leaves some of the other gaps unaddressed, particularly as regards genocide and war crimes committed in a non-international armed conflict. Hence the importance of the second initiative, that went largely unnoticed, except in a few specialised circles. Numerous States have joined an initiative to open negotiations on a multilateral treaty on mutual legal assistance for genocide, crimes against humanity, and war crimes. There are a few obstacles, including the right forum to do so, but the treaty would provide for a sophisticated regime of extradition and mutual legal assistance to implement the core obligation to prosecute or extradite all atrocity crimes.[36] In any case, the need for a revamped and more comprehensive treaty system on the obligations of States regarding the prosecution of atrocity crimes is obvious, and the current initiatives – especially if developed in a coherent fashion – have much potential to fill some gaps in the 'horizontal' international law enforcement system.

33 Payam Akhavan, 'Whither National Courts? The Rome Statute's Missing Half', (2010) 8 *Journal of International Criminal Justice* 1245.

34 Report of the International Law Commission, Sixty-fifth session (6 May–7 June and 8 July–9 August 2013), UN Doc. A/68/10, ch. XII, sect. A.2, and Annex B.

35 Leila Nadya Sadat, ed., *Forging a Convention for Crimes Against Humanity*, Cambridge University Press, 2011.

36 Ward Ferdinandusse, 'Improving Interstate Cooperation for the National Prosecution of International Crimes: Towards a New Treaty?', *ASIL Insight*, 18, 15; Amnesty International, *Universal Jurisdiction: Strengthening this Essential Tool of International Justice*, October 2012, Index: IOR 53/020/2012, p. 17.

This issue of interstate co-operation is not as technical as it may seem and is in fact linked to one of the hottest debates taking place regarding States' roles in the fight against impunity and the 'limits of universal jurisdiction', to which we now turn briefly.

The 'reasonable' exercise of universal jurisdiction

An eternal debate as regards universal jurisdiction since its rebirth in the 1990s has concerned subsidiarity, i.e., the idea that universal jurisdiction plays as a default mechanism and should only be exercised if the territorial or active nationality States (the *forum conveniens*) are unable or unwilling to exercise their jurisdiction. This debate has taken a central place in the African Union's accusations of 'abuse' of universal jurisdiction by European States and consequently at the Assembly General's Sixth Committee, where the issue of universal jurisdiction has been debated since 2009. Other issues are contentious, such as the necessity of the presence of the accused on the territory of the State wishing to exercise universal jurisdiction and the respect of immunities. On this latter issue, it seems clear that the respect by national courts of personal immunities for a few restricted incumbent senior officials while they hold office is necessary to conciliate the exigencies of international co-operation and relations with those of international criminal justice. To allow States to arrest and prosecute sitting high-level officials can only seriously disrupt international relations and severely undermine the necessary interstate co-operation and friendly relations needed to attain the common goal of accountability for the worst crimes.[37] On the presence of the accused, a growing number of States condition the exercise of jurisdiction to the presence of the accused on that State's territory after the commission of the offence or, for instance, to accused who subsequently become residents of the State. Practically speaking, in the dozens of cases that were actually brought to trial on the basis of universal jurisdiction, '[w]ithout exception the defendants had taken up permanent residence in the forum

---

37 This absolute character of personal immunities was reaffirmed by a Swiss court exercising universal jurisdiction: *Tribunal pénal fédéral, A c. Ministère public de la Confédération, B. et C.*, File Number BB.2011.140, Judgment of 25 July 2012, at para. 5.3.6.

State as refugee, exile, fugitive, or immigrant'.[38] For another thing, even for those States that do not require presence in theory, the frenzy prompted by the early Belgian and Spanish laws and practice and the diplomatic tensions that ensued are certainly acting as freezing factors for any State that might be tempted to exercise universal jurisdiction when the suspect has never set foot on their territory. This is particularly true where States have prevented or limited the possibility for private complainants to trigger the process and subjected the exercise of universal jurisdiction to the consent of a State entity, a growing trend worldwide.

Therefore, subsidiarity is arguably the most pressing concern regarding the exercise of universal jurisdiction. Subsidiarity, whether a rule of international law or a matter of good policy, should apply where a State has a concrete choice between prosecuting on the basis of extraterritorial jurisdiction and favouring the territorial State. That implies the presence of the suspect on that State's territory. Indeed, the idea of subsidiarity is closely intertwined with the obligation 'to prosecute or extradite' and comes down to what to do with a suspect on territory A who has committed crimes in State B. The debate about subsidiarity is largely based on at least three myths about the exercise of universal jurisdiction and, in fact, points to the lacunae in the interstate co-operation regime more than anything else.

The first myth is that States are aggressively pursuing the universal jurisdiction option to the detriment of territorial States. This is false. States are hesitant to embark on the universal jurisdiction journey: it is expensive, cumbersome, complicated, and generally not rewarding from an internal politics perspective and globally, as noted above, there have been a few dozen cases. Where compared to the thousands of possible fugitive war criminals, the pretension that States are aggressively pursuing universal jurisdiction is unjustified and inflated.

The second myth is that there would be real complex issues with competing jurisdictions claims and the need for a clearer hierarchy of jurisdiction in international law. Again, this is false. In fact, subsidiarity serves the interests of the two States involved. Considering the scarce resources for prosecution on the basis of universal jurisdiction and the

---

38 Luc Reydams, 'The Rise and Fall of Universal Jurisdiction', in William A. Schabas and Nadia Bernaz, eds., *Routledge Handbook of International Criminal Law*, London: Routledge, 2010, pp. 337–54, at p. 348.

comparative inexpensive costs of extradition, States where a suspect is present should naturally be favourably inclined towards the latter remedy. In fact, as noted above, extradition requests for international crimes are exceedingly rare, despite assumptions to the contrary in these discussions about competing claims for jurisdiction and, perhaps, a few exceptions recently regarding Rwanda. States confronted with the presence of international criminals on their territory are rather looking for solutions and are quite likely to welcome extradition requests.

The third myth is that we need some sort of a new principle, new conditions, even a new international mechanism to determine whether a territorial State is 'unable or unwilling' to investigate and prosecute a suspect present on a third State's territory so that universal jurisdiction could be exercised without hurting the principle of subsidiarity. This is also false. The prosecution of international crimes at the national level should remain at the interstate level and the system to determine whether State A (who has custody) should send a suspect to State B, where the crimes were committed, exists: it's called extradition.

Extradition of course has its own rules and there are a number of reasons why extradition to the territorial State will be impossible. That is the extradition language 'unwilling or unable' formula. There are issues of dual nationality and dual criminality but, most importantly, non-refoulement obligations and the ability of the custodial State to refuse extradition where the suspect would risk a flagrant denial of justice. Those considerations for instance have blocked extraditions to Rwanda for years, but they are the strict minimum, the basic reasons that will, in certain cases, put the custodial State in a well-justified position to not favour subsidiarity. The perfect system would then follow the International Court of Justice's decision in *Belgium* v. *Senegal*, according to which, as noted above, prosecution is an obligation, extradition an option.

Therefore, the importance of extradition cannot be underestimated, not only because it represents the legal framework applicable to State co-operation to ensure that justice is rendered *somewhere*, but also because it serves as the vehicle to alleviate concerns about State sovereignty raised by the exercise of universal jurisdiction. Filling the gaps in the international enforcement system is an important first step in providing national jurisdictions with the tools to contribute to closing the impunity gap.

Conclusion

It is now trite to say that the promise of the new system of international justice depends on States' capacity and will to put their legal systems to use for the global enterprise. It is also commonplace to argue that universal jurisdiction has a role to play in closing the impunity gap. Beyond the evidence and the rhetoric, many challenges remain: international obligations are inconsistent; practical and political obstacles lead to scarce prosecutions; and extradition is underused. The recent use of universal jurisdiction not only in Western States like Canada, Spain, Belgium and the like, but also by Senegal, South Africa, and Argentina, is a positive sign that the web is extending and closing on alleged war criminals. The next decades will require a move from an unduly State-centric 'no safe haven' idea into an awareness of the necessity of being a proactive member of a global system directed at a single and common goal. A more robust system of interstate co-operation would certainly greatly assist in this endeavour.

FURTHER READING

Payam Akhavan, 'Whiter National Courts? The Rome Statute's Missing Half', (2010) 8 *Journal of International Criminal Justice* 1245.

M. Cherif Bassiouni, *Introduction to International Criminal Law*, 2nd rev. edn, Leiden: Nijhoff, 2013.

Ward Ferdinandusse, *Direct Application of the International Criminal Law in National Courts*, The Hague: Asser, 2006.

Kevin Jon Heller and Gerry Simpson, eds., *The Hidden Histories of War Crimes Trials*, Oxford University Press, 2013.

Jan K. Kleffner, *Complementarity in the Rome Statute and National Criminal Jurisdictions*, Oxford University Press, 2008.

Fannie Lafontaine, 'Universal Jurisdiction: The Realistic Utopia', (2012) 10 *Journal of International Criminal Justice* 1277.

Massimo Langer, 'The Diplomacy of Universal Jurisdiction: The Political Branches and the Transnational Prosecution of International Crimes', (2011) 105 *American Journal of International Law* 1.

Roger O'Keefe, 'Universal Jurisdiction: Clarifying the Basic Concept', (2004) 2 *Journal of International Criminal Justice* 735.

Joseph Rikhof, 'Fewer Places to Hide? The Impact of Domestic War Crimes Prosecutions on International Impunity', (2009) 20 *Criminal Law Forum* 1.

Leila Nadya Sadat, ed., *Forging a Convention for Crimes Against Humanity*, Cambridge University Press, 2011.

William A. Schabas, 'National Courts Finally Begin to Prosecute Genocide, the "Crime of Crimes"', (2003) 1 *Journal of International Criminal Justice* 39.

William A. Schabas, 'Genocide Trials and *Gacaca* Courts', (2005) 3 *Journal of International Criminal Justice* 879.

William A. Schabas, 'The Contribution of the Eichmann Trial to International Law', (2013) 26 *Leiden Journal of International Law* 667.

Carsten Stahn and Mohammed El Zeidy, eds., *The International Criminal Court and Complementarity: From Theory to Practice*, vols. I and II, Cambridge University Press, 2011.

9 The United Nations Security Council and international criminal justice

David Scheffer

For almost the first half-century since its creation under the United Nations Charter in 1945, the United Nations Security Council spent relatively little of its time focusing on matters of international criminal justice. The Security Council is first and foremost the guardian of international peace and security under the Charter. It has attempted to fulfil that responsibility during a long and controversial history of mandating compliance with international law, imposing economic sanctions to coax recalcitrant nations towards acceptable behaviour, setting up peacekeeping operations to facilitate implementation of peace settlements or to defuse violent stand-offs between warring parties, and approving peace enforcement actions that might delegate to national military combat forces the task of intervening in an armed conflict or humanitarian calamity with the aim of ending it.

Original intent

One would be hard pressed to find anything, even inferentially, in the *travaux préparatoires*, or negotiating records, of the United Nations Charter – either at Dumbarton Oaks in 1944 or San Francisco one year later – that points to establishing the Security Council for the purpose of building international criminal tribunals or using judicial tools to compel compliance by individuals (of whatever allegiance). Rather, as with its predecessor, the Permanent Court of International Justice under the League of Nations, the International Court of Justice was conceived as the UN Charter's instrument of judicial remedies. But the jurisdiction of the International Court of Justice is directed towards the conduct of UN Member States and their governments and thus entails State responsibility. Absent is the typically domestic task of criminal justice that disciplines individuals for well-defined and actionable crimes. One may safely assume, based on any evidence to the contrary, that as the Second World

War came to a close and the United Nations emerged from that global war's massive assault on humankind, the idea of using the Security Council to promote international criminal justice simply had not registered with the founders of the United Nations.

Soon, however, the United Nations International Law Commission, responding to a request by the General Assembly, adopted the Nuremberg principles in 1950,[1] thus confirming that there was broad international endorsement of the illegality of atrocity crimes, namely, genocide, crimes against humanity, and serious war crimes following the Nuremberg military tribunal trials.[2] But the Nuremberg Principles were not necessarily binding at that point in history and were not explicitly endorsed by the Security Council as mandatory rules for Member States. Nonetheless, over the decades the Nuremberg Principles eventually came to be viewed as advancing and confirming customary international law.

Before the decade of the 1990s, the Council never acted solely for the purpose of ending atrocity crimes and never used its considerable powers to render international criminal justice against perpetrators. The Council's actions focused on the more conventional tools described by or otherwise enabled in the UN Charter, such as diplomatic initiatives, peacekeeping, and economic and diplomatic sanctions.

The Cold War divided three permanent members of the Council – the United Kingdom, France, and the United States – from the two remaining permanent members – the Soviet Union and, from 1971 onwards, the People's Republic of China. The threat of veto was always present and risked being used during the Cold War years, particularly if there had been any effort to subject political or military leaders of any party, government, or non-state actor that was aligned with the Western alliance or

1 UN General Assembly Resolution 177 (II), paragraph (a), directed the International Law Commission to 'formulate the principles of international law recognised in the Charter of the Nuremberg Tribunal'. The Report of the International Law Commission to the General Assembly covering its second session, 5 June to 29 July 1950, sets forth the Nuremberg Principles. See Principles of International Law Recognised in the Charter of the Nuremberg Tribunal and in the Judgment of the Tribunal, UN Doc. A/CN.4/SER.A/1950/Add.1, paras. 95–127.

2 For a discussion of 'atrocity crimes', see David Scheffer, *All the Missing Souls: A Personal History of the War Crimes Tribunals*, Princeton University Press, 2012, pp. 428–37.

the Communist powers to the scrutiny of compliance with codified law or customary law prohibiting the commission of atrocity crimes.

After the Cold War

With the collapse of the Soviet Union in 1991 and the end of the Cold War, the opportunity arose in 1992 to activate the Security Council on criminal justice challenges because the resurrected nation of Russia, fortuitously vested with the former Soviet Union's permanent membership on the Council, found political advantage in joining Western powers on certain UN ventures that confronted armed wars and humanitarian disasters. In October 1992, the Security Council tasked an independent commission of inquiry into the atrocity crimes sweeping across Croatia and Bosnia and Herzegovina,[3] where the United Nations Protection Force had been operating since early 1992.[4] Within months, as the preliminary findings of criminal conduct arrived in New York from the Commission of Experts and as other pressures mounted on the Council to react to the carnage in the Balkans, the historic step was taken in February 1993 to approve, by invoking a general reference to UN Charter Chapter VII, the establishment of the International Criminal Tribunal for the former Yugoslavia as a subsidiary organ of the Security Council.[5] Early jurisprudence of the International Criminal Tribunal for the former Yugoslavia affirmed the legitimacy of the Council's action.[6]

Standing parallel to the Security Council's initiative to create the International Criminal Tribunal for the former Yugoslavia in 1993 was the Council's sharp focus on Mohamed Fareh Aideed, a Somali warlord creating havoc and great risk for the United Nations Operation in Somalia II. The Council sought the arrest of Aideed (although not mentioning his name explicitly in pertinent resolutions) for the atrocities his militia allegedly had inflicted upon Pakistani peacekeepers in June 1993 and for other alleged crimes.[7] The operating presumption in policy circles was that

---

3 UN Doc. S/RES/780 (1992). See 'Final Report of the Commission of Experts Established Pursuant to Security Council Resolution 780 (1992)', UN Doc. S/1994/674.

4 UN Doc. S/RES/743 (1992).   5 UN Doc. S/RES/808 (1993).

6 *Prosecutor* v. *Tadić* (IT-94-1-T), Judgment, 7 May 1997, paras. 2–3.

7 UN Doc. S/RES/837 (1993); UN Doc. S/RES/865 (1993).

if captured, Aideed would be transported to a United States naval vessel for detainment and subsequent trial of an undetermined character. The sketchiness of what to do with Aideed as a matter of due process and what would constitute the proper court seemed less relevant at the time than the Council taking the initial actions to ensure his capture and removal from Somalia. The endeavour collapsed after the 'Battle of Mogadishu' on 3–4 October 1993 and the deaths of eighteen American servicemen crippled United States support for further engagement in Somalia.[8] On 16 November 1993, the Security Council required the suspension of 'arrest actions against those individuals who might be implicated but are not currently detained pursuant to resolution 837 (1993)'.[9]

Aideed remained a free man until his death in 1996. But the episode demonstrated the sea change that had occurred in the Security Council after the Cold War, namely that pursuing alleged war criminals became a natural means of exerting the Council's Chapter VII powers, particularly in conflict environments that offered no easy pathway for peace enforcement operations.

There were American-led efforts during the mid 1990s to secure Security Council support for creation of an international criminal tribunal on Iraqi atrocity crimes committed under the leadership of Saddam Hussein. But sufficient support never took hold within the Security Council to replicate what had been achieved for the atrocity crimes of the Balkans or, for that matter, the genocide in Rwanda in 1994. Nonetheless, efforts such as those concerning Aideed and Saddam Hussein, which did not result in the creation of criminal tribunals, amplified a political will within the Security Council to examine individual criminal liability in conflicts that threatened international peace and security.

The Security Council's second major exercise in tribunal building occurred in the second half of 1994 following the genocide in Rwanda earlier that year. The International Criminal Tribunal for Rwanda replicated the legitimacy of the International Criminal Tribunal for the former Yugoslavia in that the Council adopted a Chapter VII enforcement resolution to establish a subsidiary judicial organ of the Council with a limited temporal jurisdiction (calendar year 1994), limited territory

8 Mark Bowden, *Black Hawk Down: A Story of Modern War*, Berkeley: Atlantic Monthly Press, 1999.
9 UN Doc. S/RES/885 (1993).

(Rwanda and the actions of Rwandan citizens in neighbouring States), and a somewhat different configuration of atrocity crimes to investigate and prosecute.[10] It was the least that the Council could accomplish in the aftermath of the Rwandan genocide, where at least 800,000 mostly Tutsi citizens were slaughtered between 6 April 1994 and July 1994 at a pace of about 8,000 killings per day without any effective foreign military intervention being authorised or deployed by the Council. Following months of negotiations, the Council approved, in Resolution 955, the establishment of the International Criminal Tribunal for Rwanda under a Chapter VII authority. This occurred five months after the genocidal slaughter had subsided and thus was not intended as a means of stopping it or of necessarily preventing further bloodshed if violence erupted again (particularly after the temporal period of only 1994). Rather, the Council acted to achieve accountability for what had already occurred, which by then was a compelling step to take to salvage some credibility following the genocide.

Difficult choices

However, following the Council's initiatives regarding both the International Criminal Tribunal for the former Yugoslavia and the International Criminal Tribunal for Rwanda, the view emerged that the Security Council looked upon international criminal justice, and in particular the building of international or hybrid criminal tribunals, as a convenient alternative to the far more difficult choices posed by either UN peacekeeping or peace enforcement interventions.[11] That popular view is not reflected in the reality of the situations, where deciding whether and how to rapidly use armed force under Council authorisation was an option heavily conditioned in policy-making circles by political, military, logistical, and financial factors having nothing to do with justice and certainly not placated by opting for justice rather than the use of

---

10 UN Doc. S/RES/955 (1994).
11 Gary Jonathan Bass, *Stay the Hand of Vengeance*, Princeton University Press, 2000, pp. 207, 214–5; Samantha Power, *A Problem from Hell: America and the Age of Genocide*, New York: Basic Books, 2002, pp. 484, 491; Aryeh Neier, *War Crimes: Brutality, Genocide, Terror, and the Struggle for Justice*, New York: Random House, 1998, p. 112.

force. It would be an unfortunate predicament in modern history if the most powerful instrument of collective security, the UN Security Council, considered it sufficient to abandon the military component of its Chapter VII enforcement authority in favour of promoting only the seemingly less risky tool of international criminal justice. That war crimes tribunals might become a sanctuary in which the Security Council could shed its codified UN Charter responsibilities is a temptation, however, that merits constant vigilance by the Member States of the Council. The real test for the Security Council is how to advance both its traditional collective security mandate alongside its judicial powers arising under article 41 of the UN Charter.

The peace vs. justice argument also arose from the beginning of the Council's international justice era. The basic premise of the 'peace' advocates has been that the Security Council must be given full freedom and encouragement to seek peaceful resolution of conflicts *before* any judicial measures are contemplated, if at all. The primary task must be to stop the killing and indeed the atrocity crimes, even if that means granting amnesty or immunity to the perpetrators, particularly political or military leaders, in order to negotiate a successful peace deal. The premise of the 'justice' advocates is that seeking justice in fact will promote the long-term aims of peace and, even in the short-term, can isolate leaders in ways that facilitate ending combat and arriving at peace settlements.

The tension between 'peace' and 'justice' in the Council's deliberations has continued to the present day as Council members grapple with their own presumptions about what may or may not work to achieve stability during conflict situations and help ensure that the conflict will not erupt again. The short-term view might opt for seeking the end to fighting over all other objectives, while the long-term view might recognise that perpetuating a culture of impunity seriously risks further conflict and atrocity crimes. What is often overlooked is that empirically it is difficult to find examples where the worst perpetrators of atrocity crimes actually stayed their hands and engaged in meaningful talks leading to settlements simply because the international community refrained from pursuing international criminal justice. Instead, they just kept on fighting and committing heinous crimes. For example, the Government of Syria and its president, Bashar al-Assad, did not refrain from criminal warfare against his own civilian population from 2011 through at least mid-2015 while the United Nations spent years seeking a peaceful settlement and the Security Council remained deadlocked over referring the Syrian situation to the International Criminal Court.

African concerns

Although African governments were enthusiastic supporters in the creation of the International Criminal Court, and thirty-four African nations ratified the Rome Statute by 2015, the African Union turned against the Court as its early situations for investigation and prosecution centred entirely on African atrocities and as African national leaders (like Muammar Gaddafi, Omar al-Bashir, Laurent Gbagbo, Uhuru Kenyatta, and William Ruto) were indicted by the Court. The African Union waged a long campaign to unlock Security Council action under Chapter VII of the UN Charter, in accordance with article 16 of the Rome Statute, with the aim of suspending the Court's work on designated cases in Africa for at least one year (with the suspension being renewable for one-year periods thereafter based upon fresh Council approval).

The United States, France, and the United Kingdom held firm in denying any Council action to derail International Criminal Court indictments and prosecutions.[12] However, the African Union scored a victory of sorts in November 2013 when it successfully lobbied the Assembly of States Parties of the International Criminal Court to amend the Rules of Procedure and Evidence of the Court so that high political leaders, indicted by the Court and being prosecuted, could take steps to avoid having to appear during their trial proceedings.[13]

Arrests

By the mid 1990s, the Security Council's earlier creation of the International Criminal Tribunal for the former Yugoslavia and International Criminal Tribunal for Rwanda did not translate into tangible Council actions to facilitate the capture and arrest of indicted fugitives from either tribunal.

12 For a brief summary of the African initiative, see David Scheffer, *All the Missing Souls: A Personal History of the War Crimes Tribunals*, Princeton University Press, 2012, pp. 414–7.
13 Amendments to the Rules of Procedure and Evidence, ICC-ASP/12/Res.7.

The Council was exceedingly hesitant to authorise any arrest authorities to assist in the capture of accused perpetrators of the genocide in Rwanda immediately prior to the Council's decision to create the International Criminal Tribunal for Rwanda in late 1994 and continued to balk at any explicit arrest authority in the critical months when perpetrators were roaming the refugee camps in Zaire (now the Democratic Republic of the Congo).[14] Likewise, efforts to galvanise the Security Council in November 1995 to mandate a more proactive arrest authority in the wake of the Dayton Accords, which achieved relative peace in the Balkans, nonetheless failed as the major powers balked at the use of military forces deployed in Bosnia and Herzegovina to accomplish the task.

Ultimately, special operations were initiated by the United States, the United Kingdom, and a few other governments, mostly on the territory of Bosnia and Herzegovina, to assist the International Criminal Tribunal for the former Yugoslavia with arrests. Meanwhile, the European Union pressured Croatia and Serbia to capture and surrender indicted fugitives on their territory in exchange for lifting of European Union sanctions and for favourable consideration of each nation's aspirations for European Union membership. Indeed, the final two indicted fugitives of the International Criminal Tribunal for the former Yugoslavia, Ratko Mladić and Goran Hadžić, were apprehended in 2011 in Serbia and shortly thereafter the European Union facilitated further consideration of Serbia as a candidate for membership. Croatia became a Member State of the European Union on 1 July 2013, having co-operated with the International Criminal Tribunal for the former Yugoslavia years earlier by facilitating the capture or surrender of indicted fugitives on its territory.[15]

Until March 2014, the Security Council had remained consistent in its refusal to authorise UN peacekeepers or Council-authorised peace enforcement troops to assist any of the international or hybrid criminal tribunals in the arrest of indicted fugitives. This abdication of responsibility by the Council to use its considerable Chapter VII powers to assist in the enforcement of tribunal arrest warrants for two decades was consistently raised by prosecutors of the *ad hoc* tribunals in their periodic reports to the Council. Similarly, the Prosecutor of the International Criminal

---

14 See David Scheffer, *All the Missing Souls: A Personal History of the War Crimes Tribunals*, Princeton University Press, 2012, pp. 109–112.

15 Ibid., pp. 124–59.

Court, in periodic reports to the Security Council, futilely sought Council assistance to help arrest indicted fugitives in those situations that had been referred to the Court by the Security Council (Darfur (Sudan) and Libya). All such appeals regarding indicted fugitives of the International Criminal Court failed to ignite collective action by Council members, but they most likely influenced some of the unilateral actions of individual Council members to facilitate arrests, including initiatives of the United States even though it is a non-party State to the Rome Statute of the International Criminal Court.[16]

On 28 March 2014, having stressed the need for the Government of the Democratic Republic of the Congo to co-operate with the International Criminal Court, the Security Council took the significant step of authorising the United Nations Organisation Stabilisation Mission in the Democratic Republic of the Congo, acting under Chapter VII enforcement powers, to '[s]upport and work with the Government of the DRC to arrest and bring to justice those responsible for war crimes and crimes against humanity in the country, including through cooperation with States of the region and the ICC'.[17] This venture into the realm of arrest, not only for indicted fugitives of the International Criminal Court but also others 'responsible for war crimes and crimes against humanity in the country', may have finally broken through some of the long-held resistance on the part of the Security Council to vest such powers in its own agents on the ground, namely peacekeepers and national forces authorised to take enforcement actions. Still acting under Chapter VII authority, the Security Council further urged the Government of the Democratic Republic of the Congo 'to arrest and hold accountable those responsible for war crimes and crimes against humanity in the country, and *stresses the importance* to this end of both regional cooperation and cooperation with the ICC'.[18] The Security Council reiterated its new focus on arrest powers in two other central African atrocity areas in early 2014.[19]

16 See, e.g., the documentation provided at www.amicc.org/usicc/administration.
17 UN Doc. S/RES/2147 (2014), para. 4(d).
18 Ibid., para. 24 (emphasis in the original).
19 Security Council Resolution 2149 of 10 April 2014 authorised, again under Chapter VII enforcement authority, the newly-created United Nations Multidimensional Integrated Stabilisation Mission in the Central African Republic '[t]o support and work with the Transitional Authorities to arrest and bring to justice those responsible for war crimes and crimes against humanity in the country, including through cooperation with States of the region and the ICC'. Security Council Resolution 2164 of 25 June 2014 mandated

Given such recent precedents, the Council will be increasingly pressed in the future to duplicate such arrest authority in other UN peacekeeping and peace enforcement mandates, where atrocity crimes have been committed and particularly where the International Criminal Court has jurisdiction. There is an emerging pattern, at least with respect to central African situations, where the Security Council feels comfortable authorising UN peacekeeping forces to co-operate with national authorities on arrest functions relating to alleged war criminals and indicted fugitives of the International Criminal Court. The Council's authorisation still falls short of a truly proactive and even unilateral arrest function for UN troops, but what occurred in 2014 advanced international criminal justice priorities before the Security Council.

Nonetheless, the situations in the Democratic Republic of the Congo, the Central African Republic, and Mali are not the key battlegrounds of either the new Cold War or the African Union's primary concerns about the International Criminal Court centring on Libya, Sudan (Darfur), and Kenya. The Council's willingness to co-operate in the arrest of alleged war criminals in three particular countries may still prove to be the exception to the rule. Indeed, in Resolution 2148 on 3 April 2014, immediately following Resolution 2147, the Security Council declined even to mention the International Criminal Court or any arrest issues in connection with Darfur and the continuation of the African Union-United Nations Hybrid Operation in Darfur. Even though the Council had referred Darfur to the Court in 2005, the political sensitivities of enforcing arrest warrants against Sudanese leaders, particularly by a peacekeeping operation in which the African Union plays such a key role, proved reason enough to ignore the issue.[20]

the United Nations Multidimensional Integrated Stabilisation Mission in Mali, applying Chapter VII enforcement authority, to co-operate with the government on arrests, namely, 'to support, as feasible and appropriate, the efforts of the Malian authorities, without prejudice to their responsibilities, to bring to justice those responsible for serious abuses or violations of human rights or violations of international humanitarian law, in particular war crimes and crimes against humanity in Mali, taking into account the referral by the transitional authorities of Mali of the situation in their country since January 2012 to the International Criminal Court'.

20 An alternative to Security Council action on arrests is set forth in David Scheffer, 'Proposal for an International Criminal Court Arrest Procedures Protocol', (2014) 12 *Northwestern Journal of Human Rights* 229.

The historical record of reluctance of the Security Council to engage in arrest procedures for the war crimes tribunals it creates and, just as significantly, the Council's failure to provide meaningful support of any kind – financial or enforcement – for its own referrals of situations to the International Criminal Court, are stark reminders of the political limits that hamper Council engagement on international criminal justice matters. On the one hand, this can be explained as the simple reality of big power politics continuing to dominate Security Council deliberations. Where core national interests of any of the permanent five Member States are put at risk by Council action, no one should be surprised that those interests will dictate the vote of any permanent member. There is nothing inherently distinguishable about criminal justice that would override the political imperatives of a major power casting votes, including the veto, in the Security Council. Proposals to eliminate the veto power within the Council in those situations where atrocities are being addressed – so that the pathway for approval of military or even judicial interventions under Chapter VII authority can be accomplished far more easily – have not progressed and indeed have been met mostly with silence from several of the permanent five powers.

The Security Council's growing focus on the International Criminal Court

In contrast, an examination of Security Council resolutions approved from 2005 to mid-2015 reveals not only the well-recognised fact that in two such resolutions the Council referred situations to the International Criminal Court, but also that in at least twenty-nine other resolutions the Council positively noted and in some cases expressed support for the Court's work and objectives. Resolutions 1593 (2005) and Resolution 1970 (2011) are the explicit Council referrals of atrocity crimes situations in Darfur and Libya, respectively, enabled under article 13(b) of the Rome Statute of the International Criminal Court. Although by mid-2015 the Council had failed to refer any other situation, such as the Syrian atrocities that commenced in 2011[21] or the ongoing crimes against humanity

---

21 Somini Sengupta, 'China and Russia Block Referral of Syria to Court', *New York Times*, 23 May 2014, p. A3.

perpetrated by the North Korean regime,[22] there evolved during these years a steady drumbeat in Council resolutions of encouraging references to the International Criminal Court.

The Obama administration lifted the long-standing American objection to such references in Security Council resolutions. The United States, though a non-party State of the Rome Statute, became a leading proponent of using the Security Council to refer such situations as Libya and Syria to the International Criminal Court and to liberally acknowledge in Council resolutions both the Rome Statute and the Court's role in pursuing accountability for the commission of atrocity crimes.

For example, the Security Council recorded the following with respect to the International Criminal Court between 2008 and mid-2014: it noted the Rome Statute's provisions regarding sexual violence and discrimination against women and children and the commission of atrocity crimes against women and children[23] and further perpetration of atrocity crimes under the Rome Statute;[24] it noted the commitment of the Democratic Republic of the Congo to work with the International Criminal Court in holding perpetrators accountable and suggested and encouraged that UN monitoring in the country assist with this goal;[25] it acknowledged the Prosecutor's desire to launch an investigation into the situation in Côte D'Ivoire and that country's co-operation with the Court;[26] it recalled the Council's referral of the situation in Libya and called on the Libyan government to fully co-operate with and provide any necessary assistance to the Court and the Prosecutor;[27]

---

22 Report of the Commission of Inquiry on Human Rights in Democratic People's Republic of Korea, Human Rights Council, UN Doc. A/HRC/25/63.

23 UN Doc. S/RES/1820 (2008); UN Doc. S/RES/1880 (2009); UN Doc. S/RES/1960 (2010); UN Doc. S/RES/1998 (2011); UN Doc. S/RES/2068 (2012); UN Doc. S/RES/2106 (2013); UN Doc. S/RES/2122 (2013); and UN Doc. S/RES/2143 (2014).

24 UN Doc. S/RES/1894 (2009).

25 UN Doc. S/RES/1906 (2009); UN Doc. S/RES/1925 (2010); UN Doc. S/RES/1991 (2011); UN Doc. S/RES/2012 (2011); UN Doc. S/RES/2053 (2012); UN Doc. S/RES/2078 (2012); UN Doc. S/RES/2136 (2014); and UN Doc. S/RES/2147 (2014).

26 UN Doc. S/RES/2000 (2011); UN Doc. S/RES/2045 (2012); UN Doc. S/RES/2062 (2012); UN Doc. S/RES/2102 (2013); UN Doc. S/RES/2112 (2013); UN Doc. S/RES/2153 (2014); and UN Doc. S/RES/2162 (2014).

27 UN Doc. S/RES/2009 (2010); UN Doc. S/RES/2016 (2011); and UN Doc. S/RES/2144 (2014).

it noted that the destruction of property in Mali and commission of other atrocity crimes are violations of the Rome Statute and the transitional government's self-referral to the Court, encouraged entities assisting to stabilise Mali also to assist in using the Court to hold perpetrators accountable, and recalled the need for all parties concerned to co-operate with the Court following the opening on 16 January 2013 of the investigation into atrocity crimes in Mali, and under Chapter VII authority urged the Mali authorities to continue to co-operate with the Court;[28] it noted that serious human rights violations in the Central African Republic may be prosecuted under the Rome Statute and noted the Prosecutor's preliminary examination of certain acts committed since September 2012;[29] it noted that Burundi is a State Party to the Rome Statute and has obligations to fight actions that violate the Rome Statute;[30] it emphasised 'the responsibility of all States to put an end to impunity and to investigate and prosecute those responsible for genocide, crimes against humanity, war crimes and other egregious crimes perpetrated against children and highlight[ed] in this regard the contribution of the International Criminal Court, in accordance with the principle of complementarity to national criminal jurisdictions as set out in the Rome Statute'[31] and stressed 'that the fight against impunity and to ensure accountability for genocide, crimes against humanity, war crimes and other egregious crimes has been strengthened through the work on and prosecution of these crimes in the international criminal justice system, ad hoc and mixed tribunals as well as specialised chambers in national tribunals; and recognise[ed] in this regard the contribution of the International Criminal Court, in accordance with the principle of complementarity to national criminal jurisdictions as set out in the Rome Statute, towards holding accountable those responsible for such crimes, and reiterate[ed] its call on the importance of State cooperation with these courts and tribunals in accordance with the States' respective obligations'.[32]

---

28 UN Doc. S/RES/2056 (2012); UN Doc. S/RES/2071 (2012); UN Doc. S/RES/2095 (2013); and UN Doc. S/RES/2164 (2014).

29 UN Doc. S/RES/2112 (2013); UN Doc. S/RES/2127 (2013); UN Doc. S/RES/2134 (2014); and UN Doc. S/RES/2149 (2014).

30 UN Doc. S/RES/2137 (2014).

31 UN Doc. S/RES/2143 (2014).

32 UN Doc. S/RES/2150 (2014).

Presidential Statements, which must be approved unanimously by the Security Council, also provide evidence of at least the Council's rhetorical allegiance to international criminal justice objectives, as such Statements remain non-binding expressions of opinion by the Council as a collective body. Between 2007 and mid-2014, the Security Council approved at least twenty-six Presidential Statements in which the International Criminal Court was referenced favourably in connection with atrocity crimes situations erupting on the Council's agenda.[33] These included situations before the International Criminal Court, particularly Uganda and the need to arrest the indicted fugitives of the Lord's Resistance Army, the importance of the Court in the fight against crimes harming women and girls and in the struggle against crimes against civilians, the Court's work independently and through complementarity to seek justice for crimes against children, Mali's responsibility to co-operate with the International Criminal Court in prosecuting those responsible for particularly violent acts against children, the European Union's capacity to contribute to international justice through co-operation with the Court, and the importance of the international and hybrid tribunals and the International Criminal Court in the fight against impunity.

Crime of aggression

The relationship of the Security Council to the work of the International Criminal Court will become even more prominent when the crime of aggression is activated in the jurisdiction of the Court, which will occur when at least thirty States Parties of the Rome Statute ratify the 'Kampala Amendments' of 2010, and that date may arrive as early as 2017.[34] In addition to genocide,

---

33 UN Doc. S/PRST/2007/40; UN Doc. S/PRST/2008/21; UN Doc. S/PRST/2008/38; UN Doc. S/PRST/2008/48; UN Doc. S/PRST/2009/1; UN Doc. S/PRST/2009/11; UN Doc. S/PRST/2010/22; UN Doc. S/PRST/2010/25; UN Doc. S/PRST/2011/11; UN Doc. S/PRST/2011/20; UN Doc. S/PRST/2011/21; UN Doc. S/PRST/2012/1; UN Doc. S/PRST/2012/3; UN Doc. S/PRST/2012/18; UN Doc. S/PRST/2012/23; UN Doc. S/PRST/2012/28; UN Doc. S/PRST/2013/2; UN Doc. S/PRST/2013/6; UN Doc. S/PRST/2013/8; UN Doc. S/PRST/2013/12; UN Doc. S/PRST/2013/18; UN Doc. S/PRST/2014/2; UN Doc. S/PRST/2014/3; UN Doc. S/PRST/2014/4; UN Doc. S/PRST/2014/5; and UN Doc. S/PRST/2014/8.

34 Resolution RC/Res. 6. See also David Scheffer, 'States Parties Approve New Crimes for International Criminal Court', *ASIL Insight*, 14, 16.

crimes against humanity, and war crimes, the newly enforceable crime of aggression could be part of a situation referred to the International Criminal Court by the Security Council under Chapter VII authority. Because of major power politics, a referral designating aggression *per se* may be very difficult to accomplish within the Council. But once *any* atrocity crimes situation is referred to the Court, the crime of aggression potentially could be discovered as an alleged act within that situation and thus trigger investigation and prosecution by the Court provided all jurisdictional requirements set forth in articles 15 *bis* or 15 *ter* of the Rome Statute, whichever is relevant, are met.

Another provision adopted in the Kampala Amendments affirms the Security Council's power to suspend any International Criminal Court action on the crime of aggression provided the Council acts in accordance with article 16 of the Rome Statute. This provision reaffirms the Council's power to stop the Court's judicial intervention on the issue of aggression for at least one year provided nine affirmative votes and no vetoes by permanent members of the Council are cast. So the Security Council holds the potential of becoming a key player in the Court's actions with respect to the crime of aggression.

Interestingly, there is no similar provision that would provide the following: where a situation concerning aggression has been referred by either a State Party of the Rome Statute or an investigation initiated with judicial authority by the Prosecutor of the International Criminal Court, and the Council approves a resolution stating that no aggression has occurred in the same situation, then the Court may not investigate for the crime of aggression (even if a State Party or the Prosecutor had initiated the investigation). The Council still could act under article 16 of the Rome Statute to suspend an ongoing investigation of aggression by the Court, but that would be a very different political dynamic than a determination by the Council (probably shorn of any reference to legal accountability) that an act of aggression had not occurred in the first place.

There are thus encouraging signs (at least for some) that arise from the Security Council's recent history of referrals to the International Criminal Court, how it pays homage to the Court and accountability for the commission of atrocity crimes in recent years, the Council's resistance to African Union pressure to use article 16 of the Rome Statute to derail indictments and prosecutions in Libya, Sudan, and Kenya, the Council resolutions in 2014 authorising UN co-operation on arrests of indicted fugitives of the International Criminal Court and other alleged war criminals, and the prospect for Council engagement on the crime of aggression. However, the Security Council has fallen woefully short on two of the most pragmatic requirements of international criminal justice: sufficient funding to accomplish investigations and prosecutions and tough enforcement actions backing up explicit Chapter VII referrals to the International Criminal Court.

Security Council follow-through on referrals to the International Criminal Court

When the Security Council refers a situation to the International Criminal Court under the UN Charter's Chapter VII enforcement authority and in accordance with article 13(b) of the Rome Statute, there should be an expectation that the Council will follow through with tangible support for such referral in the same manner as the Council remains deeply engaged and supportive of peacekeeping and peace enforcement operations established by the Council. Such support should include financial contributions from the United Nations to the cost of the Court's investigation of the referred situation and prosecution of the cases arising therefrom, a prospect envisaged in the Rome Statute.[35] However, the Council's first two referrals, of Darfur in 2005 and Libya in 2011, explicitly precluded any UN financial support.[36] This places the entire financial burden on the Member States of the International Criminal Court to carry out a Security Council mandate that the permanent members of the Council, including the United States, Russia, and China, each of which is not party to the

---

35 Under article 115 of the Rome Statute, expenses of the Court shall be provided from two sources, one being assessed contributions made by States Parties and 'Funds provided by the United Nations, subject to the approval of the General Assembly, in particular in relation to the expenses incurred due to referrals by the Security Council.'

36 For example, operative paragraph 7 of Resolution 1953 reads: 'Recognises that none of the expenses incurred in connection with the referral including expenses related to investigations or prosecutions in connection with that referral, shall be borne by the United Nations and that such costs shall be borne by the parties to the Rome Statute and those States that wish to contribute voluntarily.' Similar language was repeated in the draft Security Council resolution seeking to refer the Syrian situation to the International Criminal Court in May 2014, but which was vetoed by Russia and China.

Rome Statute, have ordered be carried out. The methodology is deeply flawed whereby the Council refers a situation but prohibits the United Nations from contributing funds to cover the costs that the Court must incur to undertake the Council's mandate.

Logically, Council support also would include further enforcement resolutions *requesting* under Chapter VII authority that recalcitrant States (including ones not otherwise directly connected with the atrocities) co-operate with the International Criminal Court's requests for access to witnesses, for co-operation with other investigative tasks, and for execution of arrest warrants or to compel surrender of captured indictees to the Court. The Council can utilise many tools for this purpose, including holding special sessions to focus attention on the Court's needs when confronted with a government's obstructionism and adopting further Chapter VII resolutions that would inflict diplomatic or economic sanctions on non-cooperative States. It could even authorise limited military operations under Chapter VII to achieve successful arrests of certain indicted fugitives. But by mid-2015 no enforcement measures were approved with respect to the Council's referrals to the International Criminal Court.

The long game of international criminal justice requires that the Security Council remain seised of its own referral of a situation to the International Criminal Court and that it be prepared to take further enforcement actions to facilitate the Court's endeavours to achieve justice against indicted perpetrators of atrocity crimes, a goal presumably shared among Council members by virtue of the original referral. As discussed earlier, Security Council resolutions in 2014 relating to the Democratic Republic of the Congo, the Central African Republic, and Mali finally take steps in the right direction, as they authorise UN peacekeeping operations to co-operate with arrests of indicted fugitives of the International Criminal Court. But ironically these are not situations actually referred by the Security Council to the Court.

The Security Council's engagement with international criminal justice will intensify as atrocity crimes continue to define the armed conflicts and internal repression of the twenty-first century, despite all hopes to the contrary. There are no escape hatches through which Member States of the Security Council can somehow avoid the issue of accountability for the perpetrators of atrocity crimes. Acts of wilful avoidance of the issue in Council deliberations, including the use of the veto to deny referrals to the International Criminal Court, doubtless will continue, but they will not go unnoticed. After more than two decades of addressing issues of international criminal justice, the Council cannot turn back the clock. All eyes are on the Security Council as an instrument of international judicial intervention within the authority of the UN Charter.

FURTHER READING

Helena Cobban, *Amnesty after Atrocity? Healing Nations after Genocide and War Crimes,* Boulder: Paradigm Publishers, 2007.

Richard Dicker, 'The ICC at 10', (2013) 12 *Washington University Global Studies Law Review* 539.

Katherine Iliopoulos, 'The African Union and the ICC', *Crimes of War Project,* 10 July 2009.

David Kaye, 'The Council and the Court: Improving Security Council Support of the International Criminal Court', *International Justice Clinic, University of California Irvine School of Law,* 2013.

Terence McNamee, 'The ICC and Africa – Between Aspiration and Reality: Making International Justice Work Better for Africa', Discussion Paper 2/2014, Brenthurst Foundation, May 2014.

Matthias Neuner, 'The Security Council and the ICC: Assessing the First Ten Years of Coexistence', (2012) 18 *New England Journal of Comparative and International Law* 283.

William A. Schabas, *The UN International Criminal Tribunals: The Former Yugoslavia, Rwanda and Sierra Leone,* Cambridge University Press, 2006.

William A. Schabas, *An Introduction to the International Criminal Court,* 4th edn, Cambridge University Press, 2011.

David Scheffer, 'International Judicial Intervention', (1996) 102 *Foreign Policy* 34.

David Scheffer, 'The Complex Crime of Aggression under the Rome Statute', (2010) 23 *Leiden Journal of International Law* 215.

David Scheffer, *All the Missing Souls: A Personal History of the War Crimes Tribunals,* Princeton University Press, 2012.

Security Council Report, *The Rule of Law – The Institutional Framework: International Criminal Courts and Tribunals, Cross-Cutting Report,* 2015.

Part III   Crimes

Atrocity crimes (genocide, crimes against humanity and war crimes) 10

William A. Schabas

The expression 'atrocity crimes', apparently first proposed by David Scheffer,[1] and subsequently adopted by the Special Advisers to the United Nations Secretary-General on the Prevention of Genocide and on the Responsibility to Protect,[2] has emerged in recent years as shorthand for the offences that comprise the common denominator of the subject matter jurisdiction of the modern international criminal tribunals: genocide, crimes against humanity, and war crimes. Since the modern generation of international criminal courts and tribunals began activity in the mid 1990s, essentially all of the prosecutions have been for genocide, crimes against humanity, and war crimes. Exceptionally, the prosecutions at the Special Tribunal for Lebanon are for terrorist crimes under Lebanese law. The Special Court for Sierra Leone was able to exercise jurisdiction over some serious offences in the criminal law of Sierra Leone but the Prosecutor never sought indictments under the relevant provisions. And, soon, the International Criminal Court will be able to deal with the crime of aggression, a subject discussed in the chapter in this book by Benjamin and Donald Ferencz. All of the tribunals also have jurisdiction over offences related to their own operations, in particular perjury and contempt of court.

The Oxford English Dictionary defines 'atrocity' as '[a]n atrocious deed; an act of extreme cruelty or heinousness', offering Thomas Jefferson as the historical example of its first use: 'To defend themselves from the atrocities of a vastly more numerous and powerful people.' Jefferson was justifying the young American government's provision of weapons to

---

1 David Scheffer, 'Genocide and Atrocity Crimes', (2006) 1 *Genocide Studies and Prevention* 229.
2 United Nations Office on Genocide Prevention and the Responsibility to Protect, *Framework of Analysis for Atrocity Crimes, A Tool for Prevention*, New York: United Nations, 2014.

aboriginal peoples in Florida in order to protect themselves from Spanish colonialists.[3] The association with this early manifestation of 'humanitarian intervention' is intriguing because 'atrocity crimes' are the unifying principle of the modern doctrine of the responsibility to protect, defined by the United Nations General Assembly in 2005.

In international law, the tripartite classification of genocide, crimes against humanity, and war crimes can be traced to the First World War. On 24 May 1915, the United Kingdom, France, and Russia informed the Ottoman rulers of reports of 'these new crimes of Turkey against humanity and civilisation'. This was the first use of the term 'crime against humanity' in an official context although it had been employed by writers since the middle of the eighteenth century. The Treaty of Sèvres between the victors and Turkey, adopted at the Paris Peace Conference, provided for prosecution of 'massacres' but did not repeat the term 'crime against humanity'. Together with the Treaty of Versailles and some of the other post-war treaties, it also contemplated trials of enemy combatants for 'acts in violation of the laws and customs of war'. The Commission on Responsibilities that met during the Paris Peace Conference endorsed a list of these war crimes that included murders and massacres, systematic terrorism, putting hostages to death, torture of civilians, deliberate starvation of civilians, rape, abduction of girls and women for the purpose of enforced prostitution, deportation of civilians, and internment of civilians under inhuman conditions. These crimes all have their modern-day equivalents in international criminal law.

A more precise codification resulted from the post–Second World War prosecutions. In 1943, the Allied powers set up the United Nations War Crimes Commission, a body whose title suggested its work would be limited to 'violations of the laws and customs of war'. Almost immediately, delegates began to insist that the Commission also address atrocities perpetrated by enemy governments against their own civilian populations. There was no unanimity about this, however. At the London Conference, in mid-1945, where preparations were made for the Nuremberg trial of the International Military Tribunal, agreement was reached to include

---

3 *State Papers and Publick Documents of the United States, from the Accession of George Washington to the Presidency, Exhibiting a Complete View of Our Foreign Relations since that Time, including Confidential Documents*, vol. 16, Washington: Department of State, 1819, p. 183.

atrocities directed against a State's own civilians on the condition that such acts be associated with aggressive war. In so doing, the major powers that established the Tribunal, France, the Soviet Union, the United States, and the United Kingdom, could be relatively certain that atrocities for which they were responsible against civilians and ethnic minorities within their own territories would not be covered by the definition. The penultimate draft of the Charter of the International Military Tribunal contained the following:

> Atrocities against civilian populations other than those referred to in paragraph *(b)* ['violations of the laws, rules or customs of war']. These include but are not limited to murder and ill-treatment of civilians and deportations of civilians to slave labour or persecution on political, racial or religious grounds committed in any country, at any time, in pursuance of the common plan or conspiracy referred to in paragraph *(a)* above ['Initiation of a war of aggression'].[4]

Acting on the suggestion of Hersch Lauterpacht, the Conference agreed to rebrand this new category as 'crimes against humanity'.

The final judgment of the Nuremberg Tribunal issued in late-1946 confirmed that crimes against humanity could only be committed in association with aggressive war. Although referring to Nazi atrocities perpetrated during the 1930s, such as the Nuremberg laws and the infamous pogrom known as the *Kristallnacht*, the judges declined to convict for anything that occurred prior to the outbreak of the war in September 1939. Within weeks of the judgment, delegates to the first session of the United Nations General Assembly had proposed a resolution declaring that genocide was a crime under international law. Speaking to the Sixth Committee in support of the draft, Ernesto Dihigo of Cuba explained that the Nuremberg judgment had failed to address certain crimes committed prior to the war. For that reason, it was necessary to declare genocide, even committed in peacetime, to be an international crime.[5] Resolution 96(I), entitled 'The Crime of Genocide', was adopted unanimously on 11 December 1946. On a proposal by Saudi Arabia, a paragraph was added to

4 'Revised Definition of "Crimes", Submitted by American Delegation, July 30, 1945', in Robert H. Jackson, *Report of Robert H. Jackson, United States Representative to the International Conference on Military Trials, London, 1945*, Washington: Department of State, 1949, p. 394.

5 UN Doc. A/C.6/SR.22.

the Resolution mandating the preparation of a treaty. Two years later, on 9 December 1948, the Assembly agreed upon the text of the Convention on the Prevention and Punishment of the Crime of Genocide.

With the adoption of the Genocide Convention, international law comprised two distinct categories of international crime, genocide and crimes against humanity, both of them devised to cover much the same phenomenon. In a sense, they were competing concepts. On the one hand, genocide was defined in a Convention that provided for specific obligations with respect to prosecution and international co-operation. It was narrow in scope, confined to attacks on civilian populations defined by race or ethnicity and directed at their destruction. Unlike crimes against humanity, genocide applied in time of peace as well as in wartime. Crimes against humanity was much broader in two ways: victims could belong to 'any civilian population', including groups identified by politics, social class or gender, and it covered acts of persecution falling short of intentional destruction. But there was no treaty with respect to crimes against humanity. Thus, atrocities falling short of those intended to destroy a national, ethnic, racial, or religious group, if committed in peacetime, seemed to escape entirely the coverage of international criminal law.

By the end of the 1940s, war crimes in the strict sense were more fully formed. The scope of 'the laws and customs of war', initially developed in 1919, was made more extensive in the rich case law of the post–Second World War prosecutions. In 1949, the four Geneva Conventions offered a codification of the most serious war crimes, labelling them 'grave breaches'. The victims of grave breaches were, by definition, civilians, or soldiers who were *hors de combat*, essentially prisoners of war or seriously wounded combatants. But like the crimes against humanity/genocide category, war crimes also had a huge gap. They were generally deemed to apply only to international armed conflict and not to civil wars.

Over the next four decades, there was little in the way of further development of these categories of 'atrocity crimes'. With notable exceptions like the *Eichmann* case in Israel, there were almost no trials, and therefore few opportunities for judicial development. The expert body subordinate to the United Nations General Assembly, the International Law Commission, stopped its work of codification of 'offences against the peace and security of mankind' in 1954. Its attention to this project did not resume until the early 1980s. A final draft of the Code of Crimes was adopted in 1996. But by then, actual tribunals were already in operation.

Henceforth, they took the initiative in the further definition of international crimes. Beyond any doubt, the seminal event was the first ruling of the Appeals Chamber of the International Criminal Tribunal for the former Yugoslavia of 2 October 1995. In that decision, the majority confirmed that the concept of 'violations of the laws or customs of war' set out in article 3 of the Tribunal's Statute was broad enough to encompass war crimes perpetrated in non-international armed conflict. Furthermore, the Chamber declared that the nexus between crimes against humanity and armed conflict that had been proclaimed in the judgment of the International Military Tribunal was no longer applicable. Thereby, crimes against humanity, like genocide, could also be committed in peacetime.[6] Radical as they may have seemed at the time, these important holdings by the Appeals Chamber rapidly met with consensus among States. They were confirmed three years later in the definitions of crimes included in the Rome Statute of the International Criminal Court.

Crimes against humanity

When the subject matter jurisdiction of the International Criminal Court was being debated, the three broad categories of atrocity crime, namely genocide, crimes against humanity, and war crimes, were often referred to as 'core crimes' so as to distinguish them from other offences governed by international law such as piracy, trafficking in drugs and human beings, and terrorism. But if there is a 'core' of the 'core crimes' it is undoubtedly crimes against humanity. The vast majority of the indictments issued by the modern international criminal tribunals have contained charges of crimes against humanity. Most of those now serving sentences after being found guilty by the international tribunals are doing so for crimes against humanity although they may, in a minority of cases, also stand convicted of genocide or war crimes. To a large extent, crimes against humanity may be thought of as the international criminal law dimension of international human rights norms and standards. In the human rights context, 'gross and systematic violations' would be the terminology. The link between human rights law and crimes against humanity is discussed at some length in the chapter in this book by Andrew Clapham.

6 *Prosecutor* v. *Tadić* (IT-94-1-AR72), Decision on the Defence Motion for Interlocutory Appeal on Jurisdiction, 2 October 1995.

Crimes against humanity fall within the subject matter jurisdiction of all of the international criminal tribunals with the exception of the Special Tribunal for Lebanon. When the Lebanon Statute was being drafted, suggestions that terrorist bombing be prosecuted under the rubric of crimes against humanity were ultimately rejected.[7] The authoritative definition of crimes against humanity is found in article 7 of the Rome Statute of the International Criminal Court. However, each of the statutes of the other international criminal tribunals sets out a somewhat differently formulated provision for crimes against humanity. The judges of the International Criminal Tribunal for the former Yugoslavia have considered the text of article 7 of the Rome Statute to be too narrow and, consequently, inconsistent with the concept of crimes against humanity under customary international law. They have rejected it as a basis for their own interpretation of the more laconic definition of crimes against humanity in the Yugoslavia Tribunal's Statute. In particular, they dispute the requirement in article 7(2) of the Rome Statute that crimes against humanity result from an attack on a civilian population that takes place pursuant to a State or organisational policy. Individuals have been convicted by the Yugoslavia Tribunal for heinous acts, even if they were acting in relative isolation and not in pursuit of a generalised policy.[8]

Article 7(1) of the Rome Statute sets out the contextual element of crimes against humanity: 'For the purpose of this Statute, "crime against humanity" means any of the following acts when committed as part of a widespread or systematic attack directed against any civilian population, with knowledge of the attack.' It is followed by an enumeration of punishable acts: murder, extermination, enslavement, deportation or forcible transfer of population, imprisonment, torture, rape and other crimes of sexual violence, persecution, enforced disappearance, *apartheid*, and 'other inhumane acts'. The list is considerably expanded from the first codification, in the Charter of the International Military Tribunal, or the versions in the statutes of the *ad hoc* tribunals for the former Yugoslavia and Rwanda. To some extent, this is attributable to the progressive development of

---

7 Statement by Mr. Nicolas Michel, Under-Secretary-General for Legal Affairs, the Legal Counsel, at the informal consultations held by the Security Council on 20 November 2006, UN Doc. S/2006/893/Add.1.

8 *Prosecutor* v. *Kunarac* et al. (IT-96-23/1-A), Judgment, 12 June 2002, para. 98.

international human rights law. Yet in one important respect the definition in the Rome Statute may be narrower than its predecessors because the punishable act of persecution is restricted to attacks directed against 'any identifiable group or collectivity' on political, racial, national, ethnic, cultural, religious, or gender grounds, or on other grounds 'universally recognised as impermissible under international law, in connection with any act referred to in this paragraph or any crime within the jurisdiction of the Court'. It is probably reasonable to consider disability to be such a ground, but the contention that this extends to sexual orientation would be more difficult to establish, at least at the present day. The residual clause of 'other inhumane acts' is also limited by the phrase 'of a similar character intentionally causing great suffering, or serious injury to body or to mental or physical health'.

Genocide

Genocide has been described as 'the crime of crimes'. Although there is no formal suggestion of any hierarchy based upon the seriousness of the atrocity crimes in the statutes of the *ad hoc* tribunals, their practice in terms of sentencing permits a general conclusion that genocide is graver than crimes against humanity, and that the two are more serious than war crimes. When guilty pleas are negotiated, they may involve an admission of crimes against humanity in exchange for withdrawal of a genocide charge but nobody has ever offered to plead guilty to a charge of genocide if those of crimes against humanity are dropped. The Rome Statute actually provides some small indications of hierarchy: the defences of superior orders and of defence of property are permitted for war crimes but not crimes against humanity or genocide; genocide may be committed by 'direct and public incitement', even if there is no actual result, but this inchoate form of the offence does not exist for war crimes or crimes against humanity.

The word 'genocide' first appeared in late 1944 in *Axis Rule in Occupied Europe*, a study of Nazi policy authored by Raphael Lemkin. He envisaged a concept of genocide that was in many respects much closer to crimes against humanity than the definition that eventually appeared in the 1948 Convention on the Prevention and Punishment of the Crime of Genocide. The term genocide was already in common parlance during the Nuremberg trial. It appears in the record of the proceedings in several places although not in the judgment. There has never been much doubt about use of the term to describe the Nazi atrocities. However, in recent years some States have claimed the word cannot be used 'retroactively', so as to apply to events prior to adoption of the Convention in 1948. This seems driven by cynical concerns that references to the Armenian genocide of 1915 might anger the Turkish government rather than any principled understanding of the use of the term. The relevant texts could not be clearer. The 1946 General Assembly resolution, adopted unanimously, states that '[m]any instances of such crimes of genocide have occurred when racial, religious, political and other groups have been destroyed, entirely or in part', and the 1948 Convention '[r]ecogni[ses] that at all periods of history genocide has inflicted great losses on humanity'.

In contrast with the fluctuating and somewhat uncertain definitions of crimes against humanity, the definition of genocide under international law has not changed since the adoption of the Convention in 1948. The text in the statutes of the *ad hoc* tribunals and in article 6 of the Rome Statute is essentially identical to that of article 2 of the Genocide Convention. There has been unrelenting criticism of the narrowness of the definition of genocide. Nevertheless, when international lawmakers have convened, as they did in the Security Council in the early 1990s or at the Rome Conference in 1998, they have rejected attempts to enlarge the scope of the crime of genocide. This is not because of any systematic resistance to progressive developments of the law. At the very time they retained the 1948 text they also adopted definitions of crimes against humanity and war crimes that were bold and innovative. The oft-lamented shortcomings of the 1948 definition of genocide were rectified not by amendments to the text but rather by changes to the concept of crimes against humanity.

Like crimes against humanity, the definition of genocide begins with an introductory paragraph or *chapeau*: 'any of the following acts committed with intent to destroy, in whole or in part, a national, ethnical, racial or religious group, as such'. This is followed by a list of five punishable acts: killing members of the group; causing serious bodily or mental harm to members of the group; deliberately inflicting on the group conditions of life calculated to bring about its physical destruction in whole or in part; imposing measures intended to prevent births within the group; forcibly transferring children of the group to another group. Almost all of the convictions for the crime of genocide by the *ad hoc* tribunals have involved the first punishable act. Indeed, international tribunals have never applied the definition of genocide to atrocities that did not involve mass murder.

The word 'destroy' has been interpreted by the *ad hoc* tribunals as requiring physical destruction of the group. This narrow understanding of genocide has been confirmed in two judgments of the International Court of Justice.[9] That the definition should be so limited is not apparent from the text itself, notably because of the inclusion of one of the punishable acts that clearly does not require evidence of physical destruction, forcibly transferring children from one group to another. The courts have reached the conclusion whereby forms of destruction that are 'cultural' rather than physical are excluded based upon reference to the *travaux préparatoires* of the Convention. Indeed, very clear and deliberate decisions were taken by the drafters to remove references in the draft Convention to cultural genocide. Subsequently, the punishable act of forcible transfer was added as an exception to this general principle.

Whereas crimes against humanity may be perpetrated against 'any civilian population' – words included in the Nuremberg definition in order to make it clear that the concept applied to acts by Germany against its own nationals – genocide as defined in the Convention only protects a national, ethnic, racial, or religious group. The 1946 General Assembly resolution also included political groups but these were removed in the Convention. Several national legislatures have added various categories of group, including political groups, when they enact domestic statutes governing the crime of genocide.

The word 'genocide' has a rhetorical power that is unmatched by the other atrocity crimes. Victims of atrocity often insist that their persecutors be labelled *génocidaires*, even if the terms of the international legal definition do not clearly apply. They are not consoled by explanations that crimes against humanity is the more accurate categorisation. This may be explained by the very robust nature of the 1948 Genocide Convention over several decades when crimes against humanity had little

---

9 Application of the Convention on the Prevention and Punishment of the Crime of Genocide *(Bosnia and Herzegovina* v. *Serbia and Montenegro)*, Judgment, I.C.J. Reports 2007, p. 43; Application of the Convention on the Prevention and Punishment of the Crime of Genocide *(Croatia* v. *Serbia)*, 2 February 2015.

or no legal purchase, given the limitations placed upon it at Nuremberg and the absence of a proper treaty. But this is no longer the case since the dramatic expansion of the notion of crimes against humanity in recent years. At the modern international criminal tribunals, there is little or no distinction between a conviction for genocide and one for crimes against humanity. Moreover, the evolving doctrine of the 'responsibility to protect' applies to both genocide and crimes against humanity, as well as to war crimes and ethnic cleansing. Yet, even if genocide no longer has much legal significance over and above crimes against humanity, the nomenclature remains potent, cherished by victims while at the same time abhorred by perpetrators.

War crimes

The term 'war crimes' is understood in a colloquial sense to cover all of the categories of atrocity crime. Journalists will often refer to the 'war crimes tribunals' when they are discussing institutions that also deal with genocide and crimes against humanity. Precisely because it is well-understood, use of the term in this generic sense rather than in a more technical and legally accurate manner is often useful. Nevertheless, specialists appreciate the important distinctions between war crimes and the other two categories of atrocity crime.

War crimes are the oldest category of atrocity crime. Evidence of the 'laws and customs of war' can be found in the writings of all ancient civilisations. Moreover, violations of some of these laws and customs were viewed as criminal conduct, deserving of punishment. When Achilles drags Hector's body around the walls of Troy in Homer's *Iliad*, we know that he has broken the warrior's code and that some sanction awaits. Ultimately, Achilles is punished for his acts, not by an international criminal tribunal but by divine justice.

Rather than repeat the lengthy enumeration of war crimes inherited from the 1919 Commission on Responsibilities, or add to it, the Charter of the International Military Tribunal opted for a more succinct approach. It defined war crimes as 'violations of the laws or customs of war' that included, but that were not limited to, 'murder, ill-treatment or deportation to slave labour or for any other purpose of civilian population of or in occupied territory, murder or ill-treatment of prisoners of war or persons on the seas, killing of hostages, plunder of public or private property, wanton destruction of cities, towns or villages, or devastation not justified by military necessity'. Judges were left to fill in the gaps.

Article 8 of the Rome Statute provides a dramatic contrast, using 1,595 words (another fifty-one result from the amendments adopted at Kampala in 2010) to accomplish what the Nuremberg Charter did in seventy-five words. In one sense, this might be understood as a consequence of the expansion of war crimes to cover acts perpetrated in non-international armed conflict as well as in armed conflict. However, that is something that could have been easily attained with a few words. Indeed, the definition of 'violations of the laws or customs of war' in the Statute of the International Criminal Tribunal for the former Yugoslavia (itself only 111 words in length) had already been interpreted by the Appeals Chamber as covering crimes committed in non-international as well as in international armed conflict, without any explicit mention, when the Rome Statute was adopted.

Ironically, then, and despite its extraordinary length, the definition of war crimes in the Rome Statute is actually narrower in scope than its predecessors. It seems a paradox that the longer the provision, the less it actually covers. The main difference between the texts of the temporary tribunals and the Rome Statute is the absence of any residual authority left to the judges in order to address any lacunae. Article 8 does not include a phrase like the words 'included, but not limited to' that is found in article 6 of the Nuremberg Charter and article 3 of the Statute of the International Criminal Tribunal for the former Yugoslavia.

Nowhere are the shortcomings of the Rome Statute more apparent than in the provisions of article 8 dealing with prohibited weapons. Three paragraphs provide carefully worded descriptions of weapons that were prohibited historically but that in the main are rarely encountered today, such as hollow-tipped bullets and poisoned spears. The instruments of modern warfare that pose the greatest challenges, such as anti-personnel mines, cluster munitions, and blinding laser weapons, are nowhere to be found. Instead, there is a more generic provision: 'Employing weapons, projectiles and material and methods of warfare which are of a nature to cause superfluous injury or unnecessary suffering or which are inherently indiscriminate in violation of the international law of armed conflict'. The text goes on to require that these be 'the subject of a comprehensive prohibition and are included in an annex to this Statute, by an amendment in accordance with the relevant provisions set forth in articles 121 and 123'. The 1998 version of the Rome Statute contains no such annex. Moreover, when States Parties assembled at the Kampala Review Conference twelve years after adoption of the Rome Statute in order to tidy up the loose ends, an amendment with the annex envisaged by this provision was not even on the agenda. There is only one explanation: obstruction by the nuclear powers. They are concerned about the irresistible interpretation of the words 'of a nature to cause superfluous injury or unnecessary suffering or which are inherently indiscriminate'.

Article 8 of the Rome Statute makes clear what is only implied in the Statute of the International Criminal Tribunal for the former Yugoslavia: war crimes may be perpetrated in non-international armed conflict as well as in international armed conflict. A binary distinction is made within article 8, with two categories setting out the war crimes in international armed conflict and another two listing the war crimes in non-international armed conflict. Many of the punishable acts are the same, regardless of the nature of the conflict. Much judicial energy has been spent at the Court in establishing the nature of the conflict. In practice, this is of little real significance because the punishable act is identical or virtually identical in both categories. There are a few important differences, essentially because of the differences in the nature of the two types of conflict. For example, the war crime of transferring civilians into an occupied territory only really makes sense in the case of an international armed conflict.

Concluding remarks

The definitions of atrocity crimes in articles 6, 7, and 8 of the Rome Statute are the result of a consensus of the 160 States that participated in the 1998 Diplomatic Conference. In their explanations of vote at the conclusion of the Conference, only a very few delegations indicated differences of opinion with respect to the definitions of crimes. China said that the definitions of war crimes and crimes against humanity 'exceeded commonly understood and accepted customary law', adding that it opposed including non-international armed conflicts in the jurisdiction of the Court and the reference to crimes against humanity. Israel explained that had the war crime of transferring citizens to an occupied territory not been included, it would have been able to vote in favour of the Statute. Turkey said that the provisions on war crimes were not satisfactory, insisting that the Court 'should have nothing to do with internal troubles, including measures designed to maintain national security or root out terrorism'. There were also some complaints about the limited scope of some of the provisions. India protested the failure to prohibit nuclear weapons. Singapore objected to the exclusion of chemical and biological weapons. The Philippines said, without providing any further detail, that '[s]ome new definitions of war crimes constituted a retrograde step in the development of international law'.[10]

Article 10 of the Rome Statute declares that '[n]othing in this Part shall be interpreted as limiting or prejudicing in any way existing or developing rules of international law for purposes other than this Statute'. It was inserted on the initiative of the International Committee of the Red Cross. There can be no doubt that some existing international atrocity crimes are not comprised in the Rome Statute. In the case of war crimes, this is easily demonstrated, particularly with reference to the prohibited weapons provisions. Turning to genocide and crimes against humanity, the situation is more complex. Judges at the *ad hoc* tribunals have contested whether the 'State or organisational policy' requirement for crimes against humanity is actually part of customary international law, thereby broadening considerably the scope of the offence compared to its formulation in the Rome Statute.

In a similar vein, judges at the *ad hoc* tribunals have challenged a provision of the Elements of Crimes that apply to the Rome Statute whereby genocidal acts must have taken place 'in the context of a manifest pattern of similar conduct directed against that group or was conduct that could itself effect such destruction'.[11] The controversial provision in the Elements of Crimes was added in reaction to an expansive reading of the definition of genocide adopted in one of the earliest rulings on genocide by the Yugoslavia Tribunal. While the Elements of Crimes were being drafted, a Trial Chamber had concluded that there was insufficient evidence of a genocidal plan but said that the accused might have been acting alone, 'beyond the scope of the powers entrusted to him'. It said it

10 UN Doc. A/CONF.183/SR.9, paras. 11–52.
11 See, for example, *Prosecutor* v. *Popović* et al. (IT-05-88-A), Judgment, 30 January 2015, para. 436.

was 'theoretically possible' that the accused 'harboured the plan to exterminate an entire group without this intent having been supported by any organisation in which other individuals participated' and, thereby, perpetrated genocide.[12] The Elements of Crimes rule out the quite contrived and preposterous theory that international justice deal with this Lee Harvey Oswald of genocide, a mad, obsessed lunatic who is acting alone.

The 'manifest pattern' requirement of the Elements of Crimes represents a consensus of a huge number of States. It indicates the interpretation that they favour of article 6 of the Rome Statute and, by ricochet, of article 2 of the 1948 Genocide Convention. At odds with this interpretation is the one taken by several judges of the International Criminal Tribunal for the former Yugoslavia. The latter insist that their views are more consistent with customary international law. But perhaps the position taken by the former, in the Elements of Crimes, is more authoritative, given its broadly based expression of the *opinio juris* of States. At some point, this issue will arise in national prosecutions for genocide. There, domestic judges applying a text inspired by article 2 of the Genocide Convention, may have to decide which of the two positions to adopt.

Aside from what amounted to housekeeping with regard to the war crimes provision, filling a small hole left at Rome, the Kampala Review Conference did not consider any amendments to articles 6, 7, and 8 of the Statute. A few campaigners worked without success on the addition of terrorism and drug trafficking to the subject matter jurisdiction of the International Criminal Court. But in any event, although these are international crimes, they are not atrocity crimes. It would seem that the package of atrocity crimes adopted in 1998 will stand the test of time. It is unlikely to be modified or amended. Of course, that observation does nothing to detract from the ongoing controversies about the interpretation of these complex and sometimes quite enigmatic texts.

FURTHER READING

M. Cherif Bassiouni, *Crimes Against Humanity*, Cambridge University Press, 2011.
Gideon Boas, James L. Bischoff, and Natalie L. Reid, *Elements of Crimes Under International Law*, Cambridge University Press, 2009.

---

12 *Prosecutor* v. *Jelisić* (IT-95-10-T), Judgment, 14 December 1999, para. 100.

Knut Dörmann, *Elements of War Crimes Under the Rome Statute of the International Criminal Court, Sources and Commentary*, Cambridge University Press, 2002.

Paola Gaeta, ed., *The UN Genocide Convention, A Commentary*, Oxford University Press, 2009.

Ralph Henham and Paul Behrens, eds., *The Criminal Law of Genocide*, Aldershot: Ashgate, 2007.

Guénaël Mettraux, *International Crimes and the Ad Hoc Tribunals*, Oxford University Press, 2005.

Leila Nadya Sadat, ed., *Forging a Convention for Crimes Against Humanity*, Cambridge University Press, 2011.

William A. Schabas, *Genocide in International Law*, 2nd edn, Cambridge University Press, 2009.

Christian J. Tams, Lars Berster, and Björn Schiffbauer, *Convention on the Prevention and Punishment of the Crime of Genocide*, Munich: Beck, 2014.

11 Treaty crimes

Roger S. Clark

When the Rome Statute of the International Criminal Court was being negotiated, there was much discussion about whether 'treaty crimes' should be included within the jurisdiction of the Court along with the 'core crimes' of genocide, crimes against humanity, war crimes, and the crime of aggression. Ultimately, only the 'core crimes' were included. In the context of that debate, 'treaty crimes' referred to serious drug crimes as contained in United Nations treaties on the subject, and the set of 'terrorism' offences contained in a number of multilateral treaties entered into from the 1970s onwards, beginning with hijacking and other offences against aircraft. The dozen or so terrorism treaties in question were negotiated under the auspices of the United Nations and its specialised agencies, notably the International Civil Aviation Organisation and the International Maritime Organisation. These terror crimes include assaults on internationally protected persons, the taking of hostages, unlawful dealings in nuclear materials, violence at airports serving international aviation, acts against the safety of maritime navigation and on fixed platforms on the continental shelf, attacks on United Nations and associated personnel, terrorist bombings, the financing of terrorism, and nuclear terrorism. Such crimes may yet find their way into the jurisdiction of the Court, since it was understood in Rome in 1998 that their inclusion would be considered 'later'. The process for their possible inclusion is proceeding at a glacial pace and 'later' is nowhere near in sight.

I suggest in this chapter that the category of treaty crimes is in fact much broader than those that were on the table in Rome. It encompasses a multitude of infractions from the exotic to the mundane that have been regulated in bilateral and multilateral treaty practice over the last two hundred years. It is common these days to describe this area as 'transnational criminal law', as opposed to 'international criminal law' or 'international criminal law *stricto sensu*', the latter terms being commonly used to describe the Rome Statute crimes. The treaties that are the subject of this chapter are often labelled 'suppression conventions', a descriptor which emphasises their core feature. That core is a promise by the parties to make something criminal under their domestic law, to 'suppress' it. The parties also agree to institute a national/international regime of varying degrees of complexity to try to prevent or, if prevention fails, punish at the State level (rather than in an international tribunal) those who engage in the proscribed activity. Given the so far unsuccessful efforts to include some of these offences within the jurisdiction of the International Criminal Court, it seems fair to conclude that, at this stage of this development of international criminal law, there is a rather large class of crimes that are subject to domestic suppression regimes under widely ratified treaties. As yet there is no consensus that any or all of this class of crimes is suitable for inclusion within the jurisdiction of international tribunals. This is not to suggest that the omission is immutable. There is no obvious characteristic that renders them singularly inappropriate for international adjudication, or suggests that the categories are mutually exclusive. Indeed, two of the four crimes within the jurisdiction of the International Criminal Court, namely genocide and war crimes (at least so-called 'grave breaches' of the Geneva Conventions), are also 'treaty crimes' in that they have their own suppression regimes, while the other two, crimes against humanity and aggression, do not. Sometimes international drafting partakes of the random. As confidence grows in the Court, some of the other treaty crimes may well come within its jurisdiction, by amendment to the Statute.

Without going into excruciating detail on all of the treaties, I plan to discuss a representative sample of them to note the rich subject-matter involved and to suggest some recurring issues that are dealt with in them. References to the ones I discuss appear at the end of the chapter and I urge you to read some or all of them, to look for the recurring themes and to appreciate just how deeply these themes are embedded in international treaty practice. Not surprisingly, the manner in which such issues are addressed has become more sophisticated with the passage of time, but the essence resonates over two centuries of experience.

As for subject-matter, in the pages that follow, you will encounter, especially: piracy and the slave trade, damage to and stealing of submarine cables, counterfeited currency, torture, aircraft hijacking and other acts of terrorism, narcotic drugs and psychotropic substances, and transnational organised crime. In a few cases, such as torture, piracy, and the counterfeiting of currency, there was already a customary law proscription of at least some aspects of the activity in question. In such instances, the role of the suppression convention was to clarify (and possibly expand upon) the existing obligation while creating a 'suppression regime'. But in most cases in my sample, the proscription was a new one. States in Europe, the Americas and Africa did not regard the slave trade as immoral, let alone illegal, until the United Kingdom began systematically getting them to agree, either in bilateral or in multilateral negotiations, to ban the trade. The invention of the telegraph and the massive network of undersea cables that it spawned was a new problem for the law because of the possibilities this created for incompetent sailors and for thieves hunting the high seas for scrap metal treasure. Likewise, the invention of the airplane created new scope for terrorist activities and led to new conceptualisations. Globalism created new scope for human trafficking, corruption, arms trafficking, drug trafficking, and transnational crime in general. New opportunities for crime led to new efforts at its suppression.

Some representative treaty crimes

The flavour of the treaty proscriptions is best captured by quoting a few representative examples. The first 'treaty crime' that I have located is contained in article 20 of the 1794 treaty between Great Britain and the United States, known for its American negotiator as the 'Jay Treaty'. It provides that 'the Contracting Parties shall not only refuse to receive any Pirates into any of their Ports, Havens or Towns, or permit any of the Inhabitants to receive, protect, harbour, conceal or assist them in any manner, but will bring to condign punishment all such Inhabitants as shall be guilty of such acts or offences'. Piracy on the high seas was forbidden by customary international law (or 'the law of nations' as it was then known). Of necessity, all States were said to have jurisdiction over piracy on the high seas. What the treaty added was a reference to the ancillary crimes that go along with piracy, the financing of the business, the provision of supplies, the shelter of pirates on land, the fencing of stolen property, the repair of damaged vessels, and no doubt a little governmental corruption in the ports. As it turned out, all of these activities, while not amounting to piracy under international law, were already criminalised in the domestic law of both countries, but the treaty no doubt was aimed at encouraging implementation of those laws. More typical perhaps of a suppression convention is where the treaty itself creates an obligation to criminalise something not previously forbidden on the part of at least one of the treaty partners. Take this provision, Article II of a treaty entered into in 1842 between Great Britain and the Chief of Nyanibantang (West Africa), long after Britain herself had withdrawn from the slave trade:

> No persons of any colour, or wherever born, shall be taken out of the Nyanibantang country as slaves; and no person in the Nyanibantang country shall be in any way concerned in seizing, keeping, carrying, or sending away any persons for the purposes of their being taken out of the Nyanibantang country as slaves; and the Chief of Nyanibantang shall punish severely those who break this law.

Article XI of the treaty complements this basic suppression obligation as follows:

> The Chief of Nyanibantang shall, within 48 hours of the date of this agreement, make a law for carrying the whole of it into effect and shall proclaim that law, and the Chief of Nyanibantang shall put that law in force from that time for ever.

Ah, the advantages of speedy implementation when dealing with an absolute monarch – forty-eight hours for the legislative process to be effective! Levity aside, notice how fundamental the obligation is. As a practical matter, unless the treaty crime has already been criminalised under domestic law, the parties must adopt legislation domesticating the crime under national law. They must track the international proscription as closely as local conventions of law-drafting will allow. The international obligation must become the law of the land.

And consider this more recent example from the 1970 Hague Convention on the Suppression of Unlawful Seizure of Aircraft (Hijacking), done under the auspices of the International Civil Aviation Organisation. Each of the parties to the convention promises to make punishable by 'severe penalties' the following:

> Any person who on board an aircraft in flight:
> (a) Unlawfully, by force or threat thereof, or by any other form of intimidation, seizes or exercises control of, that aircraft, or attempts to perform any such act, or
> (b) Is an accomplice of a person who performs or attempts to perform any such act commits an offence (hereinafter referred to as the offence).

Keep these examples of criminal proscriptions in mind as I explore what it is beyond 'making it criminal' that these typical treaties address. One of these further requirements is typically that States 'exercise their jurisdiction' over the crimes. What does that mean? Answering this question entails thinking about two kinds of jurisdiction over persons for alleged criminal activity, called 'prescriptive' and 'enforcement' jurisdiction. I turn to this distinction.

Prescriptive and enforcement jurisdiction

Writers on international law draw a distinction between jurisdiction to prescribe (or 'legislative' jurisdiction) and jurisdiction to enforce. Prescriptive jurisdiction deals with when it is regarded by other States as appropriate for a State to apply its substantive law to a particular context and to persons alleged to have transgressed in that context. Jurisdiction to enforce deals with the appropriateness of having the executive power of a State enforce prescriptive jurisdiction, or contribute to the enforcement of prescriptive jurisdiction, either its own or that of some other State. As will be apparent from what follows, prescriptive and enforcement jurisdiction need not necessarily be in the same hands. States assist others in enforcing the others' prescriptive jurisdiction in many ways. All of the treaties address themselves to prescriptive jurisdiction and most address enforcement jurisdiction as well.

As to prescriptive jurisdiction, a distinction is made between various 'bases' of jurisdiction that are accepted as being appropriate for States to exercise their power over individuals, at least in some cases. The most common of these is territorial jurisdiction – legislative activity over what occurs within a State's boundaries and on ships and aircraft registered in the State. (Ships and aircraft are treated for these purposes as moving parts of the State.) Then there is jurisdiction based on nationality; 'active nationality' is when the actions are taken by a national; 'passive nationality' or 'passive personality' (once a controversial notion, especially in many common law countries) involves actions taken against a national who becomes the victim of the crime. Then there is 'protective' jurisdiction, which involves actions taken, in a broad sense, against the security of the State. A limited class of cases, of which piracy is the classic paradigm, gives rise under customary international law to 'universal' jurisdiction, jurisdiction that any State may exercise. Jurisdiction over treaty crimes often fits these prescriptive bases, but there is some creativity, especially in the twentieth century treaties. The bases of prescriptive jurisdiction just discussed are not exhaustive, especially in treaty practice. Universal jurisdiction, or at least a version of it, is a notable aspect of later treaties.

Thus, the Jay Treaty is dealing simply with territorial jurisdiction – it is concerned with what those assisting pirates (whether they be British, Americans or anybody else) do on British or American turf. The same is true of the promise by the Chief of Nyanibantang. 'Those' dealing in slaves in his territory are to be dealt with 'severely' by the Chief pursuant to his new law. That 'those' might not include everybody is, however, suggested by another provision in the treaty that obligates 'English people' not to break the laws of Nyanibantang. It adds that 'when they are accused of breaking the laws, the Chief shall send a true account of the matter to the nearest place where there is an English force, and the commander of the English force shall send for the English person, who shall be tried according to English law, and shall be punished if found guilty'. Notice that the English are promising implicitly that miscreants will be tried as English citizens under English law.

Article 4 of the Hijacking Convention takes another tack, or set of tacks, in respect of jurisdiction. Each party to the Convention undertakes to establish its jurisdiction notably in these two cases: (a) when the offence is committed on board an aircraft registered in that State; (b) when the aircraft on board which the offence is committed lands in its territory with the alleged offender still on board. Paragraph (a) encompasses 'territorial' jurisdiction, which is extended, non-controversially, to those aircraft registered in the State in question. But notice paragraph (b); this is a basis of jurisdiction, which I shall call 'landing state jurisdiction', seldom discussed in the literature. Yet it makes absolutely perfect sense functionally when one considers the nature of a flight by an aircraft. An aircraft has to land somewhere. The purpose of the modern terrorism suppression conventions is to ensure that there is no safe haven for the terrorist. Safe havens are minimised by having several States in a position – and obligated if someone else does not – to exercise jurisdiction. Requiring the State where a hijacked plane lands to be one of those in a position to take jurisdiction is a sensible way to achieve this. The Hijacking Convention went further and set a jurisdictional precedent that is to be found in most of the subsequent multilateral suppression conventions. It added that: 'Each Contracting State shall likewise take such measures as may be necessary to establish its jurisdiction over the offence in a case where the alleged offender is present in its territory and it does not extradite him [to any of the States previously mentioned]'. This type of jurisdiction is known as 'extradite or prosecute' or '*aut dedere aut judicare*'. It is a 'subsidiary' or 'fallback' version of universal jurisdiction, the exercise of which is triggered by the presence of the accused within the national territory. It is sometimes called 'custodial' jurisdiction, since it comes into play when the State concerned has the accused in its custody. Thus, in the case of a hijacker, even if the accused does not land the plane in the territory concerned, but he or she later travels to the territory, jurisdiction is triggered. The treaty insists that the State Party in the territory of which the alleged offender is found must, if it does not extradite that person, submit the case to its competent authorities for the purpose of prosecution. The prosecutorial authorities are obligated to make their decision in the same manner as in the case of any ordinary offence of a serious nature under the law of that State. Thus, the obligation is not necessarily to bring the person to trial. It is a requirement that a professional prosecutor make a good faith assessment of the strength of the cases and of any other considerations that indicate whether the matter should go further.

Separating the exercise of prescriptive and enforcement jurisdiction

That prescriptive jurisdiction and enforcement jurisdiction might lie in separate hands first became apparent in the slave trade treaties which typically permitted the British navy to visit and search suspected slave vessels flying the flag of the other party to the treaty. They would free the slaves and perhaps confiscate the vessel, but criminal prosecution would remain in the hands of the flag State or the State of nationality of the accused. A robust form of this division of labour appeared in Article III of the treaty with Nyanibantang (remember the Chief's obligation to criminalise the slave trade):

The officers of the Queen of England may seize every vessel or boat of Nyanibantang found anywhere carrying on the trade in slaves, and may also seize every vessel or boat of other nations found carrying on the trade in slaves in the waters belonging to the Chief of Nyanibantang; and the vessels and boats so seized shall be taken to an English possession, to be tried by English law; and when condemned shall be sold, and the produce of the sale shall be equally divided between the Queen of England and the Chief of Nyanibantang, and the slaves who were found on board shall be made free.

Notice how this provision gives the British naval vessels a right both to board Nyanibantang ships anywhere in the world, and also a right to enter the Chief's territorial waters to seize slave ships therein but hailing from other nations. Proceeds from the sale of slave ships are to be shared between the Chief and the Queen.

Similar provisions on enforcement by parties to the treaty appeared in the 1884 multilateral Convention for the Protection of Submarine Cables. Substantively, that Convention obligated parties to make it a punishable offence to break or injure submarine cables (the lines carrying telegraph signals under the sea), wilfully or by culpable negligence. Jurisdiction to prosecute such offences (jurisdiction to prescribe, in this context) lay primarily with the courts of the flag State, although sometimes with the State of nationality. On enforcement, however, Article X of the treaty read:

Offences against the present Convention may be verified by all means of proof allowed by the legislation of the country of the court. When the officers commanding ships of war, or ships specifically commissioned for the purpose by one of the High Contracting Parties, have reason to believe that an infraction of the measures provided for in the present Convention has been committed by a vessel other than a vessel of war, they may demand from the captain or master the production of the official documents proving the nationality of the said vessel.

It went on to provide for the taking of statements on board, in a form that can be used later as evidence in the country where proceedings will be taken. In short, any party to the Convention could investigate offences, which would then normally be prosecuted in courts of the flag State. There is no universal jurisdiction to prosecute under the Cables Convention.

The 1929 League of Nations International Convention for Suppression of Counterfeiting Currency added a little accretion to the mix. That Convention required the criminalisation of various depredations against currency. It insisted that no distinction should be made in the scale of punishments for offences relating to domestic currency on the one hand and foreign currency on the other. It obligated the exercise of jurisdiction to prescribe these offences, mostly on a territorial basis. The Convention then addressed the issue of extradition. Extradition is the quintessential example of one type of enforcement jurisdiction, where one State is assisting another in order that the other might exercise its prescriptive jurisdiction. First, the currency offences are deemed to be included as extraditable offences in existing or future extradition treaties between the Parties to the Convention. Moreover, Parties that do not make extradition conditional on the existence of a treaty or reciprocity are required to recognise the treaty offences as extraditable between them. Even more interesting is this provision:

> In countries where the principle of extradition of nationals is not recognised, nationals who have returned to the territory of their own country after the commission abroad of an offence referred to in [the Convention] should be punishable in the same manner as if the offence had been committed in their own territory, even in a case where the offender has acquired his nationality after the commission of the offence.

Especially in civil law countries, there is a reluctance to extradite a country's own nationals. On the other hand, most of those countries can be persuaded to exercise jurisdiction over their own on the basis of nationality jurisdiction. So the State of nationality would enforce its 'own' counterfeiting law, made pursuant to the treaty and thus a law essentially the same as the law in the place where the counterfeiting occurred.

Enforcement assistance, building on these 1884 and 1929 models, is a particular feature of the twentieth century treaties. In the Hijacking Convention, over and above the obligations to prosecute or extradite and to exercise landing State jurisdiction, there are more detailed provisions dealing with the arrest and extradition of those who are alleged to have committed offences under the treaty. There are also provisions requiring States Parties to afford one another the 'greatest measure of assistance in connection with criminal proceedings'. They must, moreover, take appropriate measures to restore lawful control of the aircraft to its lawful commander. The provisions on extradition and mutual legal assistance are often called 'mini-extradition' and 'mini-mutual-legal assistance' treaties.

Recall the provision in the Currency Convention encouraging nationality jurisdiction for the currency offences. It will be appreciated that this move to exercise 'custodial' jurisdiction over a national who returns to the fold is but a short step from what occurred with the Hijacking Convention where jurisdiction must be exercised not only over nationals in the national territory, but also over *anyone* who comes within the national territory while accused of a treaty crime. Extradite or prosecute becomes the order of the day.

More on extradition

The extradition provisions are especially interesting in the modern conventions. Many older extradition treaties that are still in force and in regular use contain a list of crimes that are 'extraditable'. These treaties were drafted before the creation of modern crimes such as terrorism offences and transnational organised crime. (Modern treaties tend to proceed on the basis of whether a crime is punishable in both requesting and requested State by a minimum penalty, often a year in prison.) Thus the modern multilateral suppression conventions tend to pick up on and expand the model discussed earlier in the Counterfeiting Currency Convention. The new model began with article 8 of the Hijacking Convention. It provides that the offence defined in the Convention shall be deemed to be included as an extraditable offence in any existing treaty existing between the Parties to the Convention in question. They undertake to include it in every extradition treaty to be concluded between them in the future. Moreover, if a State that makes extradition conditional on the existence of an extradition treaty receives a request from another State party with which it has no extradition treaty, it may consider the multilateral treaty as the legal basis for extradition for the offence. In short, it may be treated as an extradition treaty with a short list of extraditable offences, one offence only in most cases, or a set of related crimes in some of the more complex suppression treaties. Extradition is subject to the other conditions provided in the law of the requested State. States Parties to the treaty that do not make extradition conditional on the existence of a treaty are required to recognise the offence in the multilateral treaty as an extraditable offence, subject to the law of the requested State. The Commonwealth States, for example, operate among themselves on the basis of a non-treaty instrument, the 'Scheme for the Rendition of Fugitive Offenders within the Commonwealth'. It was adopted by Commonwealth Law Ministers in 1966 and amended from time to time. It functions through parallel legislation adopted in those States participating in the Scheme. It is readily adaptable to the addition of new offences in multilateral treaties to which participants in the Scheme are also parties.

As well as the nationality exception to extradition, most extradition treaties, at least since the early nineteenth century, have contained another exception to the obligation to deliver up the accused, namely that extradition need not be granted in respect of 'political offences'. Some of the more recent suppression conventions, beginning with the 1997 International Convention for the Suppression of the Financing of Terrorism, provide that none of the Convention's offences may be regarded, for the purposes of extradition or mutual legal assistance, as a political offence or as an offence connected with a political offence or as an offence inspired by political motives. Accordingly, a request for extradition or mutual legal assistance may not be refused on such a ground.

It will be recalled that Article III of the treaty with the Chief of Nyanibantang, quoted above, provided for sharing the proceeds from the sale of seized slave vessels between Great Britain and the Chief. This model reappears in some of the twentieth century treaties also. Thus, article 14 of the United Nations Convention on Transnational Organised Crime, a treaty adopted in 2000, relates to the seizure and confiscation of property and other proceeds of organised crime. It encourages States to enter into arrangements, on a regular or a case-by-case basis, to share in the disposition of such proceeds, or to contribute them to organisations involved in the fight against transnational organised crime.

Hybrid prescription and enforcement

One other feature of the Nyanibantang treaty is also worth attention; it is perhaps a hybrid of prescriptive and enforcement jurisdiction. Recall what it was that the Chief gave up to the Queen. She had the right to send her vessels into the Chief's water, to enforce the law against both the Chief's people and those of any other sovereign who were engaged in the slave trade within the Chief's bailiwick. This is enforcement jurisdiction at first sight. Enforcement jurisdiction is to be exercised both on the physical territory of the Chief's water domains and also on his flag vessels on the high seas. But notice that the treaty goes on to say that 'the vessels and boat so seized shall be taken to an English possession, to be tried by

English law'. It does not appear that the slave traders themselves are to be so tried. Be that as it may, the Chief has transferred to the British the right to apply their (prescriptive) law to the situation. In modern parlance, this is known as 'transferred jurisdiction'. It is an increasing part of the modern scene in relation to treaty crimes. For example, article 17 of the 1988 United Nations Convention against Illicit Traffic in Narcotic Drugs and Psychotropic Substances encourages parties to co-operate to suppress illicit drug traffic by sea. A flag State may, pursuant to a treaty or a more informal arrangement, authorise another State to board vessels bearing its flag and search the vessel. If evidence of involvement in illicit traffic is discovered, the State doing the boarding may 'take appropriate action with respect to the vessel, persons and cargo on board'. This enforcement provision is accompanied by article 4(1)(b)(ii) of the Convention that empowers a party to 'take such measures as may be necessary to establish jurisdiction over the offences [under the Convention] when [t]he offence is committed on board a vessel concerning which that Party has been authorised to take appropriate action pursuant to article 17'. This is prescriptive jurisdiction over persons who may have no connection with the boarding State other than the fact of boarding. (The phrase 'boarding state jurisdiction' also has a ring to it!) The United States has several such arrangements with Latin American and Caribbean States to exercise such 'delegated' or 'transferred' or 'ceded' jurisdiction. Notice how the combination of prescriptive and enforcement jurisdiction plays out in such cases. The matter begins with an enforcement action at sea, but ends with the enforcement State now gathering prescriptive jurisdiction along the way.

The right to 'visit' (board) suspected slave traders (and pirate ships) is carried forward into the 1982 United Nations Convention on the Law of the Sea. In the case of the slave trade, jurisdiction to prescribe (the obligatory exercise of which is encouraged by the treaty) remains with the flag State, as in all the nineteenth century treaties, although the naval vessel making the visit may apparently free the slaves and take appropriate evidence. For piracy, however, the Convention goes further and empowers every State to 'seize' a pirate ship or aircraft and to arrest the persons and seize the property aboard. It adds that: '[t]he courts of the State which carried out the seizure may decide upon the penalties to be imposed, and may also determine the action to be taken with regard to the ships, aircraft or property, subject to the rights of third parties acting in good faith'. One can treat the jurisdictional regime here over pirates as an example of universal jurisdiction, but given its treaty manifestation it is also possible to regard it as a species of transferred jurisdiction; parties to the 1982 Convention have ceded to other States Parties the right to apply their prescriptive law (consistent with international definitions of piracy) to captured pirate vessels of whatever origin.

Carrots, sticks and other modes of enforcement of treaty obligations against States Parties

No doubt many States enter into obligations to create treaty crimes out of altruism or to rid the world of irritations of one sort or another. Sometimes more is required. Great Britain contributed substantial sums to the Portuguese and Spanish treasuries in order to obtain Portuguese and Spanish acquiescence in treaties for the suppression of the slave trade, although those countries' actual performance on land and sea sometimes came up short. The pattern continued in the treaty with the Chief of Nayanibantang and those with similarly situated African leaders. The Nyanibantang treaty records that:

> The Queen of England, out of friendship for the Chief of Nyanibantang, and because the Chief of Nyanibantang has made this agreement, gives him the following articles, which the said Chief of Nyanibantang hereby acknowledges to have received, viz: 15 muskets; 200 pounds of gunpowder; 10 pieces of blue bafts; 11 gallons of rum; 20 pounds of tobacco; 1 yard of scarlet cloth; 1 large loaf of sugar; ½ lb. of amber, No. 2; and 250 flints.

Not a bad haul! In this case, the gift seems to have been one-off rather than annual, but in many cases annual subventions must have been contingent on continued co-operation. A modern equivalent would be annual aid payments contingent upon assistance in suppression of the drug traffic.

Are there other ways to deal with States whose euphoria for enforcing the treaty evaporates once the ink is dry on the instrument of ratification? Two examples, one from the nineteenth century and one more recent, suggest some of the possibilities for ensuring that States fulfil their obligations to suppress treaty crimes. A treaty of 1844 between Great Britain and King William of Bimbia (West Africa) contained a heavy-handed self-help provision drafted by the Superpower of the day:

> If at any time it shall appear that the Slave Trade has been carried on, through or from the territory of the chiefs of Bimbia, the Slave Trade may be put down by Great Britain by force upon that territory, and British officers may seize the boats of Bimbia, found anywhere carrying on the Slave Trade, and the chiefs of Bimbia will subject themselves to a severe act of displeasure on the part of the Queen of England.

'Severe act of displeasure' has an ominous ring!

Modern treaties eschew such unilateral action by one party and instead opt for peaceful dispute resolution. Thus, the Hijacking Convention provides that any dispute between one or more parties concerning the interpretation or application of the Convention that cannot be settled through negotiation shall, at the request of either, be submitted to arbitration. If within six months from the date of request for arbitration the parties are unable to agree on the organisation of the arbitration, any one of the parties may refer the dispute to the International Court of Justice. (States are entitled to opt out of this provision and a small minority of them have done so.) A similar provision appears in the 1984 Convention against Torture and Other Cruel, Inhuman or Degrading Treatment or Punishment. It was the jurisdictional basis for a case brought by Belgium against Senegal in the International Court of Justice. The case was an effort to require Senegal to institute a prosecution for torture against Hissène Habré, former President of Chad, who had sought asylum in Senegal. It is perhaps too much to expect in such cases that the International Court (or its theoretical enforcement arm, the United Nations Security Council) would be able to render an effective form of injunctive relief. But at least a declaration that Senegal was in breach of its suppression obligation might shame it into compliance in some fashion. In its 2012 decision, the Court conducted an extensive analysis of the obligations now commonly found in suppression treaties, including the obligation to criminalise, to extend its jurisdiction – including to those present in the State's territory who may have committed the offence elsewhere – and to conduct a preliminary enquiry when allegations have been made. Speaking of the duty to prosecute or extradite, the Court noted that '[e]xtradition is an option offered to the State by the Convention [owed to the other parties to the Convention], whereas prosecution is an international obligation under the Convention, the violation of which is a wrongful act engaging the responsibility of the State'. Senegal had clearly been procrastinating for several years and the Court highlighted that State's obligation to prosecute. The Court stopped short of saying that the alternative was to extradite *to Belgium*. Belgium was willing to act, but there were other ways to fulfil the obligation, including extradition to Chad, which had, however, shown little interest in so doing. Belgium's efforts at peaceful settlement appear to have borne fruit: in August 2012 Senegal and the African Union agreed to establish a special court within the Senegalese justice system with African judges appointed by the Union. In July 2013, Habré was charged with crimes against humanity and war crimes, along with torture, and placed in pre-trial detention.

Conclusion

There is, of course, much more that might be said about treaty crimes, both in the abstract and concerning specific instances. But I hope this general introduction will encourage you, dear reader, to dip into the originals of the treaties noted in the bibliography that follows and experience for yourself what a rich body of State practice they contain.

FURTHER READING

Neil Boister, *An Introduction to Transnational Criminal Law*, Oxford University Press, 2012.

Roger S. Clark, 'Offenses of International Concern: Multilateral State Treaty Practice in the Forty Years Since Nuremberg', (1988) 57 *Nordic Journal of International Law* 49.

Robert J. Currie and Joseph Rikhof, *International and Transnational Criminal Law*, 2nd edn, Toronto: Irwin Law, 2013.

Agreement between Great Britain and Sandibar, Chief of Nyanibantang (West Africa), 31 December 1842, 94 *Consolidated Treaty Series* 101.

Treaty between Great Britain and King William of Bimbia (West Africa) for the Abolition of the Slave Trade, 17 February 1844, 96 *Consolidated Treaty Series* 189.

Convention for the Protection of Submarine Cables, 14 March 1884 (in French), English translation in Australian Treaty Series, available at www.gc.noaa. gov/documents/seabed-icpc_1884.pdf

Convention for Suppression of Counterfeiting Currency, 20 April 1929, (1931) 112 LNTS 371.

Hague Convention on the Suppression of Unlawful Seizure of Aircraft (Hijacking), 16 December 1970, (1971) 800 UNTS 105.

United Nations Convention on the Law of the Sea, 10 December 1982, (1994) 1833 UNTS 3.

Convention against Torture and Other Cruel, Inhuman or Degrading Treatment or Punishment, 10 December 1984, (1988) 1465 UNTS 85.

United Nations Convention against Illicit Traffic in Narcotic Drugs and Psychotropic Substances, 20 December 1988, (1990) 1582 UNTS 95.

United Nations Convention against Transnational Organised Crime, 15 November 2000, (2003) 2225 UNTS 209.

Questions relating to the Obligation to Prosecute or Extradite (Belgium v. Senegal), Judgment, I.C.J. Reports 2012, p. 422.

12 Criminalising the illegal use of force

Benjamin B. Ferencz and Donald M. Ferencz

The ancient aspiration that the peoples of the earth might someday renounce war-making and 'beat their swords into plowshares'[1] seemed to get rather a significant boost with the establishment in 1945 of the UN system. Not long thereafter, the judgment of the International Military Tribunal at Nuremberg made clear that leaders responsible for crimes against peace, war crimes, and crimes against humanity could be criminally prosecuted in their individual capacities for such crimes. Consistent with the UN Charter's determination 'to save succeeding generations from the scourge of war', the General Assembly, in its first session, affirmed the principles of international law recognised by the Nuremberg Charter and judgment and called for their formulation within an International Criminal Code, to be developed for later adoption and implementation.[2]

The Cold War had a chilling effect, and it would be half a century before an international criminal code would finally emerge as the Rome Statute of the International Criminal Court. The Conference of Plenipotentiaries which met in Rome in the summer of 1998 was able to agree on granting the Court active jurisdiction over war crimes, crimes against humanity, and genocide – but not over the crime of aggression. Left unresolved in Rome were issues relating to the definition of aggression as well as

This chapter presents a summary background relating to the effort to vest the International Criminal Court with effective jurisdiction over the crime of aggression, followed by Ben Ferencz's views on illegal use of force as a crime against humanity and, finally, by observations of Don Ferencz on the Nuremberg legacy *vis-à-vis* the current status of the Court's aggression jurisdiction.

1 'And they shall beat their swords into plowshares, and their spears into pruning hooks. Nation will not take up sword against nation, nor will they train for war any more'. From the Old Testament Book of Isaiah Chapter 2, verse 4, New International Version (2011).

2 Affirmation of the Principles of International Law recognized by the Charter of the Nürnberg Tribunal, GA Res. 95(I).

whether acts of aggression ought to be determined judicially, by an independent Court, rather than by the Security Council. As a compromise, aggression was included within the Court's jurisdiction, but the Court would not be able to exercise its aggression jurisdiction until further hurdles were overcome.

The showdown on this issue would come in May and June of 2010, at a Review Conference of the Rome Statute of the International Criminal Court held in Kampala, Uganda. There, members of the Assembly of States Parties met to consider the adoption of provisions on aggression that, if made effective, would statutorily define the crime and allow the Court to exercise its jurisdiction over it. The Conference succeeded in amending the Statute so as to include a definition of aggression, but activation of the Court's jurisdiction over that particular crime was once again deferred.

The definition adopted in Kampala largely relied on a list of enumerated acts constituting aggression, as set forth in a consensus definition which had been approved by the UN General Assembly in 1974.[3] It was adopted without significant further debate, based on the formulation developed by the Working Group that preceded the Review Conference. The main issue of contention at the Review Conference concerned the conditions under which the Court might, at last, be able to exercise its jurisdiction over aggression. As in Rome, the five permanent members of the Security Council argued for exclusive Security Council control. The compromise reached in Kampala reflects the reluctance of certain States to be bound by the Court's independent jurisdiction. In the run-up to the Kampala Review Conference, Professor M. Cherif Bassiouni, who had served in 1998 as the Chairman of the Drafting Committee of the Rome Conference, publicly remarked that the sort of multi-layered jurisdictional scheme which might come out of Kampala could resemble Swiss cheese.[4] He wasn't very far off.

---

3 Definition of Aggression, UN Doc. A/RES/1974/3314. Although the 1974 definition defers to the judgment of the Security Council in making the final determination as to whether an act of aggression by a State has occurred, article 8 *bis* of the Rome Statute, as adopted at Kampala, does not.

4 For a webcast of the relevant panel discussion at which this topic was discussed, Case Western Reserve School of Law website, conference entitled 'The International Criminal Court and the Crime of Aggression', 26 September 2008, (available online at http://law.case.edu/lectures/webcast.aspx?dt=20080926).

The key provisions agreed to in Kampala are as follows: (1) If a situation is referred to the Court by the Council, the Court may exercise its aggression jurisdiction without additional limitations; (2) Unless the Council refers a situation, the Court will have no aggression jurisdiction over nationals of non-party States, nor will it have jurisdiction over acts of aggression committed on their territories; (3) Unless the Council refers a situation, the Court will have no jurisdiction over acts of aggression by States Parties which have affirmatively opted out of the Court's aggression jurisdiction. Thus, even as to Assembly of States Parties Member States, the Court's aggression jurisdiction may be limited.

Additional 'holes' in the 'Swiss cheese' that came out of Kampala may be found among the Understandings that were developed as an accompaniment to the amendments on aggression. Perhaps the most significant of them grew out of a concern by certain powerful States that criminalising aggression may have a chilling effect on potential humanitarian intervention, a euphemism for ostensibly well-intentioned international military operations that are beyond the scope of what is authorised within the letter of the UN Charter. This concern was dealt with in Understandings 6 and 7, providing that in order for an act to rise to the level associated with the crime of aggression it must be a manifest violation of the UN Charter with respect to a combination of its character, gravity, and scale – and that no one of these attributes alone will satisfy the 'manifest violation' test.[5] Thus, the door was left fairly wide open as to whether, and to what extent, conduct otherwise constituting punishable acts of aggression may be excepted from criminal culpability before the Court.

It is clear from the Understandings that some of those present in Kampala wanted to be sure that the aggression amendments would have no influence on customary international law. In this regard, it should be noted that article 10 of the Rome Statute already expressly provided that 'Nothing in this Part shall be interpreted as limiting or prejudicing in any way existing or developing rules of international law for purposes other than this Statute.' Notwithstanding the pre-existence of such unambiguous statutory language, Understanding 4 reiterates precisely the

---

5 For a complete listing of the Understandings, see Annex III of Resolution RC/ Res.6. For an excellent discussion of the import of these Understandings, see Kevin Jon Heller, 'The Uncertain Legal Status of the Aggression Understandings', (2012) 10 *Journal of International Criminal Justice* 229.

same point. On the subject of the current status of the crime of aggression in customary international law, it is noteworthy that in the case of *R* v. *Jones*, five out of five British Law Lords concurred that the crime of aggression exists in customary international law, essentially unchanged since Nuremberg.[6] Lord Bingham of Cornhill wrote the lead opinion, in which he expressed agreement that 'the core elements of the crime of aggression have been understood, at least since 1945, with sufficient clarity to permit the lawful trial (and, on conviction, punishment) of those accused of this most serious crime', adding that 'it is unhistorical to suppose that the elements of the crime were clear in 1945 but have since become in any way obscure'.[7]

Notwithstanding the already rather porous nature of the amendments proposed in Kampala, further limiting conditions were imposed, specifically intended to delay their activation. The Court will not be able to exercise its aggression jurisdiction until and unless the aggression amendments are ratified by at least thirty Assembly of States Parties members and until and unless they are re-approved by a meeting of the Assembly of States Parties, which can occur at a point in time no sooner than 1 January 2017. It should be noted in this regard that, even after thirty ratifications are achieved, there is no requirement or guarantee that the re-approval by the Assembly of States Parties will occur, nor when such re-approval may be considered – only that it not be prior to 1 January 2017. Such hurdles ensure immunity from prosecution for a potentially indefinite term,[8] and aggression remains in legal limbo – a crime without a court.

Ben Ferencz: illegal use of force as a crime against humanity

On 29 September 1947, I stood before a lectern in courtroom 600 in the Palace of Justice in Nuremberg and made the opening statement as Chief

---

6 *R* v. *Jones*, [2006] UKHL 16, [2007] 1 AC 136.

7 Ibid., para. 19.

8 For updates as to the current status of ratifications and implementation see the website of the Global Campaign for Ratification and Implementation of the Kampala Amendments on the Crime of Aggression (available online at www. crimeofaggression.info). For an online schedule showing the current deposit of instruments of ratification by country, see www.derechos.org/nizkor/aggression/doc/status.html.

Prosecutor in the *Einsatzgruppen* case. Twenty-two defendants, members of Hitler's special extermination forces – euphemistically designated 'action groups' – stood accused of methodically murdering over a million innocent men, women, and children in cold blood. I was twenty-seven years old, and it was my first case. I noted in my opening statement: 'The case we present is a plea of humanity to law.'[9] Today, a full sixty-eight years later, and in my ninety-sixth year, my goal continues to be advancing the rule of law, so that humankind may be spared the brutality of organised mass violence.

My motto is 'Law. Not War.'[10] As a combat soldier in the Second World War, I survived the major campaigns in Europe and was present at the liberation of a number of the Nazi concentration camps. I had peered into hell. That experience has been the driving force behind my life's work. I've dug up bodies with my bare hands, and have seen vengeful survivors of the camps burning their tormentors to death in the very crematoria in which their wives, mothers, fathers, sisters, brothers, and children had been reduced to ashes. I've seen corpses of murdered civilians piled high like cordwood waiting to be burned. As in the biblical story of Cain and Abel, I recall the blood of our sisters and brothers crying to me from the ground.[11]

The overriding symptom of my having experienced first-hand the unspeakable and traumatic horrors of war is my determination to do all that is in my power to work towards a world in which we have eradicated the abomination of war. We have witnessed the emancipation of women, the end of colonialism, and the criminalisation of slavery and *apartheid*. Duelling, which was recognised as an honourable response, would be ridiculed today. Men have landed on the moon. Small handheld devices now offer instantaneous communication throughout the world. When the Wright brothers tried to make their bicycles fly, they were ridiculed and taunted: 'If God wanted man to fly, He'd have given him wings!' Today,

---

9 *United States* v. *Ohlendorf* et al., 'The Einsatzgrüppen Case', (1949) 4 TWC 3, at p. 30.
10 Please see www.benferencz.org for a listing of writings, lectures, and videos by Benjamin Ferencz.
11 According to the Old Testament Book of Genesis, Cain murders his brother Abel, whereupon Cain is confronted by God, who says to him 'Your brother's blood cries out to me from the ground'. Genesis 4:10.

thousands of planes encircle the globe. I refuse to believe that humankind does not have the capacity to organise this planet so that all may live in peace and human dignity regardless of their race or creed. Doing the impossible is possible.

So what can be done to move forward?

Thucydides, the ancient chronicler of the Peloponnesian wars wrote that 'the strong do what they can and the weak suffer what they must'. Yet today, at least in certain societies, we have a different ethos, as reflected in four simple words etched in stone over the portal of the Supreme Court of the United States: 'Equal Justice Under Law.' If law is to be respected as an effective tool in defending the fundamental rights of humankind – if it is to fulfil its role in helping to protect the weak from the powerful – it should be universal in its scope and equal in its application. It must be reliable, both as to its unbiased application and as to its enforceability. The proponents in any conflict are not qualified to decide where justice lies – they are both biased. It requires the independent judgment of trained jurists, whose opinions are open to public scrutiny and approval.

We need to live up to the letter and spirit of the Charter of the United Nations and to the principles that it espouses. Its primary obligation remains to save succeeding generations from the scourge of war. The fulfilment of that universally accepted mandate requires more than lip service or platitudes. No nation and no organised group should use or threaten to use force in violation of the UN Charter. We need an enforceable rule of law, not only to protect the weak from the powerful, but to protect the powerful from themselves.

My own writings have focussed on the need for developing international law, courts, and enforcement. (Some within the international justice community referred to me as 'Mr Aggression'.) The continued delays in granting the International Criminal Court active jurisdiction over the crime of aggression makes a mockery of the Nuremberg principles. If we are to deter the killings of innocents that are the inevitable consequence of the large-scale illegal use of force, we must hold accountable those leaders responsible for forging the chain of causal events directly linked to such atrocities.

I support the ratification campaign aimed at giving the International Criminal Court active jurisdiction over the crime of aggression. Any further delays in activating the Court's jurisdiction over what the Nuremberg

Tribunal branded 'the supreme international crime'[12] encourages more crime. Aggression should not be allowed to remain in legal limbo. Perpetrators should not remain immune from prosecution.

Closing the impunity gap with respect to the illegal use of force requires accountability for perpetrators, whether domestically or internationally. As Robert Jackson, Chief Counsel for the United States at Nuremberg put it: 'The common sense of mankind demands that law shall not stop with the punishment of petty crimes by little people. It must also reach men who possess themselves of great power and make deliberate and concerted use of it to set in motion evils which leave no home in the world untouched.'[13] Nomenclature should not be decisive. Those responsible for the illegal use of force resulting in the inevitable loss of civilian life must also be held accountable for crimes against humanity.

To be punishable under the Statute of the International Criminal Court, crimes against humanity must be part of a systematic or widespread attack directed against a civilian population. It is common sense that the illegal use of armed force will inevitably leave countless innocent civilians murdered, injured, and dispossessed in its wake. As reflected in the logic of article 30 of the Rome Statute, providing that a person has intent in relation to a consequence where the person either means to cause the consequence 'or is aware that it will occur in the ordinary course of events', perpetrators must be presumed to intend the foreseeable consequences of their deeds. As the British Chief Prosecutor at Nuremberg, Sir Hartley Shawcross, put it: 'The killing of combatants in war is justifiable, both in international and in municipal law, only where the war itself is legal. But where the war is illegal ... there is nothing to justify the killing, and these murders are not to be distinguished from those of any other lawless robber bands.'[14] If the killing of combatants in an illegal war is *ipso facto* illegal, the killing of civilians must certainly also be illegal. To have a deterrent effect, international criminal law must hold perpetrators of large-scale inhumane acts accountable.

---

12 (1948) 22 IMT 411, at p. 427.

13 (1947) 2 IMT 98, at p. 99.

14 (1948) 19 IMT 458, with thanks to Matt Gillett and Manuel Ventura for drawing my attention to this quotation, cited in their joint paper: Manuel J. Ventura and Matt Gillett, 'The Fog of War: Prosecuting Illegal Uses of Force as a Crime Against Humanity', (2013) 12 *Washington University Global Studies Law Review* 523.

There is authority for the proposition that for an assault to constitute an attack 'directed against a civilian population' the civilian population must be the *primary* target of the attack.[15] Yet, none other than General Douglas MacArthur, one of the best-known military commanders of the Second World War, on more than one occasion pointed out that in the world in which we live 'civilians are the primary target in war'.[16] In modern warfare, it is increasingly unavoidable and inevitable that large numbers of civilians will be among the primary victims. To try to excuse it by calling it 'collateral damage' insults the dead and threatens the living.

The Charter of the United Nations was never given a chance. We must not forget that its fundamental purpose was 'to maintain international peace and security'.[17] What happened to the accepted moral and legal obligation that 'All Members shall settle their international disputes by peaceful means in such manner that peace and security, and justice, are not endangered?'[18] Where are the promised disarmament agreements[19] and the international military force envisaged by Chapter VII? Countless millions of innocent people have been killed in countless wars since the Charter was accepted; yet the vital components required to maintain peace and security and justice have not yet materialised. No matter what may be the political excuses, the sad conclusion is unavoidable that the Security Council, which was trusted to maintain the peace, has betrayed its trust. Who is responsible and what can be done about it?

After more than half a century of effort, the creation of the International Criminal Court in 2002 was a major step forward in the evolution of international criminal law. The Preamble to the Rome Statute set down the basic goals of the new international tribunal. Its jurisdiction was strictly limited to 'crimes of concern to the international community as a whole', which, of course, encompassed massive atrocities against women and children. It affirmed that such crimes must not go unpunished and should be effectively prosecuted. It was the declared duty of every State to end the impunity and to exercise its criminal jurisdiction over

15 William A. Schabas, *The International Criminal Court, A Commentary on the Rome Statute*, Oxford University Press, 2010, p. 153.

16 Edward T. Imparato, ed., *General MacArthur Speeches and Reports 1908– 1964*, Nashville: Turner, 2000, pp. 233, 235, 238, 247.

17 Charter of the United Nations, Preamble.

18 Ibid., article 2(3).   19 Ibid., article 26.

those responsible for major international crimes. What happened to the dream?

The Rome Statute, the basic foundational document for the International Criminal Court, is in the form of a treaty and, as such, it fully binds those States that have accepted and ratified it. Many powerful States remain unwilling to surrender their perceived sacred sovereign right to wage war whenever and however they see fit. Lawyers have no difficulty in finding objections and imprecisions in accords their clients do not wish to accept. Quibbling about ambiguous terminology offered a convenient excuse to do nothing. The truth is that many powerful States are still not ready to be bound by the restraints contained in the Rome Statute.

The current custom of belligerent nations, and militant groups, when confronted by an adversary with whom agreement on important issues cannot amicably be reached, is to turn to armed force as the only other alternative to settle their disputes. They send their young people out to kill other young people whom they do not even know and who may never have done them, or anyone, any harm. They fail to recognise that the only victor in war is Death. The practice is so irrational that it is almost incredible that people who call themselves human could act in such an irrational and inhumane way.

What needs to be done to avoid such cruelties has been articulated for a long time but the political will and ability to do what is necessary has, unfortunately, been lacking. We have failed to build the institutions that are required to maintain peace. We do not yet have clear laws, courts and enforcement mechanisms that bind everyone.

After the incredible horrors of the Second World War, the people of all countries were sick of the agony and futility of war. The attitude of the people of the United States was clearly reflected by President Harry Truman, as he went before the Assembly of the new United Nations on 23 October 1946. Speaking '[o]n behalf of the Government and people of the United States' he called upon all countries to cherish peace and develop means of settling future conflicts in accordance with principles of law and equality. He reminded the delegates that 'planning or waging a war of aggression is a crime against humanity for which individuals as well as States shall be tried before the bar of international justice'.[20]

20 UN Doc. A/PV.37.

Truman's obvious interest in strengthening the rule of law was shared by his immediate successor in the White House, Dwight D. Eisenhower, former Supreme Commander of the victorious Allied forces in the Second World War. In April of 1958, he could not have put it more bluntly: 'In a very real sense, the world no longer has a choice between force and law. If civilisation is to survive, it must choose the rule of law.'[21] On 6 January 2010, Chairman of the US Joint Chiefs of Staff, Admiral Mike Mullen, at a press conference in Washington declared: 'I would much rather prevent a war than fight a war'. Despite these repeated warnings, many powerful States, including the United States, are still unwilling to subject their own violent acts to the collective judgment of humankind; the vacillation calls for an explanation.

The United States is a great democracy. It is inevitable that its citizens will have differences of opinion on such important issues as religion, nationalism, economics, and similar causes which incite strong emotional responses. Their views are entitled to respect. The highly regarded Constitution of the United States provides that treaties entered into will be the 'supreme law of the land' but this requires approval by two-thirds of the Senate. It is understandable that persons of conservative persuasion will cling to ancient prerogatives of sovereigns to use military might to attain or protect perceived vital interests. Since elected officials may depend upon such voters in order to attain or remain in office, it is unavoidable that the political power of a small minority may have paralysing effects. That may help explain why the United States, which has always pledged allegiance to 'liberty and justice for all' and was historically a foremost champion of equal human rights for everyone, has been politically unable to carry out many of those lofty ideals. Alas![22]

It is undeniable that enforcement of criminal law serves to deter the commission of crime. Not all criminality can be eliminated but surely the enforcement of criminal law can protect humanity to a certain extent. Nuremberg branded aggression as 'the supreme international crime'

---

21 Statement by the President on the Observance of Law Day, 30 April 1958. Eisenhower had also noted that '[e]very gun that is made, every warship launched, every rocket fired signifies, in the final sense, a theft from those who hunger and are not fed, those who are cold and are not clothed'.

22 During a March 2015 lecture at Oxford University, my son Don queried whether this ideal has perhaps been supplanted in the minds of some with a worldview more nearly reflective of the notion of 'liberty and *just us* for all'.

because it incorporated all the other offences, such as rape, murder, and pillage. There has never been a war without such atrocities. Going to war as a means to power, territory, or riches, that traditionally had been a national right, was condemned as an international crime. But the widely hailed Nuremberg precedent was not implemented and bloody conflicts continued as before. If only some wars can be deterred, the effort to use the neglected power of criminal law will surely be worthwhile.

An effort to correct the recognised insufficiencies in the Rome Statute was made at a conference in Kampala, Uganda in 2010. A consensus agreement was reached after much debate (by representatives of eighty-four nations). Yet the Court still remains unable to act on the crime of aggression until the amendments have been ratified by at least thirty States and confirmed by two-thirds of the Assembly of State Parties. It cannot even begin to consider the aggression amendment until some unspecified date – after 2017. How long it will take to reach the required ratifications remains unknown. It would be prudent therefore to seek an easier and faster route to reach the desired goal.

Since crimes against humanity are already punishable under the prevailing Rome Statute, one way to deter aggression is to let it be known that individuals responsible for the illegal use of armed force in violation of the UN Charter will be prosecuted – either nationally or internationally – and charged with committing crimes against humanity.

There are several advantages in taking the crimes against humanity route. The unpopular Security Council, mandated by article 39 of the Charter of the United Nations to decide whether aggression by a State has occurred, has no similar obligation regarding crimes against humanity. Furthermore, the new categorisation is a more accurate and comprehensible designation than the perhaps less well-understood 'crime of aggression'. The statutory definition of crimes against humanity already includes a catch-all clause covering '[o]ther inhumane acts of a similar character intentionally causing great suffering'. Surely, if murder, enslavement, torture, *apartheid*, and deportation are listed as punishable crimes against humanity, the illegal use of armed force in violation of the UN Charter is equally culpable and should be equally punishable.

The suggested additional new approach does not infringe any legitimate existing rights. Force used as a last resort in self-defence remains inviolate under article 51 of the Charter of the United Nations. Security Council powers to maintain peace cannot be restricted by the International

Criminal Court or any other agency. Of course, any judicial enforcement must be by fair trial which protects all the legitimate rights of the accused.

There is yet another way to go forward. If the jurisdiction of the International Criminal Court remains paralysed or is deemed faulty, every nation State can enact its own domestic legislation to incorporate the Rome Statute crimes into their local criminal codes. The Court is thus bypassed in favour of fair local trials at the national level. In fact, the Preamble to the Rome Statute refers specifically to 'the duty of *every* State to exercise its primary criminal jurisdiction over those responsible for international crimes'.[23] Many States have already done just that and others are moving in the same direction. Local action is faster, more effective and more economical. Enforcement of international criminal law should begin at home. In time, international criminals, who today enjoy immunity, may find no place to hide.

The use of armed force that will inevitably kill large numbers of innocent men, women and children must surely be recognised, in the words of the Preamble to the Rome Statute, as a 'most serious crime of concern to the international community as a whole'. The Preamble to the Rome Statute affirms that such offences 'must not go unpunished' but should be effectively prosecuted at the national and international level.

The parties to a dispute are not competent to judge the legality of their own actions. Yet, as they had done in Rome in 1998, once again in Kampala in 2010, major powers still refused to subject the legality of their use of armed force to any independent judicial scrutiny.

There are certain acts that are so heinous that the international community simply cannot allow them to continue. For example, when piracy threatened commerce by sea, the civilised community condemned that offence as *hostis humani generis* – as offences against the whole of humanity – which could be punishable by anyone capturing the pirates. The principle of universal jurisdiction, regardless of the nationality of the offender, the victim, or the place of the crime has been expanded to apply to acts that are now universally condemned as crimes against humanity, from which no derogation is acceptable. The list of such crimes that should be criminally punishable must be expanded to deter illegal war making itself.

23 Emphasis added.

It is more important than ever to create and enforce rules to prevent the unrestrained use of armed force. The criminal law must be given a greater role to play.

Not all States are yet ready to be bound by any rules other than those specifically affirmed in their own national codes. But that is changing. For example, at a recent conference in Madrid the distinguished delegates drafted the Madrid Proposal for Discussing the Principles of Universal Jurisdiction. It called for universal jurisdiction over 'serious crimes against international law', including 'other inhuman acts such as the illegal use of force, that constitute a manifest violation of the United Nations Charter'.[24] New elaborations of crimes against humanity are a subject of important work by leading scholars, including the development of a draft convention on crimes against humanity.[25] The International Law Commission has put it on its agenda for the United Nations.[26] There is reason to hope that humane considerations will yet triumph over man's growing capacity to destroy life on this planet.

Most nations do not feel obliged to intervene in an ongoing conflict unless it is in their own self-interest. As long as combatants insist that they alone can determine the legality of their actions, their military might is not a safeguard, but a menace. The illegal use of armed force can only be curbed rationally by peaceful means. Unauthorised interventions may be morally legitimate but the illegal use of force does not become lawful just because it is done with good intentions. Let those who intervene be prepared to state their case in a court of law. The International Criminal Court and justice require that prosecutors and judges take all relevant circumstances into account. Rantings by fanatics will not be persuasive to rational minds. In the end, the court of public opinion will be decisive.

We have yet to learn that you cannot kill an ideology with a gun. Peace requires more intensive efforts to ameliorate the discontents that give rise to violence. Tolerance and compromise and compassion are indispensable

---

24 The Madrid Proposal for Discussing the Principles of Universal Jurisdiction (available online at www.fibgar.org/congreso-jurisdiccion-universal/english/propuesta.pdf).

25 Leila Nadya Sadat, ed., *Forging a Convention for Crimes Against Humanity*, Cambridge University Press, 2011.

26 Report of the International Law Commission, Sixty-sixth Session (5 May–6 June and 7 July–8 August 2014), UN Doc. A/69/10, para. 23.

norms that must be taught by every available means at every level of learning.

Hope is the engine that drives human endeavour. It provides the energy needed to do the many difficult things to establish a humane and peaceful planet. From the perspective of one who has witnessed and experienced man's inhumanity to man, I remain convinced that the illegal use of armed force, whether called 'aggression', a 'crime against humanity', or any other label, must and can be deterred by criminal law. Even at the risk of some miscarriages of justice there can be no doubt that law is better than war.

The progress towards a more rational world order has been phenomenal. Colonialism, racial discrimination, exploitation of women, and other abominations have been universally condemned. Humanitarian law is being taught in leading universities everywhere. Those who trample on human life and human dignity will, hopefully, have to explain their behaviour to a national or international court of law. Deterrence is still the primary objective. Equity, common sense, and morality should always be respected as part of our evolving legal mandate. Never give up hope and never give up.

Donald Ferencz: comments on Kampala

That I was born in Nuremberg, the son of a Nuremberg prosecutor, has much to do with my interest in the legacy of the ground-breaking trials held there.

If Nuremberg presented 'a plea of humanity to law',[27] the Kampala Review Conference did just the opposite: it presented a plea of law to humanity – *our* humanity. Activation of the Court's jurisdiction over the crime of aggression rests with the global community. To borrow a phrase from Jutta Bertram Nothnagel, the Kampala amendments are a seed for peace, waiting to be watered and grown.[28] They are the promise of Nuremberg, waiting to be fulfilled.

---

27 *United States* v. *Ohlendorf* et al., 'The Einsatzgrüppen Case', (1949) 4 TWC 3, at p. 30.

28 Jutta Bertram Nothnagel, 'A Seed for World Peace Planted in Africa: The Provisions on the Crime of Aggression Adopted at the Kampala Review Conference for the Rome Statute of the International Criminal Court', *Africa Legal Aid Quarterly*, April–June 2010, pp. 9–27.

For Robert Jackson, the International Military Tribunal represented 'one of the most significant tributes that Power has ever paid to Reason',[29] and he believed that the trial established an important and binding precedent in international law. It may be recalled that a significant part of the debate at Nuremberg focused on whether the criminalisation of aggressive war-making was essentially *ex post facto* law, since treaties such as the Kellogg-Briand Pact[30] had not provided for criminal sanctions for their breach.[31] Just after the Nuremberg judgment was rendered, in a letter of 7 October 1946 – perhaps with this in mind – Jackson reported to President Harry Truman that '[n]o one can hereafter deny or fail to know that the principles on which the Nazi leaders are adjudged to forfeit their lives constitute law *and law with a sanction*'. He went even further, emphasising that '[t]hese standards by which the Germans have been condemned will become the condemnation of *any* nation that is faithless to them'. He concluded his report by stating that the International Military Tribunal had 'put International Law squarely on the side of peace as against aggressive warfare'.[32]

As a Justice of the US Supreme Court, Jackson would have been well aware of the words etched on the portico of the building in which he worked, referenced above – Equal Justice Under Law. His message to Truman evinces his own belief that the heavy hand of powerful States clearly has no place in tipping the scales of justice in their own favour (as might be done, for example, by the use of the veto power within

---

29 (1947) 2 IMT 98, at p. 99.
30 Treaty Providing for the Renunciation of War as an Instrument of National Policy, (1928) 94 LNTS 57. When the Treaty came up for a ratification vote in the United States Senate, the one vote in opposition came from Senator John J. Blaine of Wisconsin. Knowing that the Treaty provided no meaningful sanctions and that it effectively allowed each nation to decide for itself when its interest required defending through force of arms, he called it a 'sham' and said that it contained 'the fertile soil for all the wars of the future'. See United States Congressional Record 1929, Senate, pp. 1401– 2.
31 For a short contemporaneous article addressing this issue, see 'The Chalice of Nürnberg', *Time Magazine*, 10 December 1945.
32 Robert H. Jackson, 'Report to the President by Mr. Justice Jackson, 7 October 1946', in *Report of Robert H. Jackson, United States Representative to the International Conference on Military Trials, London, 1945*, Washington: Department of State, 1949, pp. 432–40.

the Security Council).[33] Jackson could not have put his conceptualisation of 'equal justice' more plainly than in the concluding paragraphs of his opening statement at Nuremberg: 'And let me make clear that while this law is first applied against German aggressors, the law ... must condemn aggression by any other nations, including those which sit here now in judgment.'[34]

Truman's reminder to the General Assembly on 23 October 1946 that a number of its members were already bound by the principles of the Nuremberg Charter[35] was not simply a 'one-off' event. It was followed up a week later by Warren R. Austin, Chief Delegate of the United States to the United Nations, with an even more explicit statement made before the General Assembly, naming key countries, and mentioning not only trial, but punishment as well: 'Besides being bound by the law of the United Nations Charter, 23 nations, members of this Assembly, including the United States, Soviet Russia, the United Kingdom and France, are also bound by the law of the Charter of the Nuremberg Tribunal. That makes planning or waging a war of aggression a crime against humanity for which individuals as well as nations can be brought before the bar of international justice, tried and punished.'[36]

---

33 On the subject of the veto power of the permanent members of the Security Council, it may be of some small historical interest to note that in 1922, a successful American publisher named Edward Bok offered a prize of up to $100,000 for a Peace Plan Award, attracting over 52,000 submissions, including a plan proposed by Franklin Delano Roosevelt. Roosevelt's proposal for a 'Society of Nations' provided that membership of 'the five so-called Great Powers' on the Society's Executive Committee would not be permanent, but, rather, would be for an initial period of ten years. His plan contained no provision for *a veto* power, but, rather, expressed the view that 'common sense cannot defend a procedure by which one or two recalcitrant nations could block the will of the great majority'. Roosevelt's 'A Plan to Preserve World Peace Offered for The American Peace Award' is reprinted in its entirety as Appendix I in Eleanor Roosevelt, *This I Remember*, New York: Harper, 1949. For a discussion of the Bok Peace Plan Award, see Robert H. Ferrell, *Peace in Their Time, The Origins of the Kellogg-Briand Pact*, New Haven: Yale University Press, 1952, pp. 24–5.

34 (1947) 2 IMT 99, at p. 154.

35 UN Doc. A/PV.37.

36 *New York Times*, 31 October 1946.

In the fall of 1946, momentum towards codification of the Nuremberg principles was clearly building. Shortly after the conclusion of the Nuremberg trial, Francis Biddle, who had served as the lead American judge, met with President Truman, at whose behest Biddle issued a written report dated 9 November 1946. In his report, Biddle observed that '[a]ggressive war was once romantic; now it is criminal'. He urged 'that the United Nations as a whole reaffirm the principles of the Nürnberg Charter in the context of a general codification of offenses against the peace and security of mankind' – adding immediately thereafter that '[s]uch action would perpetuate the vital principle that war of aggression is the supreme crime'. He reiterated that 'sovereign immunity cannot be invoked' to protect leaders with 'lust for conquest'.[37] Truman wasted little time in responding: on 12 November 1946 he replied to Biddle, expressing the view that 'we have established for all time the proposition that aggressive war is criminal and will be so treated', adding that it was his own 'hope that the United Nations will reaffirm the principles of the Nürnberg Charter in the context of a general codification of offenses against the peace and security of mankind'.[38] The General Assembly's unanimous adoption of resolution 95(I) calling for just such a codification of offences was the fruit borne of such hopes.[39]

The Kampala amendments on aggression, if activated, could well enable the Court to serve as the very 'bar of international justice' that United States policy had pushed hard for over sixty years ago. The current obstacles that have been put in their path block the courthouse door as far as the crime of aggression is concerned, continuing a precarious *status quo*, where law cannot effectively be relied on to deter international illegal uses of force. Such a void has two unfortunate effects: it encourages those who would undertake the illegal use of force in the first instance as well

---

37 Text of Judge Biddle's report to the President, 9 November 1946, *Department of State Bulletin*, 17 November 1946, p. 954.

38 Text of letter sent by the President on November 12 to Francis Biddle, United States Member of the International Military Tribunal, *Department of State Bulletin*, 17 November 1946, p. 953.

39 Such hopes were, of course, also reflected in the pre–Second World War 'outlawry of war' movement's goal of abolishing war by way of an international code and court. See, for example, the work of Salmon O. Levinson (a Chicago lawyer who worked tirelessly to promote these concepts), *The Outlawry of War*, Chicago: American Committee on the Outlawry of War, 1921.

as those who would use violent means to address their grievances against its use because recourse to an effective judicial remedy is not an option.

The establishment of the International Criminal Court reflects the Nuremberg precedent regarding holding leaders to account for grave crimes of concern to all humankind. It is a reflection of the fact that we live in an age of humanity against crimes. Yet the characterisation of illegal war-making as a crime against all of humankind didn't begin at Nuremberg: it preceded it by almost 200 years. As early as 1758, the Swiss jurist Emmerich de Vattel wrote, in his *Law of Nations*, that the sovereign who takes his nation into an unjust war is guilty not only of a crime against his own people and the nation that he attacks, but also 'of a crime against mankind in general, whose peace he disturbs, and to whom he sets a pernicious example'.[40] Certainly, in the post-Nuremberg era, those who illegally take the law into their own hands in fomenting armed conflict – those who 'set in motion' such evils – cannot complain too loudly that they have not been put on notice that there may ultimately be a personal price to pay for such criminality.

But what of humanitarian intervention? If we criminalise uses of force that have not been authorised by the letter of the UN Charter, where does that leave us? Those who intervene militarily in the cause of true humanitarian objectives should find that they have little to fear from the Kampala amendments on aggression – but those who take it upon themselves to act in a manner which, on its face, is in violation of the UN Charter should understandably expect that they will bear the burden of proving the legitimacy of their actions. The language of article 8 *bis* of the Rome Statute, and the accompanying Understandings, make it unlikely that a *bona fide* act of humanitarian intervention would be prosecuted as an act of aggression. But there can be no 'free ride' for those who claim to have humanitarian interest on their side, as humanitarian interventions, like beauty, often exist 'in the eye of the beholder'.[41] This is

---

40 Emmerich de Vattel, *The Law of Nations*, Philadelphia: T. and J.W. Johnson and Co., 1883, Book 3, Ch. 11.

41 As a small aside, it may be noted that, according to Saddam Hussein, the invasion of Kuwait by the forces of Iraq in August of 1990 was undertaken as a matter of humanitarian intervention (in response to a purported plea for aid from 'revolutionary youth in Kuwait'), as reported in 'Iraq's Naked Aggression', *New York Times*, 3 August 1990.

not to say that the 'necessity defence' should not have a place in exonerating those who break the law where there is no reasonable choice but to do so. Such a defence exists, and for good cause, in many legal systems. But one breaks the law at one's peril, regardless of motives, and it should be up to an impartial court to determine whether the means, the motives, and the foreseeable consequence justify the actions taken.

The members of the Assembly of States Parties present at Kampala resolved, by consensus, 'to activate the Court's jurisdiction over the crime of aggression *as early as possible*'.[42] If they fail to live up to that commitment, they deserve to be seen as hypocrites.[43] And worse: by dragging their heels on ratifying agreed-upon amendments to criminalise the illegal use of force, they perpetuate the perception that 'international relations are still about who can do what to whom'.[44] Powerful States that turn their back on the effective criminalisation of aggression run the risk of looking as though they are either hiding from the law or consider themselves above it – a gift to those looking for adherents to the notion that violence is, therefore, a legitimate means for resolving perceived grievances against them.

42 Resolution RC/Res.6, p. 6.
43 Since my purpose here is to help draw attention to the respective States Parties obligation to activate the Court's jurisdiction over the crime of aggression as soon as possible, I take the liberty of listing the States Parties to the Assembly of States Parties represented in Kampala: Albania, Argentina, Australia, Austria, Bangladesh, Belgium, Bolivia (Plurinational State of), Botswana, Brazil, Bulgaria, Burkina Faso, Burundi, Canada, Central African Republic, Chad, Chile, Colombia, Comoros, Congo, Costa Rica, Croatia, Cyprus, Czech Republic, Democratic Republic of the Congo, Denmark, Djibouti, Ecuador, Estonia, Finland, France, Gambia, Georgia, Germany, Ghana, Greece, Guinea, Hungary, Ireland, Italy, Japan, Jordan, Kenya, Lesotho, Liechtenstein, Luxembourg, Macedonia (Former Yugoslav Republic of), Malawi, Mali, Mauritius, Mexico, Mongolia, Montenegro, Namibia, Nauru, Netherlands, New Zealand, Niger, Nigeria, Norway, Panama, Paraguay, Peru, Poland, Portugal, Republic of Korea, Romania, Samoa, San Marino, Senegal, Serbia, Sierra Leone, Slovakia, Slovenia, South Africa, Spain, Sweden, Switzerland, Trinidad and Tobago, Uganda, United Kingdom of Great Britain and Northern Ireland, United Republic of Tanzania, Uruguay, Venezuela (Republic of), and Zambia.
44 Robert D. Kaplan, 'Old World Order: How geopolitics fuels endless chaos and old-school conflicts in the 21st Century', *Time Magazine*, 31 March 2014, p. 26.

Some will say that death and destruction are the inevitable consequence not only of illegal uses of force, but also of the legal use of force, as authorised by the UN Charter, and, of course, they are correct. But there is a difference: those who undertake the illegal use of force should have no latitude to argue that they are shielded by either the laws of war or by the rules of international humanitarian law.

The compromise on aggression reached in Kampala has been criticised by some as being inconsistent with provisions within the Rome Statute that, as a general matter, provide that the Court may not exercise its jurisdiction over nationals of Assembly of States Parties members that have not independently ratified amendments to the Statute's core crime provisions.[45] Yet there is no denying that the original language of article 5(2) of the Statute expressly granted the Assembly of States Parties the authority for 'setting out the conditions under which the Court shall exercise jurisdiction' over the crime of aggression[46] – and that's precisely what it did in Kampala. Thus far, no ratifying State has raised any such objection to the results of the compromise achieved and agreed to by consensus in Kampala.

It has been said that 'A person stands a better chance of being tried and judged for killing one human being than for killing 100,000'.[47] Yet, notwithstanding such stark observations, not everyone is convinced that acts of aggression should be criminalised.[48] Even if the Court is granted

---

45 Rome Statute, article 121(5).

46 Article 5(2), set forth at note 10, *supra*. Confusion regarding entry into force and the Court's exercise of jurisdiction may have led some, including this author, to contrary preliminary thinking on this topic based on a literal reading, in isolation, of article 121(5), without fuller consideration of article 5(2)'s express grant of authority to the Assembly of States Parties with respect to setting out the conditions under which the Court shall exercise jurisdiction, specifically over the crime of aggression – a crime that was *already* included within the jurisdiction of the Court.

47 José Ayala Lasso, former United Nations High Commissioner for Human Rights, as quoted in the United Nations overview of the International Criminal Court. A similar observation was made by the well-known nineteenth century peace activist and former United States Senator, Charles Sumner: 'While condemning the ordinary malefactor, mankind, blind to the real character of War, may yet a little longer crown the giant actor with glory'. See, Charles Sumner, *Addresses on War*, Memphis: General Books, 2012, p. 21.

48 For example, Michael J. Glennon, 'The Blank-Prose Crime of Aggression', (2010) 35 *Yale Journal of International Law* 71, at p. 73; Beth Van Schaack,

jurisdiction over the crime of aggression, it may well be that prosecution of such cases will be rare. Nonetheless, and regardless of the likelihood of an actual prosecution for the crime of aggression, it has been observed, and is well-worth noting, that '[e]xperiments have long revealed the symbiosis of law and morality: being told that a behaviour is illegal makes it also seem more immoral'.[49] Such logic makes a compelling case for criminalising acts of aggression at both the international as well as the domestic level.

When Frank Kellogg accepted the Nobel Peace Prize on 10 December 1929 for his work on what is often referred to as the Kellogg-Briand Pact, he expressed a similar thought:

> I know there are those who believe that peace will not be attained until some super-tribunal is established to punish the violators of such treaties, but I believe that in the end the abolition of war, the maintenance of world peace, the adjustment of international questions by pacific means will come through the force of public opinion, which controls nations and peoples – that public opinion which shapes our destinies and guides the progress of human affairs.[50]

But public opinion does not exist in a vacuum. Like the wheels of justice – reputed to grind slowly – the wheels of public opinion move more effectively when given a push. If it is to be a factor in effectuating deterrence, it must be supported by an awareness of the customary law prohibition of planning or waging aggressive war as well as the statutory prohibition on acts constituting the crime of aggression, as defined within the Rome Statute and developing domestic criminal codes.

That it is political leaders themselves who are most responsible for leading nations to war was rather candidly affirmed at Nuremberg by former Reichsmarschall Herman Goering (Hitler's one-time second in command, who was sentenced to death by the International Military Tribunal):

> Naturally the common people don't want war; neither in Russia nor in England nor in America, nor for that matter in Germany. That is understood.

'In Advance of Activating The Crime of Aggression', *War Crimes Prosecution Watch*, 9 Issue 9, 28 July 2014.

49 Jan Sterling Silver, 'Can the Law Make Us Be Decent?', *New York Times*, 7 November 2012, p. A25.

50 Frank B. Kellogg's Acceptance Speech on the occasion of the award of the Nobel Peace Prize in Oslo, 10 December 1929.

But, after all, it is the *leaders* of the country who determine the policy and it is always a simple matter to drag the people along, whether it is a democracy or a fascist dictatorship or a Parliament, or a Communist dictatorship. Voice or no voice, the people can always be brought to the bidding of the leaders. That is easy. All you have to do is tell them they are being attacked and denounce the pacifists for lack of patriotism and exposing the country to danger. It works the same way in any country.[51]

The 2003 military incursion in Iraq, based on false and misleading reports of weapons of mass destruction, bears powerful witness to the continuing validity of such observations. In light of this, and recalling that complacency is a first cousin to complicity, it is to be hoped that people of goodwill may perhaps learn from this and possibly be a bit more motivated to actively engage in advancing the rule of law and holding accountable those who violate it.

The failure thus far to activate the International Criminal Court's aggression jurisdiction brings to mind not only the somewhat facetious musings of a 1938 poem by the late Stephen Vincent Benét, 'I wonder if it wouldn't simplify things to declare mankind in a permanent state of siege', but also words often attributed to Albert Einstein: 'Insanity is doing the same thing over and over again and expecting different results.'

Isn't it time for a change?

Dwight Eisenhower predicted in 1959 that 'people want peace so badly that one of these days governments are going to have to get out of their way and let them have it'.[52] Ratifying the Kampala amendments and, in addition, making aggression a punishable crime within national criminal codes might be a very good place to start.

FURTHER READING

Stefan Barriga and Leena Grover, 'A Historic Breakthrough on the Crime of Aggression', (2011) 105 *American Journal of International Law* 517.

Niels Blokker and Claus Kress, 'A Consensus Agreement of the Crime of Aggression: Impressions from Kampala', (2010) 23 *Leiden Journal of International Law* 889.

51 Gustave Mark Gilbert, *Nuremberg Diary*, Boston: Da Capo Press, 1995, pp. 278–9.

52 Radio and Television Broadcast with Prime Minister Macmillan in London, 31 August 1959.

Roger S. Clark, 'Amendments to the Rome Statute of the International Criminal Court Considered at the First Review Conference on the Court, Kampala, 31 May-11 June 2010', (2010) 2 *Goettingen Journal of International Law* 689.

Benjamin Ferencz, *Defining International Aggression, The Search for World Peace*, Dobbs Ferry: Oceana Press, 1975.

Benjamin Ferencz, *New Legal Foundations for Global Survival: Security through the Security Council*, Dobbs Ferry: Oceana Press, 1994.

Christopher Gevers and Anton du Plessis, 'Africa and the Codification of Aggression: A Pyrrhic Victory?', *Africa Legal Aid Quarterly*, April–June 2010, pp. 28–39.

Michael J. Glennon, 'The Blank-Prose Crime of Aggression', (2010) 35 *Yale Journal of International Law* 71.

Kevin Jon Heller, 'The Sadly Neutered Crime of Aggression', *Opinio Juris*, June 2010.

Carrie McDougall, *The Crime of Aggression under the Rome Statute of the International Criminal Court*, Cambridge University Press, 2013.

Jutta Bertram Nothnagel, 'A Seed for World Peace Planted in Africa: The Provisions on the Crime of Aggression Adopted at the Kampala Review Conference for the Rome Statute of the International Criminal Court', *Africa Legal Aid Quarterly*, April–June 2010, pp. 9–27.

Kirsten Sellars, *Crimes Against Peace and International Law*, Cambridge University Press, 2013.

Jennifer Trahan, 'The Rome Statute's Amendment on the Crime of Aggression: Negotiations at the Kampala Review Conference', (2011) 11 *International Criminal Law Review* 49.

Jennifer Trahan, 'A Meaningful Definition of the Crime of Aggression: A Response to Michael Glennon', (2012) 33 *University of Pennsylvania Journal of International Law* 907.

Children 13

Diane Marie Amann

Children withstand unique harms in periods of armed conflict and similar violence. Whether infants or juveniles, during such periods children often are among the most vulnerable persons. Children typically depend on their elders for sustenance, and so the loss of parents or other guardians, coupled with the destruction of homes, displacement from communities, and deprivation of basic necessities, education, or health care, affects them acutely. Some children do not survive war; others subsist along war's waysides. Still others find themselves in armed groups, where they may be required to aid or participate in combat and, at times, to endure sexual or other physical assault. In recognition of such experiences, Raphael Lemkin, a foundational figure in the development of international criminal law, once wrote: 'The permanent psychological injury and the arrest of normal development of the child victim is perhaps the most shocking and tragic result of genocide.'[1]

Stories of such children have been told and retold, not only in recent memoirs like *A Long Way Gone*, an account of armed conflicts in 1990s West Africa, but also in much older ones like the world-famous diary of Anne Frank, a European teenager who lost her battle to hide from the Holocaust.[2] Frank's story reflected a myriad of children's experiences during the Second World War. Nevertheless, early international criminal justice mechanisms paid scant attention to children's wartime plight. Neither the 1945 Charter of the International Military Tribunal, which

This chapter is written solely in my personal capacity. My thanks to Stephany Sheriff for research assistance.

1 Stephen L. Jacobs, ed., *Lemkin on Genocide*, Lanham: Lexington Books, 2012, p. 33.
2 Ishmael Beah, *A Long Way Gone: Memoirs of a Boy Soldier*, New York: Sarah Crichton Books/Farrar, Straus and Giroux, 2007; Anne Frank, *The Diary of a Young Girl*, New York: Random House/Everyman's Library, 2010.

tried accused major war criminals in Germany, nor Control Council Law No. 10, upon which twelve subsequent Nuremberg trials were based, made any mention of children. The same was true of the 1946 Charter establishing the Tokyo Tribunal. Even the seminal instrument of post-war collective security, the Charter of the United Nations, was silent with respect to children. In stark contrast were institutions established at the turn of the twenty-first century. The statutes of both the Special Court for Sierra Leone and the International Criminal Court place emphasis on crimes against children, and both courts have convicted individuals charged with such crimes. The initial focus, on the recruitment and use of child soldiers, eventually shifted towards a more comprehensive approach. International Criminal Court Prosecutor Fatou Bensouda has explained that 'in addition to focusing on children who are forced to carry arms, we must also address the issue of children who are *affected* by arms'.[3] This chapter first will trace developments that gave rise to the current emphasis, and then will examine key judgments as well as the recent move to a broader strategy. It will conclude by discussing challenges to the prevention and punishment of international crimes against children.

Towards accountability for crimes against children

Despite their charters' silence on the issue, the post–Second World War tribunals did not wholly ignore the effects of armed conflict on children. The first Nuremberg judgment contained a dozen such references. Most were brief mentions of children in the company of adults; for example, an *Einsatzgruppe* leader's statement that his unit had 'liquidated approximately 90,000 men, women and children'.[4] To the same effect were most of the five references to children in the Tokyo Tribunal's 1948 judgment.[5] Still, vulnerabilities attached to childhood were central to the Nuremberg judgment's discussions of certain Nazi practices, such as abduction and forced adoption in order to boost the number of persons presumed to possess what one witness called 'good blood of our type', and forced abortion

---

3 Fatou Bensouda, 'Children and International Criminal Justice', (2015) 43 *Georgia Journal of International and Comparative Law* forthcoming (internal quotations omitted; emphasis in the original).
4 (1948) 22 IMT 491.
5 B. V. A. Röling and C. F. Rüter, eds., *The Tokyo Judgment*, vol. 1, Amsterdam: APA University Press, 1977, pp. 96, 388–9, 396, 399.

if, in the words of another witness, 'the child's parentage would not meet the racial standards'.[6] Finding that the Nazis routinely had killed captives too young to work in concentration camps, the International Military Tribunal quoted from an official's affidavit: 'Very frequently women would hide their children under their clothes, but of course when we found them we would send the children in to be exterminated.'[7] Testimony at trial connected killings of children to the Nazis' ultimate goal: to eliminate an ethno-religious group.[8]

That annihilative intent–precisely, the 'intent to destroy, in whole or in part, a national, ethnical, racial or religious group'–was proscribed in a foremost instrument of modern international criminal law, the Convention on Genocide that the UN General Assembly approved in December 1948. The brainchild of Lemkin, this treaty aimed squarely at Second World War practices like forced adoption, and thus listed '[f]orcibly transferring children' of a protected group to another group as one of the five acts that might constitute genocide. The treaty reached criminality against future generations as well, forbidding the imposition of 'measures intended to prevent births' in a protected group.

As the onset of the Cold War stymied the enforcement of such prohibitions, States spoke more of protecting children from harm than of prosecuting harm once it occurred. The General Assembly endorsed the 1948 Universal Declaration of Human Rights, which proclaimed that '[m]otherhood and childhood are entitled to special care and assistance', and that '[a]ll children, whether born in or out of wedlock, shall enjoy the same social protection', including free education 'at least in the elementary and fundamental stages'. In 1949, States adopted the Geneva Conventions for the protection of victims of war, the fourth of which contained multiple provisions intended to assure the identification, education, health, and well-being of infants and other children, during armed conflict and under occupation.[9] The 1977 Additional Protocols to those universally ratified conventions reinforced this

---

6 (1948) 22 IMT 480.   7 Ibid., p. 503.

8 (1947) 4 IMT 337–338 (cross-examination of Ohlendorf).

9 Convention (No. IV) Relative to the Protection of Civilian Persons in Time of War, (1950) 75 UNTS 287, articles 14, 17, 23, 24, 38(5), 50, 82, 89, 94, 132. This protective array compares favourably to a legal regulation issued during the United States Civil War: its sole reference to children recommended, yet did not require, notice of attack 'so that the non-combatants, and especially the women and children, may be removed before the bombardment commences'.

regime.[10] The contours of protection took shape with the adoption of the 1989 Convention on the Rights of the Child and the 1990 African Charter on the Rights and Welfare of the Child, each of which embraced as general principles recognition of the child's rights to life and to express views in matters affecting him or her, as well as guarantees of non-discrimination and action in a child's best interests.

These latter treaties also helped to restart efforts at prohibition; precisely, prohibition of the use or recruitment of children in armed service. Additional Protocol I provides that '[p]arties to the conflict shall take all feasible measures in order that children ... do not take a direct part in hostilities', and further specifies that such parties 'shall refrain from recruiting' children under fifteen 'into their armed forces', while Additional Protocol II states that 'children ... shall neither be recruited in the armed forces or groups nor allowed to take part in hostilities'. In the Children's Convention, meanwhile, States Parties similarly promise to 'take all feasible measures' so that young persons 'do not take a direct part in hostilities', and also to 'refrain from recruiting any person who has not attained the age of 15 years into their armed forces'. The African Children's Charter follows suit, with an important innovation: whereas previous treaties limited the recruitment-and-use ban to children who had not yet attained their fifteenth birthday, this regional child rights instrument extended that ban to everyone under eighteen. Subsequent treaties, such as the 1999 Convention on the Worst Forms of Child Labour and the 2000 Optional Protocol on the Involvement of Children in Armed Conflict, also opt for the eighteen-year-old threshold.

The promulgation of these overlapping and sometimes contradictory treaties coincided with a Cold War thaw and consequent revival of the international criminal justice project begun in the Nuremberg-Tokyo era. The new tribunals drew note for pioneering jurisprudence with regard to sexual and gender-based violence – crimes that their mid-twentieth

Instructions for the Government of Armies of the United States in the Field, General Orders No. 100, article 19.

10 Protocol I Additional to the Geneva Conventions of 12 Aug. 1949, and Relating to the Protection of Victims of International Armed Conflicts, (1979) 1125 UNTS 3, articles 70(1), 76–8; Protocol II Additional to the Geneva Conventions of 12 August 1949, and relating to the Protection of Victims of Non-International Armed Conflicts, (1979) 1125 UNTS 609, articles 4(3), 6(4).

century forebears had afforded a secondary priority.[11] Like those forebears, however, the new tribunals did not dwell upon crimes against children. That changed after news dispatches and Graça Machel's 1996 UN report alerted public opinion to the prevalence of children – some younger than ten – in the ranks of national armies and rebel groups that then were waging wars across the globe.[12]

The 1998 Rome Statute of the International Criminal Court and the 2002 Statute of the Special Court for Sierra Leone, therefore, both authorised war crimes prosecutions for the conscription, enlistment, and use of children in armed forces. Yet both statutes confined the courts' jurisdiction to the recruitment or use of children under fifteen, notwithstanding the higher age limit adopted in contemporaneous child rights treaties. In other respects, however, both statutes were products of a child rights vanguard, represented at the 1998 Rome Conference by UNICEF and an active children's caucus of non-governmental organisations, and by a similar coalition in the run-up to the adoption of the 2002 Special Court Statute.[13] For example, abuse of girls and abduction of girls, proscribed under pre-existing Sierra Leonean law, were enumerated as crimes within the jurisdiction of the Special Court. An initial proposal to operate a Special Court juvenile chamber was set aside. Although that Court's statute did authorise the prosecution of children as young as fifteen, it mandated that anyone convicted of a crime committed when he or she was between

11 E.g., *Prosecutor* v. *Akayesu* (ICTR-96-4-T), Judgment, 2 September 1998; *Prosecutor* v. *Kunarac* et al. (IT-96-23 & IT-96-23/10), Judgment, 12 June 2002.

12 Impact of Armed Conflict on Children: Report of the Expert of the Secretary-General, Ms Graça Machel, submitted pursuant to General Assembly Resolution 48/157, UN Doc. A/51/306, paras. 34–62. The Machel Report inspired the establishment of an office to coordinate efforts among UN entities including the Security Council. See Office of the Special Representative to the Secretary-General for Children and Armed Conflict, *The Six Grave Violations Against Children During Armed Conflict: The Legal Foundation* (November 2009).

13 Per Saland, 'International Criminal Law Principles', in Roy S. Lee, ed., *The International Criminal Court: The Making of the Rome Statute: Issues, Negotiations, Results*, The Hague/London/Boston: Kluwer Law International, 1999, pp. 189–216, at p. 201; Ilene Cohn, 'The Protection of Children and the Quest for Truth and Justice in Sierra Leone', (2001) 55 *Journal of International Affairs* 1, at p. 19.

fifteen and eighteen years old would be subject not to imprisonment but rather to rehabilitation and societal reintegration.[14]

As for the Rome Statute, concern for young people is manifest in the very preamble: 'Mindful that during this century millions of children, women and men have been victims of unimaginable atrocities that deeply shock the conscience of humanity'. The drafters declared they were establishing the International Criminal Court 'for the sake of present and future generations'. Article 36 of the Statute requires States Parties to 'take into account the need to include judges with legal expertise on ... violence against women or children', and article 42 further authorises the Prosecutor to 'appoint advisers with legal expertise on specific issues, including ... violence against children'. Additional provisions instruct Court officials to accommodate the needs of child victims and witnesses.[15] What is more, article 26 of the Rome Statute not only excludes from the Court's jurisdiction 'any person who was under 18 at the time of the alleged commission of a crime', even as other provisions confer jurisdiction over adults for a range of crimes against children. Apparently not content simply to list so-called generic offences like killing or pillaging, which affect adults as well as children,[16] the drafters enumerated multiple child-specific crimes: genocide involving the forcible transfer of children; the crime against humanity of enslavement, defined with express reference to the trafficking of children; and, of course, the war crimes of conscription, enlistment, and use of children in armed groups. Also listed are numerous crimes that keenly affect children and future generations: prevention of births as genocide; sexual slavery, forced pregnancy, or enforced sterilisation as crimes against humanity or war crimes; and attacks on schools and hospitals as war crimes. Sexual slavery of children is expressly mentioned in the Elements of Crimes. Children similarly would suffer unique harm from the crime against humanity of persecution, if perpetrated by reason of the victim's age.

---

14 Diane Marie Amann, 'Calling Children to Account: The Proposal for a Juvenile Chamber in the Special Court for Sierra Leone', (2001) 29 *Pepperdine Law Review* 167.

15 Rome Statute, articles 54(1)(b), 68(1), (2). See also article 84 (authorising post humous revision of sentence on request of a convicted person's child).

16 Cecile Aptel, 'Unpunished Crimes: The Special Court for Sierra Leone and Children', in Charles Jalloh, ed., *The Sierra Leone Special Court and Its Legacy*, New York: Cambridge University Press, 2014, pp. 340–60, at p. 341, n.3.

Given these developments, it is little surprise that crimes against children figured prominently in the work of both the International Criminal Court and the Special Court for Sierra Leone. As discussed below, although decisions in the latter Court concentrated on child soldiering, over time the docket of the International Criminal Court grew to include additional charges involving child victims.

Special Court for Sierra Leone and crimes against children

Endemic during the 1990s civil war that wracked Sierra Leone were accounts of young people – sometimes, very young children – who toted AK-47s and committed atrocities. Typical was the 1999 report of a teenaged veteran who boasted: 'We attacked everybody. We feared nobody. We were very bold. Everybody is knowing our hot tempers.'[17] Stories of such children, and of persons of all ages victimised by their actions, stirred what has been called the 'international legal imagination',[18] and so led to the legal developments just discussed. In the end, Special Court prosecutors chose not to exercise their statutory authority to charge persons as young as fifteen; nor did they allege crimes against girls pursuant to the incorporated Sierra Leonean law.[19] Prosecutors did, however, pursue charges related to the recruitment and use of child soldiers.

The prohibition against child soldiering survived an early challenge in the Special Court. In *Prosecutor* v. *Norman*, a former Sierra Leonean government minister accused of recruiting or using children under fifteen in a pro-government militia asserted that such conduct was not criminal under customary international law. Over the dissent of one judge, a four-member Appeals Chamber held otherwise. Surveying the evolution of the prohibition contained in the Special Court's statute, the majority

17 Josep Sonah, then nineteen, quoted in Colin Nickerson, 'Albright to see Peace's High Price in Sierra Leone', *Boston Globe*, 18 October 1999, p. A1.

18 Mark A. Drumbl, *Reimagining Child Soldiers in International Law and Policy*, Oxford: Oxford University Press, 2012, p. 9.

19 Cecile Aptel, 'Unpunished Crimes: The Special Court for Sierra Leone and Children', in Charles Jalloh, ed., *The Sierra Leone Special Court and Its Legacy*, New York: Cambridge University Press, 2014, pp. 340–360, at p. 356; David M. Crane, 'Prosecuting Children in Times of Conflict: The West African Experience', (2008) 15/3 *Human Rights Brief* 11.

ruled, first, that an 'overwhelming majority of States' did not recruit such children and in fact had 'criminalised such behaviour' at the time in question, and second, that the government of Sierra Leone was on notice of this 'customary norm'.[20] One commentator saw in this 2004 decision 'the beginning of a trend … to take seriously the issue of crimes concerning children, and to prosecute those responsible for such violations, both to exact retribution from the offender, as well as to send a message of deterrence to others'.[21]

Consequent efforts at prosecution nevertheless met with mixed results. The accused in *Norman* died before the Trial Chamber's verdict issued. In that verdict, one co-accused was acquitted of the child-soldiering count, and the child-soldiering conviction of the third co-accused was overturned on appeal.[22] In contrast, in the two cases involving leaders of rebel groups, all but one accused was convicted at trial of recruiting or using child soldiers, and all five such convictions were sustained on appeal.[23] The Special Court's final trial resulted in the conviction of former Liberian President Charles Taylor on eleven counts, including a charge of aiding and abetting the rebel groups' recruitment or use of boys and girls under fifteen.[24] In 2013 that judgment, plus another imposing a sentence of fifty years in prison, withstood the accused's appellate challenge.[25] The 349-page appeals judgment detailed findings not only of systematic harms that children suffered in armed groups, but also of sexual and gender-based violence against victims described as 'women and girls', without further age differentiation.[26]

20 *Prosecutor* v. *Norman* (SCSL-04-14-AR-72(E)), Decision on Preliminary Motion Based on Lack of Jurisdiction (Child Recruitment), 31 May 2004, paras. 51–2.

21 Max du Plessis, 'Children under International Criminal Law', (2004) 13 *African Security Review* 103, at p. 108.

22 *Prosecutor* v. *Fofana* et al. (SCSL-04-14-A), Appeals Judgment, 28 May 2008.

23 *Prosecutor* v. *Sesay* et al. (SCSL-04-15-A), Appeals Judgment, 26 October 2009; *Prosecutor* v. *Brima* et al. (SCSL-04-16-A), Appeals Judgment, 22 February 2008.

24 *Prosecutor* v. *Taylor* (SCSL-03-01-T) Judgment, 30 May 2012.

25 *Prosecutor* v. *Taylor* (SCSL-03-01-A), Appeals Judgment, 26 September 2013.

26 Ibid., paras. 260–73.

Early child-specific jurisprudence of the International Criminal Court

By the time the Special Court's Appeals Chamber issued its judgment in *Taylor*, the International Criminal Court already had concluded two trials involving child-soldiering charges, against three defendants. Another person accused of crimes involving children was in custody following his surrender to the court, and a handful of others so charged remained at large.

The first International Criminal Court trial, *Prosecutor* v. *Lubanga*, pertained exclusively to allegations that the accused, a former leader of a Congolese rebel group, was responsible as an indirect co-perpetrator for the war crimes of 'conscripting or enlisting children under the age of 15 years ... or using them to participate actively in hostilities'. This singular focus signalled '[t]hat children come first, at the top of our contemporary priorities when dealing with the victims of armed conflict', one commentator wrote.[27] The focus on children drew sustained criticism, however, from victims' groups and other non-governmental organisations usually supportive of the Office of the Prosecutor; they complained in particular that despite available evidence, sexual and gender-based crimes had not been charged.[28] The Trial Chamber would echo such criticism in its post-trial judgments.

Compounding these difficulties, the reliance on child victims in *Lubanga* soon gave rise to problems of proof. The very first witness began his testimony by recanting a prior statement that he had been abducted and forced to serve as a child soldier in the defendant's militia. Trial was put on hold for a week, and eventually the witness testified in accordance with the prior statement. In its verdict, however, the Trial Chamber rejected as unreliable not just his testimony but that of all witnesses

27 William A. Schabas, 'Commentary on: Children and Armed Conflict', in Noëlle Quénivet and Shilan Shah-Davis, eds., *International Law and Armed Conflict*, The Hague: TMC·Asser Press, 2010, pp. 283–7, at p. 283.

28 Margaret M. deGuzman, 'Choosing to Prosecute: Expressive Selection at the International Criminal Court', (2012) 33 *Michigan Journal of International Law* 265, at p. 273. See Diane Marie Amann, 'Children and the First Verdict of the International Criminal Court', (2013) 12 *Washington University Global Studies Law Review* 411, at pp. 424–8.

who said they had been child soldiers. Yet it credited the testimony of two experts and of a UN official who had worked with child combatants demobilised after the Congolese conflict. Pivotal was the Trial Chamber's viewing of a video in which the defendant rallied troops while surrounded by bodyguards who, in the eyes of the judges, were 'recruits who were clearly under the age of 15'.[29] In a trilogy of 2012 decisions, therefore, the Trial Chamber: convicted the defendant of conscription, enlistment, and use in a non-international armed conflict; imposed a concurrent fourteen-year sentence; and outlined a framework for the award of reparations to victims of the crimes of conviction.

Late in 2014, a majority of the five-member Appeals Chamber sustained the conviction and sentence in *Lubanga*.[30] In so doing, it issued a number of important rulings with respect to child-soldiering crimes. First, it rejected the defence challenge to the manner by which child victims had been determined to meet the Rome Statute's age threshold. The Appeals Chamber ruled that 'it suffices that it is established that the victim is within a certain *age range*, namely *under* the age of 15 years', and further held that in the absence of precise records, age is a factual finding to be determined case-by-case.[31] It also accepted the testimony about children's ages that the judgment below credited, as well as the trial judges' finding that the rally video depicted child soldiers under fifteen.[32] Second, the Appeals Chamber clarified the relationship between 'conscripting' and 'enlisting' children. The defence in *Lubanga* had argued that the Trial Chamber erred as a matter of law when it wrote that conscription, or forcible recruitment, and enlistment, or voluntary enrolment, 'are dealt with together'.[33] The Appeals Chamber stressed that the two crimes

---

29 *Prosecutor* v. *Lubanga* (ICC-01/04-01-06), Judgment Pursuant to Article 74 of the Statute, 14 March 2012, para. 792.

30 *Prosecutor* v. *Lubanga* (ICC-01/04-01/06 A 5), Judgment on the Appeal of Mr Thomas Lubanga Dyilo against his Conviction, 1 December 2014; *Prosecutor* v. *Lubanga* (ICC-01/04-01/06 A 4 A 6), Judgment on the Appeal of Mr Thomas Lubanga Dyilo against the 'Decision on Sentence Pursuant to Article 76 of the Statute', 1 December 2014. Judge Anita Ušacka would have reversed the conviction on grounds of insufficient evidence, while Judge Sang-Hyun Song objected to the majority's treatment of child-soldiering crimes.

31 *Prosecutor* v. *Lubanga* (ICC-01/04-01/06 A 5), Judgment on the Appeal of Mr Thomas Lubanga Dyilo against his Conviction, 1 December 2014, para. 198 (emphasis in the original).

32 Ibid., paras. 207–62.   33 Ibid., para. 268.

are distinct because only conscription entails an element of compulsion, and it next found in the trial record sufficient evidence of such compulsion. A related defence argument, that conviction for conscription depended upon proof of lack of consent by the child, was dismissed; 'the elements of these crimes', the Chamber explained, 'focus on the conduct of the perpetrator'.[34]

Finally, the Appeals Chamber weighed in on how to interpret 'using ... to participate actively in hostilities', a statutory phrase with which other judges in the International Criminal Court and in the Special Court for Sierra Leone already had grappled. In *Lubanga*, the Trial Chamber majority had ruled that the phrase encompassed not only front-line combat, but also situations when 'support provided by the child to the combatants exposed him or her to a real danger as a potential target'.[35] The lone dissenter preferred a much broader interpretation. Arguing that the phrase encompassed not only supportive roles within a zone of danger, but also 'the sexual violence and other ill-treatment suffered by girls and boys', without regard to location, she wrote: 'The use of young girls' and boys' bodies by combatants within or outside the group is a war crime and as such encoded in the charges against the accused'.[36] On appeal, the defence characterised even the majority's middle-path interpretation as too broad. It endeavoured to equate 'using ... to participate actively in hostilities' with 'direct participation', an international humanitarian law concept that defines who is protected, and who may be targeted for killing, in times of armed conflict.[37] The Appeals Chamber rejected this claim of interchangeability. But it also rejected the Trial Chamber majority's construction, in favour of its own 'plain interpretation of the relevant provisions in their context'; in brief, the Appeals Chamber held that the crime of using children depends on proof of a 'link between the activity

---

34 Ibid., para. 302.

35 *Prosecutor* v. *Lubanga* (ICC-01/04-01-06), Judgment Pursuant to Article 74 of the Statute, 14 March 2012, para. 627.

36 *Prosecutor* v. *Lubanga* (ICC-01/04-01-06), Separate and Dissenting Opinion of Judge Odio Benito, 14 March 2012, paras. 16, 21 (punctuation as in original).

37 *Prosecutor* v. *Lubanga* (ICC-01/04-01/06 A 5), Judgment on the Appeal of Mr Thomas Lubanga Dyilo against his Conviction, 1 December 2014, paras. 315–20 (citing, *inter alia*, Additional Protocol I, article 51(3), which extends protections to civilians 'unless and for such time as they take a direct part in hostilities').

for which the child is used and the combat in which the armed force or group of the perpetrator is engaged'.[38]

Reluctant to delineate proscribed and permitted uses 'in view of the complex and unforeseeable scenarios presented by the rapidly changing face of warfare in the modern world', the Appeals Chamber in *Lubanga* called for case-by-case analysis.[39] It drew guidance from International Committee of the Red Cross commentaries, which included within the meaning of use 'military operations such as gathering information, transmitting orders, transporting ammunitions and foodstuffs, or acts of sabotage', as well as 'gathering and transmission of military information, transportation of arms and munitions, provision of supplies etc'.[40] Also consulted was a draft Rome Statute report, which included 'military activities linked to combat such as scouting, spying, sabotage and the use of children as decoys, couriers or at military checkpoints', and excluded 'activities clearly unrelated to the hostilities such as food deliveries to an airbase or the use of domestic staff in an officer's married accommodation'.[41] Sexual violence and other conduct of concern to the dissenter in the *Lubanga* trial judgment clearly fell outside the bounds of this construction. Within the posited meaning of use, however, was conduct for which the Trial Chamber had ruled the defendant responsible: 'the deployment of children under the age of fifteen years as soldiers and their participation in combat, as well as their use as military guards and bodyguards', as the Appeals Chamber described it.[42] Accordingly, the International Criminal Court's first trial concluded with affirmance of the judgment of conviction for crimes of child soldiering.

Acquittals in child-soldiering cases

The International Criminal Court's second trial took a turn very different from the proceedings in *Lubanga*. At issue was an attack that a rival rebel group had launched on a single day in Bogoro, a Congolese village said to harbour members of the militia over which the defendant in *Lubanga* once presided. Two leaders of that rival group stood trial in *Prosecutor*

---

38 Ibid., paras. 333, 335; see also para. 324.
39 Ibid., para. 335.   40 Ibid., para. 334.
41 Ibid.
42 Ibid., para. 340; see also paras. 341–433.

v. *Katanga and Ngudjolo*, for multiple crimes against civilians, including the use of 'children under 15 years for multiple purposes and to participate actively ... prior to, during, and following the attack'.[43] The cases were severed after trial concluded in 2012, yet in the end, both defendants were acquitted of the child-soldiering offence.

Before detailing its reasons for acquitting the defendant in *Ngudjolo* on all counts, the Trial Chamber, in a judgment subsequently upheld on appeal, emphasised its adherence to the Rome Statute provision that presumes innocence unless and until an accused is proved guilty '*au-delà de tout doute raisonnable*'–literally, 'beyond every reasonable doubt'.[44] It then ruled that essential facts had not been proved. As in *Lubanga*, judges found fault with persons who had testified that they were militia members. Concluding after extended analysis that three such prosecution witnesses were 'imprecise' and 'contradictory', the Chamber rejected their testimony in its entirety.[45] Unlike in *Lubanga*, in *Ngudjolo* the same fate befell videos introduced into evidence, all of which post-dated the attack.[46] The Trial Chamber did find that the presence of child combatants was '*un phénomène généralisé*', or 'a widespread phenomenon', during the period in question, and further that 'children under 15 years, some carrying blades, ... were present' at the attack itself.[47] Nevertheless, with respect to allegations that the accused had ordered military training for underage children or used them as bodyguards or for other purposes, the Chamber wrote in its 2012 judgment of acquittal that the credited evidence failed to establish the requisite nexus between the accused and child soldiers.[48]

---

43 *Prosecutor* v. *Ngudjolo* (ICC-01/04-02/12), Jugement Rendu en Application de l'article 74 du Statut, 18 December 2012, para. 504 (brackets around ellipsis and internal quotations omitted); *Prosecutor* v. *Katanga* (ICC-01/04-01/07), Jugement Rendu en Application de l'article 74 du Statut, 7 March 2014, para. 1025.

44 *Prosecutor* v. *Ngudjolo* (ICC-01/04-02/12), Jugement Rendu en Application de l'article 74 du Statut, 18 December 2012, para. 35. See *Prosecutor* v. *Ngudjolo* (ICC-01/04-02/12 A), Judgment on the Prosecutor's Appeal against the Decision of Trial Chamber II entitled 'Judgment Pursuant to Article 74 of the Statute', 27 February 2015.

45 Ibid., paras. 157–9, 189–90, 218–9.

46 Ibid., paras. 444, 463, 480, 500.   47 Ibid., para. 516.

48 Ibid.

The defendant in *Katanga* likewise was acquitted of child soldiering, even though he was convicted on other counts in a judgment issued early in 2014. Considerable evidence had revealed 'a significant phenomenon of the utilisation of child soldiers, aged seven to seventeen years, integrated into the ranks of different armed groups then active', the same Trial Chamber which had passed judgment in *Ngudjolo* wrote in *Katanga*.[49] During the attack on Bogoro out of which the case arose, 'children armed with guns, machetes, lances or arrows, fought alongside combatants', the Chamber continued; moreover, the evidence established that some of those children were younger than fifteen.[50] Yet no conviction issued. Doubts about some witnesses' reliability, coupled with uncertainty about specific child soldiers' ages, compelled the conclusion that the defendant on trial had not been proved responsible for the prohibited use of underage children.[51]

A more comprehensive policy on children

While these prosecutions for the recruitment and use of child soldiers were unfolding, the Court's second Prosecutor, Fatou Bensouda, assumed office. The transition marked a change in strategy. The decision to charge only child-soldiering offences in *Lubanga* had provoked objections from judges, victims, and commentators alike, and proceedings before and during trial had laid bare investigative and evidentiary challenges. Commentary also took note of the complex nature of child soldiering. Although many children were victims kidnapped into armed groups and forced to wield weapons, other children chose to do so, even though the law declined to give weight to their offers of consent; moreover, child combatants who committed international crimes victimised others, persons also deserving of redress. Increasingly, expansive interpretations of the statutory phrase 'using ... to participate actively in hostilities' were said also to expand the scope of children who might become legitimate

49 *Prosecutor* v. *Katanga* (ICC-01/04-01/07), Jugement Rendu en Application de l'article 74 du Statut, 7 March 2014, para. 1052; see also paras. 1053–9.

50 Ibid., paras. 1060, 1065; see also paras. 1061–4.

51 Ibid., paras. 1066–88. The trial judgment became final after the withdrawal of cross-appeals; the defendant is serving a twelve-year sentence on the counts for which he was convicted.

targets of warfare.[52] Perhaps in tacit recognition of considerations like these, shortly before taking office in mid 2012 Bensouda made a statement she would often repeat: 'Our focus should shift from "children with arms" to "children who are affected by the arms" in the context of the crime of enlisting and conscripting child soldiers'.[53] The Office of the Prosecutor subsequently identified 'particular attention to ... crimes against children' as one of its six strategic goals, and began preparing a Policy Paper on Children, a process that included consultations with experts in academia and civil society.[54]

International Criminal Court judges, meanwhile, agreed to enlarge the scope of proceedings in one case involving offences against children. To be precise, in 2012 judges approved a request from the Prosecutor to supplement the initial arrest warrant for a fugitive Congolese rebel leader who had been accused solely of child-soldiering crimes in 2006, at the same time as his alleged ally, the defendant in *Lubanga*.[55] Bosco Ntaganda surrendered in 2013 to face charges that he was responsible not only for the prohibited conscription, enlistment, and use of children, but also for a range of generic crimes, and for the war crimes of rape and sexual slavery perpetrated by his troops against children under fifteen in the same militia.[56] Before a Pre-Trial Chamber, he contended that 'the crimes of rape and sexual slavery against these persons are not foreseen by the Statute, as international humanitarian law does not protect persons taking part in hostilities from crimes committed by other persons

52 E.g., Roman Graf, 'The International Criminal Court and Child Soldiers: An Appraisal of the Lubanga Judgment', (2012) 10 *Journal of International Criminal Justice* 1, at pp. 16–21; Chris Jenks, 'Law as Shield, Law as Sword: The ICC's Lubanga Decision, Child Soldiers and the Perverse Mutualism of Participation in Hostilities', (2013) 3 *University of Miami National Security and Armed Conflict Law Review* 106.

53 Fatou Bensouda, 'The Incidence of the Female Child Soldier and the International Criminal Court', 4 June 2012, keynote speech before the Eng Aja Eze Foundation in New York.

54 Office of the Prosecutor, Strategic Plan June 2012–2015, 11 October 2013, para. 3.

55 *Prosecutor* v. *Ntaganda* (ICC-01/04-02/06), Decision on the Prosecutor's Application under Article 58, 12 July 2012.

56 *Prosecutor* v. *Ntaganda* (ICC-01/04-02/06), Decision Pursuant to Article 61(7) (a) and (b) of the Rome Statute on the Charges of the Prosecutor against Bosco Ntaganda, 9 June 2014, paras. 36, 74.

taking part in hostilities on the same side of the armed conflict'.[57] The Chamber disagreed. It noted that common article 3 of the 1949 Geneva Conventions protects '[p]ersons taking no active part in the hostilities', while Additional Protocol II protects 'persons who do not take a direct part or who have ceased to take part in hostilities', and forbids in particular 'rape, enforced prostitution and any form of indecent assault against persons'.[58] The Pre-Trial Chamber then proceeded to consider whether the child soldiers in question 'were taking direct/active part in hostilities at the time they were victims of acts of rape and/or sexual slavery'.[59] That framing virtually compelled a negative reply. As stated by the Pre-Trial Chamber:

> [T]hose subject to rape and/or sexual enslavement cannot be considered to have taken active part in hostilities during the specific time when they were subject to acts of sexual nature, including rape, as defined in the relevant Elements of Crimes. The sexual character of these crimes, which involve elements of force/coercion or the exercise of rights of ownership, logically preclude active participation in hostilities at the same time.[60]

The conclusion jibed with that of the Special Court for Sierra Leone trial verdict in *Taylor*, as the Pre-Trial Chamber recognised.[61] But in the earlier case the indictment had not specified sexual abuse against child soldiers; rather, the Special Court's reasoning arose out of the facts as adduced at trial, as proof of more generic charges. The confirmation of these rape and sexual slavery charges in *Ntaganda* thus was a milestone. Combined with the confirmation of additional, generic charges, it suggested a new receptivity to including, within the narrative of International Criminal Court proceedings, the full range of children's experiences amid armed conflict and analogous violence.[62]

---

57 Ibid., para. 76 (parenthetical acronym omitted).
58 Ibid., para. 77.   59 Ibid.
60 Ibid., para. 79.   61 Ibid., para. 79, n. 318.
62 The reference to 'analogous violence' is intended to encompass situations yielding to crimes that occur outside of armed conflict yet lie within the International Criminal Court's jurisdiction; for example, genocide, which may be committed in times of peace and war alike, and crimes against humanity, committed in the course of widespread or systematic attacks against civilian populations.

Challenges to prevention and punishment

It must be noted that the new charges laid in *Ntaganda* constituted an exercise of prosecutorial restraint, perhaps influenced by the actual evidence to be proffered at the trial. For the Pre-Trial Chamber's reasoning, though applied in that case to children under fifteen, invited extension in future cases to older children; indeed, to all persons in militias who have been subjected to abuses prohibited by international humanitarian law. Over time, moreover, the logic of the *Ntaganda* confirmation decision may prove a bit too neat. Accurately referring to 'the Pre-Trial Chamber's construction of a binary in which a child soldier is either subjected to sexual violence or taking direct part in hostilities', one commentator probed the boundaries of that binary: 'Is the victim only subject to sexual slavery in the moment when he or she is forced to engage in a sexual act, or for so long as the perpetrator exercises rights of ownership? And does the sexual slavery stop if the victim is made to take part in hostilities, only to resume at some future point in time?'[63] The friction inherent in such questions is salutary: it may spark an analysis of text and purpose that synthesises legal sources – not only the Geneva Conventions and other humanitarian law, but also the Children's Convention and other child rights and human rights law – in order to arrive at a deeper explication of the extent to which international law protects persons against abuse within armed groups.

This is but one jurisprudential challenge to the development of an effective structure for the prevention and punishment of international crimes against children. As the Appeals Chamber in *Lubanga* observed, even though its decision confirmed the core of criminalised conduct, it remains for future rulings to affirm the full contours of the prohibition against conscripting or enlisting children under the age of fifteen years into armed forces or groups, or using them to participate actively in hostilities.[64] Furthermore, the acquittals of some commanders charged with child-soldiering crimes point to a need for continued fine-tuning of the

---

63 Rosemary Grey, 'The Ntaganda Confirmation of Charges Decision: A Victory for Gender Justice?', *Beyond the Hague*, 12 June 2014.

64 *Prosecutor* v. *Lubanga* (ICC-01/04-01/06 A 5), Judgment on the Appeal of Mr Thomas Lubanga Dyilo against his Conviction, 1 December 2014, para. 335.

modes by which accused superiors are to be held criminally responsible for conduct committed by their subordinates.

Issues of evidence gathering and reliability loomed large in numerous cases involving children. Such cases frequently will require the presentation of witnesses who were children when alleged events occurred. To the extent that such testimony can be corroborated, by the testimony of adults and witnesses or by physical evidence, the rights both of child witnesses and adult accused will be better served. Posing a particular evidentiary hurdle is an element unique to the Rome Statute's child-soldiering crimes; specifically, that the affected children must not have reached their fifteenth birthday. Absent birth certificates or other vital records – documents often scarce in times of war – this is an especially difficult fact to prove. The use of rough markers, such as whether a boy's voice has changed, or whether a girl's breasts have developed, may have the effect of depriving some children of due protection – for example, children who have reached puberty early and thus are wrongly assumed to be fifteen or older. Considering that the two treaties raising the age threshold to eighteen enjoy more Member States than the Rome Statute, an amendment on this point may merit examination.

The International Criminal Court and related tribunals typically are set up to pursue only those persons believed to bear grave responsibility. In order to enhance prevention and punishment, international criminal justice mechanisms thus must endeavour to work with national legal systems, with the United Nations and kindred international and regional entities, and with civil society, not to mention with children themselves.[65] Also in order would be support for international instruments aimed at ending war or minimising the effects of conflict; to name a few, the treaties outlawing landmines, cluster munitions, and arms trafficking, as well as the 2010 Kampala Amendments that would make the crime of aggression punishable before the International Criminal Court. This complementary approach does not mean that all lesser offenders – let alone all child offenders – eventually must face criminal charges in some forum. To the contrary, children once associated with armed groups, not to mention

---

65 General Comment No. 12, UN Doc. CRC/C/GC/12; Virginie Ladisch, 'Children and Youth Participation in Transitional Justice Processes', (2013) 6 *Journal of the History of Childhood and Youth* 505.

other persons victimised by armed groups, may benefit far more from non-criminal means of rehabilitation, reintegration, and reconciliation.[66]

Finally, there is a need for a richer understanding of the manifold ways that armed conflict and similar violence affect children. When the evidence merits, child-specific crimes must be prosecuted to the fullest extent – not only the oft-charged child-soldiering crimes, but also offences like child trafficking, whenever they amount to crimes against humanity. Crimes that acutely affect children, such as sexual slavery or attacks on education, also must be pursued. When appropriate, allegations of generic crimes like killing and pillage ought to emphasise the impact on children.[67] In short, international criminal justice mechanisms must persist in giving priority to crimes against children, who, after all, embody the future of global society.

FURTHER READING

Diane Marie Amann, 'International Decisions: *Prosecutor* v. *Lubanga*', (2012) 106 *American Journal of International Law* 809.

Diane Marie Amann, 'Children and the First Verdict of the International Criminal Court', (2013) 12 *Washington University Global Studies Law Review* 411.

Cecile Aptel, 'Unpunished Crimes: The Special Court for Sierra Leone and Children', in Charles Jalloh, ed., *The Sierra Leone Special Court and Its Legacy*, New York: Cambridge University Press, 2014, pp. 340–60.

David M. Crane, 'Prosecuting Children in Times of Conflict: The West African Experience', (2008) 15/3 *Human Rights Brief* 11.

Mark A. Drumbl, *Reimagining Child Soldiers in International Law and Policy*, Oxford University Press, 2012.

---

66 For an analysis of such options, see, e.g., Mark A. Drumbl, *Reimagining Child Soldiers in International Law and Policy*, Oxford University Press, 2012, at pp. 168–208.

67 A trend in this direction may be discerned not only from developments at the International Criminal Court and the Special Court for Sierra Leone, but also from the many mentions of children in the second trial judgment of the tribunal established to adjudicate crimes during the Khmer Rouge regime; *Prosecutor* v. *Nuon and Khieu* (002/19-09-2007/ECCC/TC), Judgment, 7 August 2014.

Part IV   Trials

Adolf Eichmann 14

Kai Ambos

'*Un momentito, señor*', said Mossad agent Peter Malkin almost apologetically to attract the attention of a synchronised walker who was getting lost in the shadows of a small town in the province of Buenos Aires in the middle of the year 1960.[1] These were the simple but very symbolic words that started a chain of events that irrevocably changed the landscape of international criminal law. After some considerations on the historical background of the Eichmann case the chapter will analyse the main legal issues of the trial.

Historical background: from Berlin and Buenos Aires to Jerusalem

Otto Adolf Eichmann was a member of the *Schutzstaffel* ('SS'), the *Sicherheitsdienst* ('SD') and the Gestapo, all of which were declared to be criminal organisations by the Nuremberg International Military Tribunal. More importantly, in the Nazi's bureaucracy of destruction, he was the head of the section IV B 4 of the *Reichssicherheitshauptamt*, an office that resulted from the merger of the security service of the Nazi party and of the security police of the Nazi state (*Gestapo*). In this function, Eichmann organised and coordinated the deportations of the Jews to the concentration camps. The Jerusalem District Court that sentenced Eichmann to death on 12 December 1961[2] summarised his role as follows:

The chapter draws on my earlier piece in K. Ambos, L. P. Coutinho, M. F. Palma, and P. de Sousa Mendes, eds., *Eichmann in Jerusalem – 50 Years After*, Berlin: Duncker and Humblot, 2012, pp. 123–34. I am grateful to my student research assistants Jan Oberlach and Michael Zornow for important assistance.

1 Neal Bascomb, *Hunting Eichmann*, Boston: Mariner Books, 2009, p. 226.

2 *A-G Israel* v. *Eichmann*, (1968) 36 ILR 5 (District Court, Jerusalem). The sentence was confirmed by the Supreme Court on 29 May 1962; *A-G Israel* v. *Eichmann*, (1968) 36 ILR 277 (Israel Supreme Court).

We find that in the RSHA (*Reichssicherheitshauptamt*), the central authority dealing with the 'Final Solution' of the Jewish question, the accused was at the head of those engaged in carrying out the 'Final Solution'. In fulfilling this task, the accused acted in accordance with general directives from his superiors, but there still remained to him *wide discretionary* powers in planning operations on his own initiative. He was *not a puppet* in the hands of others; his place was amongst those who pulled the strings. It should be added [...] that the accused's activity was *most vigorous* in the Reich itself and in the other countries from which Jews were despatched to Eastern Europe; but it also ranged widely in various parts of Eastern Europe.[3]

Like many Nazi war criminals, Eichmann managed to escape from immediate post-war prosecution. At the beginning of 1946, Eichmann, using the aliases Otto Heninger and Otto Eckmann, escaped from American war captivity and went into hiding in a small village in the Lüneburg Heath, an area in northern Germany.[4] There he lived an inconspicuous life and enjoyed apparently widespread appreciation.[5] To convert his money from 'Reichsmark' into the 'German Mark' as the new post-war currency – he was too cautious to turn to the official occupation authorities – Eichmann bought a chicken farm and sold the eggs, making a good profit.[6] As life in Germany became increasingly risky for suspected war criminals, Eichmann fled to Genoa via Austria. Supported by smugglers, Nazi followers, sympathisers, and members of the Catholic Church, he used a well-established escape route for war criminals known as the 'rat line',[7] and obtained new identity documents and a visa for Argentina.[8]

3 Ibid., para. 180 (my emphasis).
4 David Cesarani, *Eichmann: His Life and Crimes*, London: Heinemann, 2004, p. 204.
5 Bettina Stangneth, *Eichmann vor Jerusalem: Das Unbehelligte Leben Eines Massenmörders*, Zürich and Hamburg: Arche, 2011, pp. 107–8.
6 David Cesarani, *Eichmann: His Life and Crimes*, London: Heinemann, 2004, p. 204.
7 Ibid., p. 205. There is no serious evidence that suggests that this form of escape was organised by former Nazi officials. Rather, recent research concludes that it was organised by the Holy See, originally to help the ultra-Catholic movement of Ante Pavelić and his Croatian 'Ustashas' to find a safe haven in Juan Domingo Perón's Argentina. See I. Montes de Oca, *Ustashas: El ejército Nazi de Perón y el Vaticano*, Buenos Aires: Sudamericana, 2013, Ch. 4; O. Blaschke, *Die Kirchen und der Nationalsozialismus*, Stuttgart: Reclam, 2014, pp. 235–40.
8 Here and in the following see: Bettina Stangneth, *Eichmann vor Jerusalem: Das Unbehelligte Leben Eines Massenmörders*, Zürich and Hamburg: Arche, 2011, pp. 130–3, 145–6, 163. For some time it was thought that Eichmann first

On 14 July 1950, Eichmann arrived at the port of Buenos Aires under the name of Ricardo Klement and was swiftly integrated into the German exile community, composed of many former Nazis, which helped him to find different accommodations and jobs in the coming years. Most importantly, in the group of his old comrades, he could show his true identity and convictions again, as infamously documented by a series of interviews that the Dutch journalist Willem Sassen conducted with him over several months in 1957.[9] Apparently, Eichmann felt quite safe. This may also explain why he did not seriously think about changing the surnames of his wife and his three children when they arrived in Argentina in 1952. Eichmann's wife was called Vera Liebl de Eichmann and his sons Klaus (aka 'Nicolás'), Dieter ('Tito'), Horst and Ricardo (born in Argentina two years later).[10]

However, Eichmann's new life did not last long. The Israeli secret service, Mossad, abducted him in front of his house in Buenos Aires on 11 May 1960.[11] He was then driven to a safe house, where he was thoroughly examined and interrogated.[12] On the day of the departure from Argentina, Eichmann was heavily drugged and brought to Israel in a plane of the State owned El Al airline, landing there on the 22 May.[13] The trial before the Jerusalem District Court started on 11 April 1961.[14]

The operation leading to Eichmann's capture was much less professional than the actual abduction. In fact, Fritz Bauer, a German Jew, first persecuted by the Nazis and later one of their most resolute persecutors as Chief Prosecutor of the Braunschweig district (Lower Saxony) and later of the German state Hessen, proved to be the key informant of the

travelled through the Near and Middle East before arriving in Argentina (e.g., I. de Koning, *A Study of Adolf Eichmann: Adolf Hitler's Expert in Jewish Affairs,* Newton, MA: Newton College of the Sacred Heart, 1964, p. 28, but this proved to be a red herring, cf. Stangneth, *Eichmann vor Jerusalem,* pp. 135–43.)

9 Bettina Stangneth, *Eichmann vor Jerusalem: Das unbehelligte Leben eines Massenmörders,* Zürich and Hamburg: Arche, 2011, pp. 245, 398–9.

10 Neal Bascomb, *Hunting Eichmann,* Boston: Mariner Books, 2009, p. 80.

11 Petros A. Papadatos, *The Eichmann Trial,* London: Stevens and Sons, 1964, p. 53; D. Stahl, *Nazi-Jagd: Südamerikas Diktaturen und die Ahndung von NS-Verbrechen,* Göttingen: Wallstein, 2013, p. 121.

12 David Cesarani, *Eichmann: His Life and Crimes,* London: Heinemann, 2004, p. 231.

13 Ibid., p. 234.

14 Petros A. Papadatos, *The Eichmann Trial,* London: Stevens and Sons, 1964, p. 1.

Mossad in the hunt for Eichmann.[15] He initially received the information from a man called Lothar Hermann, a German Jew exiled in Argentina. Hermann, tortured by the Gestapo, prisoner in Dachau and then exiled in Argentina, suspected that his daughter's boyfriend named Nicolás Eichmann could have some familiar relationship with the fugitive. When he finally discovered that 'Klaus' Eichmann used to live together with his mother, his brothers, and his 'uncle' Ricardo Klement in Buenos Aires, he informed Bauer.[16] He then had to use all possible tricks to overcome the broad German-Argentinean support network that Eichmann and other Nazis benefited from.[17]

Outsiders versus insiders

The Eichmann case is not only important for the law applied and the historical figure of Eichmann but also because it entailed a clash between the legal actors, the 'insiders' – that is, the prosecutor, the judge, and the defence – and the external observers, the 'outsiders' – for example, historians, philosophers, anthropologists, and persons with a similar humanities background. Hannah Arendt has perhaps been the most famous of these external observers. In a recent interview Gabriel Bach, the deputy Israeli prosecutor in the trial, had the following to say with regard to Arendt's perspective, of course different from his own as an 'insider':

> I knew nothing about Hannah Arendt before she came. She arrived a few days before the trial and I was told at the time that a philosopher from America, Hannah Arendt, had arrived and wished to write a criticism of the case – before it had even started. Something sounded a little strange to me and I made it known that I was available to meet her in order to discuss the issues she had raised. Two days later I received a reply saying

15 Ronen Steinke, *Fritz Bauer oder Auschwitz vor Gericht*, Munich and Zurich: Piper, 2013, pp. 13 *et seq.*
16 Neal Bascomb, *Hunting Eichmann*, Boston: Mariner Books, 2009, pp. 73–80.
17 There are many incredible things which deserve to be mentioned here, take just this one: The German secret service BND, safely controlled by former Nazis, already knew in 1952 about Eichmann's true identity and residence in Buenos Aires but did everything to help him and other Nazis to hide instead of helping the prosecution authorities to get hold of them (Ronen Steinke, *Fritz Bauer oder Auschwitz vor Gericht*, Munich and Zurich: Piper, 2013, p. 18).

that she was not available to talk to anyone from the Public Prosecutor's Office. This surprised me once again – I mean, she did not have to accept what we were saying, but to not be available to speak to anyone from the Public Prosecutor's Office, that was a bit strange. Even so, I gave instructions not only for her to be allowed to attend the trial on a daily basis, but also for her to be able to consult all the documents, both for the defence and the prosecution, so that she might gain some insight into any issues she might have.

And then she wrote this book... [She] not only expressed some strange ideas, but actually reproduced many of the documents she quoted in a totally distorted fashion ... Amongst other things, she wrote, for example, that we portrayed Eichmann in such a bad light that we actually minimised Hitler and Himmler's guilt. She wrote this in her book. That is also ridiculous, naturally. Of course Hitler and Himmler came up with the idea. Eichmann was responsible for carrying it out. But the fact that he was such a fanatic and that, for this very reason, he remained head of the department of Jewish affairs for the whole time does not diminish the guilt of those who had previously taken the main decisions.

All of this is very, very strange and difficult to accept... [It] is absolutely wrong to state that he was only carrying out orders in a somewhat banal fashion. We managed to actually show that in this case.[18]

It seems, then, that Hannah Arendt did not wish to know – let alone understand – the perspective of those conducting the trial. According to the latter, represented by Bach, Hannah Arendt produced an erroneous account of the trial, even distorting the 'truth' of the trial. Indeed, her account triggered a series of criticisms,[19] including personal attacks questioning her integrity as a Jew, especially since she criticised, albeit only in a small portion of her book, the role of the Jewish Councils (*Judenräte*) set up by the Nazis to better administer and control the Jewish communities in occupied territories and concentration camps.

Obviously the legal perspective and the ensuing criticism of Arendt's non-legal perspective is only half of the truth. In fact, the strictly legal perspective was of no interest to Hannah Arendt. She was concerned with understanding the Eichmann phenomenon as the 'banality of evil', that is,

---

18 The excerpts are a translation from the German interview given by Bach to *Deutschland Radio Kultur*, 7 April 2011, available online at www.dradio.de/dkultur/sendungen/thema/1431281/ (last visited 8 April 2015).

19 E.g., Jacob Robinson, *And the Crooked Shall be Made Straight: The Eichmann Trial, the Jewish Catastrophe and Hannah Arendt's Narrative*, New York: Macmillan, 1965.

as a representative of the Nazi system which could only exist and function because there were many likewise banal people, just as mediocre as Eichmann himself, who formed the workings of the system or were even converted into indispensable cogs in the Nazi machine of destruction.[20] Clearly, Hannah Arendt's critique was the cause of much concern among the prosecutors, but it is important to stress the differences of perspective. Again, her perspective came from outside the case and, furthermore, did not focus on its technical, criminal law issues but on the – from her perspective more important – sociological, psychological, philosophical, and anthropological aspects. Both of these perspectives are legitimate and perform important, yet different, functions. They reflect the tension between the interdisciplinary external vision, normally adopted by an (interdisciplinary) truth commission, and the internal legal vision of a criminal court, which is only seeking to determine whether the defendant is guilty or not.[21] Also, Arendt agreed with the final verdict (even the death penalty) and wanted by no means to write a defence of Eichmann. Her point was simply that the good versus evil dichotomy falls short of explaining the Nazis' extermination machinery. Instead, the evil is more banal, it consists of the inability to think and, thus, to judge as the centre of moral action.[22] It is the inability to reflect upon one's conduct ultimately amounting to a mere blind obedience in the execution of inhuman acts. After all, Arendt wanted to denounce 'the unlimited wickedness of ordinary men', as represented by Adolf Eichmann.[23]

---

20 For a defence of Arendt and an analysis of the expression 'banality of evil', see David Luban, 'Hannah Arendt as a Theorist of International Criminal Law', (2011) 11 *International Criminal Law Review* 621, stating that Arendt's critique 'raises questions that are still relevant today'.

21 R. Birn, 'Criminals as Manipulative Witnesses: A Case Study of SS General von dem Bach-Zelewski', (2011) 9 *Journal of International Criminal Justice* 444, at p. 474, which alludes to the 'inherent tension between historical narratives and legal requirements'.

22 M. Nogueira de Brito, 'When Thinking is Acting: The Concept of the Banality of Evil as a Key to Hannah Arendt's Political Thought', in K. Ambos, L. P. Coutinho, M. F. Palma, and P. de Sousa Mendes, eds., *Eichmann in Jerusalem – 50 Years After*, Berlin: Duncker and Humblot, 2012, pp. 89–103, at p. 93; P. de Sousa Mendes, 'Judging Eichmann to Render Justice', in ibid., pp. 107–21, at p. 120.

23 A. Aráujo, 'Hannah Arendt, Adolf Eichmann: Of Radical Evil and its Banality', in ibid., pp. 71–7, at p. 77.

Interestingly, the newly founded State of Israel demonstrated great independence in the *Eichmann* case, thereby guaranteeing that Eichmann had a fair trial. There is broad consensus in the legal literature, particularly in the English and the German literature, in this regard.[24] Eichmann was even allowed to choose any (German) lawyer he wanted, Nazi or otherwise.[25] Prosecutor Bach himself recalled that at his first meeting with Eichmann he informed him of his right to remain silent and his right to have a lawyer.[26] This cannot be overestimated given the fact that in these cases of prosecutions of mass atrocities, often of a former defeated regime, there is always a danger that the defendants are deprived of their most basic rights.

The judgment of the Jerusalem District Court – legal analysis

The indictment alleged in fifteen counts that Eichmann was guilty of crimes against the Jewish people, crimes against humanity, and membership of a 'hostile' organisation.[27] For the most part, the facts alleged were not disputed, whereas the jurisdiction of the Court and Eichmann's individual criminal responsibility was challenged on a number of grounds. In contrast, the actual requirements of his responsibility were given less attention.

The individual responsibility of Eichmann

The Jerusalem Court did not consider sufficient the fact that Eichmann had belonged to organisations declared to be criminal by the International Military Tribunal, i.e., it rejected criminal responsibility pursuant to mere *membership* in a criminal organisation. Despite Eichmann's prominent position, the Court felt that it was necessary for him to have engaged in active

---

24 See the references in Kai Ambos, *Der Allgemeine Teil des Völkerstrafrechts*, 2nd edn, Berlin: Duncker & Humblot, 2004, fn. 110.

25 Eichmann was defended by Dr. Robert Servatius (cf. Telford Taylor, *Die Nürnberger Prozesse*, 2nd edn, Munich: Heyne, 1996, p. 496; C. Große, *Der Eichmann-Prozess Zwischen Politik und Recht*, Frankfurt: Lange, 1995, p. 22.

26 In the full oral version of the interview, *Deutschland Radio Kultur*, 7 April 2011, which is not reproduced on the above indicated website.

27 *A-G Israel* v. *Eichmann*, (1968) 36 ILR 5 (District Court, Jerusalem), paras. 181–215.

conduct with a view to the commission of crimes: 'The Prosecution had to prove the Accused's membership in these organisations – and this membership is not in dispute – and in addition that the Accused *took part in the commission of crimes*, as a member of these organisations – and this *has been proved'*.[28] With this statement the Court took a far more restrictive approach than the criminal law of most western democracies which criminalise the mere membership in criminal or terrorist organisations.[29] Interestingly, the current Israeli law also broadly criminalises membership by four offences with varying phrasings, burdens of proof, and sanctions.[30]

The second substantive aspect concerns the issue of conspiracy. Given the heavy influence of English common law on Israeli criminal law[31] – only after the Eichmann trial criminal law concepts of continental Europe gained a certain importance[32] – it is little surprising that the prosecution accused Eichmann of conspiracy. However, the Court rejected this concept

---

28 Ibid., para. 215 (my emphasis).

29 See the in-depth study by I. Morozinis, *Dogmatik der Organisationsdelikte: Eine Kritische Darstellung der Täterschaftlichen Zurechnungslehre in Legalen und Illegalen Organisationsstrukturen aus Strafrechtsdogmatischer und Rechtstheoretischer Sicht Sowie ein Beitrag zur Lehre vom Tatbestand*, Berlin: Duncker and Humblot, 2010.

30 The offences are set by sections 58 and 85 of *The (Emergency) Defence Regulations 1945*, section 3 of the *Prevention of Terrorism Ordinance No. 3 of 5708-1948*, and section 147 of the Israeli Criminal Code of 1977. The Israeli Military Court of Appeal interpreted 'membership' to include passive-nominal membership (Appeal no. 7\68, *Baransi v. The Military Prosecutor*, Collection [of the Military Court of Appeal] 2, 62, at 67 [1968]). It further ruled that mere intention to join an illegal organisation is sufficient for conviction (Appeal no. 8\70, *Baransi v. The Military Prosecutor*, Collection 3, 7, at 30 [1970]). Recently, the Israeli Supreme Court has interpreted the term 'membership of a terrorist organisation' in the context of the preventive arrest of 'illegal combatants'. The Court made some effort to narrow the scope of this term, noting that: 'it is insufficient to show any tenuous connection with a terrorist organisation in order to be included within the cycle of hostilities in the broad meaning of this concept' (CrimA 6659/06, *A. v. The State of Israel*, 11 June 2008, para. 21 of Justice Beinisch's judgment).

31 *A-G Israel v. Eichmann*, (1968) 36 ILR 5 (District Court, Jerusalem), para. 189: 'in conformity with the rules of English Common Law, from which they are derived'.

32 This was mainly due to Sheneor Zalman Feller, a Jew of Romanian origin, legal practitioner and professor in Bucharest, who immigrated to Israel in

and instead demanded something 'more than mere consent' in the commission of crimes: 'We do not consider that a person who consents to the
perpetration of a criminal act or acts (for this is the essence of the conspiracy), makes himself *ipso facto* liable, without any additional ground
of responsibility, as actual perpetrator of all those acts... Such responsibility demands ... something more than mere consent, such as soliciting,
aiding, abetting, and even in the extreme case of common purpose ... at
least the presence of the Accused at the commission of the crime'.[33]

As a consequence, the type of liability actually used by the Court to
convict Eichmann was individual responsibility proper, i.e., Eichmann's
perpetration or (secondary) participation in criminal acts. To begin with,
we have a linguistic problem here. Since the judgment was originally
written in the official language of the State of Israel, Hebrew, and since
very few people can read Hebrew, the vast majority of analysts have
drawn on the English version, or another translated version.[34] This may
help to explain the terminological confusion of this part of the judgment
with regard to the mode of liability (form of perpetration or secondary
participation). The Court uses different words, which are inconsistent and
contradictory: on the one hand, it says that Eichmann is an accomplice.[35]
Here, we may tend to think of the concept of 'accomplice' that exists in
continental Europe. However, in common law and in English law 'complicity' may imply more than mere assistance to or co-operation in the main
offence as normally understood in most civil law systems.[36] The term
accomplice may also be understood in the sense of a co-perpetrator, that

1964 and became full professor at Hebrew University in 1967. He imported
some ideas from Romanian and Soviet law (he had also worked as a prosecutor in the Soviet Union), and was the PhD supervisor of Mordechai Kremnitzer
and Miri Gur Arye, who later became professors at Hebrew University and
have been very influential in some legal reforms (I am indebted to Prof. Miri
Gur Arye for sharing this information with me).

33   *A-G Israel* v. *Eichmann*, (1968) 36 ILR 5 (District Court, Jerusalem), para. 188.
34   There is also a German version in A. W. Less, ed., *Schuldig: Das Urteil Gegen
     Adolf Eichmann,* Frankfurt: Athenäum, 1987.
35   *A-G Israel* v. *Eichmann*, (1968) 36 ILR 5 (District Court, Jerusalem), para.
     194: 'everyone who acted in the extermination of Jews, knowing about the
     plan for the Final Solution and its advancement, is to be regarded as an
     accomplice in the annihilation of the millions who were exterminated'.
36   While Andrew Ashworth and Jeremy Horder, *Principles of Criminal Law,*
     7th edn, Oxford University Press, 2013, p. 419 *et seq.,* appear to understand

is a person who acts 'jointly with another' (Rome Statute, article 25(3)(a)), or the Spanish *colaborador necesario.*[37]

The judgment also speaks of the principal offender,[38] in classical common law terminology 'principal of first degree', which in civil law systems would be the direct or material perpetrator who commits the crime, in the most narrow sense of a formal-objective theory of perpetration, with his or her own hands. However, the common law only uses the term 'principal' so as to distinguish the 'secondary participant', i.e., the person who plays a less important role in the execution of the crime. It becomes clear here that the District Court did not adopt the differentiated or dualistic model of participation ('*Differenzierungsmodell*'), which distinguishes between the different forms of participation already at the level of attribution of responsibility[39] but rather opted for the unitarian

complicity in the sense of complicity or other forms of secondary participation ('principal is a person whose acts fall within the legal definition of the crime, whereas an accomplice is anyone who aids, abets, counsels, or procures a principal... Two persons can be co-principals, so long as together they satisfy the definition of the substantive offence and each of them inflicted wounds on the victim with the required fault, for example'). David Ormerod, *Smith and Hogan's Criminal Law,* 13th edn, Oxford University Press, 2011, pp. 190–1, does not make such a clear distinction ('The distinction between a joint principal and an aider or abettor is sometimes a fine one... [T]he test would be: did D2 by his own act contribute to the causation of the actus reus? If he did, he is a principal.')

37 According to article 28(2) of the Spanish Criminal Code '[*l*]*os que cooperan a su ejecución con un acto sin el cual no se habría efectuado'* would also qualify as perpetrators.

38 *A-G Israel* v. *Eichmann,* (1968) 36 ILR 5 (District Court, Jerusalem), para. 194: 'His responsibility is that of a "principal offender" who perpetrated the entire crime in co-operation with the others.' Here the Court compares this type of responsibility with that of two people who collaborate in the forging of a document (ibid.: 'Two persons may collaborate in the forging of a document, each one of them forging only a part of the document').

39 As does, at least in a terminological sense, article 25(3) of the Rome Statute, distinguishing forms of perpetration (direct, jointly with another or through another person) and secondary participation (instigation and assistance). See Kai Ambos, *Treatise of International Criminal Law,* Vol. 1, Oxford University Press, 2013, pp. 144 *et seq.*; Kai Ambos, 'Article 25', in O. Triffterer and K. Ambos, eds., *The Rome Statute of the International Criminal Court: A Commentary,* Munich: Beck, 2015, pp. 970–1021.

system of perpetration ('*Einheitstätermodell*'),[40] considering any causal contribution to the criminal result as 'perpetration' or 'commission'.[41]

The issue of the correct and precise form of responsibility is particularly relevant in our context since German scholar Claus Roxin developed the theory of control over (domination of) the act ('*Tatherrschaft*') by means of an organised power structure ('*Organisationsherrschaft*') around the same time as the *Eichmann* trial took place, taking the facts of the case as an example. However, the Jerusalem Court made no use of this theory. In fact, it could not have even known about it since Roxin's ground-breaking work was only published after the trial (in 1963).[42] Instead, Eichmann's responsibility was determined with regard to his participation in the 'Final Solution', i.e., any kind of participation, notwithstanding its concrete form (either a form of perpetration or a form of secondary participation) was deemed sufficient. Indeed, although a pure form of collective or organisational responsibility was rejected, the point of reference was the collective enterprise of the 'Final Solution'.

This follows from two considerations. On the one hand it can be inferred from the various references to the 'Final Solution' in the judgment: '[A]ll the acts perpetrated during the implementation of the Final Solution of the Jewish Question are to be regarded as one single whole,

---

40 *A-G Israel* v. *Eichmann*, (1968) 36 ILR 5 (District Court, Jerusalem), para. 197: '[W]e wish to emphasise that in any case the Accused is regarded as committing the crime itself ... whether he committed an act in order to facilitate or to aid another in carrying out the extermination ... or whether he counselled or solicited others to exterminate.'

41 Regarding the different types of the unitarian system, see T. Rotsch, '*Einheitstäterschaft' Statt Tatherrschaft*, Tübingen: Mohr Siebeck, 2009, pp. 131 *et seq.* and *passim*.

42 Roxin published his key article on 'Straftaten im Rahmen organisatorischer Machtapparate' in the German law journal 110 *Goltdammer's Archiv für Strafrecht ('GA')* (1963) 193–207 (for an English translation, see 'Crimes as Part of Organised Power Structures', (2011) 9 *Journal of International Criminal Justice* 191). He had, naturally, already worked on the article before and therefore the development of his theory was indeed parallel to the Eichmann trial which ended with the judgment of 12 December 1961. The first edition of Roxin's work for his professorial *Habilitation* (*Täterschaft und Tatherrschaft*), in which the theory of domination of the act was more broadly developed, was published in 1963 (8th edn, 2006).

and the Accused's criminal responsibility is to be decided upon accordingly'.[43] Furthermore:

> Hence, the Accused will be convicted (if no justification for his acts are found) of the general crime of the 'Final Solution' in all its forms, as an accomplice to the commission of the crime, and his conviction will extend to all the many acts forming part of that crime, both the acts in which he took an active part in his own sector and the acts committed by his accomplices to the crime in other sectors on the same front.[44]

On the other hand, the judgment refers to the Nazi organised power apparatus in which Eichmann knowingly participated:

> It was therefore clear from the outset that a complicated apparatus was required to carry out the task. Everyone who was let into the secret of the extermination, from a certain rank upwards, was aware, too, that such an apparatus existed and that it was functioning, although not everyone of them knew how each part of the machine operated, with what means, at what pace, and not even at which place. Hence, the extermination campaign was one single comprehensive act, which cannot be divided into acts or operations carried out by various people at various times and in different places. One team of people accomplished it jointly at all times and in all places.[45]

Finally, Eichmann is regarded as being responsible just like any person who knowingly participated in the Nazi criminal enterprise of the Holocaust:

> But more important than that: In such an enormous and complicated crime as the one we are now considering [the 'Final Solution', K.A.], wherein many people participated at various levels and in various modes of activity – the planners, the organisers and those executing the acts, according to their various ranks – there is not much point in using the ordinary concepts of counselling and soliciting to commit a crime. For these crimes were committed en masse, not only in regard to the number of the victims, but also in regard to the numbers of those who perpetrated the crime, and the extent to which any one of the many criminals were close to, or remote from, the actual killer of the victim, means nothing as far as the measure of his responsibility is concerned. On the contrary, in general, the degree of responsibility increases as we draw further away from the man who uses the fatal instrument with his own hands and reach the higher ranks of command, the 'counsellors' in the language of our Law. As regards the victims who did not die but were placed

---

43 *A-G Israel* v. *Eichmann*, (1968) 36 ILR 5 (District Court, Jerusalem), para. 190.
44 Ibid., para. 195.   45 Ibid., para. 193.

in living conditions calculated to bring about their physical destruction, it is especially difficult to define in technical terms who abetted whom: he who hunted down the victims and deported them to a concentration camp, or he who forced them to work there.[46]

[E]ven if we view each sector of the implementation of the Final Solution separately, there was not one sector wherein the Accused did not act in one way or another, with a varying degree of intensiveness, so that this alternative way would also lead us to find him guilty all along the front of extermination activities.[47]

From the above follows that the Court basically argued that macro-crimes of the kind in question should be dealt with in accordance with their specific nature. The ordinary structure of individual forms of liability (distinguishing between perpetration and secondary participation) does not adequately capture this specific nature since it ignores the particular relationship between the system (criminality) and the individual (criminality) in a macro-criminal context. While it is clear that inernational criminal law should be primarily be concerned with macro-criminality and that domestic criminal law is, normally, concerned with ordinary and individual criminality, the boundaries between the system and the individual level are not always clear. While ordinary domestic criminal law, at whatever level and in whatever form, always aims at the individual perpetrator, it is clear that international criminal law cannot ignore the political, social, economic, and cultural background of the criminal events ('the crime base'). Thus, it goes well beyond the establishment of mere individual responsibility. It also seems clear that the system and individual level are not mutually exclusive but rather complement each other; a one-sided focus on one or the other would not fully take into account the complexities of macro-criminality.

Be that as it may, even though Eichmann was ultimately convicted as a 'principal offender', based on his many acts of support for and co-operation in the 'Final Solution', the Court argued in favour of a kind of collective or organisational responsibility. In fact, the Court's reasoning reminds us of the concept of joint criminal enterprise that, based on the English common design theory, has experienced a kind of revival

46 Ibid., para. 197.
47 Ibid., para. 198.

in the case law of the United Nations *ad hoc* tribunals, especially the International Criminal Tribunal for the former Yugoslavia.[48]

Returning to the concept of domination of the act by means of an organised power apparatus (*Organisationsherrschaft*), the question still remains – and this issue was not analysed in the *Eichmann* trial – as to whether a person like Eichmann, who belonged to a regime's intermediate, organisational level, can have domination of the act within the meaning of this theory.[49] It cannot be denied that only the top level of the organisation, normally formally constituted as the National Defence Council, the Junta or even mere government, may exercise absolute domination *by means of* and *over* the organised power structure that is subordinate to it. In addition, this top level represents the State in a particular way and is responsible for any potential interference with fundamental rights. All other power is merely derived and, therefore, in its exercise is to be attributed to the State leadership. Only the domination of the State leadership may not be blocked from above or interfered with in any other way. In contrast, such an 'interference' is entirely possible with regard to a high or mid-level employee such as Eichmann: his orders to transport Jews to concentration camps could have been suspended or cancelled by his superiors at any time. Also, his command power over the direct executors could have been superseded by his superiors without difficulty, since the direct perpetrators, ultimately, were not responsible to Eichmann, but rather to the Nazi leadership.

48 The joint criminal enterprise doctrine was first introduced in *Prosecutor v. Tadic* (IT-94-1-A), Judgment, 15 July 1999, paras. 172 *et seq.*; recently see, *Prosecutor v. Gotovina* et al. (IT-06-90-T), Judgment, 15 April 2011, paras. 1950 *et seq.* For an analysis and critique, see Kai Ambos, *Treatise on International Criminal Law*, Vol. 1, Oxford University Press, 2013, pp. 123 *et seq.*, 160 *et seq.*, 172 *et seq.*

49 See for the following on *Organisationsherrschaft* in more detail: Kai Ambos, *Der Allgemeine Teil des Völkerstrafrechts*, 2nd edn, Berlin: Duncker and Humblot, 2004, pp. 604–5; Kai Ambos, 'Zur "Organisation" bei der Organisationsherrschaft', in B. Schünemann et al., eds., *Festschrift für Claus Roxin*, Berlin: De Gruyter, 2011, pp. 837–52, at pp. 847 *et seq.* For an analysis of the application of the doctrine with regard to the former Peruvian president Alberto Fujimori, see Kai Ambos, 'The Fujimori Judgment: A President's Responsibility for Crimes Against Humanity as Indirect Perpetrator by Virtue of an Organised Power Apparatus', (2011) 9 *Journal of International Criminal Justice* 137.

One has therefore to say that the domination over the organisation can only be established, without any doubt, in relation to those State officials acting in the background whose command power and orders cannot simply be suspended or cancelled, i.e., in relation to those who, in that sense, can dominate and govern '*without interference*'. In line with what has been said, this only occurs with the formally constituted government, that is, the actual top of the organisation, and, in exceptional cases, also with the leadership of the military and police security forces ('Generals') standing outside the civil government. We may also add that their capacity to dominate the organisation can be assumed without further ado if they themselves are the government or belong to it.

In contrast, the perpetrators that do not belong to the top of the organisation but, for example, to the mid-leadership-level, have, at best, domination over the organisation within the apparatus with regard to *their* subordinates. They do not therefore control the whole apparatus, but, at most, *part* of it. This partial domination, in any case, justifies considering them as indirect perpetrators regarding that part of the events which is effectively under their control. On the other hand, the fact that they are dependent on the top of the organisation appears to run counter to the possibility of indirect perpetration and rather in favour of co-perpetration based on the functional division of labour. Indeed, without that division of labour, the 'Final Solution' could never have been carried out. Nor could the extermination machine of a concentration camp like Auschwitz, specifically under the orders and supervision of the camp's commander Höß, have ever functioned so efficiently.

If one places the organisation at the centre of imputation of criminal responsibility and if one understands '*Organisationsherrschaft*' as domination over or by means of the (entire) organisation, partial domination, as occurs in the cases of those operating on the mid-level receiving and issuing orders, is not sufficient to establish '*Organisationsherrschaft*'. Those participants in macro-criminal activity with 'partial domination', who receive and issue orders at the same time, are therefore (at best) co-perpetrators; their possible lack of equivalence in relation to those receiving their orders (who may be the direct perpetrators) can be better accepted than their lack of domination in relation to the top of the organisation, since the latter ultimately prevents their domination over the (entire) organisation.

In any case, it seems obvious – and here the Jerusalem Court was right – that the common types of perpetration and participation may not simply be applied to acts committed in the macro-criminal context. As this criminality is characterised by a combination of individual and collective structures for attributing guilt[50] and, besides this, by an organisation that plans, coordinates and finally carries out the criminal acts, we should place the latter at the centre of our attention. The organised power apparatus is as a 'formally constituted system of injustice' at the same time part of and driving force of the 'systems injustice'. Thus, it stands at the centre of the imputation and 'collectivises' – in the sense of the dual (collective-individualistic) system of imputation recognised in international criminal law ('principle of imputation of the global act') – the classical individualistic perspective of criminal law. The top of the organisation makes use of the functionality of the apparatus in order to bring about the 'systems injustice'. It acts by means of the apparatus in conjunction with the direct perpetrators in order to achieve the organisation's supra-individual objectives, to which all members of the organisation are ultimately subordinate.

A new perspective on the *Organisationsherrschaft* may thus arise. The gist of the issue to be further explored is whether this form of responsibility may be included in the ordinary system of modes of liability as a type of indirect perpetration, or whether it should be conceived as an autonomous, self-standing form of responsibility to be applied in cases of macro-criminality.

Defences

The *Eichmann* defence brought forward a series of possible substantive or procedural grounds which would exclude criminal responsibility or impede a prosecution. The *ex post facto* or *nullum crimen* (*sine lege praevia*) objection was rejected by the District Court[51] understanding the legality principle – as the International Military Tribunal had done before it – to be an expression of general equity considerations whereby the

---

50 Kai Ambos, *Treatise on International Criminal Law. Vol. 1*, Oxford University Press, 2013, pp. 83–86.
51 *A-G Israel* v. *Eichmann*, (1968) 36 ILR 5 (District Court, Jerusalem), paras. 7–8, 19 (especially on genocide), 27.

only relevant question is whether the prosecution of the crimes at stake appears to be just. This would be clearly the case: 'It is indeed difficult to find a more convincing instance of a *just retroactive law* than the legislation providing for the punishment of war criminals and perpetrators of crimes against humanity and against the Jewish people, and all the reasons justifying the Nuremberg Judgments justify *eo ipse* the retroactive legislation of the Israel legislator.'[52]

In the Supreme Court's view, the principle of non-retroactivity had not even yet become a rule of customary international law.[53] Instead, the crimes in question had always been prohibited by customary international law so that their codification in the Israeli Nazi and Nazi Collaborators (Punishment) Law only had a declaratory effect. From this also follows that the accused must or at least should have been aware of the criminality of the acts, i.e., that the *nullum crimen* principle from a subjective perspective, focusing on a fair warning for the accused, would not have been violated either.

The superior orders defence was also rejected by the District Court for essentially a legal and a factual reason. As to the latter the Court argued that Eichmann had not acted pursuant to mere blind obedience but, mostly, whole-heartedly and willingly.[54] As to the legal admissibility of superior orders, the Court pointed out that this defence is not recognised in international criminal law for 'manifestly unlawful' orders such as the ones received and executed by Eichmann.[55] The Supreme Court understood the moral-choice-criterion (introduced by the International Military Tribunal) not as a self-standing defence but as an expression of the concepts of acting under 'constraint' or 'necessity', a defence to be dealt with in a moment.[56] Further, the Court distinguished the superior orders defence from the Act of State doctrine in pointing to the individual focus of the former as compared to the collective State focus of the latter.[57] While superior orders attributes responsibility to a natural person,

---

52 Ibid., para. 27 (my emphasis).
53 *A-G Israel* v. *Eichmann*, (1968) 36 ILR 277 (Israel Supreme Court), paras. 8, 11.
54 *A-G Israel* v. *Eichmann*, (1968) 36 ILR 5 (District Court, Jerusalem), paras. 216, 228, 231; *A-G Israel* v. *Eichmann*, (1968) 36 ILR 277 (Israel Supreme Court), para. 15.
55 Ibid., paras. 218–220; *A-G Israel* v. *Eichmann*, (1968) 36 ILR 277 (Israel Supreme Court), para. 15.
56 *A-G Israel* v. *Eichmann*, (1968) 36 ILR 277 (Israel Supreme Court), para. 15.
57 Ibid., para. 15.

Act of State entails attribution to a State. The justification of obedience to a superior order is predicated on the authority of the immediate superior, whereas the effect of an 'Act of State' relates to the supreme authority in the State. Acting under a superior order is supposed to imply a hypothetical lack of alternative performance; in contrast, an Act of State receives its binding effect through acting within the scope of the given authorisation. More generally, the Supreme Court argued that the application of this doctrine presupposes that the acts in question are lawful and do not, as the ones of the Nazi regime, violate international law and constitute international crimes. Otherwise, such acts are to be seen – in line with the so-called 'Radbruch Formula'[58] – as void.[59] In fact, '[a] State that plans and implements a "final solution" cannot be treated as *par in parem*, but only as a gang of criminals'.[60]

As for the already mentioned constraint or necessity defence, the Court took the moral choice criterion as a starting point. More concretely, the Court demanded objectively an imminent danger to the life of the subordinate for not obeying the order and subjectively that he carried out the command due to the desire to save his life and in the belief that he had no other possibility to do so.[61] As for Eichmann, the Court dismissed this latter requirement since Eichmann even exceeded his duties showing overeagerness and great ambition.

The plea of Eichmann's possibly unlawful abduction from Argentina was rejected by the Court because it would not make a difference for the jurisdiction of the Israeli courts.[62] While such an abduction might be – as an infringement of the sovereignty of the territorial State – unlawful

58 Gustav Radbruch, '"Five Minutes of Legal Philosophy" [1945]' (trans. B. L. Paulson and S. L. Paulson), (2006) 26 *Oxford Journal of Legal Studies* 13: 'The conflict between justice and legal certainty may well be resolved in this way: The positive law ... takes precedence even when its content is unjust and fails to benefit the people, *unless* the conflict between statute and justice reaches *such an intolerable degree* that the statute, as "*flawed law*", must yield to justice.'

59 *A-G Israel* v. *Eichmann*, (1968) 36 ILR 277 (Israel Supreme Court), para. 14; see also *A-G Israel* v. *Eichmann*, (1968) 36 ILR 5 (District Court, Jerusalem), para. 28.

60 *A-G Israel* v. *Eichmann*, (1968) 36 ILR 5 (District Court, Jerusalem), para. 28.

61 *A-G Israel* v. *Eichmann*, (1968) 36 ILR 277 (Israel Supreme Court), para. 15.

62 On the doctrine of *male captus, bene detentus*, which is relevant in this context, cf. C. Paulussen, *Male captus bene detentus? Surrendering suspects to the International Criminal Court*, Antwerp: Intersentia, 2010.

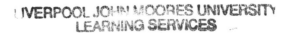

in international law, the right to a remedy or for reparations was only bestowed on the injured State and not on the abducted individual.[63] Besides, Argentina and Israel had finally reached a settlement on 3 August 1960[64] and Argentina waived its original claims.[65] In this context the District Court also dismissed any form of immunity[66] for Eichmann, in particular since he was not a political offender.[67] The Supreme Court joined in these statements substantially.[68]

Last but not least, a possible statute of limitations under Argentinean law was also considered irrelevant because the applicable law was that of Israel and it did not provide for any such limitation.[69]

FURTHER READING

K. Ambos, L. P. Coutinho, M. F. Palma, and P. de Sousa Mendes, eds., *Eichmann in Jerusalem – 50 Years After*, Berlin: Duncker and Humblot, 2012.
David Cesarani, *Eichmann: His Life and Crimes*, London: Heinemann, 2004.
C. Große, *Der Eichmann-Prozess Zwischen Politik und Recht,* Frankfurt: Lange, 1995.
Petros A. Papadatos, *The Eichmann Trial*, London: Stevens and Sons, 1964.

63 *A-G Israel* v. *Eichmann*, (1968) 36 ILR 5 (District Court, Jerusalem), paras. 40–50.
64 See the common statement of 3 August 1960, reprinted in (1968) 36 ILR 6–7: 'The Governments of Argentina and Israel ... resolve to regard as closed the incident which arose out of the action taken by citizens of Israel, which infringed the fundamental rights of the State of Argentina'.
65 Argentina originally claimed a violation of its sovereignty, demanding reparations, punishment for the kidnappers, and the return of Eichmann (David Cesarani, *Eichmann: His Life and Crimes*, London: Heinemann, 2004, pp. 235, 238; D. Stahl, *Nazi-Jagd: Südamerikas Diktaturen und die Ahndung von NS-Verbrechen*, Göttingen: Wallstein, 2013, pp. 122). On that basis the UN Security Council passed a resolution which condemned the Israeli action and requested adequate reparations to Argentina but leaving it open in which form: UN Doc. S/RES/138 (1960).
66 The Court does not make any further differentiation as to the form of immunity.
67 *A-G Israel* v. *Eichmann*, (1968) 36 ILR 5 (District Court, Jerusalem), paras. 51–52.
68 *A-G Israel* v. *Eichmann*, (1968) 36 ILR 277 (Israel Supreme Court), para. 13.
69 *A-G Israel* v. *Eichmann*, (1968) 36 ILR 5 (District Court, Jerusalem), para. 53.

Jacob Robinson, *And the Crooked Shall be Made Straight: The Eichmann Trial, the Jewish Catastrophe and Hannah Arendt's Narrative*, New York: Macmillan, 1965.

Bettina Stangneth, *Eichmann vor Jerusalem: Das Unbehelligte Leben Eines Massenmörders*, Zürich and Hamburg: Arche, 2011.

Slobodan Milošević 15

Michael Scharf

Slobodan Milošević was the President of the Federal Republic of Yugoslavia during the dissolution of Yugoslavia. From 1991 to 1999, his Serb troops and Bosnian Serb proxies fought four brutal Balkan wars. Hundreds of thousands died, most of them innocent civilians, and millions were displaced. Milošević saw himself as a modern-day Abe Lincoln, employing force in a valiant effort to hold his crumbling Yugoslavia together. Later he stood trial for the most serious crimes known to mankind – grave breaches of the Geneva Conventions, crimes against humanity, and genocide.

On 12 February 2002, the former Serb leader became the first former Head of State ever to face trial before an international criminal tribunal. With the combative Milošević acting as his own lawyer, a legal battle of epic proportions was waged at the Security Council-created Tribunal in The Hague known as the International Criminal Tribunal for the former Yugoslavia. It is often said that courts try cases, but cases also try courts. This proved to be particularly true with respect to the Milošević trial, since Milošević's primary strategy was to challenge the Yugoslavia Tribunal's legitimacy and impartiality, rather than to seek an acquittal through conventional tactics.

Although the Yugoslavia Tribunal has tried over a hundred other indicted war criminals, *Prosecutor* v. *Slobodan Milošević* was the case for which the *ad hoc* Court was created. Milošević was the highest level defendant, accused of the most serious crimes. So much was at stake.

If viewed as legitimate and fair, the Milošević trial could potentially serve several important functions in the Balkan peace process. By pinning prime responsibility on Milošević and disclosing the way the Yugoslav people were manipulated by their leaders into committing acts of savagery on a mass scale, the trial could help break the cycle of violence that has long plagued the Balkans. While this would not completely absolve the underlings for their acts, it could make it easier for victims to eventually forgive, or at least, reconcile with former neighbours who had been caught up in the institutionalised violence. This could also promote a political catharsis in Serbia, enabling the new leadership to distance themselves from the discredited nationalistic policies of the past. The historic record generated from the trial could educate the Serb people, long subject to Milošević's propaganda, about what really happened in Kosovo, Croatia, and Bosnia, and help ensure that such horrific acts are not repeated in the future.

On the other hand, a trial seen as unfair or as victor's justice could undermine the goal of fostering reconciliation between the ethnic groups living in the former Yugoslavia. The historic record developed by the trial would forever be questioned. The trial could add to the Serb martyrdom complex, amounting to another grievance requiring vengeance. And the judicial precedent would be tainted.

The Milošević trial was extremely messy. As detailed below, nearly everything that could go wrong, did go wrong. And then Milošević died just four months before his four-year trial was scheduled to wrap up. His death meant that no judgment would issue. No definitive historic record of high-level responsibility for atrocities would be published. This chapter provides an unvarnished review of the Milošević trial. Only by acknowledging its many shortcomings, can international justice improve upon its shaky performance.

A modern-day David versus Goliath?

In accordance with the rule prevailing in most common law countries, a defendant is generally permitted to decline appointed counsel and represent himself or herself if he or she is determined to be of sound mind. No decision would have a more profound effect on the course of the Milošević trial than the Yugoslavia Tribunal's ruling permitting Milošević to act as his own counsel during the proceedings.[1]

1 *Prosecutor* v. *Milošević* (IT-02-54), Transcript (Oral Ruling by the Trial Chamber), 18 December 2002, p. 14574. The Trial Chamber, however, agreed to keep the position under review, but later confirmed its ruling that Milošević could continue to defend himself: *Prosecutor* v. *Milošević* (IT-02-54), Reasons for Decision on the Prosecution Motion Concerning Assignment of Counsel, 4 April 2003. At the Trial Chamber's invitation, however, the Registrar had appointed several *amici curiae* to ensure that legal issues favouring the defence

First of all, the Tribunal's ruling significantly affected the length of the trial, as well as the amount of testimony the prosecution could present. Because the sixty-one year old Milošević was diagnosed with severe hypertension (his blood pressure was 240 over 120) and a serious heart condition, the Tribunal had to cut the number of days per week for the trial from five to three, the daily maximum number of hours for the trial from eight to four, and on several occasions adjourned for two-to-three week periods to allow Milošević to regain his strength. In an effort to try to keep the trial on track to finish in 2004, the Tribunal ordered the prosecution to pare down its witnesses, 'to the point where prosecutors claim[ed] their case [was] being emasculated'.[2] Nevertheless, the Committee for Milošević's defence, known as Slobda, accused the court of trying him to death.[3] His battle with health problems, as well as the Tribunal, boosted Milošević's underdog appeal back home in Serbia.

In addition, the decision to allow Milošević to defend himself enabled him to generate the illusion that he was a solitary individual pitted against an army of foreign lawyers and investigators. Day after day he sat alone in the courtroom behind a row of conspicuously empty desks that would ordinarily be occupied by the defence team. To get a flavour for how this played back in Serbia, according to a Serb who watched the trial proceedings on television in Belgrade: 'We cheer when he outsmarts the prosecutors. When he's defending himself all alone against the world.'[4]

In reality, Milošević, himself a lawyer who graduated near the top of his class from the prestigious University of Belgrade School of Law, had a cadre of legal counsel assisting him from behind the scenes, including some of the world's most distinguished trial attorneys. Heading Milošević's legal team were Ramsey Clark, a former US Attorney General, and Jacques Vergès, the French lawyer who defended Gestapo chief Klaus Barbie. Under their direction, and with funding from a network

would be brought to the Tribunal's attention, although the *amici* attorneys are not permitted to play any role in the actual trial proceedings.

2 Mirko Klarin, 'War Crimes Manipulation; Slobodan Milošević's Refusal to Accept Help in His War Crimes Trial is Making it Difficult to Provide him a Fair Hearing', *London Free Press*, 24 August 2002, p. F4.

3 Marc Champion, 'Court of Opinion: With Hague Case, Defiant Milošević Wins at Home; As Daily Coverage Keeps Serbs Riveted to TV, Many Feel as If They're on Trial', *Wall Street Journal*, 10 January 2003, p. A1.

4 Ibid.

of Milošević defence committees in Serbia, the United States, Britain, Russia, and France, lawyers and supporters of Milošević were able to dig up files and background on witnesses who were about to appear in court. Armed with this material, Milošević often seemed better informed than the prosecution.

Yet, the most significant ramification of the Tribunal's ruling was that it gave Milošević the chance to make unfettered speeches throughout the trial. In contrast, a defendant is ordinarily able to address the court only when he takes the stand to give testimony during the defence's case-in-chief. In the usual case, the defendant is limited to giving evidence that is relevant to the charges, and he is subject to cross-examination by the prosecution. By acting as his own counsel, Milošević was able to begin his case with eleven hours of opening argument, which included a Hollywood-quality video and slide-show presentation showing the destruction wrought by the 1999 NATO bombing campaign. The lead prosecution attorney, Geoffrey Nice QC, had shown some of the prosecution's own photos of victims of Serb atrocities during his opening, but they were not nearly as numerous or as gruesome as those Milošević presented, prompting the *New Yorker* to conclude that '[h]orror for horror, [Nice] was outdone by Milošević'.[5]

Bending over backwards to maintain the appearance of fairness, the Tribunal's judges allowed Milošević to treat the witnesses, prosecutors, and the judges in a manner that would earn ordinary defence counsel expulsion from the courtroom. In addition to regularly making disparaging remarks about the court and repeatedly brow beating witnesses, Milošević pontificated at length during cross-examination of every prosecution witness. While the Tribunal at first gave Milošević substantial leeway, the judges began to express impatience with Milošević's 'political points'. On numerous occasions, the Tribunal's presiding judge warned: 'Mr. Milošević, you are making speeches... [Y]ou're supposed to be asking questions and not making denigrating comments about the witnesses.'[6] Nevertheless, throughout the Prosecution's case, Milošević's cross-examinations averaged twice the length of the Prosecution's direct examinations.

5 Joseph Lelyveld, 'The Defendant; Slobodan Milošević's Trial, and the Debate Surrounding International Courts', *The New Yorker*, 27 May 2002, p. 82.
6 *Prosecutor v. Milošević* (IT-02-54), Transcript (Oral Ruling by the Trial Chamber), 3 December 2002, p. 13821, lines 1–4.

Summing up the impact of Milošević's trial performance, one former employee of the Tribunal stated: 'You can't help falling under his spell. He's very sharp and he's funny. It's sick, I know, given what he's there for, but he's so cynical and quick that he's had the courtroom in fits of laughter at times.'[7] The Prosecution tried to ignore the political fallout. Yet, according to the Serbian Prime Minister Zoran Đinđić: 'The prosecution says "What we care about is the law, and the fact that Milošević has hundreds of hours to promote his politics is not our problem." That's naïve.'[8]

Real justice or *Realpolitik*? Challenges to the legitimacy of the Yugoslavia Tribunal

Beginning with his arraignment before the Yugoslavia Tribunal on 3 July 2001, Milošević launched his challenge to the validity of the Security Council-created court. 'You are not a judicial institution; you are a political tool', Milošević told the panel of three judges.[9] Drawing on the commonly accepted notion that the post–Second World War Nuremberg Trials were tainted by 'victor's justice', one of Milošević's lawyers, former United States Attorney General Ramsey Clark, publicly circulated a draft brief (which included Milošević's handwritten notations), whose sole purpose appeared to be to discredit the Tribunal.

While the Nuremberg Charter precluded challenges to the legitimacy of the Nuremberg Tribunal itself, the Yugoslavia Tribunal considered the question in its first case, *Prosecutor* v. *Tadić*, in 1995. The Tribunal ruled that, although its creation by the Security Council was without precedent, it was a valid product of the Security Council under the Council's broad powers to take action to maintain international peace and security.[10] But, as Milošević himself pointed out, the judges that made that decision could not be seriously expected to decide the issue impartially, given that their

---

7 Marc Champion, 'Court of Opinion: With Hague Case, Defiant Milošević Wins at Home; As Daily Coverage Keeps Serbs Riveted to TV, Many Feel as If They're on Trial', *Wall Street Journal*, 10 January 2003, p. A1.

8 Ibid.

9 *Prosecutor* v. *Milošević* (IT-02-54), Transcript (Initial Appearance), 3 July 2001, pp. 1–2. This appearance related to the first indictment that concerned the Kosovo conflict.

10 *Prosecutor* v. *Tadić* (IT-94-1-AR72), Decision on the Defence Motion for Interlocutory Appeal on Jurisdiction, 2 October 1995, paras. 32–6.

incredibly prestigious, $150,000 (tax free) per year jobs would have been instantly extinguished if they had decided otherwise.

Having rendered that decision in the *Tadić* case, the Yugoslavia Tribunal declined to revisit the question in the *Milošević* trial. In response to Milošević's challenges to the Tribunal's legitimacy at a pre-trial hearing in August 2001, Presiding Judge Richard May responded: 'Mr. Milošević, we are not going to listen to these political arguments.'[11] Having failed to convince the Yugoslavia Tribunal to reconsider this issue, Milošević attempted to attack the legitimacy of the Tribunal in The Hague District Court. But the Dutch Court declared itself incompetent to consider the question.[12] He then took his case to the European Court of Human Rights, which ruled the application inadmissible because Milošević had failed to exhaust domestic remedies by neglecting to appeal The Hague District Court decision to the Dutch Court of Appeals.[13] That Milošević's high-powered legal team would unintentionally make such a novice legal mistake is hard to believe. It is more likely that they desired this outcome so that Milošević could make the political argument that he was being railroaded at The Hague.

Victor's justice

To the extent Milošević's goal was not to obtain a dismissal or acquittal but to publicly discredit the Tribunal, he enjoyed a greater degree of success with his argument that the Yugoslavia Tribunal, like Nuremberg, represented 'victor's justice'. In contrast to Nuremberg, however, the Yugoslavia Tribunal was created neither by the victors nor by the parties involved in the conflict, but rather by the United Nations, representing the international community of States. The judges of the Yugoslavia Tribunal came from all parts of the world, and were elected by the General Assembly, in which each of the world's 193 countries gets an equal vote. Moreover, the message of the Yugoslavia Tribunal's indictments, prosecutions, and convictions of Muslims and Croats, in addition to Serbs,

---

11 *Prosecutor* v. *Milošević* (IT-02-54), Transcript, 30 August 2001, p. 25, lines 3–5.
12 *Milošević* v. *The Netherlands*, Case No. KG 01/975, ELRO No. AD3266, Hague District Court, 31 August 2001.
13 *Milošević* v. *The Netherlands* (dec.), no. 77631/01, 19 March 2002.

was that a war crime is a war crime, by whomever it is committed; the Tribunal has self-consciously taken no sides.

On the other hand, Milošević pointed out that the decision to establish the Yugoslavia Tribunal was made by the UN Security Council, which cannot truly be characterised as a neutral third party; rather, it had itself become deeply involved and taken sides in the Balkan conflict. The Security Council had, for example, imposed sanctions on Milošević's Serbia and Montenegro, then known as the Federal Republic of Yugoslavia, which it felt was most responsible for the conflict and atrocities. Throughout the conflict, the Security Council had been quite vocal in its condemnation of Serb atrocities, but its criticisms of those committed by Muslims and Croats were comparatively muted. And most problematic of all, three of the permanent members of the Council – the United States, France, and the United Kingdom – led the seventy-eight-day bombing campaign against Milošević and Serbia in 1999. Moreover, as Milošević repeatedly observed, NATO cruise missiles specifically targeted Milošević's residence in an effort to kill him and his family.

While both the Prosecutor and the judicial Chambers of the Yugoslavia Tribunal were conceived to be independent from the Security Council, one cannot ignore the fact that the Statute provides that the Tribunal's Prosecutor is selected by the Security Council. The judges were selected by the General Assembly from a short list proposed by the Security Council. They were eligible for re-election after serving a four-year term. Moreover, the operation of the Tribunal was dependent on hundreds of millions of dollars of contributions from the United States and its Western allies. And during the Milošević trial, most of the staff of the Office of the International Prosecutor were on loan from NATO countries.

Although a creature of the United Nations, according to its first president, Antonio Cassese, the Tribunal tended to 'take into account the exigencies and tempo of the international community'.[14] Milošević suggested that this meant that the Tribunal had yielded to the objectives of the United States and other NATO powers, without whose financial and military support the Tribunal could not function. Thus, it should come as little surprise that in a survey by the polling firm Greenberg, Quinlan, and Rossner for the National Democratic Institute for International Affairs in

---

14 Seumas Milne, 'Hague is not the Place to Try Milošević', *The Guardian*, 2 August 2001.

May 2002, 80 per cent of 1,300 Serbs said they believed that the Tribunal prosecuted Serbs more vigorously than it did non-Serbs, while 57 per cent said they were convinced the Tribunal was unjust.[15]

The timing of the indictment

For evidence of the political influence of the United States on the Yugoslavia Tribunal, Milošević pointed to the all too convenient timing of his indictment. It was issued on 22 May 1999, sixty days into the seventy-eight-day NATO bombing campaign against Serbia. The indictment came down at a crucial time, when popular support for the intervention was waning in several NATO countries in the face of intense press criticism of NATO's use of cluster bombs and depleted uranium munitions, attacks on civilian trains, truck convoys, and media centres, and the accidental bombings of the Chinese Embassy in Belgrade and the territory of neighbouring Bulgaria. If this had forced a premature end of the bombing campaign, American officials feared that it might irrevocably damage the credibility of NATO, potentially leading to its demise.

After years of pressuring the Tribunal's Prosecutor not to indict the Serb leader, whose co-operation was seen as essential for the Balkan peace process, suddenly the United States was pressing for the immediate issuance of charges against Milošević, knowing that such action would bolster the political will of the NATO countries to continue the bombing campaign, and ultimately force Milošević to accept NATO's terms for Kosovo. And after years of refusing to turn over sensitive intelligence data to the Tribunal in order to protect 'sources and methods', the United States and the United Kingdom were hurriedly handing over reams of satellite imagery, telephone intercepts, and other top-secret information to help the Prosecutor make the case against Milošević.

The manner of Milošević's surrender

The newly elected President of the Federal Republic of Yugoslavia, Vojislav Koštunica, backed up by a federal court ruling, refused to permit

15 Marc Champion, 'Court of Opinion: With Hague Case, Defiant Milošević Wins at Home; As Daily Coverage Keeps Serbs Riveted to TV, Many Feel as If They're on Trial', *Wall Street Journal*, 10 January 2003, p. A1.

the extradition of Milošević to The Hague. But in a late night move that caught everyone off guard, Koštunica's political rival, Prime Minister Zoran Đinđić, instructed the Serb police under his command to secretly take Milošević to an American air base in Tuzla, Bosnia, from which Milošević was transferred by military jet to The Hague on 28 July 2001. In announcing the action, in defiance of the Supreme Court's Order, Đinđić said that he had been forced to take a 'difficult but morally correct' decision to protect the interests of Serbia. The United States and its European allies were promising $1.28 billion in aid in return for the surrender of Milošević. This led Serb newspaper headlines to proclaim that Milošević had become 'Serbia's most valuable export commodity'.[16] Immediately thereafter, a furious Koštunica protested that the extradition of Milošević was 'illegal and unconstitutional'.

Meanwhile, on board the flight to The Hague, Milošević reportedly told the tribunal officials who read him his rights: 'You are kidnapping me, and you will answer for your crimes.' In the analogous cases of *Stocké* v. *Germany*[17] and *Bozano* v. *France*,[18] the European Court of Human Rights had held that luring or abduction in violation of established extradition procedures is a human rights violation for which dismissal of charges is the appropriate remedy. But the Yugoslavia Tribunal rejected the argument in the *Dokmanović* case[19] on the ground that there does not exist a formal extradition treaty between the Tribunal and the Federal Republic of Yugoslavia. Whatever the technical legal merits of his argument, politically the timing of Milošević's irregular surrender could not have been worse for the Tribunal. He arrived at the Yugoslavia Tribunal on St. Vitus' day, the solemn holiday commemorating the historic Serb defeat to the

---

16 Konstantinos D. Magliveras, 'The Interplay Between the Transfer of Slobodan Milošević to the ICTY and Yugoslav Constitutional Law', (2002) 13 *European Journal of International Law* 661, at p. 676.

17 *Stocké* v. *Germany*, 19 March 1991, § 53, Series A no. 199.

18 *Bozano* v. *France*, 18 December 1986, Series A no. 111.

19 *Prosecutor* v. *Dokmanović* (IT-95-13a-T), 22 October 1997 (reported: '*Dokmanović* Case: Trial Chamber Denies the Motion for Release by the Accused', CC/PIO/251-E, 27 October 1997). See further, Sean D. Murphy, 'Developments in International Criminal Law: Progress and Jurisprudence of the International Criminal Tribunal for the Former Yugoslavia', (1999) 93 *American Journal of International Law* 57.

Ottoman Turks at the battle of Kosovo Polje in 1389, which figures so prominently in the Serb mythology of victimisation.

Unclean hands

To further illustrate the Tribunal's politicisation, Milošević tried to force the Tribunal to face the '*tu quoque*' argument (literally meaning 'you too'). The argument had some success at Nuremberg with respect to the charge of waging unrestricted submarine warfare levied against German Grand Admiral Karl Dönitz. In light of an affidavit obtained by Dönitz's lawyer from US Admiral Chester Nimitz, indicating that the US Navy had used the same tactic in the Pacific, the Nuremberg Tribunal decided not to impose a sentence with respect to this charge.

Drawing on the Nuremberg precedent, Milošević first complained that Franjo Tuđman, the former leader of Croatia, was never indicted by the Tribunal for the mass atrocities that Croatian troops committed against the Serbs in re-taking Serb-controlled areas of eastern Croatia. In fact, Tuđman was welcomed to the United States for cancer treatment at the Walter Reed Hospital in Washington a few months before his death in 1999.

Milošević also repeatedly raised the issue of NATO war crimes. When several respected human rights organisations urged the Tribunal to investigate the possibility that NATO had committed war crimes during the 1999 intervention, the then Prosecutor, Louise Arbour (from Canada, a NATO country), assigned the task to her Legal Adviser, William Fenrick. Fenrick was an ex-NATO lawyer, who went to the Yugoslavia Tribunal directly from his post as director of law for operations and training in the Canadian Department of Defence. Not surprisingly, Fenrick's report, which was released in June 2000, concluded that NATO had committed no indictable offences. But critics have been quick to seize upon the clause of the report that notes that the review of NATO's actions relied primarily on public documents produced by NATO, and that the authors of the report 'tended to assume that the NATO and NATO countries' press statements are generally reliable and that explanations have been honestly given'.

Finally, Milošević argued that the United States' opposition to a permanent international criminal court undermined its moral right to participate in any way in the trial of Milošević. Although there was no United States judge on the Milošević trial bench, one of the trial attorneys was a former United States Department of Justice prosecutor, and much of the evidence used by the prosecution was provided by United States authorities. According to United States officials at the time, international criminal tribunals are prone to politicisation – the very argument that Milošević was making about the Yugoslavia Tribunal.

There are several answers to Milošević's *tu quoque* challenge. First, whatever Franjo Tuđman and NATO had done, their actions did not excuse what Milošević did. Second, the Tribunal's Prosecutor at the time of the Milošević indictment, Louise Arbour, stated that she was about to issue an indictment for Franjo Tuđman just before the Croatian President passed away, demonstrating that the Tribunal was striving to be even-handed. Third, whether or not one believes NATO violated the laws of war during the 1999 bombing campaign, NATO did not systematically set out to kill and torture civilians on a mass scale – the crimes for which Milošević was accused. Fourth, established democracies have mechanisms (such as a free press, political opposition, and an independent judiciary) to examine publicly their own past, for example America's actions in Vietnam or France's use of torture in Algeria. While Serbia was willing to try Milošević for corruption, the Yugoslavia Tribunal was the only venue where his war crimes and crimes against humanity could be exposed. Finally, while these arguments might suggest that the Tribunal's Prosecutors may have been out to get Milošević, selective prosecution is never a valid defence, even in domestic trials. Milošević's ultimate fate was placed in the hands of the Tribunal's judges, not its Prosecutor. As long as history views the Tribunal's bench as independent and impartial, and the procedures as fair and equitable, the trial of Milošević should be considered credible.

Composition of the bench

Unlike most domestic systems, the Yugoslavia Tribunal's judges were not randomly assigned to cases by lot. Given that the pool of the Tribunal's judges that was available for the Milošević trial included citizens from several countries that had no stake in the Balkan conflict, the jurist picked by Judge Claude Jorda of France, the President of the Tribunal, to preside over the Milošević case represented a most unfortunate selection. The problem is that the judge selected to head the panel, Richard George May, hailed from the United Kingdom, one of the NATO countries that led the 1999 intervention against Serbia.

Judge Jorda selected Judge May for the job because May was widely viewed as the best trial judge at the Tribunal, a man uniquely capable of keeping Milošević in line and the trial moving smoothly forward. Perhaps this distinguished jurist could not be expected to recuse himself from presiding over the Milošević trial because that would be an admission of his bias, and would subvert the credibility of the Tribunal as a whole. Indeed, in none of the two-dozen cases tried before the Yugoslavia Tribunal and its sister institution the Rwanda Tribunal has a judge recused him or herself, despite numerous attempts by defendants to obtain recusal. And yet, however fair and impartial Judge May actually was, one can certainly understand why some might perceive that the 'fix is in' as long as a British judge was presiding over the trial. Then, when Judge May died of cancer two-thirds through the trial, Judge Jorda assigned as his replacement on the Milošević case a Scotsman, Iain Bonomy. In this regard, Osgoode Hall Law Professor Michael Mandel maintained that 'Milošević ha[d] about as much chance of getting a fair trial from this court as he had of defeating NATO in an air war'.

Fairness of the proceedings

In addition to an impartial bench, the validity of the trial would depend on the court allowing Milošević the equality of arms and fair procedures that the defendants at Nuremberg did not receive. But while the prosecution brought the President of Croatia, as well as several military commanders and international figures to The Hague to testify against Milošević, the defendant was rebuffed in his efforts to obtain the testimony of former President Bill Clinton, Secretary of State Madeline Albright, Special Envoy Richard Holbrooke, and NATO Generals Wesley Clark and Michael Rose. Milošević's strategy was to call such officials to the stand so he could ask them point blank: 'You embraced me as a crucial element in the peace negotiations; after the conclusion of the Dayton Accords I was mentioned as a leading candidate for the Nobel Peace Prize; how can you now argue that I am responsible for crimes in Bosnia of which you were perfectly aware at the time of Dayton'?

In an early draft of his memoir, General Wesley Clark reportedly wrote of a conversation with Milošević in which Clark asked: 'Why did you let General Mladić do what he did at Srebrenica'? According to the passage, which was cut out of the book in its final editing (presumably at the insistence of the Department of State), Clark recalled that Milošević had replied: 'Well, I warned him not to do this, but he wouldn't listen to me.'[20] Such testimony would obviously have gone a long way to proving that Milošević lacked effective control over the Bosnian Serbs who were responsible for acts of genocide in Bosnia.

With respect to the charges concerning Kosovo, Milošević sought to compare his actions with the post–September 11, 2001 American war on terrorism and its efforts to drive the Taliban and al-Qaeda from Afghanistan. As late as February 1998, the United States, and other members of the so-called 'Contact Group' (France, the United Kingdom, Germany, Italy, and Russia) were calling the Kosovo Liberation Army a 'terrorist group' and condemning the organisation's violent actions.[21] But Milošević was blocked in his quest to call Western leaders to testify about the basis for the terrorist designation, which served as the bedrock of his public justification for the use of force in Kosovo.

Another development that presented Milošević ammunition to argue that the process at The Hague was less than fair occurred when the Tribunal's appointed *amicus curiae* counsel, Michail Wladimiroff, told the press half way through the trial that Milošević's chances of acquittal 'were negligible'. Milošević charged that by giving such an assessment, Wladimiroff – who had been appointed by the Tribunal over Milošević's objections precisely to ensure that Milošević received a fair trial – had instead prejudged the Tribunal's verdict.[22] The Trial Chamber reluctantly agreed: 'The statements taken as a whole would, in the Chamber's view, give rise to a reasonable perception of bias on the part of the *amicus curiae*', Judge May said in the decision to remove Wladimiroff from the case.[23] But by that time the damage to the Tribunal's integrity had already been done.

20 Joseph Lelyveld, 'The Defendant; Slobodan Milošević's Trial, and the Debate Surrounding International Courts', *The New Yorker*, 27 May 2002, p. 82.

21 Paul Williams and Michael Scharf, *Peace with Justice: War Crimes and Accountability in the Former Yugoslavia*, Oxford: Rowman and Littlefield, 2002, pp. 176–7.

22 'Yugoslavia: Hague Tribunal Fires 'Amicus Curiae' in Milošević Case', *BBC Monitoring Europe*, 10 October 2002.

23 *Prosecutor* v. *Milošević* (IT-02-54), Decision concerning an Amicus Curiae, 10 October 2002.

Conclusion: the impact on peace and reconciliation in the Balkans

Witness by witness, document by document, the prosecution was able to construct a formidable case against Slobodan Milošević at The Hague. Convinced that exposure to the Milošević trial would have a cathartic effect on the Serb population, the United States Agency for International Development (USAID) spent $24,000 a month to broadcast the trial proceedings throughout Serbia. As noted in the *New Yorker*, 'during the trial's first couple of weeks, five channels carried the proceedings live, and more than half of all [Serbian] households were tuned in'.[24] Until Milošević's death derailed the trial, the trial proceedings were shown for up to five hours each day on Station B92 in Serbia, where it received the network's biggest market share (on average 27 per cent).

Perhaps the trial broadcasts would have achieved the hoped for effect if it were not for Milošević's refusal to play by the rules (that is, to let a lawyer defend him in the conventional manner). While his defence strategy was unlikely to win him an acquittal, it has been described by a Balkans expert as 'brilliantly cunning, designed to play on Serbia's psychological vulnerabilities and continued Serb resentment of the 1999 NATO bombing'.[25] 'You really ha[d] two trials going on at the same time, one in the court and the other in the forum of public opinion', observed Judith Armatta, an American lawyer who monitored the trial for the Coalition for International Justice, a non-profit organisation that supports international efforts to bring war criminals to justice.[26] To the extent that it was aimed not at the court of law but the court of public opinion back home in Serbia, Milošević's strategy unquestionably paid off. His approval rating in Serbia doubled during the first weeks of his trial.[27] A poll taken just

24 Joseph Lelyveld, 'The Defendant; Slobodan Milošević's Trial, and the Debate Surrounding International Courts', *The New Yorker*, 27 May 2002, p. 82.
25 Dusko Doder, 'Book Review of Slobodan Milošević and the Destruction of Yugoslavia by Louis Sell', *The Nation*, 27 May 2002, p. 25.
26 Marc Champion, 'Court of Opinion: With Hague Case, Defiant Milošević Wins at Home; As Daily Coverage Keeps Serbs Riveted to TV, Many Feel as If They're on Trial', *Wall Street Journal*, 10 January 2003, p. A1.
27 Andre Purvis, 'Star Power in Serbia; Slobodan Milošević's Performance at his War Crimes Trial has Won Him Increased Popularity at Home', *Time*, 30 September 2002, p. 46.

before Milošević's death found that 39 per cent of the Serb population rated Milošević's trial performance 'superior', while less than 25 per cent felt that he was getting a fair trial, and only 33 per cent thought that he was actually responsible for war crimes.[28] Milošević used the trial to transform himself from the most reviled individual in Serbia to number four on the list of most admired Serbs.

Does its lack of legitimacy in the eyes of so many in Serbia mean that the Milošević trial failed to achieve the goals of denying collective guilt by establishing individual responsibility, enabling the dismantlement of institutions responsible for perpetuating the commission of atrocities, establishing an accurate historical record, providing a cathartic process for victims, and deterring further instances of violence in the Balkans as well as atrocities in similar conflicts elsewhere? To answer this question, one might turn to the precedent of the Nuremberg Tribunal. Like the International Criminal Tribunal for the former Yugoslavia, the International Military Tribunal was accused of victor's justice and unfair proceedings. As the Yugoslavia Tribunal had done with Milošević, the Nuremberg Tribunal permitted Nazi leader Hermann Goering relatively free reign in his testimony. Like Milošević, the unrepentant Goering repeatedly attacked the validity of the proceedings, indulged in propaganda, and attempted to justify his policies and actions as Hitler's Reich Marshal. Indeed, history records that Goering got the better of the lead Nuremberg prosecutor, Justice Robert Jackson of the United States Supreme Court during a cross-examination that went on for two days in 1946.[29]

One of the modern myths of Nuremberg is that the German people immediately accepted the legitimacy of the Nuremberg Tribunal and its judgment. In contrast, opinion polls conducted by the United States Department of State from 1946 through 1958 indicated that a large majority of West Germans considered the Nuremberg proceedings to be nothing but a show trial, representing victor's justice rather than real justice.[30] By 1953, the State Department had concluded that

28 Joseph Lelyveld, 'The Defendant; Slobodan Milošević's Trial, and the Debate Surrounding International Courts', *The New Yorker*, 27 May 2002, p. 82; 'Q&A with Zain Verjee', Transcript, *CNN International*, 12 February 2002.
29 Telford Taylor, *The Anatomy of the Nuremberg Trials*, London: Bloomsbury, 1993, pp. 334–7.
30 Peter Maguire, *Law and War: An American Story*, New York: Columbia University Press, 2000, p. 241.

the Nuremberg and Control Council Law No. 10 trials had failed to 're-educate' West Germans. According to a de-classified 1953 State Department report: 'From the political point of view, the crux of the war criminals problem in Germany is the refusal of a large number of Germans to accept the principles underlying the [Nuremberg] trials or the findings of the trials … In spite of all the Western powers have said to the contrary, the trials are generally portrayed as acts of political retribution without firm legal basis.'[31]

Perhaps, this suggests that even if Milošević had been given a perfect trial, popular opinion in Serbia would still have regarded him as a martyr, the trial as unfair, and the testimony and exhibits as unconvincing. In the years since the Milošević trial, the Yugoslavia Tribunal has tried other high-level leaders, including Ratko Mladić, the Bosnian Serb General charged with carrying out genocidal campaigns. Each of these trials has been chaotic; perhaps that is an inherent characteristic of international trials involving high-level political and military leaders.

While perfection in international trials is impossible, international justice can do better than it did in the Milošević case. Self-representation needs to be circumscribed; stand-by counsel need to be appointed to step in when the defendant becomes disruptive, too ill to continue, or stages a boycott. Indictments need to be narrowed and cases need to be more focused so as not to drag on for years. And defendants should be tried jointly, so that the death of one does not end the case and erase the establishment of a historic record.

FURTHER READING

Gideon Boas, *The Milošević Trial: Lessons for the Conduct of Complex International Criminal Proceedings*, Cambridge University Press, 2007.

Carla Del Ponte and Chuck Sudetic, *Madam Prosecutor: Confrontations with Humanities Worst Criminals and the Culture of Impunity*, New York: Other Press, 2009.

John Laughland, *The Trial of Slobodan Milošević and the Corruption of International Justice*, London: Pluto Press, 2007.

Michael P. Scharf and William A. Schabas, *Slobodan Milošević on Trial: A Companion*, New York: Continuum, 2002.

---

31 Ibid., p. 246.

Timothy William Waters, *The Milosevic Trial: An Autopsy*, Oxford University Press, 2014.

Paul R. Williams and Michael P. Scharf, *Peace with Justice: War Crimes and Accountability in the Former Yugoslavia*, Oxford: Rowman and Littlefield, 2002.

16 Charles Taylor

Charles Chernor Jalloh

The trial of the former president of Liberia, Charles Ghankay Taylor, by the United Nations-backed Special Court for Sierra Leone, was remarkable for several reasons. First, it was the only case before the Court involving a non-Sierra Leonean. Taylor is from neighbouring Liberia, where he is alleged to be responsible for crimes even worse than those committed during Sierra Leone's civil war.[1] But Taylor, like all the other rebel leaders from his native country, has never been prosecuted for crimes committed in Liberia because the parties to that conflict effectively granted themselves amnesty.[2] Rather, he was implicated by the Special Court for supporting Foday Sankoh, the leader of a rebel army called the Revolutionary United Front, to foment a war in Sierra Leone in which numerous atrocity crimes were committed. Sankoh and Taylor made 'common cause'[3] to help each other take over their respective countries for personal and political gain.

Second, as a criminal trial, the case against Taylor was inevitably complicated. He reportedly never set foot in Sierra Leone during the time the offences for which he was charged were perpetrated. This meant that the prosecution's appropriate burden to prove the case beyond a reasonable doubt, when compared to the other cases before the Court, was going to be doubly difficult. Indeed, for most of the pre-trial and trial phases, the success of the case against Taylor appeared to hinge primarily on two expansive and controversial modes of criminal liability in international

The author is grateful to Meg DeGuzman and Alpha Sesay for helpful comments on the first draft, and to Kelly Moras for her assistance with the footnotes.

1 'Truth and Reconciliation Commission', *Consolidated Final Report*, Monrovia, 2009, pp. 151–72.
2 Chernor Jalloh and Alhagi Marong, 'Ending Impunity: The Case for War Crimes Trials in Liberia', (2005) 1 *African Journal of Legal Studies* 53.
3 *Prosecutor* v. *Taylor* (SCSL-03-01-T), Judgment, 18 May 2012, para. 25.

criminal law – joint criminal enterprise and command responsibility – neither of which requires the suspect to directly commit the acts in question. The task for the Court's prosecutors was how, using those two and other indirect theories of criminal participation such as instigating or ordering, they could link Taylor in Liberia to the offences carried out by the Revolutionary United Front and its collaborators in Sierra Leone. Interestingly, although it managed to secure Taylor's conviction for planning and aiding and abetting crimes in Sierra Leone, the prosecution failed to prove joint criminal enterprise and command responsibility.

Aside from Taylor, those persons tried by the Special Court were leaders of rebel, militia, or other organisations. Those convicted in the cases involving the Revolutionary United Front, the Civil Defence Forces, and the Armed Forces Revolutionary Council were part of the command structure of those entities. They each either committed the crimes personally or were found to have exercised *de facto* or *de jure* authority over the subordinates who perpetrated them. Thus, before Taylor's arrest, the highest profile politician charged before the Court was the former deputy defence minister, Sam Hinga Norman. He later died before judgment was rendered. Taylor's Head of State status and the fact that he had, by the time of his indictment, gained notoriety for the abuses that his forces committed against civilians in Liberia where he ascended to the presidency in August 1997, made him the most 'famous' person before the Court. As the perceived 'godfather' of the Revolutionary United Front, the stature of Taylor's case grew after Sankoh and his ruthless number two, Sam 'Mosquito' Bockarie, died before they could be tried, with the latter allegedly murdered on Taylor's orders because he knew too much. In other words, with the apex of the rebel organisation unavailable due to Sankoh's and Bockarie's deaths, Taylor became the last person standing. He thus gained in symbolic importance as a figure the prosecution could exaggeratingly blame for most of the Revolutionary United Front depravations. Yet the prosecution was unable to prove beyond a reasonable doubt – as William Schabas aptly described it – that Taylor was the 'guiding spirit', 'evil genius', or 'mastermind' who 'manipulated the war throughout the 1990s'.[4]

---

4 William A. Schabas, 'Charles Taylor Judgment Suggests a More Modest Level of Participation in the Sierra Leone Conflict', *PhD Studies in Human Rights*, 28 April 2012 (available online at: http://humanrightsdoctorate.blogspot. com/2012/04/charles-taylor-judgment-suggests-more.html).

In a still controversial decision that also made his case unique amongst the Special Court trials, Taylor was the only suspect tried in the heart of Europe at The Hague in the Netherlands, away from the seat of the Tribunal in Freetown, Sierra Leone. The decision to change the venue of his trial was taken ostensibly for security reasons. Some critics, especially many from the local civil society, including myself, vehemently contested this rationale.[5] The critics argued that Taylor – who was no longer in power – could not be a threat to an entire sub-region. Even if he was, it would have been far better, and likely less costly, for security to be bolstered in Sierra Leone and Liberia rather than move the Court's most important case away from the alleged victim communities most affected by his crimes. Similarly, Taylor was the only convict to be imprisoned outside Africa – in the United Kingdom – where he is serving a fifty-year sentence. All of the others are serving their sentences in Rwanda. Taylor's repeated requests to be sent there have so far failed.

Although not without its difficulties, many of which will be discussed, the trial is the jewel in the Special Court's crown. It is also one of the most symbolically important cases in modern international criminal law. The reason is simple. Attempts to prosecute Heads of State or Government by the *ad hoc* International Criminal Tribunals for the former Yugoslavia and Rwanda and the permanent International Criminal Court have implicated political figures of similar standing. But almost all of those trials have been marred by practical issues, procedural irregularities, or other obstacles. In contrast, with the exception of a major hiccup at the beginning of his trial and another which bookended its completion, *Prosecutor* v. *Charles Ghankay Taylor* proceeded smoothly. Today, despite the high legal and political drama that periodically characterised it, the Taylor prosecution stands as one of the better examples of a complex but successful trial of a former Head of State by a modern international criminal court.

The establishment of the Special Court for Sierra Leone

The Sierra Leone war, which started in March 1991, became notorious for some of its shocking atrocities. After several years of failed attempts

---

5 E.g., *Prosecutor* v. *Taylor* (SCSL-2003-01-PT), Civil Society *Amicus Curiae* Brief Regarding Change of Venue of Taylor Trial Back to Freetown, 9 March 2007, paras. 3–4, 13.

to make peace, President Ahmed Tejan Kabbah of Sierra Leone wrote a letter to the United Nations requesting international help to establish an independent special court to try the 'Revolutionary United Front leadership' and their 'accomplices' and 'collaborators'.[6] Sierra Leone was willing to prosecute, but lacked the legal, logistical and other resources to do so. The United Nations Security Council, which itself was tired of the Revolutionary United Front and its depravations, including attacks on its peacekeepers, acceded to the request. It asked the Secretary-General to negotiate a treaty with the Sierra Leone Government to establish an independent tribunal to prosecute those most responsible for the atrocities including the leaders who had threatened the establishment and implementation of the peace process.[7]

The United Nations and Sierra Leone consequently signed the first ever *ad hoc* penal bilateral treaty between the former and a Member State in January 2002.[8] The instrument created a special tribunal to prosecute those bearing greatest responsibility for crimes against humanity, war crimes, and other serious violations of international humanitarian law, specified in articles 2 to 4 of the Statute of the Special Court for Sierra Leone. Several offences under Sierra Leonean law relating to abuse of children and arson were mentioned in article 5 but, in practice, were never used to prosecute anyone. The Secretary-General described it as a *sui generis* court with a mixed jurisdiction and composition.[9] The Tribunal, which was the first modern one to be based in the country where the crimes were committed since the Nuremberg and Tokyo trials, was to be funded by donations and to last for three years. It began operations towards the end of 2002. It went on to prosecute several individuals from the three warring factions. At the height of its operations, the Court had two trial chambers and an appeals chamber hearing several joint trials. In a symbolic act that seemed to underscore his importance, Taylor was the only person to be tried alone by the Special Court.

---

6 Permanent Representative of Sierra Leone to the U.N., Letter dated 12 June, 2000 from the Permanent Representative of Sierra Leone to the United Nations addressed to the President of the Security Council, UN Doc. S/2000/786, Annex.

7 UN Doc S/RES/1315 (2000).

8 Agreement Between the United Nations and the Government of Sierra Leone on the Establishment of a Special Court for Sierra Leone, (2002) 2178 UNTS 138.

9 Report of the Secretary-General on the Establishment of a Special Court for Sierra Leone, UN Doc. S/2000/915, para. 9.

The indictment of Taylor

On 7 March 2003, Judge Bankole Thompson approved a seventeen-count indictment against Taylor.[10] The indictment was accompanied by an arrest warrant and request for the suspect's arrest and transfer. The documents were placed under seal. On 12 June 2003, the Trial Chamber formally granted a request unsealing them. The indictment charged him with individual criminal responsibility pursuant to articles 6(1) and 6(3) of the Statute of the Special Court for Sierra Leone. Under article 6(1), the prosecution alleged that Taylor, by his acts or omissions, planned, instigated, ordered, committed, aided and abetted, or otherwise participated with Foday Sankoh in a common plan involving the crimes charged. In addition to, or in the alternative, pursuant to article 6(3), the prosecution claimed that Taylor was criminally responsible as a superior for the crimes alleged in the indictments. The prosecution averred that he knew, or had reason to know, that his subordinates in the Revolutionary United Front and the Armed Forces Revolutionary Council/Revolutionary United Front coalition were about to carry out the crimes, or had done so, but that he failed to take the necessary measures to prevent the acts or to punish the perpetrators.

Taylor's indictment was amended twice, on 16 March 2006 and 29 May 2007. The final version, on which he was tried, contained three international crimes and eleven counts.[11] In five counts he was charged with crimes against humanity, punishable under article 2 of the Statute, namely: murder, rape, sexual slavery, other inhumane acts, and enslavement. Five other counts charged what are typically referred to as war crimes, punishable under article 3, namely: acts of terrorism, violence to life, health and physical or mental well-being of persons, in particular murder, outrages upon personal dignity, violence to life, health and physical or mental well-being of persons, in particular cruel treatment, and pillage. Finally, the last count alleged his commission of other serious violations of international humanitarian law, punishable under article 4, and in particular, conscripting or enlisting children under the age of fifteen

---

10 *Prosecutor* v. *Taylor* (SCSL-2003-01-I), Decision Approving the Indictment and Order for Non-Disclosure, 7 March 2003.
11 *Prosecutor* v. *Taylor* (SCSL-2003-01-I), Prosecution's Second Amended Indictment, 29 May 2007.

years into armed forces or groups or using them to participate actively in hostilities.

The prosecution alleged that the crimes underlying the counts were committed between the beginning of the temporal jurisdiction of the Court, on 30 November 1996, and the end of the Sierra Leone conflict, on 18 January 2002. Yet, during the trial, the prosecution presented much evidence that dated back to the period just before the war's start in March 1991. That material was not generally considered when determining his culpability. The locations pleaded in the indictment covered five of Sierra Leone's largest districts from north to south and east to west, namely: Bombali, Kailahun, Kenema, Kono, and Port Loko districts, the Western Area, as well as the capital Freetown.

The question of peace for Liberia versus justice in Sierra Leone

Taylor's indictment was first unveiled by the prosecution on 4 June 2003. He had travelled to Accra, Ghana to attend peace talks convened in the hope of ending the brutal civil war prevailing in Liberia at the time. Prosecutor David Crane arranged for the indictment to be hand-delivered to the Ghanaian High Commission in Freetown as well as transmitted directly to the Foreign Ministry in Accra. Crane asked the Ghanaian authorities to arrest Taylor and transfer him into the custody of the Special Court. He also issued a press release announcing the indictment.

The publication of the Taylor indictment was a big surprise to Ghana, host of the Liberian peace talks.[12] It was considered a public embarrassment for the Ghanaian and other authorities of the Economic Community Of West African States who were not aware of it in advance. President John Kufour of Ghana felt betrayed by his international community partners for springing a surprise on his government when negotiations had made great progress.[13] Those delicate negotiations, which were taking place as serious fighting occurred on the outskirts of Monrovia between

---

12 Priscilla Hayner, *Negotiating Peace in Liberia: Preserving the Possibility for Justice*, Centre for Humanitarian Dialogue and International Centre for Transitional Justice, November 2007, p. 8.

13 Lansana Gberie, Jarlawah Tonpoh, Efam Dovi, and Osei Boateng, 'Charles Taylor: Why Me?', *New African Magazine*, May 2006, pp. 4–5; *Prosecutor v. Taylor* (SCSL-03-01-T), Transcript, 10 November 2009, p. 31505.

Taylor forces and other factions, were thought by many to be the best hope for the restoration of peace to war torn Liberia.[14]

Not surprisingly, except perhaps to Crane, who apparently made a calculated decision to leak the indictment, President Kufour refused to act on the warrant. Instead, after some initial confusion as to whether the Ghanain authorities had even received an official copy of the indictment let alone had time to study or act on it, he gave Taylor his presidential aircraft to fly him home to Liberia. The Accra Ceasefire Agreement was signed by the Liberian Government and two other factions on 17 June 2003.[15] For various reasons, including the military and political pressure on Taylor and perhaps even the indictment, he agreed to resign from Liberia's Presidency in August. Taylor took up asylum in Nigeria, believing that by agreeing to exit the political scene under arrangements led by the African Union and the Economic Community Of West African States, he would be spared prosecution by the Special Court.

The political fallout from the indictment was immediate. Some diplomats condemned Crane's actions as ill-timed and naïve, a form of obstructionism that could stand in the way of peace in Liberia where a humanitarian catastrophe was taking place and where the suspect was still an influential player. Taylor, for his part, apparently agreed to resign so that a peace agreement could be concluded. The record is unclear as to whether he agreed to resign before he was indicted or afterwards. If the former, the concern about the effect of unveiling an indictment on a prospective prosecution would obviously be higher. It may perhaps suggest that a promise of non-prosecution was used as a carrot. On the other hand, if he agreed after the indictment was unveiled, it could suggest that the stick of prosecution could be used to hasten the departure of a recalcitrant leader who could otherwise jeopardise the chances of long-term peace.

14 Priscilla Hayner, *Negotiating Peace in Liberia: Preserving the Possibility for Justice*, Centre for Humanitarian Dialogue and International Centre for Transitional Justice, November 2007, p. 8.

15 Letter dated 18 June 2003 from the Permanent Representative of Ghana to the United Nations addressed to the President of the Security Council, UN Doc. S/2003/657.

Nigeria asylum unravels, the noose tightens around Taylor, and the dramatic arrest

The immediate impact of Crane's attempt to shame Ghana into arresting Taylor was to delay instead of hastening this. It would take another three years, much diplomatic and other advocacy efforts, as well as changed circumstances in Liberia, West Africa, and in United States foreign policy under the Bush administration before Nigeria eventually surrendered Taylor to the Court at the end of March 2006.

The final act in the Taylor arrest drama was Nigerian President Obasanjo's visit to Washington. The leader of Africa's most populous country was scheduled to meet with President George Bush at the White House on 29 March 2006.[16] Just a couple of days before, on 27 March, Nigeria, in an apparent face-saving ploy considering its prior position that it would not renege on the internationally sanctioned deal asking it to host Taylor, had announced that Taylor had suddenly 'escaped' from his villa in Calabar in southeastern Nigeria. The United States warned of 'consequences' if Taylor was not turned over. The day before the White House meeting, it was made abundantly clear that Bush would cancel the meeting with Obasanjo if the Taylor issue was not resolved. Abuja, which had expressed dismay at the 'persistent pressure' it was receiving 'to violate the understanding of 2003', reversed course.[17] Only hours later, on 29 March, Nigerian forces 'found' Taylor at a remote border post close to Cameroon. He was arrested with sacks of money ($50,000), allegedly given to him by Obasanjo, and immediately put under guard in a military jet and flown to Monrovia.[18] Obasanjo met with Bush while Taylor was on his way to Liberia, where he was arrested, upon arrival, by United Nations peacekeepers on the tarmac at Robertsfield International Airport and transferred onto a United Nations helicopter. He was flown to the Special Court premises at New England in Freetown. Nearly the whole of Sierra Leone celebrated.

---

16 Dino Mahtani and Guy Dinmore, 'US Raps Nigeria as Liberian Warlord Vanishes', *Financial Times*, 29 March 2006.

17 'Court Calls for Arrest of Liberian Ex-Leader', *Washington Post*, 27 March 2006.

18 *Prosecutor* v. *Taylor* (SCSL-03-01-T), Transcript, 10 November 2009, pp. 31521–2.

The prosecution was anxious to have Taylor arraigned. Taylor was not in a rush. He had arrived with only the clothes on his back, so he insisted to the Defence Office that his clothing be brought in from Nigeria. That was duly brought, at his own expense, by one of his former chiefs of protocol who flew on the earliest available flight. On 3 April 2006, a date negotiated by the Defence Office and the prosecution attorneys, a still visibly shaken Taylor was arraigned before Presiding Judge Richard Lussick of Trial Chamber II.[19] The charges were read out. He pleaded 'most definitely ... not guilty'.[20] In later trial testimony, he would invite Obasanjo to tell the truth about his so-called escape. He then explained that he had effectively been duped by an African 'brother'. Taylor, pressed as to reasons why, then suggested that Nigeria might have given him up because of its hope to secure a permanent seat on the Security Council, which was being discussed at the time, and Obasanjo's desire to run for a third term in office without opposition from the United States.

Taylor unsuccessfully claims immunity from prosecution

In the Taylor case, unlike most other international criminal trials, some of the preliminary legal issues were raised before he was even arrested. The first of these occurred when, as President of Liberia, he hired a Sierra Leonean lawyer, Terence Terry, to seek a quashing of the indictment. This was done even as Liberia also planned, ultimately unsuccessfully, to pursue the alternative of initiating legal proceedings against Sierra Leone at the International Court of Justice. The essence of Liberia's claim was that the issuance of an international arrest warrant against Taylor by the Special Court violated a fundamental rule of international law that provided for Taylor's immunity, as a Head of State, from criminal proceedings in foreign criminal jurisdictions. Sierra Leone had also violated the rule prohibiting it from exercising judicial power on the territory of another state, inasmuch as Liberia was not a party to the United Nations-Sierra Leone Agreement establishing the Special Court. As the tribunal was not a United Nations organ, and also not an established international penal

19 Personal observation of the author, who was present in the courtroom during Taylor's arraignment. See also *Prosecutor* v. *Taylor* (SCSL-03-01-T), Transcript, 3 April 2006, pp. 4–13.
20 Ibid., p. 15.

court, it could not impose legal obligations on a third state like Liberia. But that process did not go far because the International Court of Justice proved to not have any jurisdiction to decide the matter as Sierra Leonean consent was required and was not given.

On 23 July 2003, at the Special Court itself, Terry filed a motion asserting that Taylor, who was a sitting Head of State at the time the alleged crimes were committed, was absolutely immune from any exercise of jurisdiction by the Special Court. Denying the motion, the Court's Appeals Chamber examined the Nuremberg and Tokyo tribunal precedents, as well as the rulings in the Arrest Warrant and Pinochet cases, alongside the *amicus* briefs filed by two renowned international lawyers. It then concluded that 'the principle seems now established that the sovereign equality of states does not prevent a Head of State from being prosecuted before an international criminal tribunal or court'. In effect, the Special Court was an international criminal tribunal exercising an international mandate over international crimes. Being international, it therefore fell within one of the four exceptions that the International Court of Justice had identified. As a consequence, although no longer a president entitled to *ratione personae* immunity after having left office, Taylor's official status as a sitting president when the criminal proceedings were initiated was not a bar to his prosecution. His case was, therefore, properly within the Special Court's jurisdiction. But the Court seemed to have decided the issue in a manner that was more convenient than reflective of the existing law, avoiding the difficult issue of Liberia's third-party status to the UN–Sierra Leone Agreement.[21]

When Taylor eventually appeared before the Special Court, during his arraignment on 3 April 2006, he resuscitated the question of his immunity. He clarified that he did not recognise the Court's jurisdiction since he

---

21 *Prosecutor* v. *Taylor* (SCSL-03-01-T), Decision on Immunity from Jurisdiction, 31 May 2004. See generally Sarah M. H. Nouwen, 'The Special Court for Sierra Leone and the Immunity of Taylor: The Arrest Warrant Case Continued', (2005) 18 *Leiden Journal of International Law* 645; James L. Miglin, 'From Immunity to Impunity: Charles Taylor and the Special Court for Sierra Leone', (2007) 16 *Dalhousie Journal of Legal Studies* 21; Annie Gell, 'Lessons from the Trial of Charles Taylor at the Special Court for Sierra Leone', in Charles C. Jalloh, ed., *The Sierra Leone Special Court and its Legacy: The Impact for Africa and International Criminal Law*, Cambridge University Press, 2014, pp. 642–62.

believed his status at the time of indictment entitled him to immunity. Judge Richard Lussick reminded Taylor that he had previously contested that issue and lost. As far as the judge was concerned, the matter had been 'thrashed out' by the Appeals Chamber.[22] But Taylor was free to file motions to revisit the issue after first pleading to the charges, which he thereafter did. Interestingly, the defendant never again asserted immunity, even during the appeal of his conviction. He had realised that any further attempt to assert immunity[23] would not lead to a different outcome for his case. So he essentially gave up the fight.

The debate about where to try Taylor

After Taylor's arraignment, another controversy arose relating to the venue of his trial. All the other Special Court suspects were tried in Freetown. But, even before his initial appearance, Taylor knew that his case would be different. This was confirmed when it was rumoured that he would likely be transferred to The Hague. For that reason, on the very first day that he appeared before the Court, Taylor expressed a preference to be tried in Sierra Leone.[24] Taylor was particularly concerned about his fair trial rights and ability to obtain witnesses. The proximity of the Court to his home country, Liberia, where he had most of his family, was also naturally important to him to facilitate visits with them.

In fact, the day after Taylor's arrival in Freetown, the President of the Special Court submitted requests to the Netherlands and the International Criminal Court to facilitate the relocation of the trial to The Hague. At that point, the International Criminal Court had an empty courtroom without any defendants. Under the Special Court Statute and Rules, it could sit outside Sierra Leone whenever this would be necessary for the exercise of its functions. The Dutch government immediately agreed to host the trial, provided certain conditions could be fulfilled. This included acceptance by another State to host Taylor in the event he was convicted.

---

22 *Prosecutor v. Taylor* (SCSL-03-01-T), Transcript, 3 April 2006, p. 14.
23 For a lucid discussion, see Dapo Akande, 'International Law Immunities and the International Criminal Court', (2004) 98 *American Journal of International Law* 407.
24 *Prosecutor v. Taylor* (SCSL-03-01-T), Transcript, 10 November 2009, pp. 31547–53.

The International Criminal Court, after carrying out internal consultations and notifying its States Parties, none of whom objected to the idea, consented to the use of its facilities. A delay of several weeks then followed until the British government offered to host Taylor in the event he was convicted.

While the security rationale offered for moving the trial seemed to have some merit, there was considerable pushback from it. Matters were not helped by the Sierra Leone government appearing to contradict the Court's position. Key officials, including the vice president who had been Sierra Leone's minister of justice and attorney general during the establishment of the tribunal, Solomon Berewa, stated publicly that he did not think security was an issue. He changed his mind just days later. It was unclear what motivated the new stance. Maybe there was new information suggesting such threats were credible. The more likely scenario might have been that the decision had already been taken outside of Sierra Leone by powerful Western States.

In any event, based on what the public knows, a critical look at the security rationale for moving the Taylor case ultimately casts some doubt on its veracity. For one thing, the Special Court had in its custody other personalities who enjoyed more popular support in Sierra Leone. Yet none of them were transferred out of Sierra Leone. If anything, the threats from the supporters of Foday Sankoh, the erstwhile leader of the Revolutionary United Front who eventually died in custody, were probably greater than that of Taylor, at least to Sierra Leoneans. Thousands of former Revolutionary United Front combatants, including notorious commanders, roamed the streets of Freetown freely. Similarly, Norman, the deputy minister, was seen as a national hero for leading the Civil Defence Forces against the Revolutionary United Front. He too was detained at the Special Court facilities in Freetown. Although it is true that after his arrest, the tribunal did briefly explore the prospect of transferring him to the International Criminal Tribunal for Rwanda on account of security considerations, in the end he was kept in the same place of detention as Taylor and the rest of the other Sierra Leoneans. There were no serious security incidents from troublemaker supporters. Yet on 20 June 2006, despite the national Parliament's and civil society's attempts to forestall that decision in the hope of keeping the accused *in situ* and closer to his alleged victims, Taylor was secretly transferred to The Hague.

The dramatic courtroom walk out and the ensuing delay

Both the opening and closing of the Taylor trial were highly dramatic affairs. Each was controversial in its own way. While the first was a result of a strategy that the accused had devised with his provisional defence counsel, Karim Khan, the second can be attributed to his defence team that failed to turn in the final trial brief when it was due. The latter situation was then compounded by a short-sighted decision of the majority of Trial Chamber II to reject Taylor's final brief. This caused a disruption requiring the Appeals Chamber to intervene before deliberations on his guilt or innocence could begin. The final dramatic scene, as the curtain was drawn on the case, came from an even more surprising quarter: a judge.

Monday 4 June 2007 was supposed to be the big day for the prosecution. All openings of major trials are. It is typically a day for the prosecution to outline the bare bones of its case against the defendant, sometimes with dramatic rhetorical flourish. The defendant and his or her lawyer generally sit in the courtroom and listen to the allegations without much if any interruption, save for exceptional circumstances. They later get their turn to explain the defence case and, commensurately, enjoy the same courtesy. But in the kind of dramatic twist that came to characterise each stage of the Taylor case, when the matter of *Prosecutor* v. *Charles Ghankay Taylor* was called around 10:30 a.m. that morning in Courtroom I in The Hague, Khan dropped a bombshell: Taylor was not coming to Court. In a letter that Khan read out, Taylor explained that he had been denied equality of arms with the prosecution as well as adequate time and facilities to prepare his defence. As he believed he would not receive a fair trial, he would henceforth not participate in a 'sham' trial. He also fired Khan in favour of representing himself personally.

The problem for the judges was that Taylor was not in court. This meant that barring his being dragged into the courtroom, as the prosecution suggested, the opening could not proceed. Instead of ordering that Taylor be forced to attend, which would have caused a serious and problematic spectacle of a defendant bound and gagged, the Trial Chamber sensibly responded with an order assigning Khan to represent the defendant. But Khan insisted that it would be unethical for him to do so, even after he was threatened with contempt of court. Khan claimed that he was barred by both the Special Court's code of conduct for defence counsel and the rules of his national bar from accepting the appointment once his services had been terminated by his client.[25]

The presiding judge was not deterred, countering that 'your Code of Conduct cannot override a court order which I made a few minutes ago'.[26] The Chamber directed Khan to sit down. It then invited the prosecution to continue with its opening statement. At that point, Khan dramatically picked up his materials and walked out of the courtroom. It was at that stage, consistent with Special Court and other *ad hoc* tribunal practice that I was – as the head of the Court's Defence Office in The Hague – asked to take charge of the proceedings for the duration of the opening statements and until replacement counsel was assigned. The Court's American chief prosecutor, Stephen Rapp, then read out his opening statement. I did not make any formal objections. After the prosecution opening concluded, the Chamber adjourned the proceedings, but not before inquiring into and ordering that all of Taylor's complaints be swiftly addressed by the Court's Registrar and the Defence Office. The latter prepared an internal report setting out its independent views of the defendant's concerns, which then formed the basis for resolution of the core issues. Taylor's risky gamble, which had been largely forced by the bad decisions of the then Registrar, had paid off.

In short order, by early August 2007, the Defence Office had found and assigned new defence counsel for Taylor. It was the kind of handsomely paid defence team that the public defender's office had always internally insisted that Taylor needed to receive a fair trial. All the more so given the size and complexity of his case and its geographic divorce from the seat of the Court in Freetown and the *locus commissi delicti*. Led by Courtenay Griffiths, an unassuming but 'silver-tongued' British Queen's Counsel with a baritone voice, the team would later prove its mettle, vigorously testing the prosecution case in the courtroom. Ironically, the new defence team – unlike the previous provisional counsel – was given several months to study the thousands of pages of disclosure and to prepare for the cross-examination of prosecution witnesses. With Taylor's goals to have a top notch defence team, and adequate time for them to

25 Richard J. Wilson, ' "Emaciated" Defense or a Trend to Independence and Equality of Arms in Internationalized Criminal Tribunals?', (2003) 11/1 *Human Rights Brief* , 8.

26 Ibid.

prepare having being achieved, I convinced the suspect to end his boycott and return to court to participate in his trial. It was a big moment for the Special Court trial of Taylor.

Of war lords, super models and 'dirty-looking stones'

The trial resumed in early January 2008. The prosecution called the first of its ninety-four witnesses. Ninety-one of those witnesses were so-called crime base or linkage witnesses, while three were experts. A key highlight to the trial, at least for the Western media, which had largely ignored the oral evidence phase of the Taylor case up to that point, was the intrigue surrounding the testimony of British supermodel Naomi Campbell and American Hollywood star Mia Farrow. An apparently fearful Campbell testified about receiving rough 'dirty-looking stones' or 'pebbles' from an unknown person – a reference to the diamonds that Taylor gifted to Campbell after 'mildly flirting' with her at a dinner hosted in Pretoria by then South African President, Nelson Mandela, on 26 September 1997.[27] Besides the *viva voce* witnesses, nearly 800 prosecution exhibits were admitted into evidence, five of which were expert reports. The crux of the prosecution case took just over a year, closing finally on 27 February 2009.

For its part, the defence case opened on 13 July 2009. Twenty-one witnesses were called. Taylor, in remarkably lengthy testimony, spent over seven months on the stand between 14 July 2009 and 18 February 2010. It is not certain that giving such lengthy testimony was a wise decision. The defence, for its part, tendered about 740 exhibits, bringing to over 1,500 the documents and photographs relating to Taylor's case. In a trial that in fact lasted a total of 420 days, over the course of four calendar years, closing arguments were finally heard in February and March of 2011. By that point, the Trial Chamber had issued nearly three hundred decisions on interlocutory matters.

On 26 April 2012, just over a year after the conclusion of the prosecution and defence cases, the long awaited verdict in the Taylor case was issued. Trial Chamber II, sitting in The Hague and comprised of Judges Richard Lussick, Julia Sebutinde, and Teresa Doherty, issued a unanimous judgment. Taylor was judged guilty of five counts of crimes against humanity, five counts of war crimes, and one count of other serious

27 *Prosecutor* v. *Taylor* (SCSL-03-01-T), Transcript, 10 August 2010, pp. 45819–20.

violations of international humanitarian law. Most of the acts were perpetrated by the Revolutionary United Front rebels acting in concert with mutinying elements of the Sierra Leone Army known as the Armed Forces Revolutionary Council in the period between 30 November 1996 and 18 January 2002. Taylor was convicted as a secondary perpetrator (i.e., as a planner, aider and abettor) of murder, rape, enslavement, sexual slavery, acts of terrorism, pillage, outrages upon personal dignity, violence to life, health, and physical or mental well-being of persons. He was also found guilty of conscripting or enlisting children under fifteen years of age into the service of armed forces, or groups, and using them to participate actively in hostilities. In an interesting twist, the judges refused to use joint criminal enterprise and the prosecution failed to prove Taylor's command responsibility, both modes of liability that everyone had expected would be crucial to the outcome of the case.

Dissension on the bench: a regular (not alternate) judge?

But if the Trial Chamber was trying to avoid its significant conviction from being overshadowed by doctrinal or other debates about the shifting joint criminal enterprise theories or criminal participation that the prosecution advanced against Taylor from the beginning through to the end of trial, this was not destined to be. On this occasion, the seeds of the final trial drama came from within the judicial chamber itself. After the presiding judge concluded delivery of a long oral summary of the unanimous three-judge verdict convicting Taylor, and as the judges were rising to leave the courtroom, Alternate Judge El Hadj Malick Sow, who had been the fourth judge sitting on the case, attempted to make a public statement that he called a 'dissenting opinion'. To him, the prosecution evidence was insufficient to convict Taylor. He then insinuated that a grave procedural irregularity had occurred in that the Trial Chamber reached its guilty findings without deliberations. The curtain was drawn. Judge Sow's microphone was cut off, and in the subsequent published transcript of that day's hearing, his statement was not included because the hearing was formally completed after the presiding judge declared the session closed.

This unfortunate incident immediately triggered another firestorm of controversy among legal commentators. These turned largely on the propriety of Sow's decision to make a statement, given the established norm of silence by alternate judges in international criminal courts. Of course, article 12 of the Statute of the Special Court for Sierra Leone provided for alternate judges. Rule 16 *bis* of the Rules of Procedure and Evidence mandated that reserve judges be present for deliberations but clarified that they 'shall not be entitled to vote' on the outcome of the trial. This makes sense because the alternate judge should be able to step in at a moment's notice to ensure the continuity of a trial if, for whatever reason such as grave illness, death or sudden mental infirmity, one of the three regular judges is unable to continue sitting. That, of course, was never the situation during the Taylor case.

Some commentators, like William Schabas, seemed sympathetic to Sow's decision to speak.[28] Others, such as Michael Bohlander and myself, faulted Sow for speaking out.[29] As I argued more fully elsewhere, Judge Sow was certainly entitled to formulate his views on the sufficiency, or lack thereof, of the prosecution evidence against Taylor. He was equally entitled to share those views with his colleagues on the bench during the chamber's deliberations. But it was improper to express those opinions in public. Not surprisingly, although I was also uncomfortable with aspects of the disciplinary process that was subsequently used to declare Judge Sow unfit to sit as a judge, he seemed to have invited some sanction.[30] He later gave a media interview elucidating his views. Nonetheless, additional substance that would have justified his decision to speak out still appeared lacking.[31] It was an unfortunate end to his otherwise important service during the bulk of the historic Taylor trial. He was said to be the only judge to not miss a single day of hearings during a four-year period.

28 William A. Schabas, 'What Happened to Judge Sow?', *PhD Studies in Human Rights*, 25 May 2012 (available online at http://humanrightsdoctorate.blogspot.com/2012/05/what-happened-to-judge-sow.html).

29 Michael Bohlander, 'More on Judge Sow and the Special Court for Sierra Leone', *PhD Studies in Human Rights*, 8 October 2012 (available online at http://humanrightsdoctorate.blogspot.com/2012/10/more-on-judge-sow-and-special-court-for.html); Charles Jalloh, 'The Verdict(s) in the Charles Taylor Case', *Jurist*, 14 May 2012 (available online at: http://jurist.org/forum/2012/05/charles-jalloh-taylor-verdict.php).

30 Charles Jalloh, 'Why the Special Court for Sierra Leone Should Establish an Independent Commission to Address Alternate Judge Sow's Allegation in the Charles Taylor Case', *Jurist*, 1 October 2012 (available online at: http://jurist.org/forum/2012/10/charles-jalloh-sow-scsl.php).

31 *New African Magazine*, 18 November 2012.

In any event, on 30 May 2012, the Trial Chamber (now sitting without Judge Sow) sentenced Taylor to fifty years' imprisonment. Both the prosecution and the defence appealed. The prosecution alleged four errors while the defendant raised forty-five grounds. The bulk of the prosecution appeal asserted that the Trial Chamber, in addition to finding Taylor guilty of planning as well as aiding and abetting, should have also convicted him for ordering and instigating the commission of crimes in Sierra Leone. The prosecution also contested the Trial Chamber ruling that evidence regarding certain locations not mentioned in the indictment could be admitted. Finally, it sought an increase in his sentence from 50 to 80 years. In its view, this better reflected the gravity of his crimes and overall criminal culpability.

The defence appeal raised numerous issues. These tended to centre on the Chamber's evaluation of the evidence, some of it factual findings that the operational strategy of the rebel combatant forces, which was known to Taylor and conceived with substantial help by him, marked a deliberate terroristic campaign against Sierra Leonean civilians. It also claimed that the Chamber had misapplied the law of individual criminal responsibility, that Taylor's fair trial rights were violated in the entry of cumulative convictions and, further, that the trial judges erroneously used improper aggravating factors while ignoring favourable mitigating factors in arriving at his manifestly unreasonable sentence. It also used some of Judge Sow's contentions to challenge the guilty verdict.

Finally, as with the other controversies that came to be associated with the pre-trial and trial phases of his case, during the appeal phase, the delivery of the judgment in the Taylor case in September 2013 was marked with some rancour – at least among some international criminal lawyers – about the proper legal standard for aiding and abetting as a mode of responsibility in international criminal law. Other developments at the International Criminal Tribunal for the former Yugoslavia, especially in the Appeals Chamber judgment in the *Perišić* case, had suggested that aiding and abetting required that the accused person's contribution to the commission of the crimes could be punished only if the abettor specifically directed his assistance towards the commission of the offences in issue.[32] This was significant for the Taylor case since, with the exception of his involvement in planning a few incidents, his conviction

---

32 *Prosecutor* v. *Perišić* (IT-04-81-A), Judgment, 28 February 2013, p. 16.

turned primarily on the Trial Chamber determination that he had aided and abetted the Revolutionary United Front's commission of crimes in Sierra Leone.

The September 2013 Appeals Chamber judgment denied nearly all the substantial defence appeals save for minor reversals of convictions entered against Taylor regarding one or two locations in Kono in Sierra Leone. The Chamber also rejected the *Perišić* articulation of the legal standard for aiding and abetting liability, finding it inconsistent with customary international law. Any practical assistance by an aider-abettor which had a substantial effect on the commission of crimes will incur individual criminal responsibility. Regarding the sentence of fifty years, it was within the Trial Chamber's discretion to decline to factor into mitigation Taylor's insincere expressions of remorse and to use his abuse of trust and Head of State status as aggravating factors. Save for one exception, the Appeals Chamber also rejected the prosecution's appeal.

Overall, taking the totality of the circumstances, including the gravity of Taylor's conduct, the Appeals Chamber upheld his conviction and the sentence. Within a few days, Taylor was transferred to the United Kingdom to serve his sentence.[33] Although under standard tribunal practice he would be eligible for release after serving about one-third of his sentence, at the age of seventy years old when he was convicted, it is unlikely that Taylor will see the light of day outside where he has been housed in a hospital for his own safety.

Concluding remarks

It is still somewhat premature to definitively assess the full impact of the trial of Charles Taylor for Sierra Leone and his native Liberia, both of which are now enjoying relative serenity in the Mano River Basin of West Africa compared to the tumultuous decade of the 1990s. Yet, as the dramatic last finale for the Special Court for Sierra Leone which concluded his trial and then closed its doors in December 2013, the case was a milestone. Partly because nearly all the other indictments related to suspects who were present in Sierra Leone, they were swiftly arrested and transferred to the custody of the Tribunal. Much like the other aspects

---

33 'Liberia's Charles Taylor Transferred to UK', *BBC*, 15 October 2013.

of his trial, when it came to Taylor, matters were markedly different. In fact, although the first actual indictee of the Court, with the case number 2003–001, he was the last person to be tried. This seemed not to have been scripted. However, the coincidence of the delayed arrest and trial after the Freetown cases had been completed gave the effect of a crescendo to one of Beethoven's concertos. Here, finally, was the Sierra Leone Tribunal's most important case involving its most important accused.

From the prosecution's perspective, the conviction of Taylor was a success, even if a qualified one. From the perspective of the defendant who had insisted on his innocence, it was a major loss. For the judges, it was the Special Court's longest and most voluminous trial, with the most public spotlight and perhaps even the most external and internal pressure to get things right. The judges sifted through mountains of oral and documentary evidence and issued a reasoned opinion that generally satisfied the requirements of a fair trial under the law. Remarkably, the Taylor case was the only one at the Special Court where the bench was unanimous on all issues – three judges at the trial as well as five in the Appeals Chamber. There were no formal dissents, as there were in all of the other cases.

If nothing else, the case affirms that when there is political will, no immunity will attach to a current or former president tried before an international court for international crimes. *Prosecutor* v. *Charles Ghankay Taylor* may thus go down in history as a sizeable drop in the anti-impunity bucket, whose ripples will be felt by future African warlords and rebel leaders as well as many other Heads of State or Government further afield. Although not free of difficulty, given all the legal and political controversies that surrounded it, the trial may even prove to be a giant step towards the idea that no man or woman – no matter how powerful – is above the reach of international criminal law. At least sometimes.

FURTHER READING

Micaela Frulli, 'Piercing the Veil of Head of State Immunity: The Taylor Trial and Beyond', in Charles Jalloh, ed., *The Sierra Leone Special Court and Its Legacy: The Impact for Africa and International Criminal Law*, Cambridge University Press, 2014, pp. 325–39.

Priscilla Hayner, *Negotiating Peace in Liberia: Preserving the Possibility for Justice*, Centre for Humanitarian Dialogue and International Centre for Transitional Justice, November 2007.

Charles Jalloh, 'Immunity from Prosecution for International Crimes: The Case of Charles Taylor at the Special Court for Sierra Leone', *ASIL Insights*, October 2004.

Charles Jalloh, 'Special Court for Sierra Leone: Achieving Justice?', (2011) 32 *Michigan Journal of International Law* 395.

Charles Jalloh, 'Case Report: *Prosecutor* v. *Charles Taylor*, Appeal Judgment', (2014) 108 *American Journal of International Law* 58.

Triestino Mariniello, 'Case Report: *Prosecutor* v. *Charles Taylor*, Trial Judgment', (2013) 107 *American Journal of International Law* 424.

James L. Miglin, 'From Immunity to Impunity: Charles Taylor and the Special Court for Sierra Leone', (2007) 16 *Dalhousie Journal of Legal Studies* 21.

Sarah M. Nouwen, 'The Special Court for Sierra Leone and the Immunity of Taylor: The Arrest Warrant Case Continued', (2005) 18 *Leiden Journal of International Law* 645.

Abdul Tejan-Cole, 'A Big Man in a Small Cell: Charles Taylor and the Special Court for Sierra Leone', in Ellen Lutz and Caitlin Reiger, eds., *Prosecuting Heads of State*, Cambridge University Press, 2009, pp. 205–32.

Kathy Ward, 'Might vs. Right: Charles Taylor and the Sierra Leone Special Court', (2003) 11 *Human Rights Brief* 1.

Prosecutor v. *Taylor* (SCSL-03-01-T), Judgment, 18 May 2012.

Prosecutor v. *Taylor* (SCSL-03-01-A), Judgment, 26 September 2013.

Part V   The future

The International Criminal Court of the future 17

Hans-Peter Kaul

Allow me to start with a basic, but not unimportant question: 'When will the United States become a State Party of the International Criminal Court?' Well, it is exactly this question which was put to me in an interview by the *Süddeutsche Zeitung* – a German newspaper – published on 28 June 2012, on the occasion of the tenth anniversary of the entry into force of the Rome Statute.[1] The answer that I gave then is essentially the same as my assumption today: regrettably there is no chance that the United States will join the Court in the foreseeable future. But I assume, no, I believe that the United States will be a State Party at the latest around the year 2040, almost forty years after the entry into force of the Rome Statute – it took the United States also almost forty years to ratify the Genocide Convention.[2]

When this happens it seems quite likely to me that China will already be a member of the Court. I continue to be in regular contact with well-informed Chinese interlocutors. Already in 2003, when then

This chapter is an adapted version of remarks delivered by Hans-Peter Kaul at the International Humanitarian Law Dialogues, held in Chautauqua, New York on 26–28 August 2012. A version of these remarks was previously published in: Elizabeth Andersen and David M. Crane, eds., *Proceedings of the Sixth International Humanitarian Law Dialogs*, Washington: American Society of International Law, 2013.

1 'Wie ein argentinischer Großgrundbesitzer', *Süddeutsche Zeitung*, 28 June 2012.
2 The text of the Convention for the Prevention and Punishment of the Crime of Genocide was adopted by the United Nations General Assembly on 9 December 1948. After obtaining the twenty ratifications required by article XIII, the Convention entered into force on 12 January 1951. The United States of America ratified the Convention only on 25 November 1988. See William A. Schabas, 'Convention for the Prevention and Punishment of the Crime of Genocide', (2008) *United Nations Audiovisual Library of International Law* available online at http://legal.un.org/avl/ha/cppcg/cppcg.html.

President Kirsch and I were invited to Beijing,[3] the Legal Adviser of the Chinese Foreign Ministry told us: 'China, even as a non-State Party, wants to be regarded as a friend of the International Criminal Court. We will follow a wait-and-see policy for some time and observe whether the Court will behave as a purely judicial institution or whether it engages in politically motivated prosecutions. If the latter is not the case, the time for Chinese membership may come.' More importantly, in the next decade there will be further profound changes in China, a new leadership replacing the old guard, a more democratic society – these developments may lead to Chinese membership in the International Criminal Court system sooner than expected.

I will address three sets of issues: (1) What about the efficiency and administrative culture in the International Criminal Court of the future? (2) What are some possible or likely developments with regard to judicial proceedings or with regard to the applicable criminal law? (3) What about the relationship between the International Criminal Court of the future and States Parties, States in general or the Security Council?

It is obvious that when discussing 'The International Criminal Court of the Future', I will be bound to set out some assumptions, likely scenarios or other predictions. At the same time, there is a problem with such forecasts and prognostications. As a wise man once said – was it Einstein? – 'The problem with prognoses is that they deal with the future'. We all know that the future is unclear. Incorrect assumptions and errors are always possible. But it is my hope that such a look into the future – maybe at the International Criminal Court situation around 2030 – will be interesting, hopefully even a little bit thought-provoking.

Efficiency and administrative culture

The work of the International Criminal Court of the future will be characterised, in my view, by much more efficiency and a better work culture, this in a quite comprehensive sense – and I will give some examples. Why

---

3 Hans-Peter Kaul, 'Germany: Methods and Techniques Used to Deal with Constitutional, Sovereignty and Criminal Law Issues', in Roy S. Lee, ed., *States' Responses to Issues Arising from the Rome Statute: Constitutional, Sovereignty, Judicial Cooperation and Criminal Law*, Ardsley, NY: Transnational, 2005, pp. 65–82.

is this so? Well, not because of control efforts of States Parties but out of sheer necessity that the leadership of the Court will have to recognise or is about to recognise. One major positive factor will be for example more respect for and much better compliance with the 'One Court' principle,[4] both internally and in all contacts and communications with external stakeholders. Forgotten will be the days when admittedly objective observers, including myself, sometimes could have the impression that the Office of the Prosecutor, the Registry, and the Chambers were seeking to be separate small organisations or even kingdoms of their own. While these centrifugal tendencies occasionally have done much damage, the Court of the future will appear unified as 'One Court', with the common mission to contribute to effective investigations and judicial proceedings with regard to core crimes, and thus, to the fight against impunity. This presupposes that possible internal differences of views are settled within the Court and that its standing is not negatively affected by the perception of an internal divide at the International Criminal Court. Instead, a general atmosphere of mutual trust, confidence, and reliability between all elected officials, organs, units, and staff of the Court will contribute to more efficiency and a much better work culture.

Next point: the budget of the Court. Yes, budget preparation, financial control, and proper budget implementation – this matters. In the past decade, those involved had to learn in a difficult process of trial and error that a good budgetary process and proper budgetary means are not self-understood. Even today, the process of the preparation of the Court's annual draft budget absorbs, year after year, too much work, too much time, and often the patience of too many officials, in particular if competing priorities arise. I am, however, convinced that the International Criminal Court of the future will have a proper budget methodology, achieving a 'best practice' standardisation of the budget elaboration. Such a positive budgetary routine will set free much positive energy, in particular work capacity for the core functions of the Court, namely prosecution activities and judicial proceedings. In addition, more financial means

---

4 The so-called 'One Court' principle was originally mentioned in the Report of the Committee on Budget and Finance, ICC-ASP/3/18, para. 12, during the third session of the Assembly of States Parties in September 2004. The principle has often been recalled, most recently in Resolution ICC-ASP/11/Res.8 adopted at the 11th session on 21 November 2012, ICC-ASP/11/20, para. 33.

will facilitate the work of the Court as the forthcoming dissolution of the *ad hoc* and hybrid Courts will leave the International Criminal Court as the only international criminal justice mechanism.[5] This will alleviate the burden of the international taxpayer by around $300 to 400 million per annum.[6]

In the International Criminal Court of the future, the Registrar and the Registry will demonstrate consistently a proper understanding of their role; namely that the Registry is not an independent organ of the Court, and that the Registrar is 'the principal administrative officer of the Court, acting under the authority of the President'[7] – not less but also not more. In the future, there will be a work procedure in which the Registry without fail acts as the main service provider to the Judiciary and the Office of the Prosecutor. It will thus be a positive normalcy that all activities of the Registry, including on external relations of the Court, are aligned with the strategic and policy decisions taken by the Judiciary, the President/Presidency and, where appropriate, the Prosecutor.

It is nowadays generally recognised that international courts need strong and courageous leadership. This is true in particular for the International Criminal Court. There is more and more agreement in The Hague that the role of the President/Presidency really goes beyond protocol and representational activities. In the future, it will include – and there is no doubt in my mind – an active approach with regard to all problems and challenges facing the Court, including on difficult issues, such as the budget and the proper administration of the Court. Needless to say, the lead role of the President/Presidency must be exercised in close coordination with the Prosecutor, whose full authority over the management of his or her office shall be respected.

5 The Mechanism for International Criminal Tribunals (MICT) was established by the United Nations Security Council on 22 December 2010 to carry out a number of essential functions of the International Criminal Tribunal for Rwanda (ICTR) and the International Criminal Tribunal for the former Yugoslavia (ICTY) after the completion of their respective mandates. See www.unmict.org/

6 As approved by the Assembly of States Parties, the Court's 2013 budget totals €115,120,300. See ICC-ASP/11/Res.1.

7 Article 43(2) of the Rome Statute states 'The Registry shall be headed by the Registrar, who shall be the principal administrative officer of the Court. The Registrar shall exercise his or her functions under the authority of the President of the Court'.

In the future, the Court will have to live up to two other requirements: first, a consistent practice of 'trust but verify' that the tasks and challenges arising are indeed addressed. Second, there will have to be more respect for basic work requirements, such as discipline, diligence and punctuality, reliability, respect for deadlines and cost awareness, observance of the working hours, and no absence from work without proper notice and permission. Non-compliance with the aforementioned is particularly unfair to all who do their job as usual.

There is, however, a related necessity for the elected officials of the Court, including the judges: the leadership of the International Criminal Court of the future will have a much better understanding of how important it is to motivate the staff, to encourage all concerned. One has to lead by example to take the personnel with you. Experience shows that good work morale and staff feeling appreciated at work is the most important factor for efficiency and performance. This is valid for Google and Apple; it is also valid for the International Criminal Court of the future.

There is another development which, quite soon, will foreseeably enhance the work culture and efficiency of the International Criminal Court; already in 2015/2016 the Court will have – and here I use a term coined by Ben Ferencz – its own 'Temple of Law',[8] namely permanent premises which are in full conformity with the functional, organisational, security, and other needs of the Court. Maybe I am allowed to mention, in all modesty, that from 2003 to quite recently, I have invested enormous work and efforts to drive this project ahead, the key parameters of the premises, the site, the financing, professional project management, and the international architectural competition. Only on 24 August 2012, a contract was awarded to the construction company. The International Criminal Court will thus be the first international criminal court in the history of mankind that will have its own purpose-built permanent premises, built for generations to come. As this project is currently on track, there is, as usual, no more acknowledgement of my ground-laying role – but I do not mind – maybe they will invite me to the inauguration ceremony.

---

8 Hans-Peter Kaul, 'Über Hoffnung und Gerechtigkeit', *Fakultätsspiegel der Kölner Juristischen Fakultät* (ed. by Verein zur Förderung der Rechtswissenschaft an der Kölner Juristischen Fakultät), Cologne, 2008/2009, pp. 83–93, at p. 91.

Judicial proceedings and applicable criminal law

In this part, the main part of this presentation, I will set out some possible or likely developments that, in their combined effect, will probably make the judicial proceedings at the International Criminal Court of the future much more efficient and expeditious. In the International Criminal Court of the future, Chambers will have certainty to receive the necessary resources to properly and expeditiously carry out their functions. It is expected that not a single hearing, if necessary simultaneous hearings of Chambers on the same day, will be delayed or adjourned because of lack of courtroom support staff or other necessary resources.

Second, victims' participation,[9] and the related current practice of the Court, will undergo significant change to a more meaningful participation.[10] The current practice is, in my view, largely characterised by a deplorable lack of genuine victims' participation. Instead of such genuine participation, that may enable victims to see justice being done, with the related potential of healing, there exists a bureaucratic, slow and costly system of victims' admission, in which the victims are at best 'virtually' present. They are routinely represented by a new sub-category of counsel, the so-called legal representatives of victims,[11] who all too often do not maintain proper contact with the victims represented. In the future, various ways and means will be explored to achieve more proximity, to bring the victims closer to effective participation in the judicial proceedings, in particular:

---

9 There are numerous articles on victims' participation. *Ex multis*, see Elisabeth Baumgartner, 'Aspects of victim participation in the proceedings of the International Criminal Court', (2008) 90 *International Review of the Red Cross* 409; Marianna Pena, 'Victim participation at the International Criminal Court: Achievements Made and Challenges Lying Ahead', (2009–2010) 16 *ILSA Journal of International and Comparative Law* 497.

10 Trial Chamber V recently issued a decision which promotes a modified understanding of the application process for victims who wish to participate in the proceedings. See *Prosecutor* v. *Ruto* et al. 9ICC-01/09-01/110, Decision on Victims' Representation and Participation, 3 October 2012 and *Prosecutor* v. *Muthuara* et al. 9ICC-01/09-02/110, Decision on Victims' Representation and Participation, 3 October 2012.

11 Article 68(3) of the Rome Statute and Rules 89–91 of the Rules of Procedure and Evidence.

- through the possibility of collective participation: intervention of elders or community leaders who represent a group of victims throughout the proceedings;
- through more consistent appearance of victims in hearings, also as witnesses;
- through the presence of elders of affected communities or the presence of victims elected as representatives of victims' groups in the courtroom or in the gallery; to this end, a network of NGOs could assist the victims and the Court in facilitating the organisation of those visits to the Court;
- through *in situ* hearings of Chambers or judges in which they receive orally and directly 'representations' or the 'views and concerns' of victims;
- and through the holding of confirmation of charges or trial hearings or parts thereof *in situ*.

These measures[12] could and will be as simple and practical as possible to create real opportunities for the victims to see that their suffering is indeed acknowledged and that serious efforts are being made to prosecute their tormentors.

In the Court of the future, proceedings will be much more expeditious than they are today. In particular, two somehow related problems that have already caused many complications and delays will no longer exist: first, so-called 'phased investigations' in which the Office of the Prosecutor seemingly seeks to assemble just enough evidence to achieve the next threshold – instead of working full power *ab initio* to achieve evidence 'beyond reasonable doubt'.[13] Second, the questionable practice

---

12 It is clarified that the various ways and means to ensure effective participation of victims in the judicial proceedings as set out above are based on existing provisions of the Rome Statute and do not require, in the view of the author, any amendment of the present provisions of the Statute or of the Rules of Procedure and Evidence. It should be noted, however, that there exist knowledgeable experts who are of the view that the Rome Statute's system of victims' participation is essentially 'irreparable' and thus structurally unable to form a basis for any effective and meaningful participation of victims of core crimes.

13 Regarding the question of evidence 'beyond reasonable doubt' see also Trial Chamber II's most recent judgment in *Prosecutor* v. *Ngudjolo*

to request time and again redactions across the board, in hindsight often excessive, inconsistent, and unfair to the defence.

With regard to so-called 'phased investigations', there is still an Appeals Chamber decision explicitly allowing the continuation of investigations after the confirmation of charges.[14] Fortunately, there is a recent decision in the *Mbarushimana* case clarifying the position of the Appeals Chamber on this point by specifying that 'the investigation should largely be completed at the stage of the confirmation of charges hearing'.[15] I have argued that it is 'risky, if not irresponsible'[16] for the Prosecutor only to gather the minimum amount of evidence needed to move to the next phase of the proceedings,[17] and it is my expectation that the quality of investigations will improve as the Court goes forward.

An investigation as focused and effective as possible *ab initio*, with a strong investigation team, will also largely eliminate a problem that until now continues to plague pre-trial proceedings in particular – namely, pervasive, often exaggerated or precautionary redactions, which have often been a major problem. In particular in pre-trial proceedings, their consideration has absorbed inordinate time and energy of all concerned. However, if investigations are more advanced or almost complete before cases are commenced, then the need for such extensive redactions can be eliminated. Witnesses in vulnerable locations have time to be moved,

---

(ICC-01/04-02/12-3), Jugement Rendu en Application de l'article 74 du Statut, 18 December 2012.

14 *Prosecutor* v. *Lubanga* (ICC-01/04-01/06), Judgment on the Prosecutor's Appeal against the Decision of Pre-Trial Chamber I entitled 'Decision Establishing General Principles Governing Applications to Restrict Disclosure Pursuant to Rule 81(2) and (4) of the Rules of Procedure and Evidence', 13 October 2006, para. 54.

15 *Prosecutor* v. *Mbarushimana* (ICC-01/04-01/10), Judgment on the Appeal of the Prosecutor against the Decision of Pre-Trial Chamber I of 16 December 2011 entitled 'Decision on the Confirmation of Charges', 30 May 2012, para. 44.

16 For further comments on this issue, see Susana SáCouto and Katherine Cleary et al., *Investigative Management, Strategies, and Techniques of the International Criminal Court's Office of the Prosecutor*, as part of the War Crimes Research Office, International Criminal Court Legal Analysis and Education Project, Washington, 2012, at p. 64.

17 *Prosecutor* v. *Ruto* et al. (ICC-01/09-01/11), Decision on the Confirmation of Charges Pursuant to Article 61(7)(a) and (b) of the Rome Statute, 23 January 2012, para. 47 (dissent).

disclosure consent forms can be obtained, tactical decisions can be made as to whether using vulnerable witnesses is necessary, etc. Redactions will be used in a limited and much more pragmatic way than they are now. Therefore, in the future, disclosure – in unredacted form – of all relevant material will probably take place immediately after the confirmation of charges hearing. Trial proceedings will commence two or three months thereafter, that is, after the defence is afforded a reasonable time to prepare its case.

I also foresee much more effective investigations and co-operation work in the Office of the Prosecutor through maybe a doubling of the staff in the Investigation Division (currently 111 positions) and in the Jurisdiction, Complementarity and Cooperation Division (currently thirty-two positions, only fifteen professional positions).[18] There will also be – there is already – an emerging awareness among States Parties about the following: with this limited staff for investigations and co-operation necessities – and please do not forget: these staff are also entitled to annual leave, to training, some may need time off for legitimate reasons, etc. – how is it possible with around 100 staff to fully cover the investigation and co-operation necessities for eight situations, fourteen outstanding arrest warrants, or another eight situations under preliminary examination? Consequently, as an International Criminal Court judge now serving for almost a decade, as somebody who knows our Court, also as a former Vice-President, I fully encourage Ms Bensouda, our distinguished Prosecutor, to seek in the years to come such a doubling of her staff, in particular in these key areas. The work of Chambers, which are on the 'receiving side', is fully dependent on effective and professional investigations, prosecutions and related co-operation efforts. I am also quite confident that the Assembly of States Parties will approve these increases to the staff of the Office of the Prosecutor. They will understand this compelling necessity reflected in a picture often used at the Court, namely, that: 'The Office of the Prosecutor is the engine, professional and effective investigations are the fuel of the Court.' Yes, I believe that the International Criminal Court of the future will have more than enough fuel in this regard.

18 The approved Programme Budget of the Court for 2013 foresees 111 positions (including seventy-nine professional staff) in the Investigation Division and thirty-two positions (including fifteen professional staff) in the Jurisdiction, Complementarity, and Co-operation Division.

Already the combined effect of all these positive changes on the judicial proceedings will make them more convincing and more expeditious. Positive change is also possible with regard to the future work of the judges. It is indeed my expectation that a careful pre-selection of the judge candidates through the Advisory Committee on nomination of judges,[19] established by last year's Assembly of States Parties held in New York, will increase the chances that only judge candidates who, beyond the necessary formal qualifications, have also a solid inner compass and proven commitment to the cause of international justice may be elected as judges of the International Criminal Court of the future.[20]

Improvements are also possible in the work methodology of the Appeals Chamber. The Appeals Chamber of the future should and will in my view leave behind the somewhat minimalistic approach of decisions on appeal, in which all too often a tendency has become obvious to seek an 'easy way out'. The Appeals Chamber of the future will hopefully demonstrate a consistent will to consolidate the jurisprudence of the Court with substantial decisions clarifying the complex issues as they arise.

On the basis of these positive developments, which may occur as a result of sheer necessity or more insight and experience, or even both, it is quite likely, at least in my view, that proceedings and trials will be in the future more expeditious. As with many cases at the International Criminal Tribunal for the former Yugoslavia, it took International Criminal Court Chambers in the two first trials five to six years to come to a verdict or come close to a formal judgment. Pre-trial proceedings took regrettably around ten to twelve months. In my view, this is unsatisfactory. It will mean significant progress if the duration of the trial of mass crimes can

---

19 ICC-ASP/10/Res.5, para. 19. The paragraph reads as follows: '[The Assembly of States Parties] [w]elcomes the report, adopted by the Bureau pursuant to paragraph 25 of resolution ICC-ASP/9/Res.3, decides to adopt the recommendations contained therein, and requests the Bureau to start the process of preparing the election, by the Assembly of States Parties, of the members of the Advisory Committee on nominations of judges of the International Criminal Court in accordance with the terms of reference annexed to the report'.

20 Ibid., para. 20 reads as follows: '[The Assembly of States Parties] [e]mphasises the importance of nominating and electing the most highly qualified judges in accordance with article 36 of the Rome Statute; for this purpose encourages States Parties to conduct thorough and transparent processes to identify the best candidates'.

be reduced at the International Criminal Court of the future to approximately three years, in particular through proper case management. This includes, first and foremost, a strong role and control of the proceedings by the judges. It means also streamlining and accelerating the disclosure process and dealing expeditiously with the related issue of redactions, to which I have already referred. The overall time for trials could be reduced, however, as well through the use of a single judge[21] for the preparation of the Court proceedings and the use of case managers and legal officers with specialised knowledge on, for example, victims' participation and protection issues. Likewise it is in my view not impossible to reduce, through focused work of all concerned, the length of pre-trial proceedings maybe to around six months. Here, I would like to refer in particular to my earlier comments on the need to abandon the practice of the so-called 'phased investigations'. Needless to say, in the future there will also be many *imponderabilia* and unforeseen developments which may cause delays. The task, however, is clear: as the duration of judicial proceedings is one of the most corrosive factors for the standing of the Court, all must be done to come closer to a trial 'without undue delay' as referred to in article 67 of the Statute.[22]

The quality of the judicial proceedings will also be better because judges, legal support staff, and others may have benefitted from regular and professional training seminars organised, in particular, by the International Nuremberg Principles Academy.[23] The mandate of this new institution will be to promote, to disseminate, and to implement the legal and moral legacy of the Nuremberg trials, and of Robert H. Jackson, Telford Taylor,

---

21 Articles 39(2)(b)(iii) and 57(2)(b) of the Rome Statute, Rules 7 and 132 *bis* of the Rules of Procedure and Evidence, and Regulation 47 of the Regulations of the Court. The Rules of Procedure and Evidence were amended through Resolution ICC-ASP/11/Res.2 adopted at the eighth plenary meeting, on 21 November 2012, by including Rule 132 *bis*, allowing for the designation of a single judge for the purpose of preparing the trial.

22 Article 67(1)(c) of the Rome Statute: 'In the determination of any charge, the accused shall be entitled to a public hearing, having regard to the provisions of this Statute, to a fair hearing conducted impartially, and to the following minimum guarantees, in full equality: ... (c) To be tried without undue delay.'

23 The International Nuremberg Principles Academy is a project based on the German Government's Coalition Agreement of 26 October 2009, Chapter V, Item 6, Protecting Human Rights – Promoting the Rule of Law. The city of Nuremberg acts as a leading partner. For more information see the website: www.museums.nuremberg.de/academy/index.html.

Whitney Harris, Benjamin Ferencz, H. W. William (Bill) Caming, and others. Such training seminars for International Criminal Court members will probably be one main support activity of this new Academy, which hopefully will be founded already in 2013. Another important support activity of the Academy for the International Criminal Court will be customised information work on the objectives and functioning of the Court, tailored to the needs of specific target groups.

With regard to the substantive criminal law applicable before the International Criminal Court of the future, one significant development is already generally known: at the end of this decade the International Criminal Court will have, at least to a certain extent, a somewhat symbolic jurisdiction with regard to the 'supreme international crime', the crime of aggression.[24] The necessary thirty ratifications of the Kampala amendments and the necessary affirmative vote of at least two-thirds of the States Parties will not be difficult to achieve. Germany will ratify the amendments at the latest in 2013.[25]

It is, however, my assumption that the Court may not have yet, even around 2030, a concrete case in which a crime of aggression pursuant to articles 8 *bis* and 15 *bis* and *ter* of the Rome Statute will be prosecuted. Why? Well, experience shows that quite obvious crimes of aggression reaching the high threshold of article 8 *bis* such as, in the past, the Iraqi invasion of Kuwait and the crimes against peace, such as the German attack on Poland on 1 September 1939, are not committed very often. The existence of International Criminal Court jurisdiction with regard to the crime of aggression, even only to a limited extent, will nevertheless have significant positive effects: whenever there is a questionable use of armed force against another State, international commentators or media will raise the question whether the leadership persons in question may have committed a crime of aggression. One can hope that this may reduce or contain, at least to a certain extent, the readiness of political or military leaders to use brutal armed force for their goals.

---

24 Articles 5, 8 *bis*, 15 *bis*, and *ter* of the Rome Statute.
25 On 29 November 2012, the German Parliament (Bundestag) in its final reading unanimously approved the ratification bill on the amendment of the Rome Statute in order to include the crime of aggression. This step now enables the final ratification procedure to be completed in due course. [Germany's Acceptance of the amendment to the Rome Statute is dated 3 June 2013 – WS].

With regard to crimes against humanity pursuant to article 7 of the Statute, it is my hope that the current majority jurisprudence[26] established in the Kenya cases will have become obsolete and overturned by future decisions. To blur or to do away with the fundamental difference between crimes against humanity and multiple ordinary crimes is in my view simply wrong. A vague formula that any kind of non-state actor may qualify as an 'organisation' within the meaning of article 7(2)(a) of the Statute, that 'has the capability to perform acts which infringe on basic human values',[27] remains totally unconvincing to me. In the future, it will hopefully become clear that this type of jurisprudence, which also brings along the risk of extending jurisdiction indefinitely and beyond its capacity, is not sustainable. In this regard, however, I note with appreciation that more recent decisions have consciously shied away from using the aforementioned formulation.[28]

The jurisdiction of the Court of the future will continue to be limited to the four core crimes as enumerated in article 5 of the Statute. Further attempts to include terrorist crimes as such and suggestions to include financial crimes in the Court's jurisdiction will go nowhere. Other mechanisms will have to be found to prevent impunity for enormous financial crimes that seemingly continue to be committed almost day by day.

States, the Security Council, and the International Criminal Court

The International Criminal Court of the future – this is the first point – will be stronger and more accepted because around the year 2030 it will probably have around 140 State Parties or more, and not 121 as today. What is even more important is that there will be a much more positive

---

26 *Prosecutor* v. *Ruto* et al. (ICC-01/09-01/11), Decision on the Confirmation of Charges Pursuant to Article 61(7)(a) and (b) of the Rome Statute, 23 January 2012.

27 Ibid., para. 184.

28 *Situation in the Republic of Côte d'Ivoire* (ICC-02/11-14-Corr.), Corrigendum to 'Decision Pursuant to Article 15 of the Rome Statute on the Authorisation of an Investigation into the Situation in the Republic of Côte d'Ivoire', 15 November 2011, para. 46; *Prosecutor* v. *Ntaganda* (ICC-01/04-02/06), Decision on the Prosecutor's Application under Article 58, 13 July 2012, para. 24.

attitude of the States Parties towards 'their' Court. Forgotten will be the current attempts of some State Parties organised in the so-called 'G5'[29] or 'G6'[30] to impose a 'Zero Nominal Growth' policy on the Court – this despite the fact that the workload is constantly increasing and also despite the fact that the sums that may be saved through such a policy are ridiculously small. They are indeed irrelevant compared, for example, to the costs of fire brigades in capitals of States Parties or the costs of one single tank. Furthermore, the expected shutting down of the *ad hoc* tribunals, of the Special Court for Sierra Leone, of the Special Tribunal for Lebanon, and of the Extraordinary Chambers in the Courts of Cambodia in the near or foreseeable future will dramatically reduce the costs for international criminal courts and alleviate the budget of State Parties by at least $300 million per year. Governments and Finance Ministries of States Parties will gradually understand that henceforth more funds are available and that complementary International Criminal Court jurisdiction is soon worldwide the only remaining mechanism to promote more criminal justice. There is therefore good hope that there will be enough breathing space to provide the International Criminal Court in the decades to come with a solid financial basis.

There is a further area in which a change of the behaviour of States Parties towards the International Criminal Court is necessary and likely to come about. This concerns a quite obvious, if not excessive, current tendency of certain States Parties and their delegates to micro-manage, interfere in internal matters of the Court, or demand excessively all kinds of written reports on all kinds of complex issues. This problem is compounded by the activities of a significant number, yes, a proliferation

---

29 During the budget preparations for the 2012 draft budget, in early autumn 2011, the United Kingdom took the initiative to establish an informal group of five major contributors ('G5') to the Court's budget consisting of the United Kingdom, Japan, Italy, France, and Germany. On 28 October 2011, this newly founded G5-group submitted a quite critical and restrictive paper on the 2012 Budget entitled 'Zero Nominal Growth Approach' demanding far-reaching and drastic budget reductions of more than €20 million. Objective observers were particularly astonished that also Germany, which in previous years and until then had regularly supported the draft budget of the Court, had joined this group.

30 In 2012, Canada joined the group of the G5 whose overall aim continued to be to limit the ICC budget.

of subsidiary bodies for inspection, evaluation, and investigation of the Court, concerning its efficiency and economy. Believe it or not, in 2012, there exist some twelve to fifteen such bodies, working groups, or sub-groups.[31] Needless to say, this imposition of additional work often absorbs almost entirely the working time of senior officials and staff, thus having a detrimental effect on the regular functioning of the Court. There is, however, light at the end of the tunnel: there are hopeful indications that in the next years it will be possible to (re-)establish a fair balance between the independence of the Court and the legitimate desire of States Parties to provide oversight management as foreseen in the Statute.

A fundamental strengthening of the International Criminal Court may also become possible in a crucial, if not decisive, area: arrest actions supported much more vigorously by State Parties or even non-State Parties such as the United States. Informed observers have for some time noted a growing awareness in the international community that the total dependence on effective international co-operation, notably with regard to arrest and surrender to the Court, needs to be addressed. Currently, only six warrants of arrest have been executed and fourteen remain outstanding. This points to the necessity that States one day will form or make available task forces to arrest suspects for the Court, just as it is now routine to use such forces against armed criminals domestically. The fact that the United States has recently sent a small number of military advisers to Uganda to train forces for the possible arrest of Joseph Kony and his commanders is encouraging and a step in the right direction. Other measures will have to follow.

For the International Criminal Court of the future, there is also room for improvement in its relationship with the Security Council – and in

---

31 According to an informal document dated 23 May 2012, put together by the Ambassador of Switzerland to the Netherlands, The Hague Working Group consists of the following sub-groups: Victims and Affected Communities and Trust Fund for Victims, Independent Oversight Mechanism, Complementarity, Strategic Planning Process, Cooperation, Legal Aid, Budget, Reparations, Study Group on Governance, Increasing the Efficiency of the Criminal Process, and Budgetary Process. Furthermore, the New York Working Group consists of the following sub-groups: Peace and Justice, Geographical Representation and Gender Balance in the Recruitment of Staff of the Court, Arrears, Plan of Action for Achieving the Universality, and Full Implementation of the Rome Statute.

the treatment of the Court in particular by the five permanent members. The Court is an independent and non-political institution, acting in the interest of the international community – it should not be treated as a political instrument of the Council. To use the Court as a tool of the Council will inevitably politicise it, make it controversial, and damage its chances of becoming a universal institution. One must hope especially that future Security Council referrals of situations will be decided upon with wisdom and a visible sense of responsibility. In my humble view, this means in particular that the responsibility of the Council to support the work and intervention of the International Criminal Court does not end with the adoption of the referral resolution under Chapter VII of the UN Charter. Why is it not possible, as Hans Corell has suggested, that the Council may adopt, if necessary, a resolution under Chapter VII ordering the Government of Sudan to arrest and surrender the Sudanese suspects sought with an international warrant of arrest? Furthermore, article 24 of the Charter of the United Nations leaves no doubt that the Security Council, when exercising its authority for the maintenance of inter-national peace and security, acts on behalf of the Members of the United Nations. The logical consequence of this is, at least in my view, that the costs of International Criminal Court interventions after a Security Council referral should be borne by the United Nations, and not by States Parties alone.

Perspectives and outlook

I believe that in a foreseeable time, around the year 2030, we will see a stronger, more effective International Criminal Court, working more successfully in a more favourable international environment. Yes – and I am prepared to admit this quite openly – there are problems and weaknesses at the current Court, yes, progress and positive change continue to be difficult, setbacks are possible. Compared with the violent crises in this world, compared with the forces of *Realpolitik* as explained by Cherif Bassiouni, the Court will always be small and weak, more a symbol, more moral authority than real might.

But 'the International Criminal Court of the Future' is possible despite so many difficulties. It is encouraging that the abbreviation 'ICC' has become, in only ten years, a universally recognised symbol. The Court has become some kind of worldwide visible lighthouse for the message, that nobody, no President or general, is above the law and that there shall be no impunity for core crimes, regardless of the rank or nationality of the perpetrator. This is the standard-setting message of the International Criminal Court and one should not underestimate its impact. It is only logical that this message is not to the liking of those who continue to regard the use of brutal armed force as a possible means for their political objectives.

To conclude, yes, steadfastness and patience, much patience will be necessary to achieve 'The International Criminal Court of the Future'. And even after 2015, when my office as judge will have ended, I will follow the development of the Court with hope and in good spirit. And should it happen that the positive changes that I have mentioned take too long, then I may, if necessary, pass away – but still with hope and in good spirit. So be it!

FURTHER READING

Hans-Peter Kaul, 'Towards a Permanent Criminal Court: Some Observations of a Negotiator', (1997) 18 *Human Rights Law Journal* 169.

Hans-Peter Kaul, 'Special Note: The Struggle for the International Criminal Court's Jurisdiction', (1998) 6 *European Journal of Criminal Law and Criminal Justice* 48.

Hans-Peter Kaul, 'Der Internationale Strafgerichtshof: Das Ringen um seine Zuständigkeit und Reichweite', in Horst Fischer and Sascha Rolf Lüder, eds., *Völkerrechtliche Verbrechen vor dem Jugoslawien-Tribunal, Nationalen Gerichten und dem Internationalen Gerichtshof*, Berlin Verlag Arno Spitz GmbH, 1999, pp. 177–91.

Hans-Peter Kaul, 'The International Criminal Court: Jurisdiction, Trigger Mechanism and Relationship to National Jurisdictions', in Mauro Politi and Giuseppe Nesi, eds., *The Rome Statute of the International Criminal Court: A Challenge to Impunity*, Aldershot: Ashgate, 2001, pp. 59–64.

Hans-Peter Kaul, 'Preconditions to the Exercise of Jurisdiction', in Antonio Cassese, Paola Gaeta and John RWD Jones, eds., *The Rome Statute of the International Criminal Court: A Commentary*, Oxford University Press, 2002, pp. 583–616.

Hans-Peter Kaul, 'The International Criminal Court after Two Years', (2005) 99 *American Journal of International Law* 370.

Hans-Peter Kaul, 'Der Internationale Strafgerichtshof nach fünf Jahren – Ein Erfahrungsbericht aus Richterlicher Sicht', (2007) 13 *Zeitschrift für Internationale Strafrechtsdogmatik* 494.

Hans-Peter Kaul, 'The ICC and International Criminal Cooperation – Key Aspects and Fundamental Necessities', in Mauro Politi and Federica Gioia, eds., *The ICC and National Jurisdictions*, Farnham, UK: Ashgate, 2008, pp. 85–92.

Hans-Peter Kaul, 'The International Criminal Court – Its Relationship to Domestic Jurisdictions', in Carsten Stahn and Goran Sluiter, eds., *The Emerging Practice of the International Criminal Court*, Leiden: Brill, 2009, pp. 31–8.

Hans-Peter Kaul and Claus Kreß, 'Jurisdiction and Cooperation in the Statute of the International Criminal Court', (1999) 2 *Yearbook of International Humanitarian Law* 143.

Situation in the Republic of Kenya (ICC-01/09), Dissenting Opinion of Judge Hans-Peter Kaul, 31 March 2010.

Challenges to international criminal justice and international criminal law 18

M. Cherif Bassiouni

In 1950, Professor Georg Schwarzenberger wrote an article expressing his doubts about the existence of international criminal law.[1] In response, Professor Gerhard O. W. Mueller responded that international criminal law exists because it is being taught in universities.[2] The Schwarzenberger approach reflects the positivist school, which in turn incorporates political realism. Thus, international criminal law exists only when States want it to exist. In other words, international criminal law does not exist *per se* – but only to the extent that States want it to exist and that this is reflected in positive international law. The proponents of the philosophical perspective advance the same claim for international law in general. This is the legacy of the 1648 Westphalian approach, which still lingers on in world affairs.[3] The Mueller approach reflects the natural law philosophical approach, founded on higher values and overarching principles that should control State-action.[4] These opposing views are both, to some extent, correct. Anything international is by its very nature conditioned by State interests and, maybe because of that, is *sui generis* and mostly *ad*

1 Georg Schwarzenberger. 'The Problem of an International Criminal Law', (1950) 3 *Current Legal Problems* 263, at p. 295.
2 Gerhard O. W. Mueller and Edward M. Wise, *International Criminal Law*, London: Sweet and Maxwell, 1965.
3 Gene M. Lyons and Michael Mastanduno, eds., *Beyond Westphalia?: National Sovereignty and International Intervention*, Baltimore and London: Johns Hopkins University Press, 1995; Cornelius J. Murphy, Jr., 'The Sovereign State and Universal Peace', (1971) 47 *Notre Dame Law Review* 57. For a more recent academic perspective reflecting the political realism perspective, see Mohamed S. Helal, 'Justifying War and the Limits of Humanitarianism', (2014) 37 *Fordham Law Review* 551.
4 Brendan F. Brown, ed., *The Natural Law Reader*, New York: Oceana, 1960; Lloyd L. Weinreb, *Natural Law and Justice*, Cambridge: Harvard University Press, 1987.

hoc. But that does not mean that State interests always, and with respect to everything international, are devoid of or not subject to considerations based on higher values and enduring principles.[5]

In the course of time, particularly after the Second World War, the establishment of the United Nations and the development of international human rights law, international law has sought to reconcile conflicting and competing State interests while at the same time identifying commonly shared interests that reflect certain higher values and enduring principles.[6] As is evident from what follows, history does not repeat itself; precedents are not comparable and are not necessarily binding upon States' future conduct. Yet somehow, since 1648, there is evidence that commonly shared values have influenced the collective decision-making processes of States, notwithstanding State interests. In contemporary times, this is evident in matters of international trade and other areas where the common and mutual interest of States exists. In fact, in those areas much progress has been made in collective decision-making. Not so, however, in other areas where such mutuality of interest is evident, as is the case in the fields of human rights, international criminal justice, and international criminal law.

By the Mueller postulate international criminal law and international criminal justice not only exist, but by now they are both doing very well. The number of universities and particularly law schools teaching these subjects and related ones has increased significantly since the 1990s. This is also true of the number of books, law review articles and doctoral dissertations on these subjects,[7] not to mention the number of persons who have

---

5 For a radically different position, which insidiously, yet not unconvincingly, attacks human rights, see Eric A. Posner, *The Twilight of Human Rights Law*, Oxford University Press, 2014. Conversely, a proponent of a more nuanced and qualified State-interest perspective approached human rights in a more analytical and methodological approach; see Myres S. McDougal, 'Law and Minimum World Public Order: Armed Conflict in Larger Context', (1984) 3 *UCLA Pacific Basin Law Journal* 21.

6 An advocate of a similar perspective was the late Myres McDougal, founder of the Yale World Order School: Myres S. McDougal, Lung-chu Chen, and Harold D. Lasswell, 'Human Rights and World Public Order: Human Rights in Comprehensive Context', (1977) 72 *Northwestern University Law Review* 227. In contrast, see Philip C. Jessup, *A Modern Law of Nations*, New York: Macmillan, 1948.

7 M. Cherif Bassiouni, *Introduction to International Criminal Law*, 2nd rev. edn, The Hague: Brill, 2013, Bibliography xvii–cx.

worked at or have transited through international criminal justice institutions, United Nations commissions of inquiry, other fact-finding bodies, and various inter-governmental organisations and non-governmental organisations. By this yardstick, one should conclude that international criminal law and international criminal justice are well-established and capable of withstanding the challenges of *Realpolitik* in the era of globalisation.[8] But this is not the case, as described below.

These reflections, many of which are based on my personal experience, are intended to demystify some idealisation of international criminal justice and international criminal law. More importantly, it is intended to show to the proponents of international criminal justice and international criminal law the techniques employed by the *realpolitician* to constrain, manipulate, and sometimes subvert the goals of accountability and justice reflected in international criminal justice and international criminal law, in terms of process and outcomes. This understanding is needed by the proponents of international criminal justice and international criminal law to avoid certain pitfalls, and to enhance the attainment of the value-oriented goals of international criminal justice and international criminal law.

International criminal justice: evolution and challenges

The international criminal justice balloon that has been soaring in the skies in the last two decades, infused with the exalting experiences of the *ad hoc* Tribunals for the former Yugoslavia and Rwanda, and the mixed model tribunals of Sierra Leone, Cambodia, Lebanon, Kosovo, and East Timor, has gradually deflated. The only air left in that shrinking balloon is that of the International Criminal Court. Even so, all of these experiences require a sober assessment as they all carry with them a baggage of *Realpolitik*, which conditioned their establishment, determined their mandates, and constrained their operations and outcomes. Thus, how effective and convincing these experiences will be as solid precedents for the future is not as certain as it appears to the proponents of international criminal justice. The reason for that is that international criminal justice institutions though related in some respects are distinguishable because

---

8 M. Cherif Bassiouni, ed., *Global Issues and Its Impact on the Future of Human Rights and International Criminal Justice*, Antwerp: Intersentia, 2015.

that is the way that its *Realpolitik* architects have made it to be. Rather than being incremental pieces of an overall architecture in which various components build upon one another, we have witnessed a careful distinction made by the *realpolitician* as between each institution, probably for the very purpose of not establishing a complementary architecture of international criminal justice.

Conversely proponents of international criminal law and international criminal justice want to solidify for posterity the experiences of the last two decades. But will our collective *desideratum* produce that reality? It is in this respect that one has to assess how historical precedents have or have not been foundational in the gradual development of international criminal justice and international criminal law. We all rely on 'Nuremberg', the International Military Tribunal, notwithstanding the fact that it was a victor's tribunal, as has always been the case throughout history.[9] We seldom refer to its faults and its weaknesses including a historic distortion that has never been corrected, namely the indictment of two German Generals for the Katyn Forest massacre of 12,000 Polish officers who were actually killed by the Red Army and not by the Wehrmacht.[10] To some it may be a small detail, but to those who see the integrity of the legal processes of international criminal justice as uncompromising, such details are vital. Justice is about truth and it cannot be built on the distortion of the truth, or miscarriages of justice in individual cases. No detail or individual miscarriage is small enough to go uncorrected. Justice should be applied in an uncompromising and uncompromised manner. This historic error, and any others, should be corrected so that no such error is ever repeated and allowed to withstand the test of time.

The other major precedent of the Second World War, the International Military Tribunal for the Far East, the 'Tokyo trial', is seldom referred to with the same authority as its European counterpart and inspiration. Maybe it is because of the flaws of the International Military Tribunal for

---

9 Robert H. Jackson, *Report of Robert H. Jackson, United States Representative to the International Conference on Military Trials, London, 1945*, Washington: Department of State, 1949; Telford Taylor, *Final Report to the Secretary of the Army on the Nuremberg War Crimes Trials Under Control Council Law No. 10*, Washington: Government Printing Office, 1949.

10 J. K. Zawodny, *Death in the Forest: The Story of the Katyn Forest Massacre*, South Bend: Notre Dame University Press, 1962.

the Far East or because of the Western cultural bias that only that which is in the West counts.[11] Most likely the 'Tokyo trial' and others in the Far East are conveniently placed in the waste bin of history in the hope that the use of the atomic bomb by the United States on two civilian cities, Hiroshima and Nagasaki, is also placed in that bin.[12]

The two precedents or, more appropriately, the two experiences of the International Military Tribunals, have been absorbed differently by their respective peoples. The German people, because of their Western Christian cultural values, have accepted responsibility and atoned for their misdeeds. For all practical purposes, they have metabolised and digested the experience and its sequels, even making it their own as they prosecuted over 50,000 Germans in their national system and continue to do so to date. The radically different Japanese culture has always perceived the Tokyo trials and their sequels as being a way in which the victors punished the losers by trampling on their dignity. Unlike their German counterparts, Japanese culture, and in particular military culture, stems from a different code of human conduct and particularly a different military code.[13] The defeated should never surrender but die in combat and those who do not die in combat should be allowed the dignity of ritual suicide or *seppuku*. But to put their leaders on trial is the ultimate indignity for the individuals in question and the ultimate humiliation of that nation as a whole. This is why controversies still exist in modern Japan about the burial place of those who were convicted in the post–Second World War proceedings, that many in that country would like to move to a burial place that honours their spirits. Contemporaneously, revisionist history is presently at work to deny that the Japanese armed forces placed an estimated 300,000 women from occupied countries in sexual slavery either

11 John A. Appleman, *Military Tribunals and International Crimes*, Indianapolis: Bobbs-Merrill, 1954, p. 259; B. V. A. Röling and C. F. Rüter, eds., *The Tokyo Judgment*, vol. 1, Amsterdam: APA-University Press, 1977, pp. 965, 971–3, 988–9; see also Neil Boister and Robert Cryer, *The Tokyo International Military Tribunal: A Reappraisal*, Oxford University Press, 2008.

12 Martin Sherwin, *A World Destroyed: The Atomic Bomb and the Grand Alliance*, New York: Alfred A. Knopf, 1974; Richard Falk, 'State Terror Versus Humanitarian Law', in Mark Selden and Alvin Y. So, eds., *War and State Terrorism: The United States, Japan, and the Asia-Pacific in the Long Twentieth Century*, Lanham, MD: Rowman and Littlefield, 2004, pp. 41–61.

13 Nitobe Inazō, *Bushido: The Soul of Japan*, Tokyo: Teibi Publishing, 1908.

in Japan or in other countries;[14] and, also questioning the atrocities committed against civilians in the Chinese occupied city of Nanjing (Nanking) in 1937, what is commonly referred to as the 'Rape of Nanking'.[15] Time is on the Japanese revisionists' side as most of these victims, who are euphemistically if not insultingly referred to as 'comfort women', and other victims, particularly those of Nanjing, are gradually passing away by reason of age.

The efforts of Japan to erase the memory of the International Military Tribunal and its sequels, are best reflected in the 1953 San Francisco Peace Treaty which required that all Japanese detainees, otherwise referred to as 'War Criminals', be returned to Japan where they would be held in a Tokyo prison. Less than a year later, in 1954, they were all released irrespective of their remaining sentences. Two of those convicted by the Tribunal then became Prime Minister and Minister of Foreign Affairs. In contrast, Rudolph Hess was tried before the International Military Tribunal. He had been imprisoned in England as of 1941 when he flew alone into Scotland to try and arrange a peace treaty between Germany and England. He was, therefore, not involved in anything done by the Nazi regime after that time. But he was sentenced to life imprisonment and remained the only prisoner at Spandau prison in Germany until his death in 1987, at the age of ninety-three.[16]

If caught alive, Hitler would have surely been prosecuted for all the three crimes in the Charter of the International Military Tribunal, namely: crimes against peace, war crimes, and crimes against humanity. In contrast, Emperor Hirohito, who lived in the Royal Palace across the moat separating his residence from General Douglas MacArthur's headquarters in Tokyo, was never charged with any crime.[17] His uncle, Prince Asaka, who directed what happened in 1937 in Nanjing (estimates range from 40,000 to 300,000 civilians killed and countless women raped) was also never charged with any crime.

14 Susan Brownmiller, *Against Our Will: Men, Women, and Rape*, New York: Bantam Books, 1975, pp. 54–9.
15 Iris Chang, *The Rape of Nanking: The Forgotten Holocaust of World War II*, New York: Basic Books, 1997.
16 Norman J. W. Goda, *Tales from Spandau: Nazi Criminals and the Cold War*, New York: Cambridge University Press, 2007.
17 Douglas MacArthur, *Reminiscences*, New York: McGraw Hill, 1964.

At the International Military Tribunal, it served the Soviet Union's interests to blame Germany for the Katyn Forest massacre, much as it served the interests of the United States to overlook the responsibility of Emperor Hirohito and Prince Asaka. It also served the interests of the United States to overlook what was committed in Hiroshima and Nagasaki; much as it served the interests of the United Kingdom to overlook the firebombing of the city of Dresden on 13–15 February 1945, resulting in 22,000 to 25,000 majority civilian deaths.[18] Another telling observation, now all but forgotten, is that the International Military Tribunal was established by treaty. Its terms and the contents were intensely negotiated by the four major Allies meeting in London (United States, Soviet Union, United Kingdom, and France). Subsequently, nineteen other States acceded to the treaty. Not so for the International Military Tribunal for the Far East, established pursuant to a Proclamation issued unilaterally by General Douglas MacArthur in his capacity as Supreme Allied Military Commander in the Far East. Why the difference? *Realpolitik* prompted the United States to select this legal approach in order not to allow the Soviet Union, which had only entered the war with Japan three weeks before its end, to have any say about the Tribunal and about the occupation of Japan. Whatever the political judgment on these two institutions may be, they were established pursuant to different legal bases, as were their sequels in terms of the European Allied subsequent prosecutions, which differed from those that occurred subsequent to the International Military Tribunal for the Far East. Surely these are not apples and oranges but they are slightly different types of apples or oranges.

All of this is to say that we are still struggling with the imperfections of the precedents that we try to rely upon to build a solid and durable foundation for international criminal justice. It is a constant struggle between the *realpolitician* and those who advocate for the pursuit of international criminal justice as the embodiment of higher values and enduring principles that so many of us believe are part of the accretional process of human civilisation.[19] There is no doubt that this struggle is ongoing, as

18 E.g., Paul Addison and Jeremy A. Craig, eds., *Firestorm: The Bombing of Dresden, 1945*, Lanham, MD: Ivan R. Dee, 2006; Marshall DeBruhl, *Firestorm: Allied Airpower and the Destruction of Dresden*, New York: Random House, 2006.

19 M. Cherif Bassiouni, 'Challenges Facing a Rule-of-Law-Oriented World Order', (2010) 8 *Santa Clara Journal of International Law* 1; M. Cherif Bassiouni, 'The

it has always been, though not because history repeats itself but because people repeat their conduct and also repeat their mistakes. This is why each experience is separate and distinguishable, though we must try to keep them linked to one another in order to establish a credible historic record that will not be so easy for *realpoliticians* to overlook, whenever it is more convenient to their political purposes.

Suffice it to note that the two institutions established by the Security Council, namely the International Criminal Tribunal for the former Yugoslavia and the International Criminal Tribunal for Rwanda, were *ad hoc*, were created for each specific conflict, occurring on a specific territory, for a specific group of people and for a limited period of time. Both institutions have now ended their proceedings and moved into their winding-down and closing phase. Other contemporary international criminal justice initiatives referred to as the mixed model tribunals have all been separate and distinct from one another though having similar characteristics. The mixed model tribunals were circumscribed to a given conflict, on a given territory, relating to an identifiable group of persons, for a limited period of time but with different applicable norms and procedures. With the exception of the Special Tribunal for Lebanon, which has not accomplished much of anything other than on paper, all other mixed model tribunals have accomplished something and have now reached closure. They and other similar experiences in the post–First World War and post–Second World War eras stand isolated and institutionally unrelated. All of them have some similarities, but each one of them is different enough to make it distinguishable from the others. The reason is simply that *Realpolitik* makes it so in order to avoid the vertical accretional build up that international criminal justice would otherwise have.

Each one of these institutions has a baggage of *Realpolitik*, which is often buried in the processes leading to the ending of the conflicts that brought about these international criminal justice institutions. What we see is the establishment of the institution, but what we don't see is how they came about and what compromises were made. Following are some illustrative observations:

Perennial Conflict Between International Criminal Justice and Realpolitik', (2006) 22 *Georgia State University Law Review* 541.

- In Rwanda, the genocide started in April 1994. Within three months the Hutu extremists killed an estimated 800,000 Tutsi. The United Nations commander in Rwanda, Lieutenant-General Roméo A. Dallaire (Canada), kept notifying Under-Secretary-General Kofi Annan that the genocide was impending.[20] Annan was in charge of the Department of Peacekeeping Operations. These reports were kept under wraps because Annan knew that President Bill Clinton was in no mood to deal with another peacekeeping operation after having ordered the withdrawal of 35,000 United States troops from Somalia following that country's rebels shooting down a Blackhawk Helicopter and killing fifteen American servicemen.[21] For these political reasons, the news of the impending genocide in Rwanda was never made public. When Annan became Secretary-General, he had a United Nations report published on that episode that partly accepts responsibility.[22] Had it not been for these political factors, the Security Council would likely have increased peacekeeping forces in Rwanda and that might have saved thousands of lives. Yet even after the Rwanda Tribunal's establishment and the definitive evidence of genocide, there was no international victim compensation programme established. In fact, none was ever created in any post-conflict justice situation.[23]
- In Cambodia, the Khmer Rouge killed an estimated 1.7 to 3 million or more persons, which is between 21 per cent and 37 per cent of Cambodia's pre-war population.[24] The Khmer Rouge were supported at the time by China while the Viet Cong, with whom the United States was at war in Vietnam, was opposed to the Khmer Rouge. Consequently, the United

20 Roméo A. Dallaire, *Shake Hands with the Devil: The Failure of Humanity in Rwanda*, New York: Da Capo, 2003.
21 Mark Bowden, *Black Hawk Down: A Story of Modern War*, New York: Signet Books, 1999.
22 Report of the Independent Inquiry into the Actions of the United Nations During the 1994 Genocide in Rwanda, UN Doc S/1999/1257, Enclosure.
23 The Rome Statute of the International Criminal Court provides victim representation at its proceedings and it has a voluntary trust fund for victims. See: William A. Schabas, *The International Criminal Court: A Commentary on the Rome Statute*, Oxford University Press, 2010.
24 See Yale University, Cambodian Genocide Programme, available online at: www.yale.edu/cgp/; William Shawcross, *The Quality of Mercy: Cambodia, Holocaust and Modern Conscience*, rev. edn, New York: Simon and Schuster, 1985.

States did nothing while the carnage was ongoing (1975–1985). It took until 2003 for the United Nations to begin establishing the Extraordinary Chambers in the Courts of Cambodia, which was when the United States supported it. By then, most of the perpetrators had died and only five elderly ones remained alive to be tried. No truth commission was ever established because it would have pointed out the responsibility of China as well as the United States's failure to act, for the reasons stated above. Unlike the Rwanda Tribunal, however, which has established a meritorious legacy, as is the case for the Yugoslavia Tribunal, the Cambodian experience is merely window dressing.

- The Special Tribunal for Lebanon established in 2007 falls in the same category as the Cambodia Tribunal though it is clearly, at least at this point, at an even lower level since no one has yet been prosecuted. It is the only international tribunal in history set up for the killing of a single person, Lebanon's President Rafiq Hariri, on 14 February 2005, and the others with him on that occasion. The only reason it was established was because the United States wanted to do so, to get at the al-Assad regime in Syria. Yet interestingly enough the United States has done precious little when it comes to preventing that regime from the killing of some 200,000 persons since 15 March 2011, and creating several million refugees. To the credit of the United States, it did try to put an end to that conflict but it has been thwarted by the geopolitical interests of Russia and Iran. Most likely these interests will also have an impact on future accountability in connection with that conflict.

- Sierra Leone/Liberia is another telling example, though the Special Court for Sierra Leone has effectively prosecuted the main perpetrator in that conflict, Charles Taylor. He and those working with him caused the deaths of an estimated 300,000 people and the rape of an estimated 30,000 women in these two countries over the period 1996–2002. All of that for the extraction of what are now called 'Blood Diamonds' which were mostly smuggled, cut, and sold through the reputable firm of DeBeers, headquartered in England and with roots in South Africa's *apartheid* regime.[25] The proceeds were then laundered, allegedly through the United Kingdom's Isle of Mann corporations and trusts as well as Swiss numbered bank accounts and shell corporations. These funds

25 E.g., Greg Campbell, *Blood Diamonds: Tracing the Deadly Path of the World's Most Precious Stones*, New York: Basic Books, 2004; John L. Hirsch, *Sierra*

were used to purchase weapons from dealers who allegedly obtained them from Ukraine and other former Soviet Union sources. But when the conflict had reached the high level of victimisation mentioned above, the United Nations sponsored a ceasefire and peace treaty with Charles Taylor, referred to as the Lomé Agreement. To everyone's surprise, the deal included amnesty for Charles Taylor. It is on that basis that Nigeria offered asylum. The two were disconnected for political face-saving but it was understood that Nigeria would offer asylum. The reactions of certain governments and international civil society was condemned by the Special Representative of the Secretary-General but the amnesty nonetheless remained in the Lomé agreement. Legally it is still in force, but it is presumably legally superseded by the provision in the statute of the Special Court for Sierra Leone that denies the application of the amnesty to those charged before the Court. The United States favoured the establishment of the Sierra Leone Court and having Charles Taylor brought to trial. He was convicted and sentenced to fifty years in prison. That sentence has been upheld on appeal. But there is no judgment on the seizure of his assets, estimated at several hundred million dollars, that were produced by the 'Blood Diamonds'. No matter what the politics of that situation were and any heretofore unknown deals with Charles Taylor, the Tribunal acquitted itself in an exemplary way and the people of Sierra Leone and Liberia, more than any other victimised society since the 1990s, have felt justice. In a strange way, that which started as an unjust manipulation of accountability turned out to be the opposite.

These are only a few examples of the hidden histories of international criminal justice in the last two decades. There is certainly much more to be said about the mixed model tribunals as well as the two *ad hoc* tribunals established by the Security Council. What these stories reveal is that *Realpolitik* has always been active in undermining the pursuit of justice. Only the determination and tenacity of the proponents of justice have been able to snatch those accomplishments from the jaws of the *realpolitician*. To them goes the credit and to them we owe the merits of

Leone: *Diamonds and the Struggle for Democracy*, Boulder: Lynne Reiner, 2001; Lucinda Saunders, 'Rich and Rare are the Gems They War: Holding DeBeers Accountable for Trading Conflict Diamonds', (2001) 24 *Fordham International Law Journal* 1402.

what was accomplished, no matter how limited some may say that it is. To have had any such institutions is in itself an accomplishment that must be acknowledged and more importantly those who have made it possible must not be forgotten.

All of this leaves us, in terms of present international criminal justice institutions, only with the International Criminal Court, and so far its record is understandably mixed. It is the lone institution in a field surrounded by the remains of similar institutions, including some that have long been forgotten. One of these is the first manifestation of international criminal justice in history, namely the 1474 Breisach Trial of Peter von Hagenbach. Peter was an Alsatian (some say Dutch) *condottiere* hired by the Duke of Burgundy, to whom the City of Breisach had been mortgaged by Duke Sigmund of Further-Austria in the Treaty of St. Omer in 1469. That Duchy was part of the German Holy Roman Empire. Burgundy is far from Breisach and the Duke was not about to take actual possession of this far away German city. Instead, he hired what today we would call mercenaries to take over the city and to exact taxes to be sent to him. When the local Germans were unwilling to do so, he ordered his chief mercenary, Peter, to have his hired mercenaries sack the city, burn whatever they wanted, kill whomever they wanted and rape whomever they wanted. The German city's resistance succeeded in having the other members of the Holy Roman Empire, also Germans, understandably sympathise with them and support them against the foreign French Duke and his mercenaries. They sent troops to seize Peter and the remaining mercenaries in Breisach, and they set up the world's first truly international tribunal.[26] It consisted of twenty-six judges each one representing a principality of that Empire. They prosecuted Peter for 'crimes against the laws of God and nature', as was the case with their former young Emperor Conradin von Hohenstaufen (then believed to be fifteen to sixteen years old) who in 1268 was charged with the same crime after he and his troops lost the battle of Tagliacozzo (near Naples) against Charles D'Anjou, who ruled Naples on behalf of the French Bourbon King with the

26 See M. Cherif Bassiouni, *Introduction to International Criminal Law*, 2nd rev. edn, The Hague: Brill, 2013, p. 29, fn. 99; M. Cherif Bassiouni, *Crimes Against Humanity*, Cambridge University Press, 2011, pp. 594–5; Georg Schwarzenberger, *International Law: As Applied by International Courts and Tribunals*, vol. 2, London: Stevens & Sons, 1968, pp. 462–6.

support of Pope Clement IV in Rome. Conradin was trying to reclaim the Kingdoms of Naples and Sicily that his father Frederic II had ruled as part of the Holy Roman Empire. Conradin lost the war to Charles D'Anjou.[27] Conradin was executed but had he hired a *condottiere* like the Duke of Burgundy, it would have been him that would have been killed instead of the young Emperor. Just as Peter von Hagenbach was punished *in lieu* of the French Duke of Burgundy and was sentenced to death by drawing and quartering.

At his trial, Peter sought to present in his defence a written directive from the Duke of Burgundy, ordering him to do what he did. In a paradoxical way, the Breisach trial of 1474 took the same position as article 8 of the Charter of the International Military Tribunal as is also the case with article 33 of the Statute of the International Criminal Court, 'Superior Orders and Prescription of Law'.[28] Peter could not rely on the orders he received from his superior as a defence. But the Duke was never prosecuted for the very same reason that Heads of States were never prosecuted until the International Criminal Tribunal for the former Yugoslavia and International Criminal Tribunal for Rwanda, unless they were first militarily defeated. At Nuremberg the *Führerprinzip* was rejected. The norm was established in article 27 of the International Criminal Court Statute, though the International Court of Justice still holds to the position of customary international law recognising the temporal immunity of Heads of States.[29] Sitting Heads of States have yet to be brought to trial before an international criminal justice mechanism. Only former Heads of States or the ones defeated in war have ever been prosecuted so far.[30]

The 1268 trial of Conradin von Hohenstaufen was as much a travesty of justice as that of Peter von Hagenbach in 1474 although for different

---

27 The French Bourbon King became King of Naples and Sicily by Papal grant, thus removing these possessions from the Holy Roman Empire (namely, the German principalities).

28 E.g., Aubrey M. Daniel III, 'The Defense of Superior Orders', (1973) 7 *University of Richmond Law Review* 477, at p. 481; William H. Parks, 'Command Responsibility for War Crimes', (1973) 62 *Military Law Review* 1, at pp. 69–73.

29 Arrest Warrant of 11 April 2000 (*Democratic Republic of the Congo* v. *Belgium*), Judgment, *I.C.J. Reports 2002*, p. 3, paras. 58 and 78.

30 See, however, *Prosecutor* v. *Muthaura* et al. (ICC-01/09-02/11), Decision on the Confirmation of Charges Pursuant to Article 61(7)(a) and (b) of the Rome Statute, 23 January 2012; *Prosecutor* v. *Kenyatta* (ICC-01/09-02/11), Decision on the Withdrawal of Charges against Mr Kenyatta, 13 March 2015.

reasons. Conradin was tried for exercising the Holy Roman Empire's legitimate claim of what we would today call 'self-defence' to regain the twin kingdoms of Naples and Sicily that had belonged to the Empire of which he was the Head of State. Peter was carrying out his superior's legitimate orders at a time when no law required him to do otherwise. And yet both of these proceedings relied on this exalted formula of 'crimes against the laws of God and nature'. But with respect to Peter's trial, it should be noted that the historic evolution of the prohibition of violence against civilians and persons *hors de combat* as well as other protections of what we now call international humanitarian law had evolved in multiple civilisations since the fifth century BCE. This is evident in the Chinese writings of Sun Tzu in *The Art of War, The Book of Manu* in India in the fourth century BCE and in some recorded evidence of the Mayan civilisation in South America, also in the fourth century BCE. Rules of conduct in warfare were established by Prophet Muhammad in 630 CE and Islam's first Caliph, Abu-Bakr, in 637 CE, and in the Middle Ages in Europe in the 'Laws of Chivalry'.[31] These ideas, values, norms, and rules reflect certain higher values and enduring principles that have not migrated from one civilisation to the other. Thus, it can be said that they reflect the commonly shared values of humankind. No one, of course, can empirically prove that these commonly shared values of earlier times have informed modern international humanitarian law as it developed beginning in 1864 and particularly after the Second World War. Nevertheless, one can advance the proposition, on the basis of human intuitive and intellectual deduction, that the similarity of ideas, values, norms, and rules that has emerged so consistently over time in so many different civilisations that have not borrowed from one another reflect commonality. But this does not mean that evolution and consolidation of commonly shared values, that ripened into the normative prescriptions of international criminal law, eluded the control or influence of State interests.

The modern evolution of international criminal law and its enforcement can best be seen in the post–First World War events applicable to international criminal law and international criminal justice.[32] At the end

---

31 M. Cherif Bassiouni, ed., *A Manual on International Humanitarian Law and Arms Control Agreements*, Ardsley: Transnational, 2000.

32 See M. Cherif Bassiouni, 'World War I: "The War to End All Wars" and the Birth of a Handicapped International Criminal Justice System', (2002) 3 *Denver Journal of International Law and Policy* 244.

of the First World War the exalted formula of 'crimes against the laws of God and nature' surfaced again though under a new formulation based on the words of the preamble of the 1907 Hague Convention with Respect to the Laws and Customs of War on Land namely: 'Crimes Against the Laws of Humanity'. Even if that formula never resulted in being recognised as a valid legal basis for individual criminal responsibility after the First World War, it became that after the Second World War.[33] After the First World War, the two main objectors were the United States and Japan, relying on a positivistic approach that no specific international law norm contained such a formulation.[34] But some twenty-five years later, the US made short shrift of this positivistic approach and relied on the more flexible one, which reflected the views of naturalists, when it insisted that the subject matter jurisdiction of the International Military Tribunals contain 'Crimes Against Peace' and 'Crimes Against Humanity', categories that never before had been specifically posited as international crimes. Considering other positions adopted by the United States since then, this radical change of position in 1945–1946 was not due to an awakening to the imperatives of higher values and enduring principles, but to a policy shift based on State interest.

After the First World War, the proposition of trying a certain number of persons of the then defeated Turkish Ottoman Empire, who during the First World War and more particularly in 1915 were responsible for the killing of an estimated 250,000 to 1 million defenceless Armenian civilians for 'Crimes Against Humanity', was deemed by the US as contrary to positive law.[35] At the time it was simply put aside because of the political

---

33 See M. Cherif Bassiouni, *Crimes Against Humanity*, Cambridge University Press, 2011; Geoffrey Robertson, *Crimes Against Humanity: The Struggle for Global Justice*, London: Penguin Books, 2000; Leila Nadya Sadat, ed., *Forging a Convention for Crimes Against Humanity*, Cambridge University Press, 2011.

34 See 'Commission on the Responsibilities of the Authors of War and on Enforcement of Penalties, Report Presented to the Preliminary Peace Conference, 29 March 1919', (1920) 14 *American Journal of International Law* 95.

35 For the position of the United States Representative in Paris, Robert Lansing (who became Secretary of State), see M. Cherif Bassiouni, *Crimes Against Humanity*, Cambridge University Press, 2011, p. 92; 'Annex II. Memorandum of Reservations Presented by the Representatives of the United States to the Report of the Commission on Responsibilities', (1920) 14 *American Journal of International Law* 127.

interests of the United States and Europe after the rise of the Bolshevik Revolution in Russia, as it was called in 1917. For the Western Allies, having the support of Turkey in preventing Communist Russia's access to the Mediterranean was far more important than prosecuting its public officials for 'crimes against humanity'. The way that *Realpolitik* played its role was most telling for its blatant disregard of that atrocity.

The victorious Allies of the First World War had signed a treaty with Turkey, the Treaty of Sèvres, in 1920, that included the right to try and punish the perpetrators of these crimes. They replaced it in 1923 with the Treaty of Lausanne, which eliminated the trial and punishment provision of the Treaty of Sèvres and added an unpublished protocol that provided amnesty to the perpetrators of the 'Crimes Against the Laws of Humanity'. An apocryphal story is a telling commentary on this tragic experience. Hitler, visiting the Wehrmacht's headquarters near the border of Poland prior to that country's invasion in 1939, told sceptical senior Wehrmacht commanders, who were concerned about the responses of England and France to the invasion of hapless Poland, '[a]nd who now remembers the Armenians?' The story is right about the meaning of this historic injustice and how it was ignored; even to date the historic record has not been officially established. Examples such as these abound throughout history. Depending on how it suits the victor, the outcome is either impunity or accountability, not because it is the right thing to do, but because it suits States' interests, and that of course flies in the face of respecting higher values and enduring principles.

Step-by-step, however, progress was made. If nothing else, *Realpolitik* was forced to achieve its goals in more subtle ways. Such was the case with the post–First World War prosecution of Kaiser Wilhelm II for what was then the beginning of the quest for holding Heads of State responsible for what we now call the crime of aggression.[36] France and Belgium, which had particularly suffered from the Kaiser's invasion of

---

36 For a contemporary champion of criminalising aggression and a former post-Nuremberg prosecutor, see Benjamin Ferencz, *Defining International Aggression: The Search for World Peace*, New York: Oceana, 1975; M. Cherif Bassiouni and Benjamin Ferencz, 'The Crime Against Peace and Aggression: From Its Origins to the ICC', in M. Cherif Bassiouni, ed., *International Criminal Law: Sources, Subjects, and Contents*, 3rd edn, vol. 1, The Hague: Martinus Nijhoff, 2008, pp. 207–42. This article was published before the Kampala Conference, which drafted a new definition for aggression in 2010.

their countries and the war conducted on them, wanted him prosecuted. The United States had little interest in the matter. But not so for England. The Kaiser was one of Queen Victoria's grandchildren and she was particularly fond of her twelve grandchildren, especially the one that she referred to as 'Willy', as well as his cousin the Czar of Russia, Nicholas, also affectionately called by his grandmother 'Nicky'. In fact, there is a compilation of the correspondence of cousins 'Nicky and Willy' prior to and during the course of the First World War.[37] That exchange ended in 1917 with 'Nicky's' demise at the hands of the Communists.

The demand for the prosecution of Kaiser Wilhelm was 'a bridge too far', as the saying goes. To prosecute a Head of State was novel, but to prosecute a Head of State who was also a monarch, when most European Heads of State were monarchs, and particularly one who was closely related to an ally in the war, namely England, was to say the least a politically impossible task. How this situation was addressed is a tribute to the finesse of English *Realpolitik*. A very skilled representative of Whitehall drafted article 227 of the Treaty of Versailles, which states '[t]he Allied and Associated Powers publicly arraign William II of Hohenzollern, formerly German Emperor, for a supreme offence against international morality and the sanctity of treaties'. The headlines of French and Belgian newspapers declared that the Kaiser who had launched this terrible war of aggression and conducted it so fiercely against the French and Belgian people would be brought to trial for the 'supreme offence against international morality and the sanctity of treaties'. The people of France and Belgium, along with others around the world, were at least satisfied and content that justice would prevail and that the maker of that terrible war would be deservedly punished. The Kaiser, who had sought refuge in the Netherlands, a monarchy related to his own, was residing in a castle about forty kilometres from the Belgian border. The governments of France and Belgium clamoured that he should be extradited for trial before a specially constituted international tribunal pursuant to article 227 of the Treaty of Versailles. But when a delegation representing England, France, and Belgium went to the Netherlands, they were faced with the simple fact that there was no such crime, whether international or domestic,

---

37 Catherine Clay, *King, Kaiser, Tsar: Three Royal Cousins Who Led the World to War*, New York: Walker, 2007; Marc Semenoff, ed., *Correspondance entre Guillaume II et Nicolas II, 1894–1914*, Paris: Plon, 1924.

that was called 'a supreme offence against international morality and the sanctity of treaties'. Thus, if it was not an international crime and it certainly was not a crime under Dutch law, then how could the Netherlands grant the extradition of the Kaiser? England came out of it smelling like a rose, as Queen Victoria's grandson would not be extradited and would therefore not be prosecuted. France and Belgium blamed the Dutch and the whole thing ended as a tempest in a teapot.

What few people know, however, is that shortly after that diplomatic *denouement*, an American Lieutenant-Colonel from Texas in the 42nd Infantry 'Rainbow' Division, who was stationed about forty kilometres from the castle where the Kaiser was enjoying his Dutch asylum, believed what he read in the papers.[38] And, he decided to act in the good old Texan tradition. He rounded up a few Texan soldiers, filled up a couple of Model T Ford trucks, drove the forty kilometres, and went into the castle to seize the Kaiser and bring him back so that he could be tried. To his surprise, as he went into the castle he found a senior British officer who was officially named the 'liaison officer with the Dutch military'. The higher ranking British officer found a way to convince the Texan Lieutenant-Colonel to go back to where he came from whereupon his superior officer informed him that he had left his post without authorisation and could therefore be considered as having gone AWOL (Absent Without Official Leave), which is subject to a military court martial. Instead, he was offered an immediate discharge. He accepted and was immediately returned home. The Kaiser's informal seizure and submission to international justice, pursuant to article 227 of the Treaty of Versailles, failed and the *Realpolitik* goal of England to keep him protected succeeded.

Admittedly, the way the question of the Kaiser's accountability before a special international tribunal was handled has to be considered as an act of finesse of *Realpolitik* unlike so many other situations in which the political interests of States have been simply thrown out openly in the face of the pursuit of international criminal justice. Suffice it to mention that while the Security Council referred the Darfur and Libya cases to the International Criminal Court, in Resolution 1593 of 2005 and Resolution 1970 of 2011 respectively, it has never done anything

---

38 James F. Willis, *Prologue to Nuremberg: The Politics and Diplomacy of Punishing War Criminals of the First World War*, Westport, CT: Greenwood, 1982, p. 85.

to enforce the International Criminal Court's orders for the surrender of those persons charged with crimes and for whom arrest warrants were issued. Incongruously, the Security Council mandated the referral and yet at the same time refrained from enforcing the actions of the International Criminal Court, which were made pursuant to these same referrals. Few have noticed that in December 2014, the International Criminal Court Prosecutor decided to suspend the pursuit of the Darfur situation because the Security Council failed to enforce the Court's arrest warrants. The Prosecutor probably intended to embarrass the Security Council and cause it to take action. Instead, the Security Council in the most insidious way, having taken *de facto* note of the International Criminal Court's naïve action, turned around and started to dismantle the United Nations peacekeeping operation in Darfur by turning over control of that region to the same government whose Head of State and other senior officials have been the subject of the International Criminal Court's arrest warrants. And so it is that in a situation where an estimated 200,000 to 300,000 people have been killed, over 1,000,000 people made refugees, and a large number of women raped, impunity for the perpetrators persists.

Unlike other historic situations where States sacrifice justice for their political ends, this was for an even less dignified purpose – the cost of the peacekeeping operation. If the United Nations could save about $1 billion a year for the maintenance of a full-fledged peacekeeping mission in Darfur in exchange for compromising international criminal law, then it was good and done. Of course that was not a United Nations decision *per se*. It was a consequence of the States' reluctance to fund peacekeeping operations. The upshot was no funding means no peacekeeping. But to avoid further atrocities, the co-operation of President el-Bashir's government was necessary. To obtain it meant to bring about a certain situation where he would not be under a realistic threat of prosecution. That was not obvious impunity and it was not interference in the International Criminal Court's judicial process. It was, however, a *de facto* outcome.

The same situation arises with respect to Libya where no trials have taken place under 'complementarity' and there has been no surrender by Libya to the International Criminal Court of those persons indicted. It appears that the same situation is likely to arise in Syria even though the Bashar al-Assad regime is believed to be responsible for the deaths of over 100,000 civilians and the displacement, internally or as refugees, of several million people. Impunity under one guise or another is always the carrot that is being dangled before those who have the power to end conflicts. For the *realpolitician* it is always how to achieve the cessation of conflict, euphemistically referred to as 'peace', in exchange for impunity. Sometimes it is done with the finesse displayed in the artful drafting of article 227 after the First World War and sometimes it is done in more crass ways, as in the cases of Sudan, Libya and, I predict, also Syria, although who knows what genial formula some *realpolitician* will come up with.

Another historic example of how *Realpolitik* operates to obstruct international criminal justice is what happened after the First World War with respect to war crimes. In this case, there was no doubt that war crimes existed in positive international law. The Treaty of Versailles contained two articles on the prosecution of the defeated German Power, namely 228 and 229, for violations of the 'laws and customs of war' irrespective of rank and position. In preparation, an international commission was established in 1919, 'The Commission on the Responsibility of the Authors of the War and on Enforcement of Penalties'. It drew up a list of 12,000 to be prosecuted (some reports put that number as high as 20,000). The victorious Allies, led by England, thought the number was too high and the list was brought down to 895 (again, reports vary from some 850 to 895). Even so, England still thought that this was too much. As the haggling over the numbers proceeded, by 1922, the Allies still could not reach agreement. Three years after the end of the war, the drive for the establishment of military trials for the defeated Germans waned significantly.

England then spearheaded an initiative, aimed at convincing Germany to take over the task of prosecution. Germany agreed to have the proceedings conducted pursuant to its 1871 Code of Criminal Procedure, which meant that the Prosecutor-General had a certain discretion as to which cases would be brought to trial. Prior to that he convinced the Allies to further bring down the number of those to be submitted for his consideration. The Allies agreed and only forty-five names of the 895 were submitted. In turn, he selected twelve. The trials were conducted before the Supreme Court of Germany sitting in Leipzig. Six persons were convicted and the highest sentence was four years, for two submarine Lieutenants under an officer who ordered the sinking of a Red Cross ship carrying 600 wounded, then surfacing the submarine to fire at rafts that held survivors.

These facts are mentioned because there was no question under the laws and customs of maritime warfare that this type of conduct was the most heinous of all crimes conducted in time of war on the high seas.[39]

Between 1919 and 1923 the political climate had changed. The determination of the victorious Allied governments had also changed. The perception that the defeated Germany was unjustly treated under the Treaty of Versailles also became more solidified among Germans. Thus, for Germany to prosecute its own hardly found domestic political support. But to prosecute twelve at home with low sentences was better than 895 before an Allied Tribunal that could enforce death sentences and long-term imprisonment. Yet international criminal law norms were clearly established, as were the facts evidencing the violations. The number of victims was significant. Chemical weapons were used. None of that really mattered and political expedience prevailed.

Realpolitik and the bureaucratisation of international criminal justice and international criminal law

Since the 1990s the sophistication of *Realpolitik* has moved away from open opposition to international criminal justice to a more concealed way. The new technique involves using international bureaucracy to achieve political ends. In other words, if all international criminal justice initiatives are brought under the operational control, that is, the bureaucratic and financial control of the United Nations, then it becomes much easier to manipulate outcomes by instrumentalising the political and bureaucratic processes of this institution. In broad terms, if institutions like the two *ad hoc* tribunals, the mixed model tribunals, the International Criminal Court, United Nations commissions of inquiry, fact-finding bodies, special procedures, and human rights treaty mechanisms are all dealt with in the same administrative way and by the same bureaucracy, subject to the same financial constraints and regulations, then the appearance of impartiality, fairness, and non-politicisation is maintained. But if anyone

39 Sheldon Glueck, *War Criminals – Their Prosecution and Punishment*, New York: A.A. Knopf, 1945; *Empire* v. *Dithmar* et al., 'Hospital Ship "Llandovery Castle"', (1921) 16 *American Journal of International Law* 721; Dirk von Selle, 'Prolog zu Nürnberg (Die Leipziger Kriegsverbrecherprozesse vor dem Reichsgericht)', (1997) 19 *Zeitschrift für Neuere Rechtsgeschichte* 193.

knows how to politically and bureaucratically manipulate these processes then outcomes can be controlled. This applies to how institutions, bodies, mechanisms, and missions are structured, how they are staffed, how they operate in the field, how they are funded and the internal constraints to which they are subject. All of that put together determines outcomes that may not have an apparent or direct link to international criminal justice though they definitely impact on it. Thus, for example, if a commission of inquiry is established and does not properly collect evidence usable by an international criminal justice mechanism, particularly the International Criminal Court, that evidence may be lost or it may become unusable by the prosecutors of the international criminal justice mechanism in question.[40]

On the whole, it is an obvious and fair observation to say that the bureaucratic system of the United Nations is cumbersome and costly. It is also slow. This means that international criminal justice institutions necessarily start with these three deficits. The International Criminal Tribunal for the former Yugoslavia and the International Criminal Tribunal for Rwanda have cost in excess of $2.5 billion and $2 billion, respectively, for a total of $4.5 billion. The two tribunals have cumulatively indicted 254 persons. The average cost per person is therefore $17.7 million. It becomes inevitable that governments as well as supporters of international criminal justice are compelled to ask whether or not the cost of pursuing international criminal justice is something that the international community or the United Nations or the given institution, if created by treaty like the International Criminal Court, can afford. And if, as in the case of the International Criminal Court, the higher costs may be assumed by a limited number of States, to what extent will these States have a greater say so within the institution than others. Without going into specific numbers it has to be evident to the International Criminal Court's Assembly of State Parties that what seems like an annual cost of $150 million and a staff of over 800 persons to deal with six or seven

---

40 For the history of the thirty commissions of inquiry established by the Human Rights Council and the unexplainable diversity of its standards on evidence collection, see: M. Cherif Bassiouni and Christina Abraham, eds., *Siracusa Guidelines for International, Regional and National Fact-Finding Bodies*, Antwerp: Intersentia, 2013.

ongoing cases involving less than a dozen defendants in custody is not a good cost–benefit ratio.

Maybe more importantly in these instances is whether the choices of Arusha and The Hague, which are not the two locations where the Rwanda and Yugoslavia conflicts took place, were the most appropriate ones. There is no doubt that these expenditures benefited the host countries of Tanzania and the Netherlands as opposed to Rwanda and any of the three most directly involved States of the former Yugoslavia (Bosnia, Croatia, and Serbia). More importantly, what was the impact of these proceedings on their respective local populations, which have produced the perpetrators who in turn have been the cause of the victimisation, which is the subject of the proceedings? Surely the purposes of international criminal justice include closure for the victims and their families, deterrence against similar violations in the future, and retribution against those who have committed such crimes. Can it be said that hoped for post-conflict justice outcomes of international criminal justice institutions like the International Criminal Tribunal for the former Yugoslavia and International Criminal Tribunal for Rwanda, located far from where the crimes were committed and without any technique of dissemination of these proceedings and their outcomes to the victim populations, have been produced in any measureable way? Admittedly, deterrence is difficult to measure, as is the sense of closure for victims, but without achieving any of these post-conflict justice goals, is reconciliation between opposing communities likely? Is the prevention of such future conflict enhanced? If these value-oriented goals are not achieved then the cost–benefit analysis of these international criminal justice institutions becomes limited to the very basic institutional cost that relates to the number of persons brought to justice. That is unquestionably not the value-oriented goal of international criminal justice. But this is precisely what is produced from the establishment of these international institutions and their bureaucratisation within a system as unwieldy as that of the United Nations.

This is not the place to lay bare all of the bureaucratic failings of the United Nations system – this has been done many times over the decades. In the end, all of the reform efforts have been swallowed in the quicksand of bureaucracy, never to be seen again. The United Nations system is not suitable for the administration of international criminal justice, no more than it is suitable for an international legislative process to develop international criminal law norms and procedures. With respect to the latter, it has to do with the sporadic political and bureaucratic processes that bring about the slow and uncoordinated elaboration of treaties by disparate persons with scant expertise in international criminal law and without continuity in legislative policy. The former is also linked with bureaucracy, politics, and the haphazard way in which United Nations support staff are assigned to these tasks despite lack of experience and knowledge of the nature of the work involved. Special internal procedures can easily cure most of these problems. Some illustrations follow.

As one who served on the world's first commission of inquiry after the Second World War experiences and subsequent to the Cold War period, I can attest to the difficulties I first encountered as Chair of the Security Council Commission on the former Yugoslavia.[41] Even though the mandate was extraordinarily broad, it could not be achieved if personnel and financial resources were unavailable. And that was the way in which the *Realpolitik* interests of some of the Security Council States were achieved. During its two-year existence, the Commission never received a penny from the United Nations for any investigative activity, for any investigative personnel, or for any expenses related to its mandate. The only United Nations funds made available were to pay for the *per diem* of the commissioners when they were on mission and for anywhere between two and five secretariat staff personnel. The entire cost of investigations, of establishing a database, of collecting and documenting the evidence, and of preparing the final report and annexes (the largest Security Council report in history, consisting of over 3,500 pages, backed by 79,000 documents, 300 hours of video tape, and 3,000 pictures) was all done through funds that I personally raised and by the good will of governments who contributed personnel and some funding.[42] If it were not for the government and private funders and for personnel contributed by governments the Commission could never have accomplished its task. And without it

41 M. Cherif Bassiouni, 'The Commission of Experts Established Pursuant to Security Council Resolution 780: Investigating Violations of International Humanitarian Law in the Former Yugoslavia', (1994) 5 *Criminal Law Forum* 279; M. Cherif Bassiouni, 'The United Nations Commission of Experts Established Pursuant to Security Council Resolution 780 (1992)', (1994) 88 *American Journal of International Law* 784.

42 'Final Report of the Commission of Experts Established Pursuant to Security Council Resolution 780 (1992)', transmitted by letter dated 24 May 1994, from

there would have never been enough evidence to convince the Security Council to establish the International Criminal Tribunal for the former Yugoslavia, which in turn was the impetus for the International Criminal Tribunal for Rwanda. Both were important factors in bringing about the International Criminal Court.

In the case of the Yugoslavia Commission, the situation was clear and it is difficult to argue with the fact that there was zero funding. In addition, I encountered numerous politically motivated bureaucratic hurdles in establishing the Commission's database and in conducting field missions. At the time, the goal was to negotiate an end to the conflict and to establish the foundations for future peaceful relations between the warring factions. It was all about a political settlement, it was not about justice. In fact, justice was then perceived as an impediment to the achievement of a political settlement. One only has to consider how incongruous it was to have Lord David Owen and former Secretary Cyrus Vance (though more the former than the latter) engage in negotiations with the Heads of State of Serbia, Croatia, and Bosnia as well as the rump State of Republika Srpska while the Commission was investigating those very persons and others in their respective regimes with whom they were negotiating for war crimes and crimes against humanity.

The irony was noted by visitors to the Palais des Nations, the United Nations headquarters in Geneva. The political team headed by Owen was on the first floor of the first bâtiment and the investigating commission that I chaired was on the fifth floor of the last bâtiment. One was pursuing a political settlement with all of its implications on accountability while the other was pursuing accountability with all of its implications on the prevention of impunity and the achievement of justice. The only way the two could co-exist was if the former was unencumbered by the latter, and that meant that the latter could not be allowed to move at a pace that would outdistance the former. At that time cessation of hostilities was a priority. It could only be achieved by a political settlement. Why the politicians and United Nations bureaucrats serving these political interests saw a contradiction between the two was simply a matter of their myopia. The issue was not peace versus justice. It was simply a question of timing. And if the politicians and their bureaucratic servants

the Secretary-General established pursuant to Security Council Resolution S/RES/780, dated 6 October 1992, UN Doc S/1994/674.

would have understood that simple fact, the pursuit of justice could have gone on unhindered. But maybe this is a naïve vision on my part. Maybe the pursuit of *Realpolitik* is, in the minds of its practitioners, incompatible with the pursuit of justice.

In time, one of those prime political settlement negotiators, Slobodan Milošević, the former President of Serbia, was brought to trial before the International Criminal Tribunal for the former Yugoslavia as were Radovan Karadžić the former President of Republika Srpska and Ratko Mladić who was the commander of the Srpska forces and also a General in the Serbian Army (the first died during the trial while the two others are still presently on trial). But that was after the Dayton Peace Accords in 1995.[43]

My Yugoslavia experience was prior to the establishment of the United Nations Office of High Commissioner for Human Rights. Later, when I chaired the United Nations Commission of Inquiry for Libya, in 2011, things had bureaucratically changed. My difficulties with that bureaucracy led me to relinquish the chair of the Commission to my colleague Phillipe Kirsch, the former President of the International Criminal Court, while remaining as a member.[44] The political stakes when I was chair of the Libya commission were difficult. The Commission's first report was very well received by the United Nations Member States in Geneva, to the point where the original three-hour session for my presentation of the report and discussion thereof was extended to six hours because forty-three governments wanted to express their appreciation for the work of the Commission. But this was before Qaddafi had been killed. The conflict was still open and NATO was still desperately trying to help the rebels even though it had no regime-change mandate from the Security Council. A United Nations Commission report made by well-known and reputable commissioners based on evidence could only favour the position of those who were pursuing a regime change in Libya.

---

43 'General Framework Agreement for Peace in Bosnia and Herzegovina', (1996) 35 *ILM* 75; Paola Gaeta, 'The Dayton Agreements and International Law', (1996) 7 *European Journal of International Law* 147.

44 M. Cherif Bassiouni, ed., *Libya From Repression to Revolution: A Record of Armed Conflict and International Law Violations, 2011–2013*, The Hague: Martinus Nijhoff, 2013, for a description of the work of the Commission, its reports and subsequent events.

The moment Qaddafi was killed and the regime collapsed, the major powers' interest in Libya waned. NATO and other States simply allowed the country to disintegrate to the point where it has now become a failing State. This change of political events resulted in the original staff, that had performed so well, being bureaucratically disbanded, thus halting the Commission's investigations. To select a new staff meant that job descriptions had to be filled, put up on a website, a selection process had to be established and finally, three months later, a new staff was constituted that had no experience with the country or with the prior investigation. It was at this point that I resigned in protest. But that had no impact on the Human Rights Council or for that matter on the Office of the High Commissioner. My successor had to do whatever he could under those circumstances and acquitted himself excellently. By the time he delivered the final report of the Commission the whole exercise took less than an hour, with only a few States in attendance at that session. This is by no means a reflection of the work of the Commission or its Chair but it is such a telling manifestation of how political interests can drive the pursuit of justice.

Another factor that is also very little known and relates to something akin to bureaucratic manipulations is the use of security concerns as a way of curtailing international criminal justice investigations. Because international criminal justice institutions are subject to the administrative control of the United Nations bureaucracy it follows that if somebody in the security department opposes the conduct of an investigation in a given territory at a given time for security reasons that investigation cannot be conducted. This means that if there is an investigation that needs to be conducted at a given time and place, because pertinent evidence may no longer be available, the prohibition for United Nations investigators to go to the field jeopardises accountability. In the former Yugoslavia, in Afghanistan, where I was the UN's independent expert on Human Rights in 2004–2005, and in Libya in 2011, I encountered such hurdles repeatedly and it was only through ingenuity that I was able to get around them. That is not the case with respect to the International Criminal Tribunal for the former Yugoslavia, International Criminal Tribunal for Rwanda, and the International Criminal Court. They could not go where they wanted, when they wanted, and they could not have access to the best evidence where and when it could have been secured. They were frequently forced to rely on secondary evidence or on evidence that gave the opportunity to the defendants to question it.

The challenges to international criminal law

International criminal justice relies on international criminal law and that too has its challenges. International criminal law is a complex legal discipline consisting of several components bound by their functional relationship in the pursuit of certain value-oriented goals.[45] These goals include the prevention and suppression of international criminality, enhancement of accountability and reduction of impunity, and the establishment of international criminal justice. Each of these components derives from one or more legal disciplines and their respective branches, including international law, national criminal law, comparative criminal law and procedures, and international and regional human rights law. These legal disciplines are distinguished on the basis, *inter alia*, of their subjects, contents, scope, values, goals, and methods. Thus, they cannot be easily reconciled. Nevertheless, the different components that make up international criminal law constitute a more or less functional whole, even though lacking in the doctrinal cohesiveness and methodological coherence found in other legal disciplines whose relative homogeneity gives them a more defined systemic nature. Thus, there is something that can be called the system of international criminal law, derived from the functional relationship that exists between the different components of this discipline and the value-oriented goals it seeks to achieve. This is evident in the scholarly writings on international criminal law.

The processes of international law reflect the delicate balance between the principles of national sovereignty and the need to regulate the multifaceted relations and interests of States with one another and with those of the international community. Interstate processes, however, are primarily designed for States. As a result they are not particularly well-suited to the needs of international criminal law whose subjects are individuals.

---

45 E.g., M. Cherif Bassiouni, *Introduction to International Criminal Law*, 2nd rev. edn, The Hague: Brill, 2013; Antonio Cassese, *International Criminal Law*, 2nd edn, Oxford University Press, 2008; Robert Cryer, Håken Friman, Darryl Robinson, and Elizabeth Wilmshurst, *An Introduction to International Criminal Law and Procedure*, 3rd edn, Cambridge University Press, 2014; Jordan Paust, M. Cherif Bassiouni, Michael Scharf, Jimmy Gurule, Leila Sadat, and Bruce Zagaris, *International Criminal Law: Cases and Materials*, 4th edn, Chapel Hill, NC: Carolina Academic, 2014.

Moreover, international co-operation in penal matters regulates State-to-State relations rather than national legal processes. International criminal law's norms are directed towards States even though their proscriptions apply to persons. But their enforcement is essentially dependent upon State action and upon interstate co-operation.

National criminal justice systems, their diversity notwithstanding, work on the premise that a legislative authority exists that has the power to bind its subjects, namely individuals and private legal entities. They rely on coercive means to enforce legal proscriptions. These powers extend to the national territory and only extraterritorially in a very limited context. Enforcement of national criminal law rests first with a law enforcement and prosecutorial apparatus designed to prevent and control unlawful behaviour and second with a judiciary that adjudicates guilt in accordance with pre-established, specific laws and procedures. Thus, the method, scope, content, and processes of national criminal justice systems significantly differ from and cannot be co-mingled with those of international law. A new comprehensive legal system of international criminal law has to be put in place, but that depends on the willingness of States to do so. So far it appears lacking, except with respect to certain international criminal activities that are essentially performed by individuals who are not acting as State agents.

This explains why there are so many conventions containing so many substantive and procedural norms on such crimes, i.e., drug trafficking and terrorism. In contrast, there are far fewer international conventions and substantive and procedural norms that apply to international crimes requiring State action. This is particularly evident in connection with international criminal law conventions containing obligations requiring States to undertake enforcement through their national legal systems. Such undertakings include the duty to criminalise the proscribed conduct, prosecute its violators, extradite accused, or convicted perpetrators of these crimes to States seeking to prosecute or execute sentences of conviction, and provide legal assistance to States investigating the commission of these crimes. Such normative provisions, for the reasons stated above, are always stronger when they apply to non-state actors.[46]

---

46 M. Cherif Bassiouni, 'The New Wars and the Crisis of Compliance with the Law of Armed Conflict by Non-State Actors', (2008) 98 *Journal of Criminal Law and Criminology* 712.

Interstate co-operation in penal matters is the legal regime applicable between States for the enforcement, at the interstate level, of their respective domestic criminal laws. In this regime, States rely on bilateral and multilateral relations, as well as on their respective national legislation. The techniques and the modalities are the same as those employed by States with respect to the national and interstate enforcement of international criminal law legal obligations and the enforcement of international judicial bodies' orders and judgments. International judicial bodies that, in many respects, have to go through the intermediation of States to enforce their orders and judgments, rely on national laws and national legal institutions. Thus, in this situation, the enforcement of international judicial orders and judgments will be as effective as the national legal institutions on whose intermediation the execution of the international mandates depend.

Each of the different components of international criminal law impacts on the others. If a given norm is not precisely defined, its enforcement, whether through the 'direct enforcement system' (international criminal justice) or the 'indirect enforcement system', will be weakened. For the same reasons interstate co-operation in penal matters will also be weakened. If a number of norms pertaining to the same subject are formulated in different ways in different treaties, they too will impact on their enforcement. As an example, there are at present eighteen international conventions that deal with terrorism and thirteen that deal with drug trafficking. These conventions contain norms on interstate co-operation in penal matters but these norms are all posited differently. This for example gave rise to a significant issue involving the United States and the United Kingdom on one side and Libya on the other in connection with the bombing of Pan Am Flight 103 on 21 December 1988. The applicable convention, namely the 1971 Montreal Hijacking Convention, provides, in article 5, that jurisdiction lies in the State in which the offense occurred. Article 7, on the other hand, gives jurisdiction to the State with custody of the accused. The Montreal Convention does not indicate which State has priority, nor does it declare the unarticulated premise that both prosecution and extradition must be based on fairness and effectiveness. Thus, Libya claimed that it had jurisdiction, as did the United States and the United Kingdom. Libya relied on the language of the Convention, which gave it priority, while the United States and the United Kingdom claimed that Libya would not prosecute effectively. Libya responded that if extradited, its nationals would not be tried fairly. The matter went before the International Court of Justice, which was to no avail because the political process trumped the legal process when the Security Council voted to support the United States and the United Kingdom against Libya. It took ten years to resolve the political stalemate.[47] Notwithstanding that, to date the Montreal Convention's provisions on jurisdiction have never been amended.

Two other examples of normative lacunae are in the Genocide Convention. Social and political groups are excluded from the protection offered by the Convention. As a result, the killing of an estimated 1,000,000 Khmer in Cambodia by other Khmer cannot be considered genocide because a social group is not specifically protected. The same is true for any political group that is targeted for extermination. This was clearly the intention of the Soviet Union in 1948 not to include social and political groups in the definition of genocide because that is precisely what the Communist Party at the time was doing. Notwithstanding the passage of time during the deliberations of the *Ad Hoc* and Preparatory Committees of the General Assembly for the establishment of an International Criminal Court as well as during the Diplomatic Conference, I consistently urged

---

47 M. Cherif Bassiouni, *International Extradition: United States Law and Practice*, 6th edn, New York: Oxford University Press, 2014, at p. 417; *Questions of Interpretation and Application of the 1971 Montreal Convention arising from the Aerial Incident at Lockerbie (Libyan Arab Jamahiriya v. United Kingdom), Preliminary Objections, Judgment*, I.C.J. Reports, 1998, p. 9; *Questions of Interpretation and Application of the 1971 Montreal Convention arising from the Aerial Incident at Lockerbie (Libyan Arab Jamahiriya v. United States), Preliminary Objections, Judgment*, I.C.J. Reports, 1998, p. 115; *Questions of Interpretation and Application of the 1971 Montreal Convention arising from the Aerial Incident at Lockerbie (Libyan Arab Jamahiriya v. United Kingdom), Provisional Measures, Order of 14 April 1992*, I.C.J. Reports 1992, p. 3; *Questions of Interpretation and Application of the 1971 Montreal Convention arising from the Aerial Incident at Lockerbie (Libyan Arab Jamahiriya v. United States), Provisional Measures, Order of 14 April 1992*, I.C.J. Reports 1992, p. 114; *Questions relating to the Obligation to Prosecute or Extradite (Belgium v. Senegal), Judgment*, I.C.J. Reports 2012, p. 422. See also Michael P. Scharf, 'Terrorism on Trial: The Lockerbie Bombing Criminal Proceedings', (2000) 6 *ILSA Journal of International and Comparative Law* 355; Omer Y. Elagab, 'The Hague as the Seat of the Lockerbie Trial: Some Constraints', (2000) 34 *International Lawyer* 289.

Member States to amend the definition of genocide to include social and political groups as protected categories, but to no avail.[48] The concern of States was that the overall definition of genocide could be limited to a narrower context such as a city, as opposed to an entire country. This was something that I had included in the Final Report of the former Yugoslavia's Commission to the Security Council. The bottom line is that almost seventy years later, and notwithstanding the high number of victims resulting from the very type of policies intended by the Genocide Convention, there is still no willingness on the part of States to extend criminal responsibility for such conduct to State actors who carry out such State policies.

Another example of States' reluctance to criminalise the conduct of State actors in what some refer to as 'atrocity crimes' is evident in the absence of a convention on crimes against humanity.[49] An effort spearheaded by a number of academics, led by Professor Leila Sadat, has been working with the International Law Commission and particularly Professor Sean D. Murphy who is its special rapporteur on a crimes against humanity convention.[50] This notwithstanding the fact that this international crime is deemed *jus cogens* and was included in the Charter of the International Military Tribunal and the Statutes of the International Military Tribunal for the Far East, the International Criminal Tribunal for the former Yugoslavia, the International Criminal Tribunal for Rwanda and the International Criminal Court, as well as the normative instruments applicable to the mixed tribunals identified above. But this too is not without political purpose.[51] The absence of a convention on crimes against humanity suits the purposes of many governments whose State actors engage in systematic and/or widespread arbitrary arrest and detention, torture, extrajudicial executions, and other forms of persecution.

48 M. Cherif Bassiouni, *The Legislative History of the International Criminal Court: Introduction, Analysis and Integrated Text of the Statute, Elements of Crimes and Rules of Procedure and Evidence*, vol. 1, Ardsley: Transnational, 2005.

49 David Scheffer, 'Atrocity Crimes Framing the Responsibility to Protect', (2007) 40 *Case Western Reserve Journal of International Law* 111.

50 Leila Nadya Sadat, ed., *Forging a Convention for Crimes Against Humanity*, Cambridge University Press, 2011.

51 M. Cherif Bassiouni, *Crimes Against Humanity*, Cambridge University Press, 2011, pp. 594–5.

The fact that there are eight international instruments that define crimes against humanity with slight variations is also a way of creating vagueness as to the specificity of the norm. This in turn limits its effective enforcement at national levels and raises questions as to whether 'complementarity' under the International Criminal Court Statute's article 17 can be satisfied.

It should be noted, however, that the International Law Commission is presently considering such a convention after the passage of over sixty years since the United Nations had resolved to adopt an international Code on Crimes Against the Peace and Security of Mankind. That long-standing effort came to naught by 2001, proving once again that if *Realpolitik* can drag things out in time, international interest in it will wane and die. The reader should be mindful of the *Realpolitik* tergiversations over the drafting of this code of international crimes, which started after the post–Second World War experiences in international criminal justice. It was clear then that substantive international criminal law norms on such crimes as aggression, genocide, crimes against humanity, and others were lacking and that this was impeding the effectiveness of international criminal justice as well as national enforcement of international crimes.

As a brief illustration of the tortuous process that went on between 1947 and 2001:

- *1946*, the General Assembly adopts a resolution on the Nuremberg Principles;
- *1950*, a committee is established to prepare a Draft Code of Offences Against the Peace and Security of Mankind;
- *1950*, the General Assembly establishes a separate committee to develop a statute for an International Criminal Court;
- *1952*, work on the Draft Code makes progress but, the General Assembly severs the definition of aggression from the Draft Code's mandate and establishes another committee to define it (that committee consisted of government representatives instead of independent experts);
- *1953*, the committee for the International Criminal Court completes its work but the General Assembly tables it because the Committee on the Draft Code had not completed its work;
- *1954*, the Committee on the Draft Code completes its work but the General Assembly tables it because aggression had not yet been defined by the other committee;

- *1974*, when the committee to define aggression completes its work after twenty-two years;[52]
- *1977*, a draft statute on the establishment of the International Criminal Court was prepared by this writer at the request of the Commission on Human Rights, Committee on Southern Africa, for a specialised international criminal court for the enforcement of the 1976 *Apartheid* Convention;[53]
- *1978*, the General Assembly asks the International Law Commission to revisit the Draft Code, tabled in 1954; between 1978 and 2001, the International Law Commission produced several technically unsatisfactory texts of the revised 1954 Draft Code, and finally reduced that codification work to less than one page, but the General Assembly never voted on it (the codification effort, which started in 1950, lingered on until 2001 and died of old age);

---

52 Aggression is the equivalent of 'Crimes Against Peace', prosecuted at Nuremberg and Tokyo. But the 1974 definition was never embodied in a treaty nor did the Security Council ever act upon it. Only the International Criminal Court contains an amendment to its statute, adopted in Kampala in 2010, that defines the crime of aggression. But whether that provision will ever become effective under the Court's norms on when amendments become effective and with respect to each State Party, it is unlikely that this crime will ever be more than textual language.

53 M. Cherif Bassiouni and Daniel Derby, 'Final Report on the Establishment of an International Criminal Court for the Implementation of the Apartheid Convention and other Relevant International Instruments', (1981) 9 *Hofstra Law Review* 523; William A. Schabas, *The International Criminal Court: A Commentary on the Rome Statute*, Oxford University Press, 2010; M. Cherif Bassiouni, *The Legislative History of the International Criminal Court: Introduction, Analysis and Integrated Text of the Statute, Elements of Crimes and Rules of Procedure and Evidence*, vol. 1, Ardsley: Transnational, 2005; Claus Kreß and Flavia Lattanzi, eds., *The Rome Statute and Domestic Legal Orders*, vol. 1, *General Aspects and Constitutional Issues*, Baden-Baden: Nomos and Ripa di Fagnano Alto, Italy: il Sirente, 2000; Claus Kreß, Bruce Broomhall, Flavia Lattanzi, and Valeria Santori, eds., *The Rome Statute and Domestic Legal Orders*, vol. 2, *Constitutional Issues, Cooperation and Enforcement*, Baden-Baden: Nomos and Ripa di Fagnano Alto, Italy: il Sirente, 2005; Otto Triffterer, ed., *Commentary on the Rome Statute of the International Criminal Court, Observers' Notes, Article by Article*, 2nd edn, Munich: C.H. Beck; Baden-Baden: Nomos; Oxford: Hart, 2008.

- *1989*, a proposal was made by Trinidad and Tobago at the General Assembly Special Session on Drugs to have a special international criminal court for drug offences (the proposal was championed by the late Arthur N. R. Robinson, former President of Trinidad and Tobago, with whom I worked on the draft of the resolution). The resolution was forwarded to the International Law Commission;
- *1993*, the International Law Commission produced a draft modelled after the 1977 text mentioned above for the enforcement of the Apartheid Convention;
- *1993*, the International Law Commission's text was first used by the General Assembly's *Ad Hoc* Committee for the Establishment of an International Criminal Court in 1994 but not so during the Preparatory Committee meetings which started work in 1995 on what was finally adopted in Rome in 1998.

If a benign interpretation is to be given as to why there is no policy on the development of international criminal law norms, on the uniformity of similar norms contained in different instruments, and on the absence of continuity in the policy-goals sought to be achieved by international criminal law, then it could simply be that the international legislative process is dysfunctional. Another benign explanation could be that this very process takes place at different times, at different venues, and that its participants are different government officials, usually diplomats, who are not the same at these different occasions. Moreover, they may not be knowledgeable of international criminal law, something that also makes for a dysfunctional process that produces deficient results. Even so, one would have to assume that after almost seventy years of such a dysfunctional international legislative process some remedies would have been found. The fact that none were undertaken may well attest to another way by which *Realpolitik* accomplishes its ends by making international criminal law a system containing a number of deficiencies and weaknesses that can best be exploited by those in a position to do so and that is usually the most influential States.

Towards a new strategy on international criminal law and international criminal justice

Is humankind condemned to repeat its mistakes? Not necessarily if one accepts the postulate that everything is relative. We have made progress in the institutionalisation of memory, monitoring of events, anticipating catastrophic occurrences, developing preventive and curative measures, providing accountability for what we now call international crimes by eliminating or minimising impunity, and the institutionalisation of international criminal justice through various mechanisms founded on international criminal law.[54] All of this enhances the prospects of peace by strengthening the prospects of justice. This endeavour is necessarily relative, both in terms of what it can accomplish and what its outcomes are likely to be, under changing circumstances to which international criminal justice and international criminal law would apply. That is why it is important to identify the failures and successes of the past, assess them in their relative contexts and rely upon them to solidify the foundation of an overall system of international criminal law and international criminal justice. For certain this is not an easy task. It requires a balanced assessment of past and present in order to determine what is best for the future, bearing in mind, as Shakespeare said, that 'past is prologue'.

Regrettably, in international criminal law and international criminal justice, past is not always prologue because there are those who are preventing it from being such. But for those who are engaged in the building of the legal and institutional architecture and functionality of international criminal law and international criminal justice it is important to link past, present, and future. And, to have the ability to distinguish between what can and cannot be done in order that we may have the ability, the strength, and the courage to struggle for what can be done and to accept what cannot be done. And be ready to resume the struggle another day. Our legacy is what subsequent generations will rely upon to continue the struggle, even though it may appear to some that their efforts may be like the proverbial Sisyphus rolling the rock up the hill, only to see it fall back. The secret of success is the ability of succeeding generations of those committed to international criminal law and international criminal justice to roll that rock back up the hill time and time again until it finally sits at the top and does not roll down.

54 Priscilla Hayner, *Unspeakable Truths: Confronting State Terror and Atrocity*, 2nd edn., New York: Routledge, 2011; Jane E. Stromseth, *Accountability for Atrocities: National and International Responses*, Ardsley, NY: Transnational, 2003; M. Cherif Bassiouni, ed., *Post-Conflict Justice*, Ardsley, NY: Transnational, 2002; Neil Kritz, ed., *Transitional Justice: How Emerging Democracies Deal with Former Regimes*, Washington: US Institute of Peace Press, 1995.

What is the best strategy to move forward? Surely we must pursue the same beaten path that we have pursued so far and for so long. This includes the strengthening of international criminal law norms and procedures as well as the International Criminal Court, which will soon be the only remaining international justice institution. But all of this has its limitations as history teaches us. We need a new strategic approach, one that the International Criminal Court Statute contemplated, namely, what it refers to in article 17 as 'complementarity'. As Chairman of the Diplomatic Conference's Drafting Committee, I can attest to the fact that complementarity was viewed by most States at the diplomatic conference and prior to that at the *Ad Hoc* and Preparatory Committees of the General Assembly (of which I was vice-chair) as a way of giving priority to the national jurisdiction of the States Parties. But in order for States Parties to exercise their national jurisdiction, they must have national implementing legislation and the capacity to investigate, prosecute, and adjudge, in a fair and effective manner. The capacity of most of the world's States is not at this level. We must therefore focus efforts on strengthening national capacity through technical and financial assistance, and to enhance the capacity of their national legal systems. This in turn will strengthen their legal systems and enhance the prospects of democracy, freedom, and justice for their peoples.

The future strategy of international criminal justice must focus on national systems by first developing their substantive norms and having those incorporated in their criminal laws. In addition, the development of jurisdictional mechanisms as between States, which are on a vertical basis with international criminal justice institutions, must change to being on a horizontal basis as between States in order to make inter-state co-operation in penal matters effective. This includes extradition, mutual legal assistance in obtaining evidence, and other modalities of international co-operation in penal matters such as recognition of foreign penal judgments, transfer of sentenced persons, enforcement of sentences and penal judgments abroad, and other forms of co-operation. In short, the new strategy should emphasise this shift in focus from the internationalisation to the nationalisation of accountability for international crimes.

I would be remiss at the conclusion of these observations not to insist upon the need to press for the international enforcement of the United Nations Declaration of Basic Principles of Justice for Victims of Crime and

Abuse of Power.[55] As the United Nations Independent Expert, appointed
in 1998, who prepared the text that was adopted by the General Assembly
in 2005, I can also attest to the fact that opposition by major States to
the Declaration was politically motivated. Japan in particular was fearful
that it would be used by the 'comfort women', the United States was concerned that it would give rise to claims by the Native Americans and by
African Americans, the United Kingdom and other former colonial powers
were equally anxious about the prospective claims of former victims of
colonial periods, and Turkey was worried that the case of the Armenians
would be raised once again. Many States were concerned about their torture practices and other practices which violate international humanitarian law, international human rights law, and international criminal law.
These States were successful in delaying the adoption of the Declaration
between 2000 and 2005. Finally, when it was adopted, the United Kingdom
made a statement at the General Assembly that reflected many of these
governments' concerns, namely the binding legal nature of the resolution.
The statement was to the effect that the resolution was recommendatory
and not binding. Maybe in their minds it would simply whither away as
is the case with the 1974 General Assembly consensus resolution on the
definition of aggression.

Realpolitik is no more willing to accept a limitation on the use of power
than it is on recognising the rights of victims of States' abuses of power.
Thus, there is no accountability for aggression and no redress for the victims of international crimes other than through the benevolence of those
States willing to do so on a voluntary basis.

As Machiavelli said, 'There is nothing more difficult to take in hand,
more perilous to conduct, or more uncertain in its success, *than to take
the lead in the introduction of a new order of things'*. That is the challenge
of international criminal justice and international criminal law. But the
proponents of international criminal justice and international criminal
law have no choice but to persevere. Their convictions condemn them to
keep on trying, no matter what the outcomes may be.

There is no better way to conclude these reflections than to quote the
following:

---

55 Declaration of Basic Principles of Justice for Victims of Crime and Abuse of
    Power, UN Doc. A/RES/40/34; M. Cherif Bassiouni, 'International Recognition
    of Victims' Rights', (2006) 6 *Human Rights Law Review* 203.

If you see a wrong you must right it:
with your hand if you can (meaning action),
or, with your words (meaning to speak out),
or in your heart, but that is the weakest of faith.

(Prophet Mohammed)

If you want Peace, work for Justice.

(Pope Paul VI)

The world rests on three pillars: on truth, on justice and on peace.

(Rabban Simeon ben Gamaliel, Abot 1, 18)

A Talmudic commentary adds to this, saying:

The three are really one. If justice is realised, truth is vindicated and peace results.

FURTHER READING

M. Cherif Bassiouni, ed., *Post-Conflict Justice*, Ardsley: Transnational, 2002.

M. Cherif Bassiouni, *Crimes Against Humanity*, Cambridge University Press, 2011.

M. Cherif Bassiouni, *Introduction to International Criminal Law*, 2nd rev. edn, The Hague: Brill, 2013.

M. Cherif Bassiouni and Christina Abraham, eds., *Siracusa Guidelines for International, Regional and National Fact-Finding Bodies*, Antwerp: Intersentia, 2013.

Neil Boister and Robert Cryer, *The Tokyo International Military Tribunal: A Reappraisal*, Oxford University Press, 2008.

Geoffrey Robertson, *Crimes Against Humanity: The Struggle for Global Justice*, London: Penguin Books, 2000.

Leila Nadya Sadat, ed., *Forging a Convention for Crimes Against Humanity*, Cambridge University Press, 2011.

Telford Taylor, *Final Report to the Secretary of the Army on the Nuremberg War Crimes Trials Under Control Council Law No. 10*, Washington: Government Printing Office, 1949.

Final Report of the Commission of Experts Established Pursuant to Security Council Resolution 780 (1992), transmitted by letter dated 24 May 1994, from the Secretary-General established pursuant to Security Council Resolution S/RES/780, dated Oct. 6, 1992, UN Doc S/1994/674.

Index